PLANTING SEEDS OF KNOWLEDGE

The Environment in History: International Perspectives
Series Editors: Stefania Barca, *University of Santiago de Compostela*;
Kieko Matteson, *University of Hawai'i at Mānoa*; Christof Mauch, *LMU Munich*;
Helmuth Trischler, *Deutsches Museum, Munich*

ENVIRONMENT AND SOCIETY

Recent Titles:

For a full volume listing, please see the series page on our website: http://berghahnbooks.com/series/environment-in-history.

Planting Seeds of Knowledge

Agriculture and Education in Rural Societies in the Twentieth Century

Edited by

Heinrich Hartmann and Julia Tischler

berghahn

NEW YORK · OXFORD

www.berghahnbooks.com

First published in 2023 by
Berghahn Books
www.berghahnbooks.com

© 2023 Heinrich Hartmann and Julia Tischler

Library of Congress Cataloging-in-Publication Data
Names: Hartmann, Heinrich (Professor of history), editor. | Tischler, Julia,
  1982- editor.
Title: Planting seeds of knowledge : agriculture and education in rural societies
  in the twentieth century / edited by Heinrich Hartmann, Julia Tischler.
Description: First edition. | New York : Berghahn Books, 2023. | Series:
  Environment in history : international perspectives; Volume 24 | Includes
  bibliographical references and index.
Identifiers: LCCN 2023000717 (print) | LCCN 2023000718 (ebook) | ISBN
  9781805390107 (hardback) | ISBN 9781805390114 (ebook) Subjects: LCSH:
  Agricultural education--History--20th century. | Agriculture--Research--
  History--20th century. | Education, Rural--History--20th century.
Classification: LCC S531 .P62 2023 (print) | LCC S531 (ebook) |
  DDC 630.71--dc23/eng/20230417
LC record available at https://lccn.loc.gov/2023000717
LC ebook record available at https://lccn.loc.gov/20230007180

British Library Cataloguing in Publication Data

A catalogue record for this book is available from the British Library

ISBN 978-1-80539-010-7 hardback
ISBN 978-1-80539-011-4 ebook

https://doi.org/10.3167/9781805390107

Contents

Illustrations

Figures

Table

Acknowledgements

This volume is the outcome of an intense and rewarding collective project. In our effort to provide a global perspective on the role of knowledge and education in farming, we invited scholars from around the world to participate. We had the chance to discuss our contributions during two authors' workshops that were held virtually in June and November 2020 in the midst of the COVID-19 pandemic. We thank all authors for the intense debates and their generous and constructive feedback.

We furthermore wish to thank our corresponding editors at Berghahn Books, foremost Amanda Horn, for their guidance and patience in navigating us through the publication process. This publication project has been made possible thanks to funds contributed by the Heisenberg Programme of the German Research Foundation (DFG) as well as the University of Basel.

A great note of thanks goes to our language editor, Patrick Grogan, whose expertise and meticulous work greatly improved the linguistic quality, and in many cases even the scholarly quality, of our individual contributions. We thank Tessa Hille and Andrina Sommer for their support with the index, proofs and other formal aspects of this publication.

 INTRODUCTION

Planting Seeds of Knowledge

Agriculture and Education in Rural Societies in the Twentieth Century

Heinrich Hartmann and Julia Tischler

In June 1914, forty white farmers from South Africa travelled across the United Kingdom to obtain first-hand knowledge on modern farming techniques. Marvelling at the research stations and admiring the pedigree livestock at various breeding centres, the 'Boer farmers' concluded that the days of the 'old-type farmer who thought whatever his grandfather had done was good enough' were over.[1] A year earlier, D.D.T. Jabavu, a prominent black educator from South Africa's Cape Province, had embarked on a journey to the United States to visit the famous Tuskegee Institute in Alabama. He closely observed the Institute's outreach activities, which included short courses, conferences and the work of so-called Negro Farm Demonstrators, who were trying to free African-American farmers from the exploitative cotton plantation system.[2] Upon his return, Jabavu lobbied the South African government for the establishment of agricultural colleges and demonstration services that would contribute towards improving the eroding so-called native reserves.[3] In 1962, seventeen-year-old Erdal Pakünlüer left his village near the Turkish city of Bursa to travel to Switzerland as part of a Turkish government programme designed to give young farmers the opportunity to observe mechanized farming techniques.[4] However, soon after his arrival, Erdal realized that his Swiss hosts were quite reluctant to share their knowledge and were only interested in him as a casual labourer. With his work obligations for the farmers leaving him with no time to study or attend classes, it became clear that disseminating knowledge was not in the interests of all the participating parties. It was only after the Turkish ambassador intervened that the Swiss farmers started to share some of their insights with Erdal and other participants in the programme.[5]

The Boer farmers, Jabavu and Erdal were not eccentric scientophiles, but formed part of a broad movement promoting agricultural education and the application of scientific knowledge in farming that was profoundly transnational. For centuries, agricultural knowledge travelled alongside crops and livestock breeds as they were exported to new environments.[6] Centuries-old trade schemes as well as European imperial expansion, colonial domination and frontier management all gave rise to and promoted such exchanges.[7] However, we argue in this volume that important quantitative and qualitative shifts unfolded in the late nineteenth and twentieth centuries. In this period, not only were agricultural techniques at the centre of transnational knowledge transfers, but broader conceptions of rural social engineering in a modernizing world also became the subject of transnational conversations. As such examples show, farmers and rural dwellers across the world increasingly sought out scientific knowledge – including from abroad – in order to improve local farming practices. Revolutions in transport and communications, a deeper international integration of markets for agricultural produce, rising mass literacy and a growing belief in improvability through scientific knowledge at least partially accounted for the global proliferation of agricultural and rural education initiatives in the late nineteenth and early twentieth centuries.[8]

Agricultural research and education emerged out of shared experiences of fundamental transformations in the countryside, as the rise of industrial capitalism, the commercialization of farming, intensified global trade and rapid urbanization challenged existing agricultural practices and rural livelihoods. Experts, government officials and rural producers all sought out new and improved agricultural methods that would boost farmers' outputs. Meanwhile, poorer farming families found themselves increasingly squeezed off the land that they had worked, unable to muster the inputs and capital required to compete under the new, commercialized agrarian regimes. Formalized knowledge, building on claims to universal applicability, was invoked by governments, experts and farmers to respond to the imperatives of production increase and global economic competition. At the same time, rural education also constituted one strategy to ameliorate the condition of those whom agricultural commercialization had left behind. Many governments and urban elites, driven by fears of social unrest or eugenic concerns, sought to contain these struggling producers in the countryside rather than allow them to crowd the cities. The dramatic changes affecting agrarian labour regimes throughout much of the world impacted billions of rural dwellers, who constituted the world's demographic majority until as late as 2007.[9] Agricultural and rural education offer unique insights into the ways in which farmers, rural elites and agents of the rising nation states attempted to manage these transformations. Although they were among the earliest responses, rural and agricultural education initiatives have rarely been studied, and even less so from a transnational perspective.

This volume examines the rising importance of formalized agricultural knowledge and its transnational circulation in the twentieth century. Various food emergencies, in conjunction with the global political conflicts and economic crises of the twentieth century, make the previous century, especially its first half, one focal point of the chapters in this volume. Across the world, agricultural colleges, village schools, farmers' associations, home economics movements, children's clubs and agricultural extension services mushroomed with the broadly shared aim of transforming both farming practices and rural living conditions. Sharing the conviction that farming should be subjected to rational and universally valid principles, rural elites, farmers, scientists and governments developed forms of education that were strikingly similar in otherwise very different parts of the globe. The latter half of the twentieth century witnessed significant advances in agrarian knowledge and science, as well as an increase in state intervention, including through training and advisory services for farmers. At the same time, the history of agricultural knowledge and education evades straightforward periodization and is not easily absorbed into a grand narrative of the increasing dominance of mechanized, capital-intensive and large-scale farming advocated in the programmes of the mid-twentieth century's Green Revolution. These developments were always reversible to some degree and played out very distinctly in different countries. Furthermore, collectivist agriculture did not lose its appeal, while projects of land reform proliferated in the second half of the twentieth century with the aim of undoing land concentration and/or promoting family farming as an economically favourable alternative to large-scale farming. Various postcolonial governments also experimented with repeasantization schemes.[10]

This volume foregrounds different forms of agricultural education and knowledge communication in order to undercut overly simplified categorizations such as 'experts' and 'laypeople' or 'scientific' and 'practical' knowledge. Rather than examining knowledge-making in laboratories, universities or other institutions associated with the rise of science, it explores the ways in which knowledge has been communicated on the ground. As the chapters in this volume show, farming is not simply an economic activity, but a culturally charged way of life that has often been seen as a nation's last bastion of traditional values and true identity. As such, this volume investigates both the circulation of technical agricultural knowledge, which underpins the pursuit of rational economic goals such as increased production,[11] and the broader social and political intentions that this has entailed.

In the period under investigation, governments around the world grew increasingly interested and interventionist in relation to questions of agricultural knowledge, especially at a time of rising international conflicts over food and corresponding attempts to enhance agricultural productivity through the introduction of new technologies.[12] This became obvious with the mid-twentieth century's Green Revolution, but similar tendencies could already be observed for earlier mechanization initiatives or cooperative movements that enjoyed the support of a growing number of international expert networks and organizations.[13] This new interest of national governments and transnational expert networks was not confined to Europe and North America, but also extended to the colonial world.[14] Reflecting how agrarian knowledge dissemination was for many experts a global goal, each contribution in this volume highlights transnational borrowings and exchanges while zooming in on parts of Europe, the Americas, the Indian subcontinent or Africa. In this manner, they are able to show that the observable similarities between different rural knowledge regimes were not, or at least not primarily, the result of the diffusion of hegemonic North Atlantic theories of modernization to the rest of the world, as large sections of the existing historiography suggest. Instead, they can be traced back to multidirectional forms of knowledge exchange that were just as likely to see local experiences redefining global approaches.

Agricultural and Environmental History, the History of Knowledge and Global History: The Chapters in This Volume

This volume addresses key debates in agricultural history and the history of knowledge, as well as colonial and global history, bringing bodies of literature into conversation that have remained surprisingly distinct. In examining agrarian transitions, agricultural and rural history have traditionally focused on the classic means of production: land, labour and capital.[15] Knowledge, as an increasingly important production factor valued by farmers, experts and governments alike, has received far less attention. In his history of the scientization of German agriculture in the twentieth century, Frank Uekötter has described how the increasing appreciation of knowledge as a 'key resource' ('Schlüsselressource') in modern agriculture contributed to the establishment of new types of educational institutions.[16] Similarly, Auderset and Moser have discussed the 'agrarian-industrial knowledge society' ('agrarisch-industrielle Wissensgesellschaft'), examining the ways in which agricultural research and development changed farming practices and boosted outputs in different Western European contexts.[17]

Our volume broadens the history of science and knowledge in agriculture by highlighting their profoundly transnational character, showing that innovations in agricultural practice were seldom the result of narrow national developments. Furthermore, our focus on education and communication adds fresh perspectives to the historiography of agrarian knowledge and science. By relying mainly on the information that state institutions have collected, such as statistics, censuses and other macrolevel data,[18] much of the existing research disproportionately favours top-down understandings of knowledge flows, assigning peasant knowledge only a residual and rarely active character. Peasants' perspectives have been notoriously difficult to investigate, given a lack of sources. At the same time, there have been branches of peasant studies, often focusing on colonial contexts, that have applied innovative methodologies to overcome this bias and study agricultural production and rural politics from below. Such studies, often relying on oral history and ethnographic fieldwork, have tried to invert dominant perspectives on agricultural development by emphasizing peasant knowledge and innovation.[19] Rather than siding with either 'top-down' or 'inversion'-oriented perspectives, this volume focuses on education as a hinge between science and practice, politics and farming, as well as experts and rural dwellers, with the aim of studying the practical application of formal knowledge. Our emphasis on the *communication* of knowledge allows us to study the interface between experts, state actors, farmers and rural communities. The multiple tensions that official interventions almost invariably caused provide important insights into prevailing local practices, conversations and movements in the realm of agricultural education. In many sociopolitical contexts around the world, agricultural education schemes were a coproduction of local actors – including farmers' associations and rural cooperatives that were often led by regional economic elites – and representatives of the state.

Debates around agricultural knowledge have always, at least implicitly, also been about farmers' use of soil, animals, plants and water. This volume contributes to innovative strands of environmental history that have explored this nexus by shedding light on forms of environmentalism that emerged from or in response to agricultural practices. As agricultural production intensified, rural producers searched for what are today called sustainable methods to ensure that future generations would also be able to live on and from the land.[20] On the other hand, conservation also became a platform for the (colonial) state to intervene in rural areas, especially in arid contexts, with officials blaming peasant producers for their allegedly harmful agricultural practices, such as shifting cultivation or overstocking.[21] Another prominent strand of research has explored the environmental impact of intensive, commercially oriented farming as it spread across the world. This has included deforestation, desertification, erosion and a loss of biodiversity, the consequences and associated challenges of which affected farming populations have been forced to confront and contain in order to save their deteriorating livelihoods.[22] Environmental as well as knowledge history offer us the opportunity to question narratives that present agrarian modernization as a one-directional, teleological process by shifting our attention to the multiplicity of potential bodies of knowledge or technological solutions. Given that there have always been many possible trajectories for processes of mechanization or innovation, environmental history allows us to evaluate and question the specific models over which stakeholders fought or negotiated.[23] While our focus on knowledge prioritizes social over environmental dynamics, the chapters in this volume also address the ways in which agricultural education has moderated farmers' interactions with their material environment.

Global history has largely neglected farmers and rural contexts, typically seeking transnational entanglements and exchanges in urban or industrial settings.[24] This volume demonstrates the ways in which rural areas became 'globalized', including through farmers comparing themselves with their counterparts in other countries, experts exchanging problem diagnoses and solutions across borders and governments looking abroad in their search for new ways to integrate rural producers politically and economically. We thereby build on a recent and increasingly robust historiography on rural reform, development and agricultural science from a transnational perspective. Studies in this field have explored the various ways in which national governments have attempted to integrate rural populations through development initiatives.[25] Furthermore, by highlighting the manifold entanglements between different geographical contexts and/or comparing the application of agricultural knowledge or technologies in different locations,[26] such studies have demonstrated the merits of looking beyond national frameworks of analysis – albeit largely in relation to a European or North American context.

Although rural development interventions were in many respects foreshadowed by agricultural development schemes in colonial contexts, the continuities between imperial and international agrarian development have only been partially explored.[27] As previous scholarship has shown, imperial governments intervened in agricultural production from the late nineteenth century onwards with an interest in increasing colonial revenues, often violently enhancing productivity through mandatory quotas or taxation.[28] The interwar period saw a first phase of colonial 'development' policy, during which colonial governments drew up comprehensive plans to increase cash crop production and simultaneously 'uplift' rural producers.[29] In relation to this context, this volume builds on debates on the broader relationship between science and colonialism. While earlier research cast science as an integral component of authoritarian colonial rule – focusing on how important it was for officials and experts to construct colonized populations as backward and inferior, as well as how local bodies of knowledge were systematically misunderstood and eclipsed in the process – more recent studies have questioned this dichotomizing perspective. As Beinart, Brown and Gilfoyle, among other scholars, have argued, colonial science drew on the knowledge of the colonized to a significant degree, sometimes quite consciously. Various studies have since pointed to the interdependent and hybrid character of knowledge production in the colonies.[30]

The chapters in this volume explore the communication of agrarian knowledge in both colonial and international contexts. Highlighting transnational entanglements while also offering comparative perspectives, they analyse the often strikingly similar ways in which methods of education and knowledge dissemination – model villages and farms, extension services, schools or publications – were implemented in heterogeneous local contexts. The volume thus makes a case against Western-centric perspectives of knowledge dissemination from a North Atlantic core. Rather than comparing the 'West' and the 'rest' or focusing on the ways in which 'Western' models have been supposedly imposed without challenge on colonial and postcolonial settings, the volume examines rural and agricultural knowledge circulation as an opportunity to overcome dichotomies that have informed the historiography on modernization in the twentieth century. Whereas identifying a 'great divergence' that pits Europe and the United States in opposition to the rest of the world might be helpful for explaining the dynamics of the industrial world, it offers only limited analytical value when examining how rural lifeworlds have changed.[31]

Renegotiating Global Knowledge in Rural Societies in the Twentieth Century

The chapters in this volume advance existing research on several key themes in the field of rural and agricultural knowledge circulation. First, they analyse the role of the (nation or colonial) state as well as international organizations in generating and communicating knowledge relevant to agriculture and rural issues. Science and education have never been neutral endeavours, but are always embedded in specific – and contested – visions of what role agriculture should play within the modern nation and in the development of rural society. Second, they analyse the mechanisms through which knowledge has been negotiated among and between different social groups – farmers, rural inhabitants, scientists and state officials – as well as the ways in which supposedly universal scientific truths have travelled between societies, and been modified and adapted to the very different social and environmental contexts in which they have been applied.

The Governmentality of Agricultural Knowledge: The Nation State and the Colonial State

As recent historiography has shown for various countries, rural areas came into the focus of attempts to govern populations in a more centralized manner and subject them to novel forms of social engineering.[32] Since at least the late nineteenth century, emerging nation states have developed a profound interest in expanding their authority by modernizing supposedly backward rural peripheries. Rural dwellers' access to education was often markedly inferior to that of their urban peers, and they frequently remained effectively excluded from higher education institutions. The opening of village schools, vocational training centres and other rural educational institutions were evidence of government efforts to offset these disparities and at the same time extend the state's reach into remote areas and political constituencies.[33] Moreover, governments intervened in rural economies in order to control and boost food production, with many departments of agriculture in the nineteenth and early twentieth centuries founded with the explicit goal of increasing agricultural productivity.[34] This became particularly evident in times of crisis. As several chapters in this volume (Geronymaki, Ribi Forclaz and Hartmann) show, the two World Wars and the food shortages they caused became major catalysts for state-led agricultural education initiatives.

Various examples suggest that agricultural and rural education programmes could also form part of an attempt by government or transnational elites to stifle rural radicalism. As Olsson has shown for Mexico and the US South, agrarian populist movements of the late nineteenth and early twentieth centuries, which demanded land reform and redistribution, were displaced by much more conservative, reformist agendas – for instance, in the form of the US-based country life movement – that hailed science and production increase, but shunned questions of social justice.[35] Similarly, South African agricultural policy from the interwar period became increasingly shaped by white officials and experts who believed that starving black rural dwellers, who had been squeezed into entirely inadequate reserves, did not need more land, but only had to be taught how to farm better.[36] Rural education interventions could even serve as a counterinsurgency strategy, as Geronymaki (in this volume) shows in the case of the Greek state's post-Second World War conflict with communist rebels and their supporters among the peasantry. Compared to land reform or other possible strategies for addressing the 'agrarian question', agricultural and rural education often constituted a more cautious and conservative response. The chapters in this volume draw out the ambiguities inherent in agricultural and rural education, which oscillated between the encouragement of change and the containment of social unrest.

Previous historiography has discussed the ways in which 'the rural' became a constitutive imaginative space for rising nation states.[37] Many agricultural schools and village teachers constructed particular notions of 'the village' and 'the rural', and invited new scholarly perspectives on the countryside, for instance, by conducting or encouraging anthropological and sociological surveys. Young farmers' clubs in the United Kingdom, for example, played an important role in the conducting of surveys, while Turkish village institutes promoted the idea of the village as a stronghold of Turkish culture (see Hartmann in this volume). In Latin America, members of the rural middle class assumed the strongly moralist agendas of 4-H programmes to distinguish themselves from urban elite culture (see Pernet in this volume).[38] This double-edged process – governments and elites spreading education in rural areas, yet at the same time defining rural societies as remote, backward and uneducated – has been observed for different societies around the world and points to the tensions and ambiguities inherent in nation-building processes. The orientalization of rural societies, which often accompanied delineations of class, ethnicity and/or race, could be a transnational process in which urban-based elites and experts in different countries exchanged analyses of common rural problems and proposals to address them (see Grunert in this volume). Urban orientalist projections were particularly tangible in rural development programmes. To other reformers, the 'remote countryside' represented a repository of alternative forms of knowledge, with the rediscovery of traditional knowledge feeding into antimodernist agendas that promoted the village as a utopian societal vision.[39] From the perspective of othered rural communities, the sense of being part of local counterknowledge advanced against the universalizing impositions of science could even strengthen local or regional identity constructions (see Fischer and Hartmann in this volume).

In many contexts, farmers came together to advance the agricultural science movement themselves. Although demonstration agents and agricultural schools could be met with a significant degree of scepticism, as the chapter by Horrocks, Martin and Merchant shows in the case of the postwar United Kingdom, many farmers also attached hopes of social advancement and citizenship to the idea of improved agriculture. One prominent example of the inherent ambiguities of agricultural education was the aforementioned Tuskegee Institute in Alabama, which became a global model for the education of black or colonized peoples. While its founder, Booker T. Washington, a former slave, promoted agricultural education as a path to black emancipation, his opponents denounced his pedagogy as a basic labour education designed to uphold white supremacy in the US South as well as in colonial Africa (see Mark-Thiesen in this volume).[40] Similarly, agricultural education projected patriarchal gender norms, with demonstrators and schools usually catering exclusively for men and boys, who were seen as the agents of modern, commercial farming.[41] Women and girls, by contrast, were relegated to a separate sphere of rural domesticity that often sat uneasily with their actual responsibilities on the farm. However, as the example of rural women in South Africa (see Tischler in this volume) shows, many found ways to appropriate rural education to their own ends in their efforts to enhance the wellbeing of their families as well as their own social status. Domestic training, which in many countries formed an integral component of the rural education package, thus sheds light on the construction of – and contestations over – gendered norms that increasingly defined rural divisions of labour and responsibilities.

The Rise of the Agricultural Sciences and Their Local Contestations

By the late nineteenth century, farmers, governments and experts in many parts of the world were convinced that '[t]he era of self-taught or parent-taught farmer ha[d] gone' and that agriculturalists required institutionalized instruction by formally qualified teachers.[42] However, this view has sat uneasily with longstanding, and still-enduring, understandings of being a farmer as an inherited identity rather than an acquired capability. As the chapters in this volume show, the claimed universal validity of scientific agricultural knowledge was in fact often disputed. Knowing how to farm was, and still often is, the result of intergenerational knowledge transmission within the family.[43]

The rise of formalized agricultural knowledge coevolved with novel channels of knowledge exchange. Besides village schools and rural colleges, farmers' associations and cooperatives emerged as new agents of knowledge transmission in many regions of the world, some of them filling the void left by the dissolution of older feudal structures.[44] In the late nineteenth and early twentieth centuries, under the impact of transport and communications revolutions and a phase of globalization that had seen the integration of widely dispersed agricultural markets, farmers, governments and experts began looking beyond the borders of their own countries to an unprecedented degree.[45] They sought insights and inspiration via new opportunities for exchange, such as on expert tours, in specialist journals, in partnership with international organizations or at international exhibitions and conferences.[46]

However, farming had long been cold-shouldered by established scientific institutions. Well into the twentieth century, many farmers and rural communities were still being left to develop their own methods of generating and disseminating knowledge. While initiatives like the Danish folk schools, South African agricultural societies, British young farmers' clubs, 4-H clubs in the United States or Turkish village institutes sought to systematize and empower such efforts,[47] the academic world of the classical university remained reluctant to take up questions of plant breeding, animal husbandry or rural sociology. Established disciplines and institutions, including departments of economics and social or natural sciences, regarded agriculture and rural societies as remnants of the past. Agriculture, as an example of applied science and a mix of different disciplinary approaches, did not fit into the classical divisions that defined existing higher education systems. Agronomists had never been fully part of the *Bildungsbürgertum* (the educated middle class), nor did they invariably integrate into the new economic elite who had built their prosperity on industrial production. In many countries, original institutional forms, such as the Canadian agricultural colleges or the US land-grant colleges (see Part I in this volume) thus evolved outside of or in parallel to conventional academic institutions.[48] While these new institutions were testament to the nation state's increased interest in matters of agricultural research and education, their proponents would frequently have to fight for the recognition of agriculture as a genuine scientific field.

As the chapters in this volume illustrate (see Part III especially), the communication of scientific knowledge was never a one-way street. While several chapters take official programmes run by (colonial) governments or international organizations as a starting point, they emphasize the significant impact of local appropriation and negotiation. The tensions that official interventions almost inevitably caused offer important insights into local practices of and engagement with agricultural education. While experts and officials tried to teach rural families supposedly rational ways of farming and living, rural dwellers brought their own logics to agricultural education and innovation. In her seminal book on the industrial ideal in US agriculture, Deborah Fitzgerald points to the nonlinearity of rural knowledge production and asks where and how historians can locate rationality[49] – whether on the macrolevel, where government agents and experts strive to optimize productivity and secure societal benefits from agriculture, or on a more individual level, where farmers attempt to secure their own subsistence in the long run. Similarly, examples of knowledge being contested at farm demonstrations show that it could make perfect sense for a farmer not to undertake recommended investments, not to pursue the latest technological advances or not to listen to advisers, demonstrators or village teachers.[50] The chapter by Horrocks, Martin and Merchant on farm demonstration in the United Kingdom as well as Doyle-Raso's chapter on the technological choices made by farmers in Uganda when confronted with global regimes of wetland knowledge reflect the dialogic character of rationality in rural contexts. With their priorities set on securing their own subsistence or commercial future, farmers' frequently alleged conservatism was often the result of rational risk calculation.[51]

Examples of local resistance or appropriation point to the contradictions that arose between the universalist claims inherent in scientific knowledge and the highly place-specific nature of agricultural production, which varies according to local soil types and microclimates as much as according to prevailing labour arrangements, family structures, cultural preferences and land tenure practices. As Auderset (in this volume) illustrates, experts frequently confronted these tensions when they favoured industrial models of modernization and adhered to a Taylorist illusion that cast agriculture as one modern profession among others, and conceptualized technical knowledge as a tradable commodity that is interchangeable across time and space.[52] By contrast, the chapters in this volume consider 'global' knowledge to be socially and spatially embedded in local contexts in the same way as 'local' bodies of knowledge.[53] What has distinguished scientific agricultural knowledge is less how it has been shaped into government programmes than its inherent universalizing claims and the positions of power it has consequently adopted. Analysing formalized processes of knowledge communication does not mean playing off the global against the local, but critiquing these positions without presupposing that power is to be found on only one side. 'Transnationalism' itself, as several of the chapters in this volume illustrate (Pernet, Ribi Forclaz, Fischer and Auderset), became an important distinguishing factor with which experts could legitimize their authority on the basis of their international careers and foreign experience.[54] Indeed, many of the individuals discussed in this volume modelled their actions on the experience they had gained in or from other countries. The chapters all explore mechanisms through which individuals established themselves as experts, thereby challenging frequently invoked concepts – foremost, the notion of dissemination – to show that on the ground, it was often far from clear who was actually the expert and who was on the receiving end of expertise. Not only did agriculturists often initiate improvements or technological innovations themselves, but their experiences also fed into the bodies of knowledge that were being curated by formally qualified experts and officials. As Horrocks, Martin and Merchant as well as Grunert show in this volume, agricultural extension, demonstrations, shows and competitions were also opportunities for state actors to keep themselves informed about farmers' problems and problem-solving methods.

Methodologically, historians' quest for rural *Eigensinn* (stubborn self-reliance) and non-elite knowledge has often been hampered by a lack of documentation, as farmers have rarely spoken for themselves in the sources at hand. Existing research has thus tended to focus on the formal side of agricultural knowledge and rural education, but most agricultural knowledge is transmitted informally – within families or by learning on the job.[55] As social historians who share an interest in the history of knowledge, the authors in this volume address the challenge of examining different bodies of knowledge by reading relevant administrative records, newspapers, project reports, school records and letters both with and against the grain to discern farmers' perspectives. Moreover, as several chapters in this volume demonstrate (especially that by Horrocks, Martin and Merchant), oral history is a particularly constructive methodology for addressing such deficits.[56]

The Structure of the Volume

Part I. In Institutions: Brokering Contested Knowledge

The first part of this volume investigates specific institutions and programmes that were established to improve rural production and livelihoods, including their scope and contested nature. In colonial situations (Preeti and

Mark-Thiesen) as well as in the post-Second World War development era (Ribi Forclaz and Hartmann), new programmes to improve rural life proliferated, with their implementation brokered by a multitude of local agents, including government officials, demonstrators, schoolteachers and village headmen. Although such programmes provoked counterreactions, these did not always take the form of open resistance. Local actors expressed their discord with proposed or newly introduced measures through various responses, including refusing to adhere to prescribed techniques, declining to apply a technology in the suggested manner or formulating local alternatives to top-down programmes.

All of these aspects contributed to the negotiation of *mētis* in the sense of James Scott, a form of knowledge derived from practical experience and embedded in local contexts, between peasant and expert populations.[57] Part I focuses on the ways in which processes of negotiation and contestation defined the limits of development programmes, thereby challenging common historiographical perspectives on the expertise that steered such plans. Instead of understanding expert knowledge as exclusive and all-powerful, Part I sheds light on its ephemeral nature and instrumentalization in the competition between different institutional settings. Whereas in some cases (Preeti and Ribi Forclaz) a general lack of trust between outsiders and local populations prevented a constructive dialogue between different knowledge regimes, in other cases social cleavages within rural populations accounted for the limits of rural development projects.

Focusing on the Imperial Agricultural Research Institute in the remote village of Poosah in Bihar, India, Preeti discusses the imperatives and limitations of agricultural research and training in British-ruled India. While the Institute promoted plants and techniques that were intended to maximize colonial revenues, its geographical isolation and top-down approach to transmitting scientific knowledge significantly undermined its capacity to meet its aims. The Booker Washington Institute in Liberia, which Mark-Thiesen explores in her chapter, was founded in 1929 and constituted an unusual case of agricultural knowledge circulation whose aims were shaped by imperialism, but were presented as fostering national self-determination. While its white US philanthropic sponsors supported the Institute as a means to promote the advancement of African rural dwellers through practical training, Liberian leaders were suspicious – not least because the expansion of agricultural and industrial education in Liberia coincided with an emergent US-owned rubber empire in the country and the related fear that the black-led state would be effectively turned into a US protectorate. Arguably, it was not until agricultural (and manual) education became firmly associated with the 'traditional' Indigenous population that the fears of urban dwellers and Liberian officials were assuaged and support for the Institute was won.

Discussing the role played by wartime relief agencies and early postwar international organizations in agricultural development, Ribi Forclaz shifts the focus to a European case study, albeit one that bears some similarities to colonial interventions. Ribi Forclaz unpacks the social and political challenges faced by the agricultural rehabilitation programme that was introduced by the United Nations Relief and Rehabilitation Administration (UNRRA) in war-ravaged, postfascist Italy. Trusting that the importation of farm machinery, cattle, fertilizers, pesticides and seeds would lead to the rehabilitation of Italian agriculture, UNRRA officials ignored structural conditions on the ground, the enduring influence of regional agricultural institutions inherited from the fascist regime as well as the needs and wishes of Italian farmers themselves. The UNRRA's short-lived programme, Ribi Forclaz argues, thus exemplifies the lack of control that international aid organizations had over the actual trajectory of Italian agricultural development.

Hartmann's chapter examines programmes to turn Turkish farmers into modern entrepreneurs with the capacity to compete on the global market after the Second World War and two decades of protectionism. The efforts of the government of Prime Minister Adnan Menderes to modernize Turkish farming by inviting international experts to serve as advisers on rural development and by disseminating scientific knowledge via new educational institutions confronted a myriad of existing institutions – foremost the so-called village institutes, whose foundation dated back to the Atatürk era. Considered an independent, anti-authoritarian instrument of grassroots rural development, this uniquely Turkish approach to modernization attracted international interest and was eventually co-opted into the Marshall Plan-funded agricultural extension service and educational programmes for the rural middle and lower classes. As such, the village institutes represent an example of how local institutions in Turkey and beyond had the potential to shape large-scale, international programmes.

Part II. Across Borders: Transnational Expertise and Entangled Bodies of Knowledge

The chapters in Part II address the question of how knowledge moves in space – across national boundaries as well as within societies and cultures. While several chapters focus on the translation of knowledge – highlighting the ways in which specific bodies of knowledge have been transferred from one national context and adopted in another (Plantinga and Zwarts, and Pernet) – others foreground more circular movements of knowledge back and forth between different countries (Auderset and Grunert). All chapters engage with visions of modernization in agriculture as well as the specific policies associated therewith. Rural communities were defined as backward and subjected to wide-ranging reforms, while experts increasingly modelled agricultural production on industrial ideals of efficiency, mechanization and commercialization. All chapters discuss specific schemes for improving agricultural practices, interventions that often ran counter to the idiosyncrasies of the local contexts in which they were applied.

Grunert analyses rural reforms implemented in the period from 1910 to 1940 in Poland and Yugoslavia, where measures targeting peasant self-organization, agricultural production, and the processing and selling of agricultural products in countries such as Denmark, the Netherlands, Norway, Germany and Switzerland served as examples for rural development. Grunert's chapter investigates several proposed or completed model facilities – including model villages, model farmhouses and experiment stations – as didactic tools through which knowledge on specific aspects of rural life such as housing, education, healthcare and agrarian work was communicated. Rural models were often a reflection of how academics and urban elites orientalized rural communities. However, it is also true that rural inhabitants valued the orientation provided by models and that experts, in turn, recognized the necessity of local adaption. As such, model facilities were never exact copies of pre-existing facilities abroad.

In a similar vein, Plantinga and Zwarts discuss the adaptation of international bodies of knowledge – in this case, mainly from Germany and the United States – in Dutch farming from 1890 to 1970, a period when agriculture in the Netherlands was undergoing rapid specialization. Zooming in on the examples of fertilizer use as well as the application of business economics and scientific work management to commercial farming, Plantinga and Zwarts' chapter analyses the ways in which the emerging Dutch agricultural knowledge infrastructure, despite its openness towards scientific knowledge from abroad, also took into account local variations in farming practice and soil type. But after the Second World War, they argue, the decentralized infrastructure of local schools, extension services and farmers' societies was superseded by national organizations that often disregarded local specificities.

Auderset similarly examines efforts to transplant knowledge from one country to another, highlighting how agricultural work became a subject of intense interdisciplinary scientific inquiry after the First World War. Focusing on the circulation of scientific knowledge on agricultural working practices between Western Europe and North America, he explores the ways in which knowledge claims were constantly reinterpreted, redesigned or re-embedded within specific patterns of agricultural thought and practice as they travelled back and forth across the Atlantic. Offering in-depth insights into efforts to apply Taylorism and scientific management to the United States' Farm Work Simplification Program in the 1940s and to postwar European agriculture, Auderset's chapter shows how knowledge on farm labour became a field of contestation between different visions for aligning agriculture with industrial modernity.

In Latin America, US institutions and experts were not only influential as producers of knowledge, but also actively intervened in rural reform. Pernet's chapter discusses attempts in Costa Rica to replicate the US 4-H agricultural youth clubs, foremost through the Inter-American Program for Rural Youth (PIJR), an effort that was spurred on by fears of social upheaval in rural Latin America in the wake of the 1959 Cuban Revolution. Pernet's analysis adds nuance to previous studies that have examined the PIJR as one of a number of US interventions in Latin America during the Cold War or as a mere instrument of capitalist expansion, arguing instead that the Costa Rican 4-H clubs (or 4-S clubs, as they were known nationally) were not simply a top-down imposition by powerful external actors. The development approaches of Latin American modernizers were closely interlinked with US programmes, but they were also embedded in distinct sociopolitical contexts. As such, despite their underpinnings in US ideology, rural youth clubs could gain popularity in Latin America because they offered their members a much-needed space for sociability as well as a chance to acquire practical, income-generating skills. When the PIJR was dissolved in the 1970s, the 4-S movement in Costa Rica had become sufficiently entrenched in the fabric of rural life to continue without US support.

Part III. On the Ground: Translating Bodies of Knowledge in Rural Communities

Part III emphasizes the perspectives of rural dwellers during their encounters with various experts – government officials, scholars and representatives from international organizations – who were attempting to transform how rural communities farmed and lived. The chapters in Part III highlight how outcomes on the ground could be radically different from the results that experts had envisaged. In so doing, they also foreground methodological concerns and make use of alternative, nonstate sources, read official records or expert accounts against the grain (Tischler and Fischer) or turn to oral history (Horrocks, Martin and Merchant). Because translations often – quite literally – failed, language and linguistic evidence can be extremely insightful when exploring the limits and implications of rural education programmes, as the different case studies show. Through such perspectives, the chapters not only highlight the ways in which some rural education programmes failed, were misunderstood or were rejected wholesale, but also show that 'targeted populations' often appropriated outside interventions, tweaking them to fit their own interests.

Tischler's chapter discusses the ways in which rural women in South Africa responded to domestic training programmes that state authorities promoted as a counterpart to agricultural education initiatives for men. Domestic training promoted distinct and hierarchical gender roles that limited rural women to reproductive work within the home. Notions of domesticity, which were heavily derived from North American experiences, contradicted traditional gender roles in many African cultures, according to which women were assigned the main responsibility for agricultural production. Furthermore, by juxtaposing the experiences of black women in the eastern Cape Province with those of women in white farming communities in the Free State and triangulating these with research on other parts of the globe, Tischler's chapter also shows that emerging contestations were rooted in the processes of agricultural labour itself. Aware that their productive labour was crucial to the viability of farming, black and white rural women in South Africa, as in many other parts of the world, refused to have their existence reduced to reproductive work within the home.

Sally Horrocks, John Martin and Paul Merchant discuss the interactions between scientists, farmers and agricultural advisers in the United Kingdom from 1950 to 1990, a period that saw dramatic productivity increases. Analysing extended biographical interviews, the authors highlight the importance of sociability, arguing that knowledge communication relied on the advisers' development of personal relationships with farmers, as the advisers were well aware. For farmers, the advisers' lectures and meetings offered an opportunity for social interaction as much as for learning about the latest agricultural science. The close relationships between farmers and agricultural advisers ensured that the agrarian knowledge that was generated and refined in their interactions flowed in both directions; nevertheless, as the authors highlight, it was rare for this knowledge to 'travel back to centres of agricultural science' (p. 286).

Analysing the spread of rice farming across southeastern Uganda in the colonial and postcolonial periods, John Doyle-Raso focuses on aspects of language in the interactions between local farmers and Ugandan and foreign officials. After the British colonial authorities had established demonstration farms and intensified their promotion of rice cultivation during the Second World War, the post-independence Ugandan government collaborated with China to construct new demonstration farms. Doyle-Raso argues that changes in the landscape, languages and markets of southeastern Uganda are evidence of how farmers used their knowledge – sometimes as an instrument of cooperation, sometimes as a means of asserting control – to influence the development and operation of demonstration farms and the spread of rice farming. By analysing place names, translations and other aspects of language that were relevant to local rice production, the chapter also reveals the power dynamics that characterized the farming of rice. As Doyle-Raso argues, farmers were empowered by access to translations of scientific knowledge, which they combined with local bodies of knowledge, but their knowledge also subjected them to exploitation by successive governments intent on boosting Uganda's position in the global rice market.

Georg Fischer's chapter examines the role of agricultural knowledge in domestic and international agendas of development, agrarian colonization and Indigenous 'integration' in Bolivia in the 1950s. The Cotoca settlement programme, which formed part of the United Nations' Andean Indian Project (AIP) and was vigorously supported by Bolivia's revolutionary government, combined the goals of increasing agricultural production by settling under-populated areas with 'modernizing' the Indigenous population of the Bolivian highlands through their migration to the agriculturally fertile lowlands, where agricultural education and community development measures were also to be implemented. Fischer's chapter highlights the broader governmentalist aims that came with agricultural education as well as the unforeseen consequences of social engineering as experts and settlers negotiated their own visions of rural development. Agricultural knowledge communication in Cotoca, Fischer argues, was a 'constant [attempt] to reconcile the high modernist ambition … [of] agrarian colonization … with the experiences and expectations of the communities that were supposed to become the bearers of a self-sustaining development process' (p. 340).

Heinrich Hartmann is Professor for Social and Economic History and the History of Technology at the Helmut Schmidt University in Hamburg. He has written a monograph, *Eigensinnige Musterschüler* (Campus, 2020), on expert knowledge in Turkish rural development in the twentieth century and has a broader research focus on European development programmes in the Mediterranean.

Julia Tischler is Associate Professor of African history and co-director of the Centre for African Studies at the University of Basel, Switzerland. With a focus on the history of Southern Africa, she has published on questions of development, settler colonialism, environmental history, race and agriculture. Her first monograph dealt with the history of the Kariba Dam on the border between Zambia and Zimbabwe. She is currently working on a monograph on the history of agricultural progressivism in South Africa.

Notes

1. Cullen Library, University of the Witwatersrand, A73 MacDonald (vol. 1), 'Science in Agriculture', *Daily Graphic*, 27 June 1914. On the role of science in Cape progressivism, see Brown, 'Agriculture in the Natural World', 111.
2. Zimmerman, *Alabama in Africa*, 22; see also Hersey, *My Work Is That of Conservation*.
3. Jabavu, *The Black Problem*.

4. Letter, Turkish ambassador to Switzerland, Zeki Küneralp, to the head of the Swiss programme, Karl Ketterer, Archives of the Migros Genossenschaftsbund, G MT II.021.
5. Ibid.; see also Hartmann, "'Wir wünschen Ihnen mit diesem Türken guten Erfolg'", 41–62.
6. Isett, *State, Merchant, and Peasant*, 1644–862; Brakensiek, 'Das Feld der Agrarreformen um 1800', 101–22; Zimmermann, 'Bäuerlicher Traditionalismus', 219–238.
7. Woods, *The Herds Shot Round the World*; Carney and Rosomoff, *In the Shadow of Slavery*; Crosby, *The Columbian Exchange*; Ehret, *An African Classical Age*; Maddox, *Sub-Saharan Africa*, 23–102; McNeill, 'Biological Exchanges in World History'.
8. Some of these developments have been associated with the 'first wave of globalization' that began in the 1870s; see Nützenadel and Trentmann, *Food and Globalization*; Langthaler, 'Landwirtschaft vor und in der Globalisierung', 135–69; Krausmann and Langthaler, 'Nahrungsregime und Umwelt in der Globalisierung', 85–106; Jachertz and Nützenadel, 'Coping with Hunger?'; Amrith and Clavin, 'Feeding the World'.
9. United Nations, 'Urban and Rural Areas'.
10. See Hartmann's chapter on Turkey in this volume. One of the first development experts to promote reforming land tenure as a means of increasing agricultural productivity was W. Arthur Lewis; see Unger, *International Development*, 109. Two prominent examples of postcolonial land reform and peasant development are Tanzania's Ujamaa programme and Zimbabwe's land reforms; see Lal, *African Socialism in Postcolonial Tanzania*; Moyo, 'Three Decades of Agrarian Reform in Zimbabwe', 493–531.
11. Nützenadel and Trentmann, *Food and Globalization*; Langthaler, 'Landwirtschaft vor und in der Globalisierung'; Langthaler and Krausmann, 'Globale Nahrungsregime aus historisch-sozialökologischer Sicht'.
12. Harwood, *Technology's Dilemma*; Mooser, 'Moderne Landwirtschaft', 15–22; Mooser, 'Das Verschwinden der Bauern', 23–35; Kluge, *Bauern, Agrarkrise und Volksernährung*.
13. Pan-Montojo and Mignemi, 'International Organizations and Agriculture', 237–53; Mignemi, 'Italian Agricultural Experts as Transnational Mediators', 254–76; Lynch-Dungy, 'The Global Agricultural Crisis and British Diplomacy', 297–319; Ribi Forclaz, 'Shaping the Future of Farming', 320–39.
14. Conte, *Highland Sanctuary*, 96–99.
15. Federico, *Feeding the World*; Tauger, *Agriculture in World History*; Bairoch, 'Les trois révolutions agricoles', 317–63.
16. Uekötter, *Die Wahrheit ist auf dem Feld*, 105; Fitzgerald et al., 'Roundtable: Agricultural History', 92, 569–604, esp. 573–74.
17. Auderset and Moser, *Agrarfrage*.
18. In Fitzgerald's words: 'It was numbers, not narratives, that became the dominant language in agricultural knowledge.' Fitzgerald, *Every Farm a Factory*, 35.
19. However, few historians in this field have focused explicitly on agricultural knowledge, with most concentrating on the politics of rural resistance; cf. Williams, 'Taking the Part of Peasants', 131–54; Schäfer, *Guter Rat ist wie die Glut des Feuers*; Feierman, *Peasant Intellectuals*; Fliege, *Bauernfamilien zwischen Tradition und Moderne*; Beinart and Bundy, *Hidden Struggles in Rural South Africa;* Ranger, *Peasant Consciousness and Guerrilla War in Zimbabwe*; Richards, *Indigenous Agricultural Revolution*. For a recent, broad-ranging assessment of peasants in global history, see Vanhaute, *Peasants in World History*.

20. Mulwafu, *Conservation Song*; Beinart, *Rise of Conservation in South Africa*, 499–516.
21. Davis, 'Of Deserts and Decolonization'; Davis, *Resurrecting the Granary of Rome*. For an early discussion of the concept of environmental orientalism, see Sawyer and Agrawal, 'Environmental Orientalisms', 71–108. On African contexts, see e.g. Anderson and Grove, *Conservation in Africa*.
22. For a global synthesis, see Ross, *Ecology and Power in the Age of Empire*, esp. 307–350. See also Ax et al., *Cultivating the Colonies*; Jacobs, *Environment, Power, and Injustice*; Isaacman and Roberts, *Cotton, Colonialism, and Social History in Sub-Saharan Africa*; Adas, 'Continuity and Transformation', 191–207; D'Souza, 'Water in British India', 621–628; Fernando, 'Famine in a Land of Plenty', 291–320.
23. Lyautey, Humbert, and Bonneuil, 'Introduction', 7–20.
24. Unger, 'Agrarwissenschaftliche Expertise', 552–579, here 553–554.
25. Van de Grift and Ribi Forclaz have examined rural interventions in interwar Europe as a form of governance by which national governments attempted to raise food production, improve rural living standards and integrate rural populations; Van de Grift and Ribi Forclaz, *Governing the Rural*. See also Vivier, *The State and Rural Societies*. Rodgers has discussed progressive-era knowledge exchanges in the areas of rural reform and, to a lesser extent, education within a North Atlantic framework; Rodgers, *Atlantic Crossings*. On agrarianism as an Eastern European movement, see Müller and Harre, *Transforming Rural Societies*. On agrarian reform in 'the Euro-American World', see Regan and Smith, *Agrarian Reform and Resistance in an Age of Globalisation*.
26. Jonathan Harwood has compared 'Europe's Green Revolution' with the green revolutions in the formerly colonized world; Harwood, *Europe's Green Revolution and Others Since*.
27. See e.g. Scott, who has pointed to the continuities between agricultural development schemes in colonial Tanzania and post-independence Ujamaa rural development; Scott, *Seeing Like a State*.
28. See e.g. the rich scholarship on the cash crop revolution after the abolition of the slave trade in colonial Africa: Austin, 'Vent for Surplus or Productivity Breakthrough?', 1,035–1,064; Hill, *Studies in Rural Capitalism in West Africa*. Zimmerman has analysed a cotton cultivation scheme in German-ruled Togo, highlighting the degree of coercion and the racist message inherent in programmes of agricultural improvement that delegated particular forms of agrarian labour to specific communities based on their skin colour; Zimmerman, *Alabama in Africa*.
29. Tischler, 'Agriculture', 119–150; Van Beusekom, *Negotiating Development*; Hodge, *Triumph of the Expert*; Cooper, *Africa since 1940*; Moon, *Technology and Ethical Idealism*; Conte, *Highland Sanctuary*, 96–98. Beinart wrote a seminal study on rural development and the conservation movement in the settler-colonial context of South Africa; Beinart, *Rise of Conservation in South Africa*. See also Unger, *Entwicklungspfade in Indien*; Unger and Frey, 'Rural Development in the Twentieth Century'; Bernal, 'Cotton and Colonial Order in Sudan', 96–118; Bonneuil, 'Pénétrer l'indigène', 199–223.
30. Beinart, Brown, and Gilfoyle, 'Experts and Expertise in Colonial Africa Reconsidered', 413–433. Among others, the authors criticize McCracken ('Experts and Expertise in Colonial Malawi', 101–116) and Fairhead and Leach (*Misreading the African*

Landscape). Studies highlighting the interdependence of 'local' and 'scientific' knowledge include, among many others, Tilley, *Africa as a Living Laboratory*; Harries, *Butterflies and Barbarians*; von Hellermann, 'Reading Farm and Forest', 89–114.

31. Pomeranz, *The Great Divergence*; Landes, *Wealth and Poverty of Nations*; Bairoch, *Economics and World History*.
32. Van de Grift and Ribi Forclaz, *Governing the Rural*.
33. Adams, 'Rural Education and Reform between the Wars'; Brassley, Burchardt, and Thompson, *The English Countryside between the Wars*, 36–52; Ashby and Byles, *Rural Education*.
34. Harwood, *Technology's Dilemma*; Harwood, *Europe's Green Revolution and Others Since*.
35. Olsson, *Agrarian Crossings*, 31–36.
36. Tischler, 'Education and the Agrarian Question'.
37. For instance, there is a robust historiography in relation to France, including the seminal works of Jacques and Mona Ouzouf as well as Eugen Weber; Ouzouf and Ouzouf, *La république des instituteurs*; Weber, *Peasants into Frenchmen*; see also Aldenhoff-Hübinger, 'La politisation des campagnes', 163–176. Merkel-Hess has examined the Chinese nation state's rural self-understanding; Merkel-Hess, *The Rural Modern*.
38. Similarly, the US land-grant universities played an important role in conducting surveys; see Thompson, 'Agricultural Education in the Interwar Years'; Brassley, Burchardt, and Thompson, *The English Countryside between the Wars*, 53–72, 60; Cravens, '"Waist Deep in the Big Muddy"', 241–268; Yıldırmaz, *Politics and the Peasantry in Turkey*.
39. Treitel, *Eating Nature in Modern Germany*; Barton, *The Global History of Organic Farming*, 80–93.
40. On Tuskegee's legacy in the US South, see Harlan, *Booker T. Washington*. On Tuskegee's colonial reverberations, see Zimmerman, *Alabama in Africa*.
41. On gender roles in modern farming, see e.g. Jones, *Gender and Rural Modernity*; Osterud, *Putting the Barn before the House*; Neth, *Preserving the Family Farm*; Jensen, *With These Hands*; Verdon, 'The Modern Countrywoman', 86–107; Jellison, *Entitled to Power*; Jensen and Ambrose, *Women in Agriculture*.
42. South African Dept. of Agriculture and Forestry, Division of Agricultural Education and Research, 'Vocational Training in Agriculture', SAB LON 236, A 138/1, Vol. II, c. October 1946. On agriculture's transition to a science, see Hillebrand, 'Books and Dirt in a Transatlantic World', 90–103.
43. For an in-depth study of agricultural knowledge generation and communication among Shona women in Zimbabwe, see Schäfer, *Guter Rat ist wie die Glut des Feuers*. See also Fliege, *Bauernfamilien zwischen Tradition und Moderne*.
44. Vári, 'Ländliche Genossenschaften in der Habsburgermonarchie', 255–98; Vári, *Herren und Landwirte*; Holec, 'Agrardemokratie als Versuch eines Dritten Weges', 41–54; Müller and Harre, 'Agrarianism as Third Way', 14–23; Bódy, 'Weder Demokratisierung noch Diktatur', 225–52.
45. Nützenadel and Trentmann have highlighted the ways in which markets for agriculture produce and food became increasingly internationally integrated; Nützenadel and Trentmann, *Food and Globalization*.
46. Jones, 'Seeing Is Believing', 37–51.

47. Rodgers, *Atlantic Crossings*, 354–57; Karaömerlioğlu, 'The Village Institutes Experience in Turkey', 47–73; Thompson, 'Agricultural Education in the Interwar Years', 53–72.
48. The US land-grant colleges were created as a result of the first Morrill Act of 1862, which gave each state the right to grant land for the establishment of institutions that would teach 'practical' science (namely agriculture) instead of instruction in the liberal arts tradition, which was widely associated with the European university system; Marcus, *Service as Mandate*.
49. Fitzgerald, *Every Farm a Factory*, 33–50.
50. Marcus, *Agricultural Science and the Quest for Legitimacy*; Danbom, 'The Agricultural Experiment Station and Professionalism', 246–55.
51. Scott has famously argued that the peasant moral economy has not followed macroeconomic reasoning. Instead, peasants' first priority has been to secure their own subsistence before investing in their farms. As he describes, there can be perfectly rational reasons for this seemingly antimodernist and non-innovative behaviour; Scott, *Moral Economy of the Peasant*.
52. Auderset and Moser, *Agrarfrage*.
53. Livingstone, *Putting Science in Its Place*.
54. Rodogno, Struck and Vogel, 'Introduction', 1–20.
55. Brassley, 'Agricultural Education, Training and Advice', 260–61.
56. In relation to British history, there is a strong research tradition among social historians of applying oral history methods to gain insights into the knowledge of farmers and their attempts to improve their agricultural practices; see Evans, *Ask the Fellows Who Cut the Hay*; and Evans, *Horse in the Furrow*.
57. Scott, *Seeing Like a State*, 6 and 311.

Bibliography

Adams, Caitlin. 'Rural Education and Reform between the Wars', in Paul Brassley, Jeremy Burchardt and Lynne Thompson (eds), *The English Countryside between the Wars: Regeneration or Decline?* (Woodbridge: Boydell Press, 2006), 36–52.
Adas, Michael. 'Continuity and Transformation: Colonial Rice Frontiers and Their Environmental Impact on the Great River Deltas of Mainland Southeast Asia', in Edmund Burke III and Kenneth Pomeranz (eds), *The Environment and World History* (Berkeley: University of California Press, 2009), 191–207.
Aldenhoff-Hübinger, Rita. 'La politisation des campagnes à travers agrarisme et protectionnisme à la fin du 19e siècle en Europe (Allemagne, France, Italie)', in Jean-Luc Mayaud and Lutz Raphael (eds), *Histoire de l'Europe rurale contemporaine: Du village à l'État* (Paris: Armand Colin, 2006), 163–76.
Amrith, Sunil, and Patricia Clavin. 'Feeding the World: Connecting Europe and Asia, 1930–1945', *Past & Present* 218(8) (2013), 29–50.
Anderson, David, and Richard H. Grove. *Conservation in Africa: Peoples, Policies and Practice*. Cambridge: Cambridge University Press, 1988.
Ashby, Arthur W., and Phoebe G. Byles. *Rural Education: A Study of Oxford County, England, Conducted in 1920 under the Auspices of the Oxford National Education Association and the Horace Plunkett Foundation*. New York: Oxford University Press, 1923.

Auderset, Juri, and Peter Moser. *Die Agrarfrage in der Industriegesellschaft: Wissenskulturen, Machverhältnisse und natürliche Ressourcen in der agrarisch-industriellen Wissensgesellschaft (1850–1950)*. Cologne: Böhlau, 2018.

Austin, Gareth. 'Vent for Surplus or Productivity Breakthrough? The Ghanaian Cocoa Take-off, c. 1890–1936'. *Economic History Review* 67(4) (2004), 1035–64.

Ax, Christina Folke, Niels Brimnes, Thode Jensen and Karen Oslund (eds), *Cultivating the Colonies: Colonial States and Their Environmental Legacies*. Athens, OH: Ohio University Press, 2014.

Bairoch, Paul. 'Les trois révolutions agricoles du monde développé: Rendements et productivité de 1800 à 1985'. *Annales ESC* 44 (1989), 317–63.

———. *Economics and World History: Myths and Paradoxes*. New York: Harvester Wheatsheaf, 1993.

Barton, Gregory A. *The Global History of Organic Farming*. Oxford: Oxford University Press, 2018.

Beinart, William. *The Rise of Conservation in South Africa: Settlers, Livestock, and the Environment 1770–1950*. Oxford: Oxford University Press, 2003.

Beinart, William, Karen Brown, and Daniel Gilfoyle. 'Experts and Expertise in Colonial Africa Reconsidered: Science and the Interpretation of Knowledge'. *African Affairs* 108(432) (2009), 413–33.

Beinart, William, and Colin Bundy. *Hidden Struggles in Rural South Africa*. Johannesburg: Ravan Press, 1987.

Bernal, Victoria. 'Cotton and Colonial Order in Sudan: A Social History with Emphasis on the Gezira Scheme', in Allen Isaacman and Richard Roberts (eds), *Cotton, Colonialism, and Social History in Sub-Saharan Africa* (Portsmouth: Heinemann, 1995), 96–118.

Bódy, Zsombor. 'Weder Demokratisierung noch Diktatur: Die kontrollierte Politisierung der ländlichen Unterschichten im Ungarn der Zwischenkriegszeit', in Eduard Kubů, Torsten Lorenz, Uwe Müller and Jiří Šouša (eds), *Agrarismus und Agrareliten in Ostmitteleuropa* (Berlin: Berliner Wissenschaftsverlag, 2013), 225–52.

Bonneuil, Christophe. 'Pénétrer l'indigène: Arachide, paysans, agronomes et administrateurs coloniaux au Sénégal (1897–1950)'. *Études rurales* 151/152 (1999), 199–223.

Brakensiek, Stephan. 'Das Feld der Agrarreformen um 1800', in Eric J. Engstrom, Volker Hess and Ulrike Thoms (eds), *Figurationen des Experten: Ambivalenzen der wissenschaftlichen Expertise im ausgehenden 18. und frühen 19. Jahrhundert* (Frankfurt: Peter Lang, 2005), 101–22.

Brassley, Paul. 'Agricultural Education, Training and Advice in the UK, 1850–2000', in Nadine Vivier (ed.), *The State and Rural Societies: Policy and Education in Europe, 1750–2000* (Turnhout: Brepols, 2008), 259–78.

Brassley, Paul, Jeremy Burchardt and Lynne Thompson (eds). *The English Countryside between the Wars: Regeneration or Decline?* Woodbridge: Boydell Press, 2006.

Brown, Karen. 'Agriculture in the Natural World: Progressivism, Conservation and the State. The Case of the Cape Colony in the Late 19th and Early 20th Centuries'. *Kronos* 29 (2003), 109–38.

Carney, Judith, and Richard Rosomoff. *In the Shadow of Slavery: Africa's Botanical Legacy in the Atlantic World*. Berkeley: University of California Press, 2011.

Conte, Christopher A. *Highland Sanctuary: Environmental History in Tanzania's Usambara Mountains*. Athens, OH: Ohio University Press, 2004.

Cooper, Frederick C. *Africa since 1940: The Past of the Present*. Cambridge: Cambridge University Press, 2014.

Cravens, Hamilton. '"Waist Deep in the Big Muddy": Land-Grant Social Scientists and Modernity from the Country Life Movement to the Cold War', in Alan I. Marcus (ed.), *Service as Mandate: How American Land-Grant Universities Shaped the Modern World, 1920–2015* (Tuscaloosa: University of Alabama Press, 2015), 241–68.

Crosby, Alfred. *The Columbian Exchange: Biological and Cultural Consequences of 1492*. Westport, CT: Praeger, 1972.

Danbom, David B. 'The Agricultural Experiment Station and Professionalism: Scientists' Goals for Agriculture'. *Agricultural History* 60(2) (1986), 246–55.

Davis, Diana K. *Resurrecting the Granary of Rome: Environmental History and French Colonial Expansion in North Africa*. Athens, OH: Ohio University Press, 2007.

———. 'Of Deserts and Decolonization: Dispelling Myths about Drylands. Pastoralism, Uncertainty and Resilience'. *PASTRES*, 30 October 2020. Retrieved 25 October 2022 from https://pastres.org/2020/10/30/of-deserts-and-decolonization-dispelling-myths -about-drylands.

D'Souza, Rohan. 'Water in British India: The Making of a "Colonial Hydrology"'. *History Compass* 4(4) (2006), 621–28.

Ehret, Christopher. *An African Classical Age: Eastern and Southern Africa in World History, 1000 BC to AD 400*. Charlottesville: University of Virginia Press, 2001.

Evans, George E. *Ask the Fellows Who Cut the Hay*. London: Faber, 1965.

———. *The Horse in the Furrow*. London: Faber, 1967.

Fairhead, James, and Melissa Leach. *Misreading the African Landscape: Society and Ecology in a Forest-Savanna Mosaic*. Cambridge: Cambridge University Press, 1996.

Federico, Giovanni. *Feeding the World: An Economic History of Agriculture*. Princeton: Princeton University Press, 2008.

Feierman, Steven. *Peasant Intellectuals: Anthropology and History in Tanzania*. Madison: University of Wisconsin Press, 1990.

Fernando, M.R. 'Famine in a Land of Plenty: Plight of a Rice-Growing Community in Java, 1883–84'. *Journal of Southeast Asian Studies* 41(2) (2010), 291–320.

Fitzgerald, Deborah. *Every Farm a Factory: The Industrial Ideal in American Culture*. New Haven: Yale University Press, 2003.

Fitzgerald, Deborah, Lisa Onaga, Emily Pawley, Denise Phillips and Jeremy Vetter. 'Roundtable: Agricultural History and the History of Science'. *Agricultural History* 92 (2018), 569–604.

Fliege, Thomas. *Bauernfamilien zwischen Tradition und Moderne: Eine Ethnographie bäuerlicher Lebensstile*. Frankfurt: Campus, 1998.

Harlan, Louis R. *Booker T. Washington: The Wizard of Tuskegee*. New York: Oxford University Press, 1983.

Harries, Patrick. *Butterflies and Barbarians: Swiss Missionaries and Systems of Knowledge in South-East Africa*. Oxford: James Currey, 2007.

Hartmann, Heinrich. '"Wir wünschen Ihnen mit diesem Türken guten Erfolg": Die Migros als Akteur der ländlichen Entwicklung in der Schweiz und in der Türkei in den 1960er Jahren'. *Schweizerische Zeitschrift für Geschichte* 70(1) (2020), 41–62.

Harwood, Jonathan. *Technology's Dilemma: Agricultural Colleges between Science and Practice in Germany, 1860–1934*. Frankfurt: Peter Lang, 2005.

———. *Europe's Green Revolution and Others Since: The Rise and Fall of Peasant-Friendly Plant Breeding*. New York: Routledge, 2012.

Hersey, Mark. *My Work Is That of Conservation: An Environmental Biography of George Washington Carver*. Athens, GA: University of Georgia Press, 2011.

Hill, Polly. *Studies in Rural Capitalism in West Africa*. Cambridge: Cambridge University Press, 1970.

Hillebrand, Justus. 'Books and Dirt in a Transatlantic World: Negotiating Agricultural Knowledge in Nineteenth-Century Maine and Westphalia', in Joe Regan and Cathal Smith (eds), *Agrarian Reform and Resistance in an Age of Globalisation: The Euro-American World and beyond, 1780–1914* (New York: Routledge, 2018), 90–103.

Hodge, Joseph M. *Triumph of the Expert: Agrarian Doctrines of Development and the Legacies of British Colonialism*. Athens, OH: University of Ohio Press, 2007.

Holec, Roman. 'Agrardemokratie als Versuch eines Dritten Weges mitteleuropäischer Transformation', in Helga Schultz and Angela Harre (eds), *Bauerngesellschaften auf dem Weg in die Moderne: Agrarismus in Ostmitteleuropa 1880 bis 1960* (Wiesbaden: Harrassowitz, 2011), 41–54.

Isaacman, Allen, and Richard Roberts (eds). *Cotton, Colonialism, and Social History in Sub-Saharan Africa*. Portsmouth: Heinemann, 1995.

Isett, Christopher. *State, Merchant, and Peasant on the Manchurian Frontier, 1644–1862*. Stanford: Stanford University Press, 2007.

Jabavu, Davidson Don Tengo. *The Black Problem: Papers and Addresses on Various Native Problems*. Alice: Lovedale Institution Press, 1920.

Jachertz, Ruth, and Alexander Nützenadel. 'Coping with Hunger? Visions of a Global Food System, 1930–1960'. *Journal of Global History* 6 (2011), 99–119.

Jacobs, Nancy. *Environment, Power, and Injustice*. Cambridge: Cambridge University Press, 2009.

Jellison, Katherine. *Entitled to Power: Farm Women and Technology, 1913–1963*. Chapel Hill: University of North Carolina Press, 1993.

Jensen, Joan M. *With These Hands: Women Working on the Land*. New York: Feminist Press, 1981.

Jensen, Joan M., and Linda Ambrose (eds). *Women in Agriculture: Professionalizing Rural Life in North America and Europe, 1880–1965*. Iowa City: University of Iowa Press, 2017.

Jones, Elizabeth B. *Gender and Rural Modernity: Farm Women and the Politics of Labor in Germany, 1871–1933*. Aldershot: Ashgate, 2009.

———. 'Seeing Is Believing: Sites/Sights of Agricultural Improvement in Germany (1840–1914)'. *Rural History* 30(1) (2019), 37–51.

Karaömerlioğlu, Asım. 'The Village Institutes Experience in Turkey'. *British Journal of Middle Eastern Studies* 25(1) (1998), 47–73.

Khan, Farieda. 'Rewriting South Africa's Conservation History: The Role of the Native Farmers Association'. *Journal of Southern African Studies* 20(4) (1994), 499–516.

Kluge, Ulrich. *Bauern, Agrarkrise und Volksernährung in der europäischen Zwischenkriegszeit: Studien zur Agrargesellschaft und -wirtschaft der Republik Österreich 1918–1938*. Stuttgart: Steiner, 1988.

Krausmann, Fridolin, and Ernst Langthaler. 'Nahrungsregime und Umwelt in der Globalisierung (1870–2010)', in Karin Fischer, Johannes Jäger and Lukas Schmidt (eds), *Rohstoffe und Entwicklung: Aktuelle Auseinandersetzungen im historischen Kontext* (Vienna: New Academic Press, 2016), 85–106.

Krausmann, Fridolin, and Ernst Langthaler. 'Globale Nahrungsregime aus historisch-sozialökologischer Sicht'. *Rural History Working Papers* 33 (2016).

Lal, Priya. *African Socialism in Postcolonial Tanzania: Between the Village and the World.* Cambridge: Cambridge University Press, 2017.

Landes, David S. *The Wealth and Poverty of Nations: Why Some Are So Rich and Some So Poor.* New York: W.W. Norton & Company, 1998.

Langthaler, Ernst. 'Landwirtschaft vor und in der Globalisierung', in Reinhard Sieder and Ernst Langthaler (eds), *Globalgeschichte 1800–2010* (Vienna: Böhlau, 2010), 135–69.

Livingstone, David N. *Putting Science in Its Place: Geographies of Scientific Knowledge.* Chicago: University of Chicago Press, 2003.

Lyautey, Margot, Léna Humbert and Christophe Bonneuil. 'Introduction: Un renouveau de l'histoire contemporaine des mondes agricoles et espaces ruraux', in Margot Lyautey, Léna Humbert and Christophe Bonneuil (eds), *Histoire des modernisations agricoles au XXe siècle* (Rennes: Presses Universitaires de Rennes, 2021), 7–20.

Lynch-Dungy, Madeleine. 'The Global Agricultural Crisis and British Diplomacy in the League of Nations in 1931'. *Agricultural History Review* 65(2) (2017), 297–319.

Maddox, Gregory. *Sub-Saharan Africa: An Environmental History.* Santa Barbara: ABC-CLIO, 2006.

Marcus, Alan I. *Agricultural Science and the Quest for Legitimacy: Farmers, Agricultural Colleges, and Experiment Stations, 1870–1890.* Ames: Iowa State University Press, 1985.

———. (ed.). *Service as Mandate: How American Land-Grant Universities Shaped the Modern World, 1920–2015.* Tuscaloosa: University of Alabama Press, 2015.

McCracken, John. 'Experts and Expertise in Colonial Malawi'. *African Affairs* 81(322) (1982), 101–16.

McNeill, John R. 'Biological Exchanges in World History', in Jerry Bentley (ed.), *The Oxford Handbook of World History* (Oxford: Oxford University Press, 2011), 325–42.

Merkel-Hess, Kate. *The Rural Modern: Reconstructing the Self and State in Republican China.* Chicago: University of Chicago Press, 2016.

Mignemi, Niccolò. 'Italian Agricultural Experts as Transnational Mediators: The Creation of the International Institute of Agriculture'. *Agricultural History Review* 65(2) (2017), 254–76.

Moon, Suzanne. *Technology and Ethical Idealism: A History of Development in the Netherlands East Indies.* Leiden: Brill, 2007.

Mooser, Josef. 'Das Verschwinden der Bauern: Überlegungen zur Sozialgeschichte der "Entagrarisierung" und Modernisierung der Landwirtschaft im 20. Jahrhundert', in Daniela Münkel (ed.), *Der lange Abschied vom Agrarland: Agrarpolitik, Landwirtschaft und ländliche Gesellschaft zwischen Weimar und Bonn* (Göttingen: Wallstein, 2000), 23–35.

———. 'Moderne Landwirtschaft: Einführende Bemerkungen zu langfristigen Weichen-stellungen und Phasen der agrarischen Modernisierung seit dem 18. Jahrhundert', in Karl Ditt, Rita Gudermann, and Norwich Rüße (eds), *Agrarmodernisierung und ökologische Folgen: Westfalen vom 18. bis zum 20. Jahrhundert* (Paderborn: Schöningh, 2001), 15–22.

Moyo, Sam. 'Three Decades of Agrarian Reform in Zimbabwe'. *Journal of Peasant Studies* 38(3) (2011), 493–531.

Müller, Dietmar, and Angela Harre. 'Agrarianism as Third Way: Between Fascism and Communism and between Capitalism and Collectivism', in Dietmar Müller and Angela Harre (eds), *Transforming Rural Societies: Agrarian Property and Agrarianism in East Central Europe in the Nineteenth and Twentieth Centuries* (Innsbruck: Studienverlag, 2011), 14–23.

———. (eds). *Transforming Rural Societies: Agrarian Property and Agrarianism in East Central Europe in the Nineteenth and Twentieth Centuries.* Innsbruck: Studienverlag, 2011.

Mulwafu, Wapulumuka. *Conservation Song: A History of Peasant-State Relations and the Environment in Malawi, 1860–2000.* Cambridge: White Horse Press, 2010.

Neth, Mary C. *Preserving the Family Farm: Women, Community, and the Foundations of Agribusiness in the Midwest, 1900–1940.* Baltimore: Johns Hopkins University Press, 1998.

Nützenadel, Alexander, and Frank Trentmann (eds). *Food and Globalization: Consumption, Markets and Politics in the Modern World.* London: Bloomsbury, 2008.

Olsson, Tore C. *Agrarian Crossings: Reformers and the Remaking of the US and Mexican Countryside.* Princeton: Princeton University Press, 2017.

Osterud, Nancy Grey. *Putting the Barn before the House: Women and Family Farming in Early Twentieth-Century New York.* Ithaca: Cornell University Press, 2012.

Ouzouf, Jacques, and Mona Ouzouf. *La république des instituteurs*, Paris: Seuil, 1992.

Pan-Montojo, Juan, and Niccolò Mignemi. 'International Organizations and Agriculture 1905–1945: Introduction'. *Agricultural History Review* 65(2) (2017), 237–53.

Pomeranz, Kenneth. *The Great Divergence: China, Europe, and the Making of the Modern World Economy.* Princeton: Princeton University Press, 2000.

Ranger, Terence. *Peasant Consciousness and Guerrilla War in Zimbabwe: A Comparative Perspective.* London: James Currey, 1985.

Regan, Joe, and Cathal Smith (eds). *Agrarian Reform and Resistance in an Age of Globalisation: The Euro-American World and beyond, 1780–1914.* New York: Routledge, 2018.

Ribi Forclaz, Amalia. 'Shaping the Future of Farming: The International Labour Organization and Agricultural Education, 1920s to 1950s'. *Agricultural History Review* 65(2) (2017), 320–39.

Richards, Paul. *Indigenous Agricultural Revolution: Ecology and Food Production in West Africa.* London: Hutchinson, 1985.

Rodgers, Daniel T. *Atlantic Crossings: Social Politics in a Progressive Age.* Cambridge, MA: Belknap Press, 1998.

Rodogno, Davide, Bernhard Struck, and Jakob Vogel. 'Introduction', in Davide Rodogno, Bernhard Struck and Jakob Vogel (eds), *Shaping the Transnational Sphere: Experts, Networks and Issues from the 1840s to the 1930s* (New York: Berghahn Books, 2015), 1–20.

Ross, Corey. *Ecology and Power in the Age of Empire: Europe and the Transformation of the Tropical World.* Oxford: Oxford University Press, 2017.

Sawyer, Suzana, and Arun Agrawal. 'Environmental Orientalisms'. *Cultural Critique* 45 (2000), 71–108.

Schäfer, Rita. *Guter Rat ist wie die Glut des Feuers: Der Wandel der Anbaukenntnisse, Wissenskommunikation und Geschlechterverhältnisse der Shona in Zimbabwe.* Herbolzheim: Centaurus Verlag und Media UG, 1998.

Scott, James C. *The Moral Economy of the Peasant: Rebellion and Subsistence in Southeast Asia.* New Haven: Yale University Press, 1976.

———. *Seeing Like a State: How Certain Schemes to Improve the Human Condition Have Failed.* New Haven: Yale University Press, 1998.

Tauger, Mark B. *Agriculture in World History.* Abingdon: Routledge, 2010.

Thompson, Lynne. 'Agricultural Education in the Interwar Years', in Paul Brassley, Jeremy Burchardt and Lynne Thompson (eds), *The English Countryside between the Wars: Regeneration or Decline?* (Woodbridge: Boydell Press, 2006), 53–72.

Tilley, Helen. *Africa as a Living Laboratory.* Chicago: University of Chicago Press, 2011.

Tischler, Julia. 'Education and the Agrarian Question in South Africa, c. 1900–40'. *Journal of African History* 57(2) (2016), 251–70.

———. 'Agriculture', in Stefano Bellucci and Andreas Eckert (eds), *General Labour History of Africa: Workers, Employers and Governments, 20th–21st Centuries* (Woodbridge: James Currey, 2019), 119–50.

Treitel, Corinna. *Eating Nature in Modern Germany: Food, Agriculture, and Environment, c. 1870 to 2000.* Cambridge: Cambridge University Press, 2017.

Uekötter, Frank. *Die Wahrheit ist auf dem Feld: Eine Wissensgeschichte der deutschen Landwirtschaft.* Göttingen: Vandenhoeck & Ruprecht, 2010.

Unger, Corinna. 'Agrarwissenschaftliche Expertise und ländliche Modernisierungsstrategien in der internationalen Entwicklungspolitik, 1920er bis 1980er Jahre'. *Geschichte und Gesellschaft* 41(4) (2015), 552–79.

———. *Entwicklungspfade in Indien: Eine internationale Geschichte 1947–1980.* Göttingen: Wallstein, 2015.

———. *International Development: A Postwar History.* London: Bloomsbury, 2018.

Unger, Corinna, and Marc Frey. 'Rural Development in the Twentieth Century: International Perspectives'. *Comparativ* 27(2) (2017), 7–14.

'Urban and Rural Areas'. 2007. United Nations website. Retrieved 25 October 2022 from https://www.un.org/en/development/desa/population/publications/pdf/urbanization /2007_urban_rural_chart.pdf.

Van Beusekom, Monika. *Negotiating Development: African Farmers and Colonial Experts at the Office du Niger, 1920–1960.* Oxford: Oxford University Press, 2002.

Van de Grift, Liesbeth, and Amalia Ribi Forclaz (eds). *Governing the Rural in Interwar Europe.* Abingdon: Routledge, 2018.

Vanhaute, Eric. *Peasants in World History.* Abingdon: Routledge, 2021.

Vári, András. *Herren und Landwirte: Ungarische Aristokraten und Agrarier auf dem Weg in die Moderne, 1821–1910.* Wiesbaden: Harrassowitz, 2008.

———. 'Ländliche Genossenschaften in der Habsburgermonarchie zwischen lokaler Eigeninitiative und Mitwirkung der Elite', in Eduard Kubů, Torsten Lorenz, Uwe Müller and Jiří Šouša (eds), *Agrarismus und Agrareliten in Ostmitteleuropa* (Berlin: Berliner Wissenschaftsverlag, 2013), 255–98.

Verdon, Nicola. "'The Modern Countrywoman": Farm Women, Domesticity and Social Change in Interwar Britain'. *History Workshop Journal* 70(1) (2010), 86–107.

Vivier, Nadine (ed.). *The State and Rural Societies: Policy and Education in Europe, 1750–2000*. Turnhout: Brepols, 2008.

Von Hellermann, Pauline. 'Reading Farm and Forest: Colonial Forest Science and Policy in Southern Nigeria', in Ricardo Roque and Kim A. Wagner (eds), *Engaging Colonial Knowledge: Reading European Archives in World History* (Basingstoke: Palgrave Macmillan, 2012), 89–114.

Weber, Eugen. *Peasants into Frenchmen: The Modernization of Rural France, 1870–1914*. Stanford: Stanford University Press, 1976.

Williams, Gavin. 'Taking the Part of Peasants: Rural Development in Nigeria and Tanzania', in Peter C.W. Gutkind and Immanuel Wallerstein (eds), *The Political Economy of Contemporary Africa* (Beverley Hills: Sage, 1976), 131–54.

Woods, Rebecca. *The Herds Shot Round the World: Native Breeds and the British Empire, 1800–1900*. Chapel Hill: University of North Carolina Press, 2017.

Yıldırmaz, Sinan. *Politics and the Peasantry in Turkey: Social History, Culture and Modernization*. London: I.B. Tauris, 2017.

Zimmerman, Andrew. *Alabama in Africa: Brooker T. Washington, the German Empire, and the Globalization of the New South*. Princeton: Princeton University Press, 2012.

Zimmermann, Clemens. 'Bäuerlicher Traditionalismus und agrarischer Fortschritt in der frühen Neuzeit', in Jan Peters (ed.), *Gutsherrschaft als soziales Modell: Vergleichende Betrachtungen zur Funktionsweise frühneuzeitlicher Agrargesellschaften* (Munich: Oldenbourg, 1995), 219–38.

 PART I

In Institutions
Brokering Contested Knowledge

 CHAPTER 1

An Imperial 'Shrine' to Agrarian Research and Education

Decoding the Imperial Agricultural Research Institute, Pusa, in Bihar, 1905–36

Preeti

Bihar, an agrarian state in eastern India, is located on one of the world's most fertile alluvial plains, an area that is drained by the Ganges and its tributaries. However, colonial India in general – and colonial Bihar in particular – had a history of famine, reflecting poorly on British colonial administration. Recurring famines until the final decades of the nineteenth century made the colonial government reconsider its disdainful attitude towards Indian agriculture. To overcome this heritage of famine, drought, poverty and disease, colonial India required modern technology to counterbalance its 'ancient dependence' on subsistence agriculture.[1] Agricultural education, another essential tool in this regard, fell under the domain of the colonial Department of Agriculture. There were few agricultural colleges in India before the First Famine Commission Report (1880), barring some exceptions like the agriculture college in Patna, the capital of Bihar, which opened in 1876. Agricultural classes were also offered at the Shibpur Engineering College in Howrah from 1895–96. Colleges providing instruction in agriculture were thus almost unknown in India and had few precedents to serve as a guide. Nevertheless, John A. Voelcker, an agricultural chemist at the Royal Agricultural Society of England, expressed a common sentiment among colonial experts in his *Report on the Improvement of Indian Agriculture*: 'Suffice it to say here I am distinctly in favour of giving an agricultural education in India, rather than of sending Natives to England to study.'[2] Ideas were borrowed from different countries, including Germany, France, Britain, Japan and the United States.[3] The United States in particular had demonstrated to the world how beneficial a well-organized department of agriculture could be for those who derived their living from the soil.

By the end of the nineteenth century, all European imperial powers had reached the conclusion that colonial domination and capitalistic penetration would generate material gain. Furthermore, by this point, science and technology had aided colonial powers like Britain to establish a level of suzerainty throughout their empires that could not have been achieved through force alone. Postcolonial thinkers like Michel Foucault and Edward Said have demonstrated that science was increasingly being viewed as an agent of cultural imperialism that supposedly reflected the dominance and superiority of the West.[4] A sense of awe and hegemony, it was widely held, would ultimately arise from 'technological prowess', at the 'base' of which stood 'places of research and teaching in science'.[5] In British-ruled colonial India, where agriculture was generating the highest revenues of any economic sector,[6] scientific intervention in this field represented a supposedly logical next step. The British colonial administration believed that the 'primitive age-old technologies' used by local farmers could not exploit the resources of the land as efficiently as the instruments of Western science.[7] At the heart of the British colonial agenda thus lay the importation of Western science and technology to Indian soil. Since the first half of the nineteenth century, the emphasis in Britain had been on laboratory-based agriculture, which had been developed at its colleges and universities. Although more than half a century behind, colonial India opened its first and ultimately pre-eminent agricultural research institute in 1905 at Pusa, which more than a century later continues to be one of the best agriculture institutes in India. However, there has yet to be a full study – or even an article – discussing its initial three decades, when it rose to prominence before its headquarters were transferred to Delhi in 1936, a period that this chapter will examine.[8]

In 1892, imperial scientists met at an open site in Poosah (later renamed Pusa), a seemingly sleepy village in Bihar about 50 miles north of the present-day state capital, Patna. This land had long been owned by the colonial government, but it was only in the 1900s that the then Viceroy of India, Lord George Nathaniel Curzon, would eventually put it to use for the construction of Pusa.[9] With the agreement of the Bengal presidency, in which Bihar was located until 1912, the central government selected the Poosah estate as the site that would fulfil its agricultural needs through the establishment of an agricultural research institute, experimental farm and agricultural college.[10] Curzon decided to use a £20,000 donation (which was followed by an additional £10,000) from Henry Phipps, a US philanthropist from Pittsburgh, for the development of an agricultural department at Pusa that would be responsible for purchasing the equipment for the new research laboratory.[11]

The period from 1888 to 1905 marked Curzon's imperial apotheosis, a time during which he embarked on his effort to bring scientific research more closely under the control of the colonial government. Aware that agricultural research had been receiving insufficient financial support from the central government since the creation of the colonial Department of Agriculture in

1881, Curzon believed that a more centralized control and direction of scientific exploration and research could better capitalize on colonial government investment in science. In his speech at its inaugural ceremony, he expressed his hope that Pusa would become a nucleus for agricultural activities, research and education that would benefit the entire British Empire and attract the best talents from India and abroad.[12]

Unlike his predecessors, Curzon was determined to apply scientific research in a more organized manner, especially towards the aims of preventing famine[13] and promoting Indian exports to Britain and other parts of the British Empire. Curzon – like the Institute's influential economic botanist, Sir Albert Howard – wanted Pusa to focus on applied science rather than the pure sciences. For the latter, Britain could already rely on its nineteenth-century institutes like Rothamsted Research Station (established in 1843) or Cirencester Agricultural College (1845). In contrast to Britain, however, India promised rich geographical diversity that could be mined for applied knowledge. Furthermore, as a colony, it offered the infamous 'elbow room' that would allow for an unhindered pursuit of scientific knowledge.[14]

Pusa's Curriculum

By providing research training to its students, the Imperial Agricultural Research Institute's aim was to formulate solutions to agricultural problems that would enhance British hegemony on the Indian subcontinent. In contrast to the provincial agricultural colleges, Pusa was to occupy the role of an institute of postgraduate learning. It aimed to enable its students, through postgraduate courses of the highest possible standard, to qualify for the best appointments in specialist branches of agricultural science, not only in India but also in neighbouring colonies (such as Burma, Sri Lanka, Indonesia and Malaysia). Facilities similar to those available to students in Europe would be made available to Indians who wished to qualify for the Indian agricultural service. Pusa was the only institution in India that offered facilities for postgraduate instruction in all branches of agricultural science.[15] At the heart of its teaching lay instruction in research methods. In a letter, Lord Minto, the Viceroy of India from 1905 to 1910, explained:

> Our scheme provides that experiment and research work should proceed hand in hand with educational work; the two are dependent one upon the other if the best work is to be done in either; and the progress of each will be greatly hampered if the staff of Provincial Departments is not strengthened by the appointment of the Superintendents of farms, and the specialists recommended by us.[16]

If Pusa was to set the premier standard for agricultural research in India and become the pre-eminent centre for postgraduate training in the agricultural sciences, it was necessary for it to employ researchers and teachers of the highest available calibre. For the colonial government, this implied that 'higher research staff at Pusa must remain English for a considerable period if the Institute were to do its work properly'.[17] In short, this meant that senior faculty were recruited mainly from Britain. For example, Hugh Martin-Leake had trained at the University of Cambridge before arriving in India in 1901 as a botanist for the Bihar Indigo Planters Association. He joined the Indian Agricultural Service at the newly established Pusa in 1904.[18] Another eminent faculty member at Pusa was Sir Albert Howard, who later became renowned as the father of organic farming in India. He was employed at Pusa as an economic botanist from 1905 to 1924, when he left to become the director of the Institute of Plant Industry in Indore.[19] The recruitment of Martin-Leake and Howard offer an insight into the high calibre of academic staff at Pusa, reflecting that it was never meant to serve as a standard research institute. However, it is a significant irony that researchers from Europe, most of whom had yet to put their feet on Indian soil before being recruited, were deemed capable of mastering Indian agrarian conditions. Nonetheless, partly as a result of their supposed racial supremacy as white men, they were recruited directly into senior posts.

Pusa was supposed to place agricultural research in India on a new pedestal. Prior to its establishment, agricultural research in colonial India had been, in the words of MacLeod, 'fitful and uncoordinated, and always at the mercy of uninstructed and un-sympathetic officials, whose one cannon of criticism has been the solvency of the annual balance-sheet'.[20] To remedy this unsatisfactory state of affairs, no expense was spared in making Pusa's agricultural research follow its preordained trajectory towards becoming the 'Rothamsted of the East'.[21] Pusa was designed to contribute towards finding solutions to the major problems of tropical agriculture,[22] such as soil crust formation. It comprised the following five departments: (1) an experimental farm, which served as a model for similar facilities run by provincial governments; (2) an agricultural research laboratory, a research station for investigating agricultural problems relating to the cultivation and improvement of the numerous field and garden crops grown in India; (3) an agriculture college, in which the principles and practices of Indian agriculture would be taught to produce graduates who could reliably conduct agricultural experiments and improvement work in any province of colonial India; (4) a library containing a wide range of agricultural and scientific literature; and (5) a cattle breeding farm for the improvement of the local breed of cattle and the growth of herds. There was also a museum, where wheat, barley, oats and pulses of many varieties were displayed in numerous glass pots.[23] Besides these facilities, Pusa was also equipped with herbaria and lecture rooms.

Pusa's initial focus was on improving and developing agricultural research, experimentation, demonstration and education.[24] To this end, specialized courses lasting two years for each of the main branches of agricultural science – agricultural chemistry, mycology, entomology, agricultural bacteriology and botany – were started.[25] By 1915, the Institute's scientific staff consisted of a director (a position that incorporated the additional role of agricultural adviser to the colonial government), an agricultural chemist, an agricultural bacteriologist, an economic botanist, an economic entomologist, a mycologist, a pathological entomologist and an agriculturist, who was in charge of managing the farm. The Entomological Department of Pusa's Central Research Station and College assisted the provincial departments with their most pressing investigations and with the training of competent Indian assistants for deployment to the provinces. Similarly, Pusa's Botanical Department provided mycologists for several provincial botanical departments.

Pusa's Contribution to Agriculture

Land has always been the Indian economy's most important source of revenue generation and at the base of its production.[26] The British administration and intelligentsia considered research to be vital for increasing the productive capacity of the soil in order to feed and generate employment for India's rapidly growing population.[27] In Pusa's first few years, experts were appointed to conduct crop-specific research on cotton, wheat, tobacco, indigo, sugar cane and jute, but no researchers concentrated on rice until 1911.[28] The general tendency at Pusa was 'to grow more saleable crops and less food crops, i.e. to [generate] money rather than food out of the land'.[29] This meant that rice, albeit a staple food for the majority of Indians, was ignored as long as it continued to fetch a lower price than other cash crops.

Since the 1860s, Britain had also been interested in reducing its dependence on the United States for supplies of wheat and cotton. Whereas in the period from 1871 to 1875, Britain had received only 1.9 per cent of its total wheat imports from India, this figure rose to 17.6 per cent by 1911–15.[30] It was no coincidence that Pusa gained much of its reputation from its world-famous wheat varieties, which were the subject of some of the earliest research undertaken by its Department of Economic Botany from 1906. Leslie C. Coleman, Director of Agriculture for Mysore, commented that the so-called Pusa 12 wheat boosted harvests by 10 to 25 per cent, particularly in parts of the United Provinces, Bihar and Punjab.[31] Across India, Pusa wheats already covered more than two million acres of land within fifteen years, an advance that was much quicker than those of the other main wheat types grown in India.[32] Pusa 4 was distributed on a large scale in eastern Punjab, Sind, the

United Provinces, the Shimla Hill States and Rajputana. Wheat, particularly Pusa 4, Pusa 12 and Pusa 52, was being grown on over six million acres of Indian land by the 1930s,[33] while some of the Pusa wheats were also being cultivated in Australia.[34] Moreover, scientists and cultivators in different parts of the world were showing considerable interest in Pusa wheats, with seeds being dispatched to South Africa, Nigeria, Java, Uganda, Sudan, Argentina, Canada, France, Australia and elsewhere.[35]

The demand for Pusa wheats from other parts of India and abroad was so high that it exceeded the Institute's supply capacity. One of the fundamental reasons behind the success of Pusa wheats in Bihar, as A.C. Dobbs, Director of Agriculture for Bihar and Orissa, explained, was that Pusa 12 could grow comparatively unaffected by the vagaries of the soil and the monsoon. Meanwhile, Pusa 114 was rust-resistant, which increased its popularity in the Sind region. Special measures were undertaken by Sir Albert Howard, who was in contact with Sir Albert Humphries (a well-known miller in England), in an effort to boost the quality of Pusa wheats so that they would fetch a higher price on the British market.[36] Furthermore, as Howard explained, 'methods which have proved successful in wheat were now being applied in India to crops like cotton, rice, jute and sugarcane, and important results have already been obtained'.[37] By broadening its research specializations, Pusa was thus undertaking a wide variety of research on topics ranging from cash crops to fungicides and insecticides, manuring and soil aeration. In the first three decades of the twentieth century, for example, the cultivation of sweet potatoes, a relatively new crop, was popularized in Bihar through Pusa's research efforts.[38] The Institute's success in this regard ultimately lay in demonstrating the significance of the use of high-quality seeds and proper manuring as well as the prevention of crop disease.[39]

Tobacco was regarded as another industry that was in need of an overhaul through the application of Western science and technology. From 1910, four years after Pusa's opening, until 1920, Bihar became the headquarters of the Imperial Tobacco Company and the Peninsular Tobacco Company. At the request of the latter, Pusa conducted much research on identifying tobacco that was suitable for the Bihar cigarette industry.[40] By contrast, because Pusa officials were aware of the global collapse in the profitability of natural indigo production after the invention of synthetic dye in Germany, indigo research at Pusa was more or less abandoned from around 1920, with the Institute's scientists shifting their attention to sugarcane and other crops.[41] A British indigo planter, Minden J. Wilson, had written in his 1908 *History of Behar Indigo Factories* on how the success of sugarcane operations in Bihar since the turn of the century had transformed the province's agricultural production.[42] The Sugarcane Breeding Station, a Pusa substation that was established in 1912 in Coimbatore in the Madras Presidency, became famous for its research.[43] By the

1930s, sugar cane had become one of the most popular crops in India by luring cultivators with the promise of ready cash.

As discussed above, Pusa was established with the aim of serving as a hub for applied science. In their efforts to develop their own 'improved' crop strains and to 'improve' existing agricultural practices, scientists based in colonial India would attempt to set the agenda for agricultural experiments instead of blindly following imported solutions from Europe or the United States. Indeed, the popularity of adaptive empiricism among the scientists at Pusa demonstrates that not all of its officials and agriculturists were asserting the superiority of the technology that divided the supposedly rational, active and progressive British from the seemingly irrational and passive 'natives'.[44] For example, Howard voiced his detestation of artificial fertilizers:

> While the application of chemical and other manures has undoubtedly increased production, its very success has worked a considerable amount of mischief and has done much to obscure the real factors on which growth depends. I will confine my remarks to nitrogen and phosphorus, the two substances on which vast sums are now spent or rather wasted.[45]

Through local influence, Howard became convinced of the benefits of organic farming and devoted his life to spreading its virtues through his publications. He recommended applying organic matter in any form, including farmyard manure, cow dung, oil cake or indigo *seeth* (refuse). Indigo *seeth*, which was considered 'the most expensive form of organic nitrogen',[46] was used as a fertilizer for Pusa's tobacco plots. By 1910, Howard was able to grow crops almost disease-free without the aid of artificial chemicals, fertilizers or 'all the other expensive paraphernalia of the modern Experiment Station'.[47] A further renowned faculty member was Dr John W. Leather, the agricultural chemist to the colonial government, who arrived at an estimate of the quantity of water consumed by plants that allowed him to devise corresponding methods for economizing water use. He would be remembered for initiating the first series of permanent manorial and rotational experiments in India.[48]

Pusa's experts aimed to make agricultural research accessible to the poor Indian peasantry. Regardless of whether this stated aim was fulfilled or not, their research findings from their diverse fields of study were indeed made available across a wide range of publications released by the Institute. These included the journals *Agricultural Journal of India*, the *Journal of the Central Bureau of Animal Husbandry* and *Dairying in India* as well as the irregular *Pusa Bulletins* and various memoirs by faculty members. When officials and experts such as William H. Moreland or Martin-Leake reported on their agricultural experiments and innovations, their preferred mode of communication was through the *Agricultural Journal of India*. However, as was observed in an anonymous article in the *Indian Agriculturalist*, 'what the Indian *ryot* [peasant] requires is practical information conveyed in simple language, and obviously the expensive English-language publications with their artistic plates are from his point of view absolutely useless'.[49] Pusa experts attempted to solve this problem by disseminating 'modern' knowledge in the form of magazine or journal articles containing practical information on agricultural techniques in English, Hindi, Urdu or, occasionally, vernaculars in the hope that these articles would be within the epistemological reach of poor peasants.[50] Efforts were also made to distribute short circulars or leaflets with specific and locally relevant knowledge in almost every province.[51] But here, once again, the Pusa scientists misconceptualized Indian farmers as a single, literate mass; Leather, for example, was only prepared to recognize as an 'agriculturist' a 'man whose general education would enable him to assimilate such information'.[52]

Student Cohorts: Pusa's Direct 'Beneficiaries'

Only graduates of Indian universities or agricultural colleges or those who had undergone training in agriculture and its allied branches at a British university or recognized agricultural college were eligible for admission to the specialized courses at Pusa. To its postgraduate courses, Pusa admitted students from across India, many of whom were nominated by local governments and came from the upper castes and classes of Indian society. Because Pusa issued no stipends,[53] an overview of the students who attended these courses provides us with a window into understanding the caste and class dynamic at play at Pusa.

Although the colonial government never promised Pusa graduates jobs in the colonial government service, most of the alumni were absorbed into this sector or found work for the princely states. Whatever the colonial government's intentions behind imparting agricultural education were, it became in many respects 'just' another avenue for the emerging middle class to secure a job – and not necessarily an agricultural job. The students who could shoulder the costs of an agricultural education came from either nonagricultural emerging middle-class or absentee *zamindars* (landlords) families, or were local government nominees who were pursuing a path into the government service.[54] It is an irony that an educational institution that was projected as an instrument for cutting across the barriers of caste and class turned out to be an esoteric and elitist institute serving the Indian elite, a role that was directly opposed to its stated aim of serving as a national centre for agricultural education for all Indians. In reality, this discrepancy had already been confirmed on 28 March 1897, when the colonial government passed a resolution declaring 'that agricultural degrees, diplomas or certificates should be placed upon the same footing as corresponding literary or science degrees in qualifying for admission to

Government appointments and more particularly those connected with land revenue administration.'[55] As such, just under a decade before Pusa's opening, it appears to have already been the intention of the colonial government to encourage graduates of agricultural research institutes to follow nonpractical, white-collar careers.

Sir Edward J. Russell, the director of Rothamsted Experimental Station, correctly judged that the most significant difference between agricultural colleges in India and those in the West was that most Western graduates returned to the land to practise farming. By contrast, Indian agricultural graduates desired nonpractical posts, in which their impact on practical agriculture would be negligible.[56] This explains the relatively limited influence exerted by Indian agricultural colleges on cultivation practices. As Russell argued: 'Until good students from the agricultural colleges settle on the land as farmers the Colleges cannot be expected to exert much influence on village life.'[57] But there were also complaints, including from government officials, about farmers who had supposedly trained at an agricultural college, but who were unable to cultivate a good-quality crop.

The colonial education system did not recognize agriculture as a skilled profession or grant it the corresponding respect. Furthermore, agricultural students themselves were so dismayed by the prevailing status of the peasantry that they preferred to find relatively lowly white-collar roles such as clerical work. As a well-to-do landed proprietor in Madura appropriately claimed, 'the cleverest son is sent to the Law, the next into Government employ, the dullest one goes to Agriculture or else to Trade'.[58] This view was based on the assumption that 'any old fool' would instinctively know how to farm and would therefore be able to make the most of the soil and the available resources with no intelligence required.[59] Many Indians thus held a disdain for physical work, believing that 'men of talent' were not supposed to be exposed to the hardships of the open field, a hierarchy between mind and hand that can be constantly observed throughout the archival record.

Since the formal teaching of practical agriculture occurred in a 'haphazard [and] amateurish manner' in colonial India, agricultural education offered more of a theoretical overview of various branches of science and failed to create an appreciation for science as a transformative tool for improving practical farming.[60] Many of the parents of former students at agricultural colleges reflected how it had been as a result of this type of education that their sons had left behind their ancestral pursuits. Furthermore, the insensitivity shown by modern-minded *pandits* (scholars) towards agriculture was cited as another cause of agricultural decline and the decreasing respect for agricultural work under British rule.[61] In addition, as an anonymous writer in *The Indian Agriculturist* reasoned, a career in the government service paid better, making it an obvious choice over agricultural labour: 'So long as the rate of salaries the Government servants withdrew was not reduced, very few persons of education would be found taking to farming.'[62]

Responses in the Popular Press

Indian intellectuals made extensive use of the press to vent their opinions on the poor state of agriculture in colonial India. One such person was Narendranath Gangulee, Professor of Agriculture and Rural Economics at the University of Calcutta, who ruefully described how:

> Since Lord Curzon's regime, the Government of India seems to have realized the value of fostering systematic research in agricultural science, but whatever results may have been accomplished, in our laboratories, Research Institutes and Government Farms, they are of no use unless proofs of their practical value are brought home to the cultivators.[63]

The colonial government intended Pusa as a pedestal on which the triumphs and glories of the colonizers and the instruments of colonization would be displayed. Because it had been conceived as a hub for applied agricultural science, as discussed above, its chief purpose was to engender a transition from agricultural practices rooted in informal knowledge to science-based agriculture. Against a commonly held perception among intellectuals on both sides of the colonial divide, Indian farmers never saw science and technology as an external imposition, but rather as a useful mechanism with which to achieve a certain level of autonomy and self-sufficiency. However, Pusa did appear elitist in the eyes of most Indians due to its association with the upper echelons of Indian society and its hegemonic role in the field of research.[64] Even prior to its opening, Pusa became embroiled in controversies relating to its elevated status and doubtful capacity to deliver equally for the benefit of all of India's provinces. In March 1904, the newspaper *Varthamani* rejected the idea of having one centralized institute to engage with agrarian problems pertaining to 2 million square miles of land that was varied in multiple respects. On the contrary, it suggested a decentralized system of agricultural colleges and experimental farms across the length and breadth of the colony.[65] *Swadeshimitran*, a Tamil daily, came up with similar recommendations, arguing that Lord Curzon would have to forego his top-down diffusionist attitude if the colonial government was serious about immediate agrarian improvement. Instead, his government would have to spend a significant portion of its education budget on the establishment of village schools while also opening large teacher training colleges in each province that would train Indian teachers to impart agricultural education in the village schools.[66] Other newspapers proposed a range of suggestions for how Henry Phipps' donation could be used. The 7 April 1905 edition of *Lokopakari*, a Tamil weekly, called for this money to be utilized to improve irrigation channels, predicting that if it was spent on Pusa, it would disproportionately benefit European planters.[67]

In testimony to the 1926 Royal Commission on Agriculture, Babu Arikshan Sinha, General Secretary of the Muzaffarpur-based Bihar Provincial Kisan Sabha (Bihar Provincial Farmers' Assembly), described the common attitude towards Pusa among Indians:

> The PUSA Research Institute has been of no benefit to us. We do not know what good it has as yet done for the poor ratepayers particularly the tenants, although it has devoured a huge sum of money in its huge buildings and big establishment … In our opinion this Pusa Research Institute has been a sheer waste of public money without any '*Ma Bap*' [guardians] to enquire into this huge wastage.[68]

India has its own longstanding indigenous traditions of information collection and dissemination that coexist with the modern press.[69] As an institute that was supposed to benefit the entire colony, Pusa caught the attention of many local vernacular newspapers and magazines. Nevertheless, because it was located at a remote location that was connected to the outside world by a single small railway station with few trains, it was not able to attract the best talents from across the colony. Time and again, criticism aimed at the decision to establish a central research institute like Pusa in such a remote region resurfaced. *The Searchlight*, a triweekly English language newspaper from Patna, published the following article on 19 June 1927 in an attempt to respond to these complaints:

> Pusa had alternatively been the spoilt child and the Cinderella of the Government institutions … The majority of influential men in India had never clearly grasped its real function and owing to geographical isolation few had first-hand knowledge of its work. Educated public opinion was needed to take up arms in its defence.[70]

The article then went on to correctly recognize that Pusa's role was to conduct research for the benefit of the whole of India and that it should not favour one province over the others. However, a single institution of relatively small size in a colony like India, which covered an enormous area with a range of climates and soils, could hardly fulfil the purpose for which it was intended. Pusa had proven of far greater benefit to its home province, Bihar, and nearby provinces such as Orissa, the United Provinces and Punjab than to Madras and, to a lesser extent, Bombay and the Central Provinces. As such, Pusa was not accessible to the majority of agriculturists across India. The 1926 Royal

Commission on Agriculture also acknowledged this when it found that Pusa had failed in some of its core objectives because of its geographical isolation.

Indians had high hopes of reaping wider benefits from agricultural improvement, which would supposedly prevent famine and create employment. Nevertheless, there were socioeconomic challenges that were more immediate and the solutions for which did not require the long-term development of scientific agriculture in India. For example, as *Dainik Basumati* declared on 21 November 1922, the dilapidated huts of the poor peasantry required urgent attention,[71] as did the eradication of a range of diseases. Ordinary people did not understand the language of botany, chemistry or entomology, but they did want quick and achievable solutions to their problems.[72]

Negative comparisons between agriculture in India and the rest of the world, a theme that was recurrent in the press in the late nineteenth and early twentieth centuries, reinforced the disaffection among Indians. The Calcutta newspaper *Sri Sri Vishnu Priya-O-Ananda Bazar Patrika* opined on 2 February 1911 that, with India being an agricultural country, it was the primary duty of the colonial government to implement agrarian improvement. Although the government had taken various steps in this direction since 1900, the newspaper argued that those endeavours were mostly confined to the realm of 'scientific research', which lay beyond the comprehension of the illiterate peasantry. A gap was thus evident between the propagators of this form of knowledge and its supposed practitioners. Seemingly, the British were less concerned about the receptibility of scientific knowledge than with applying it themselves to extract and siphon off Indian resources for export to Britain and its other colonies.

Sri Sri Vishnu Priya-O-Ananda Bazar Patrika did not deny the need for scientific research, but it argued that as long as proper measures were not adopted for training the peasantry and putting scientific theory to practical use, the miseries of the Indian people would not be alleviated. Aggravating this problem was the high cost of scientific research. The newspaper thus argued in favour of the government 'curtail[ing] its expenditure on scientific researches [*sic*] and try[ing] to induce the peasantry to devote themselves to the improvement of their practical training in agriculture'.[73]

When compared with other types of research or higher education institutions in India, enormous sums were being spent on Pusa and other elite agricultural research institutes, money that the colonial government could not afford. In a colony with tight budgetary constraints and many competing and pressing challenges, a limit had to be set on such expenditure. Moreover, as demonstrated in the demands formulated in local newspapers, ordinary Indians were likewise facing financial challenges; for them, scholarly status was required less than straightforward ways to earn a livelihood. It was in this context that the Calcutta-based newspaper *Ananda Bazar Patrika* lamented on 19 July 1922 that the hard-earned money of poor Indian subjects was, year after year, evaporating like vapour on agricultural research, an endeavour that had offered them nothing in return.[74] The ongoing economic crisis, a state of affairs that was even acknowledged by British officials, resulted in the regular airing of grievances as Indians saw the colonial government's limited funding being 'wasted' on an extravagant research institute like Pusa, which even in its own province of Bihar remained an isolated outpost.

Conclusion

An elite project such as Pusa was not aloof from the agenda of colonial expansion. Pusa was intended to serve as a fountainhead of agricultural science that would 'rescue' Indian agriculture in the same manner as other forms of science had aided other industries. Scientific research and agricultural education were thought to promote crop rotation and improve soil health while offering a boost to British resource extraction. The close association between science, technology and imperialism was thus becoming increasingly important for the development of agriculture and commerce in colonial India. The colonial government's standard agricultural reform strategy was to invite foreign experts and then to seek and implement their advice. It was an irony that while the colonial government claimed that science would increase Indian autonomy and self-sufficiency, the British Raj continued to rely on hiring Western experts, mostly from Britain, further underlining its tacit agenda of white supremacy. It seems likely that most British officials did not believe that Indians were capable of engaging with 'modern science'. Furthermore, even Pusa's Indian students themselves were typically more concerned with securing white-collar government jobs than pursuing a career in agriculture. Generally, until the second half of the 1930s, Pusa continued to face opposition across India due to its location and privileged status. In 1936, two years after its main building was damaged during a severe earthquake, the Institute was moved to Delhi – 'much to the delight of everyone who worked there'.[75]

Preeti completed her BA and MA in History at Kirori Mal College, University of Delhi, in 2012 and 2014. She completed her M.Phil at the Zakir Husain Centre for Educational Studies (ZHCES), Jawaharlal Nehru University, in 2016. In 2022, she completed her Ph.D. at the Department of History, University of Sussex, having been awarded the Chancellor's International Research Scholarship. Her research interests include the history of education in South Asia, agrarian history, and the history of science and modernity.

Notes

1. MacLeod, 'Scientific Advice for British India'.
2. Voelcker, *Report on the Improvement of Indian Agriculture*, 309.
3. Randhawa, *A History of Agriculture in India*.
4. Harrison, 'Science and the British Empire', 56–63.
5. Pyenson, 'Cultural Imperialism and Exact Sciences', 5.
6. Washbrook, 'Law, State and Society in Colonial India', 650.
7. Preeti, 'Agriculture as Knowledge', 527.
8. Historians such as Madhumita Saha have written about postcolonial Pusa.
9. Curzon served as Viceroy of India from 1899 to 1905.
10. Clouston, 'The Report of the Royal Commission on Indian Agriculture', 920.
11. Burns, 'The Imperial Agricultural Research Institute', 431. See also Headrick, *Tentacles of Progress*.
12. Burns, 'The Imperial Agricultural Research Institute', 431.
13. Baber, *Science of Empire*, 215.
14. Prakash, 'Science Gone Native', 155.
15. 'Royal Commission on Agriculture in India'.
16. Revenue & Agriculture Department., Agriculture Branch., No. 7, August 1906, Part. A. Lord Minto to John Morley, 26 July 1906.
17. 'Pusa as Research Station', 8.
18. Singh, 'Science, Hindi Print and Agricultural Improvement', 222; Kumar, '"Modernization"'.
19. On Sir Albert Howard, see Barton, 'Sir Albert Howard'; and Barton, 'Albert Howard and the Decolonization of Science'.
20. MacLeod, 'Scientific Advice for British India', 364.
21. Ibid., 364.
22. Lawrence, 'Indian Agriculture', 252.
23. 'Eighth Annual Report of the Patna College', 13.
24. Clouston, 'The Report of the Royal Commission', 920.
25. Bihar State Archives, File No. 5A-II of 1923, Government of Bihar and Orissa, Ministry of Education. 'Post-Graduate Courses at the Agri-Research Institute Pusa and Diary Farm at Bangalore'.
26. Washbrook, 'Law, State and Society in Colonial India', 650.
27. Temple, *India in 1880*, 82–85; Tallents, *Census of India*; MacLeod, 'Scientific Advice for British India'.
28. Prey, 'Impact of Agricultural Research', 435.
29. Russell, 'Science and the Indian Peasant', 662.
30. Turner, 'Agriculture, 1860–1914', 135.
31. Coleman, 'Indian Agricultural Development', 3.
32. Howard and Howard, *India of Today*, 36.
33. Burt, 'Science in the Service of Indian Agriculture', 533.
34. Burns, 'The Imperial Agricultural Research Institute', 431.
35. Howard, *Sir Albert Howard in India*.
36. Russell, *Report on the Work of the Imperial Council of Agricultural Research*, 27.
37. Howard, 'Agriculture and Science', 173.

38. Das, 'Changel', 23.
39. Kale, *Introduction to the Study of Indian Economics,* 209.
40. Howard and Howard, 'The Improvement of Tobacco Cultivation in Bihar', 13.
41. Kerkhoff-Sinha, *Colonising Plants in Bihar.*
42. Wilson, *History of Behar Indigo Factories.*
43. 'Breeder's Gift to India', 138.
44. Ghosh, 'Scientific Knowledge and Practices of Green Manuring', 306.
45. Howard, 'Soil Aeration in Agriculture', 17.
46. Ibid., 17.
47. Ross, *Cultivating the Colonies,* 35.
48. Basu, Bose and Basu, *History of Science in India Vol. V.*
49. *The Indian Agriculturist,* 8.
50. See the essay 'Our Modernity' in Chatterjee, *Empire and Nation.*
51. 'Second Report on the Introduction of Improvements into Indian Agriculture', 4–5.
52. Singh, 'Science, Hindi Print and Agricultural Improvement', 228.
53. Bihar State Archive, File No. 5A-II of 1923, Government of Bihar and Orissa, Ministry of Education. 'Post-Graduate Courses at the Agri-Research Institute Pusa and Diary Farm at Bangalore'.
54. National Archive of India, Education Department, Health and Land Branch/1930/7-8/A. 'The Establishment of Sub-stations to Remedy the Deficiencies of Pusa in Relation to the Problems of Tropical India, August 1930'.
55. Department of Education, Bengal, 'Third Quinquennial Review of Education', 92.
56. Russell, *Report on the Work of the Imperial Council of Agricultural Research,* 61.
57. Ibid., 61.
58. Voelckar, *Report on the Improvement of Indian Agriculture,* 379.
59. 'The ABC of Agriculture', 85
60. Department of Agriculture, Bihar and Orissa, 'Report on Agricultural Activities, 1915–16', 53.
61. Voelcker, *Report on the Improvement of Indian Agriculture,* 379.
62. *The Indian Agriculturist,* 421.
63. Gangulee, 'The Problem of Increased Food-Production', 140.
64. Chakrabarti, *Western Science in Modern India,* 148.
65. Deepak Kumar Collection (DKC). *Varthamani,* 17 March 1904, 122.
66. DKC, *Swadeshmitran,* 3 April 1905.
67. *Lokopakari,* 7 April 1905. See also 'Modern Agricultural Research', 2.
68. 'Royal Commission on Agriculture in India', 257–258.
69. Codell, 'Introduction', 107.
70. 'Pusa as Research Station: Director's Evidence', *The Searchlight,* 8.
71. DKC, Native Newspapers Report, Bengal No. 47 of 1922. *Dainik Basumati,* 21 November 1922, 939–40.
72. DKC, *Sasilekha,* 20 January 1911, 159; *Sadhvi,* 1 February 1911, 193.
73. DKC, Native Newspapers Report, Bengal No. 29 of 1910, *Sri Sri Vishnu Priya-O-Ananda Bazar Patrika,* 2 February 1911, 138.
74. DKC, Native Newspapers Report, Bengal No. 30 of 1922, *Ananda Bazar Patrika,* 19 July 1922, 596.
75. Sen, 'Scientific Enquiry in Agriculture', 209.

Bibliography

Baber, Zaheer. *The Science of Empire: Scientific Knowledge, Civilization, and Colonial Rule in India*. New York: State University of New York Press, 1996.

Barton, Gregory A. 'Sir Albert Howard and the Forestry Roots of the Organic Farming Movement'. *Agricultural History* 75(2) (2001), 168–87.

———. 'Albert Howard and the Decolonization of Science: From the Raj to Organic Farming', in Brett M. Bennett and Joseph M. Hodge (eds), *Science and Empire: Knowledge and Networks of Science across the British Empire, 1800–1970*. New York: Palgrave Macmillan, 2011, 163–86.

Basu, R.N., T K. Bose and Chandra Sekhar Basu, *History of Science in India Vol. V: Agricultural Science*. Kolkata: Ramkrishna Mission Institute of Culture, 2014.

'Breeder's Gift to India'. *Journal of Heredity* 28(4) (1937), 138.

Burns, W. 'The Imperial Agricultural Research Institute'. *Nature* 139 (1937), 431–32.

Burt, Bryce C. 'Science in the Service of Indian Agriculture'. *Science and Culture* 1(10) (1936), 530–40.

Chakrabarti, Pratik. *Western Science in Modern India: Metropolitan Methods, Colonial Practices*. Ranikhet: Permanent Black, 2010.

Chatterjee, Partha. *Empire and Nation: Selected Essays*. New York: Columbia University Press, 2010.

Clouston, David. 'The Report of the Royal Commission on Indian Agriculture'. *Journal of the Royal Society of Arts* 78(4051) (1930), 918–34.

Codell, Julie F. 'Introduction: The Nineteenth-Century News from India'. *Victorian Periodicals Review* 37(2) (2004), 106–23.

Coleman, Leslie C. 'Indian Agricultural Development'. *Agricultural Journal of India* (1918), 1–9.

Das, Arvind N. 'Changel: Three Centuries of an Indian Village'. *Journal of Peasant Studies* 15(1) (1987), 3–60.

Department of Agriculture, Bihar and Orissa. 'Report on the Agricultural Activities of Government in Bihar and Orissa for the Year 1915–16 Ending the 30th June 1916'. Patna: 1916.

Department of Education, Bengal. 'Third Quinquennial Review of Education in Bengal 1902–03 to 1906–07'. Calcutta: 1907.

'Eighth Annual Report of the Patna College', *Chanakya Society* 1 (1918).

Gangulee, Narendranath. 'The Problem of Increased Food-Production in India'. *Modern Review* 23(2) (1918), 138–42.

Ghosh, Sanjukta. 'Scientific Knowledge and Practices of Green Manuring in Bengal Presidency, 1905–1925', in Ezra Rashkow, Sanjukta Ghosh and Upal Chakrabarti (eds), *Memory, Identity and the Colonial Encounter in India: Essays in Honour of Peter Robb* (New Delhi: Routledge India, 2017), 298–319.

Harrison, Mark. 'Science and the British Empire'. *Isis* 96(1) (2005), 56–63.

Headrick, Daniel R. *The Tentacles of Progress: Technology Transfer in the Age of Imperialism, 1850–1940*. New York: Oxford University Press, 1988.

Howard, Albert. 'Soil Aeration in Agriculture'. *Agriculture Research Institute, Pusa, Bulletin* 61 (1916), 1–22.

———. '"Agriculture and Science" in the Presidential Address to the Thirteenth Indian Science Congress'. *Agricultural Journal of India* 21(3) (1926), 171–82.

Howard, Albert, and Gabrielle Howard. 'The Improvement of Tobacco Cultivation in Bihar'. *Agricultural Research Institute* 50 (1915), 1–19.

———. *India of Today: The Development of Indian Agriculture, Vol. 8.* Bombay: Oxford University Press, 1927.

Howard, Louise E. *Sir Albert Howard in India.* Emmaus: Rodale Press, 1954.

Kale, Vaman Govind. *Introduction to the Study of Indian Economics: Vol. I Fifth Edition.* Poona: Arya Bhushan Press, 1925.

Kerkhoff-Sinha, Kathinka. *Colonising Plants in Bihar (1760–1950): Tobacco betwixt Indigo and Sugarcane.* Delhi: Partridge India, 2014.

Kumar, Prakash. '"Modernization" and Agrarian Development in India, 1912–52'. *Journal of Asian Studies* 79(3) (2020), 633–58.

Lawrence, Henry S. 'Indian Agriculture'. *Journal of the Royal Society of Arts* 56(2880) (1908), 246–66.

MacLeod, Roy M. 'Scientific Advice for British India: Imperial Perceptions and Administrative Goals, 1898–1923'. *Modern Asian Studies* 9(3) (1975), 343–84.

Prakash, Gyan. 'Science Gone Native in Colonial India'. *Representations* 40 (1992), 153–78.

Preeti. 'Agriculture as Knowledge: Delegitimizing "Informal" Knowledge through Colonial Pedagogy in Bihar, 1880–1930'. *History of Education* 51(4) (2022), 522–40.

Prey, Carl E. 'The Impact of Agricultural Research in British India'. *Journal of Economic History* 44(2) (1984), 429–40.

Pyenson, Lewis. 'Cultural Imperialism and Exact Sciences: German Expansion Overseas 1900–1930'. *History of Science* 20(1) (1982), 1–43.

Randhawa, Mohinder Singh. *A History of Agriculture in India: Vol. III, 1757–1947.* New Delhi: Indian Council of Agricultural Research, 1983.

Ross, Corey. *Cultivating the Colonies: Agriculture, Development, and Environment.* Oxford: Oxford Scholarship Online, 2017.

'Royal Commission on Agriculture in India: Abridged Report'. Bombay: Government Central Press, 1928.

Russell, Edward J. *Report on the Work of the Imperial Council of Agricultural Research in Applying Science to Crop Production in India.* Delhi: Manager Publication, 1937.

———. 'Science and the Indian Peasant'. *Journal of the Royal Society of Arts* 87(4512) (1939), 662–81.

Second Report on the Introduction of Improvements into Indian Agriculture. Calcutta: Superintendent Government Printing, 1910.

Sen, Srabani. 'Scientific Enquiry in Agriculture in Colonial India: A Historical Perspective', *Indian Journal of History of Science* 45(2) (2010): 199–240.

Singh, Charu. 'Science, Hindi Print and Agricultural Improvement in Colonial North India', Ph.D. dissertation. New Delhi: Jawaharlal Nehru University, 2015.

Tallents, P.C. *Census of India, 1921, Vol. II.* Patna: Superintendent Government Printing, 1923.

Temple, Richard. *India in 1880.* London: William Cloves and Sons, 1880.

'The A B C of Agriculture', *The Indian Agriculturist* 12(7) (1887).

The Indian Agriculturist 13(31) (1888).

Turner, Michael. 'Agriculture, 1860–1914', in Roderick Floud and Paul Johnson (eds), *The Cambridge Economic History of Modern India, Volume II: Economic Maturity, 1860–1939* (Cambridge: Cambridge University Press, 2004), 133–60.

Voelcker, John A. *Report on the Improvement of Indian Agriculture*. London: Eyre & Spottiswoode, 1893.

Washbrook, David A. 'Law, State and Society in Colonial India'. *Modern Asian Studies* 15(3) (1981), 649–721.

Wilson, Minden J. *History of Behar Indigo Factories*. Calcutta: Calcutta General Printing Company, 1908.

 CHAPTER 2

Transferring Formal Agricultural Education to Liberia in the 1920s

Cassandra Mark-Thiesen

State-led development oriented around the establishment of agricultural research stations and the expansion of public agricultural education became a key pursuit of colonial and independent governments across the African continent during the interwar period. At the time, the New York-based Phelps-Stokes Fund's reports on education in West, Southern and Equatorial Africa, which were produced 'at the request of mission boards and with the approval of governments', were widely considered to represent the blueprint for African education. One such report, *Education in Africa*, which was published in 1922 and was written by the Phelps-Stokes Fund's educational director Thomas Jesse Jones, 'exerted probably greater influence on African education than any other single element' in subsequent generations.[1] In a context in which export agriculture was being used as a vehicle to open up domestic colonial economies, Jones and other foreign educationists aimed to convince government officials on the continent that, with the help of greater public investment, local populations could play a bigger role in this apparently opportune endeavour. As Jones explained in the report, 'economic prosperity and the educational development of the [Indigenous] people are inextricably interwoven'.[2] This was an agenda that was seemingly even more acute in the independent but politically isolated black-led West African state of Liberia, which was perceived by many observers as a US protectorate.[3] Having already gained international attention as a case study for the benefits (and challenges) of US-sponsored African self-rule, Liberia was a particularly instructive testing ground for this kind of experiment. However, there were persistent and 'serious problems of finance and organisation confronting the government'.[4] The founding in 1929 of the country's first vocational and agricultural school, the Booker Washington Agricultural and Industrial Institute (BWI), was a direct outcome of Liberia's conforming to the Phelps-Stokes Fund's guidance.

As this chapter will demonstrate, the founding of the BWI highlights the tensions that emerged as US educationists zealously tried to expand public (including agricultural and manual) education in Liberia as a means of strengthening the project of republican governance in Africa in front of a doubtful international community. Nevertheless, in doing so, they frequently sidestepped many principles of sovereign rule and applied a racialized lens onto the issue of economic development. An analysis of speeches at the BWI's inaugural ceremony and local newspaper reports thereon captures the struggles of the Liberian government in a variety of arenas to shape the transfer of agricultural education that was being enacted by US philanthropic agencies and religious missions. Finally, this chapter affirms that, while a variety of policies underpinned manual and agricultural training in Africa during the interwar period, its ultimate purpose in Liberia was to develop a labour force that was expected to (independently and incentivized by regular wages) serve the newly established US-owned and US-managed Firestone Tire and Rubber Company plantation, which remains the largest contiguous rubber plantation in the world.

The first section of this chapter addresses the imbalanced nature of the collaboration between US and Liberian educationists during the 1920s. This was a period defined by the arrival of the rubber producing giant, the bureaucratic centralization of Liberia's public administration, and the further integration of agricultural education into local curriculi and its eventual systematic expansion into the rural interior – all processes that laid the groundwork for the transfer of formal agricultural education. The following section articulates the issue of racism in the US–Liberian relationship and illuminates how, during the 1920s, the Liberian government attempted to resist the impending dominance of a racialized version of agricultural and industrial training. In spite of the missionaries' wish to display the benefits of interracial cooperation to broader West Africa, power struggles persisted behind closed doors. Finally, an analysis of speeches from and press coverage of the BWI's inaugural ceremony shows that, whether in a purely rhetorical manner or not, US educationists had to move closer to the Liberian government's expectations in connection with mutual cooperation. For instance, they indirectly addressed its concerns about the threat to the sovereignty of the Liberian state and its desire to delink agricultural development in Liberia from racialized imaginaries of development in the US South.

US–Liberian Collaboration on Expanding Public Education

The Phelps-Stokes Fund-sponsored African Education Commission's 1922 report implied that the conditions facing most rural Africans shared much in common with contemporary African American life in the US South as well as with conditions in the United States during its early colonial days. Such supposedly lowly circumstances, Jones argued in the report, demanded the type of self-reliant community education that would lead to a bottom-up improvement in socioeconomic conditions. It is hardly a coincidence that this era saw unprecedented strides in the expansion of public schooling to the Liberian interior. As one member of the Fund saw it, the 'urban character of much of the educational work in Africa' was not only misplaced, but also failed to realize the continent's economic potential, which was based on agricultural and mineral wealth.[5] In his report, Jones presented agricultural and industrial education as the solution to previous errors in judgement.[6]

As they witnessed colonial officials in neighbouring territories gradually shifting from a strategy of exploitation to a burgeoning developmentalism via an emphasis on agricultural training and research, Liberian educationists initially fully expected to steer a similar course within their own territory. On 22 April 1921, just one year after the Commission's visit and prior to the publication of its official report, the Liberian government introduced the Public School Act, which reconstituted the national Board of Education.[7] This unified the various (Episcopal, Methodist, Lutheran and Catholic) missionary and religious associations conducting educational work in Liberia under the nominal authority of the Secretary of Public Instruction.[8] This consolidation of the public administration of education was intended to showcase a government finally taking more initiative in the management of 'the great problem of public education in Liberia'.[9] In 1923, the Liberian president, Charles D.B. King, explained that '[i]f adopted and enforced the proposed plan will give to the educational interest of Liberia a greater impetus as well as inspire confidence and a larger amount of financial support from the foreign educational boards in the United States who hold in trust considerable sums of money for education in Liberia'. Government officials anticipated that fundraising in the United States would enable them to deliver positive results. But the founding of the (American) Advisory Committee on Education in Liberia revealed that US educationists had designs on direct involvement in this process of educational transformation.

Indeed, the introduction of state-led rural development policies in Liberia cannot be understood without exploring the contemporary international context, in particular US–Liberian diplomatic relations. At the beginning of the twentieth century, Liberia was faced with repeated provocations and attempts at territorial encroachment – some successful, others not – by the British and French Empires. Warding off these attacks came at a significant economic and administrative cost to the bullied Liberian state. Against this backdrop, Liberia officially adopted its own form of indirect rule in 1905, featuring a novel form of territorial statehood following decades of emphasis on convincing immigrants from within the African diaspora in the Americas to join the loose collection of settlements limited to the coast and the land running alongside the

Saint Paul River. From around the turn of the century, government officials made their first attempts to exert 'effective occupation'[10] over the hinterland, with agriculture being envisioned as the main arena through which to integrate, educate and ultimately profit from the work of rural inhabitants. As part of this agriculture-led transformation in approach to state-building and development, Liberian officials increasingly looked to the United States for guidance and protection.[11] According to the historian David McBride, Liberia was one of the largest recipients of US technical assistance among nation states in the Atlantic world with large populations of African descent, having hosted 'science-based projects of U.S. philanthropy, government, or business' since the late nineteenth and early twentieth centuries.[12] This meant that instead of exclusively deploying funds, US institutions preferred to transfer knowledge via trained US 'experts'. This would also prove to be true for US influence in interwar education in Liberia.

Members of the Phelps-Stokes family had already played a hand in the formation of Liberia in the 1820s, when they backed the settlement of free and manumitted African Americans in this corner of West Africa. A century later, the family's wealth continued to give it a say in Liberia's domestic affairs, especially in the realm of education. Among other impacts, its philanthropic wealth helped to give life to the Advisory Committee on Education in Liberia, which was founded in 1926. This committee, rather than the Board of Education, would come to lead the process of expanding public education. In doing so, it followed a similar blueprint to that of the Advisory Committee on Native Education in British Tropical Africa (established in 1923), with related institutions supporting both bodies. In Liberia, these included representatives of the Phelps-Stokes Fund, the American Colonization Society, the New York Colonization Society, the Boston-based Trustees of Donations and the foreign mission boards of the Protestant Episcopal Church, the Methodist Episcopal Church and the United Lutheran Churches of America.[13] However, Liberians were excluded from the Advisory Committee on Education in Liberia. Thus, even though members of the 1922 African Education Commission had lamented that the 'educational welfare of the people [of Liberia] has been left almost entirely to foreign mission societies', with the country continuing to rely on educational funding from the United States, it was precisely these circumstances that would ultimately help to fast-track their recommendations.[14]

Liberia's Secretary of Public Instruction, a trained physician of Bassa origin named Benjamin W. Payne (c. 1875–1940), made every effort to negotiate with his foreign counterparts on an equal footing.[15] In June 1927, members of government were 'kindly invited' to New York to attend a set of conferences organized by the Advisory Committee to determine Liberia's educational future.[16] Despite the Committee expressing a desire to 'assist' the Liberian government,[17] asymmetries in (public) Liberian versus (private) foreign representation, its narrow interpretation of 'expertise' and the location it chose to discuss these crucial matters – Payne had to travel for several months, via Germany, before arriving in New York to participate in the deliberations – were all signs of the dominant role that would be assumed by US actors in Liberian education over the following decades.

A key point on the agenda of the New York conferences was the appointment of the white Alabamian James Longstreet Sibley as educational adviser to the Liberian government. In the Liberian press, Payne declared that Sibley's 'duties are in an advisory capacity and have nothing to do with the administrative management of the Department as such, neither do they infringe upon or undertake to do, the duties of the Secretary of Public Instruction as set forth in the School Act'.[18] According to Payne, authority over local schools and their administration remained 'resting as heretofore with the officials of the Government'.[19] In reality, however, control over the funding of education, and its ultimate purpose and practices, were firmly in the grip of the US 'experts'; indeed, their hold was actually tightening. For example, whereas Liberian officials had still been debating the extent to which agricultural and industrial training should be promoted nationwide alongside a liberal arts education, Sibley and his deputy proposed the former as the most important priority for the country's education system for the foreseeable future, as discussed in the following section.[20] In the end, Sibley and his deputy also implemented the agenda originally laid out by the Board of Education, namely to coordinate the disorganized and scattered coastal schools by bringing the education policies of the various churches as well as that of government in line with one another.[21] Furthermore, as discussed above, the expansion of educational services into the rural interior remained a central part of their mission.

During this process, foreign educationists made much publicity of their sham 'interracial cooperation' with Liberian government officials, to set an example for broader West Africa. As Sibley explained it, 'the relationship of whites and natives [Africans] in Monrovia is also going to have considerable bearing on the future of relationships between the two groups all along the West Coast'.[22] However, behind the scenes, consultation with Liberian experts, whether formally trained or not, continued to be an anomaly. Expertise was continuously sourced from outside the continent, with the Fund regularly tapping into its network of reputable partner institutions on the east coast of the United States. It was no different when it came to developing textbooks to meet the novel demands of national education planning in Liberia. Covering topics from hygiene and physiology to geography and pedagogy, these English-language textbooks were intended to be 'more suitable and adoptable [adaptable] to local conditions and national ideals than those at present in use', but this overlooked the fact that only a minority of the country's rural population spoke the official language. Every single one of the expert authors who were chosen to capture Liberian culture came from either Columbia University in New York,[23] an important centre for sociological studies on, as well as rural education for, poor African Americans that had long benefited from donations from the Phelps-Stokes family,[24] or from 'a committee of [US] teachers with a knowledge of educational conditions and requirements in Liberia and other parts of West Africa'.[25] Knowledge that had not originated from within or adjacent to the (US) academy did not seem to feature in these deliberations whatsoever.

Given this unseemly imbalance in power, it is understandable that Liberian government officials pursued even the smallest opportunity to garner some prestige from the project. In 1928, for example, Payne announced a modest, but widely publicized, government promise to make an annual contribution of US$150 towards the publication of a new newspaper, the *Liberia Educational Outlook*, which would be aimed at an audience of government officials and teachers. Here again, the Advisory Committee repeated its familiar tactic of overstating the Liberian government's involvement in the project.[26] Actually, the newspaper's managing editor was the aforementioned Sibley, who would ultimately also become the BWI's first principal, although William H. Thomas, the associate editor, and Charles C. Dennis Sr., the printer, lent the newspaper a limited degree of local character. While President King described it in a speech as an interesting and well-written newspaper focusing on Liberia's educational challenges that was 'published by the Advisory Committee',[27] George J. Hill has more accurately described it as 'his [Sibley's] new newsletter.[28] Due to Sibley's unexpected death in 1929, the *Liberia Educational Outlook* was ultimately a short-lived experiment. Nevertheless, its content provides additional 'everyday' insights into the negotiations and contestations that accompanied the transfer of a contemporary US version of vocational and agricultural education to Liberia.

Race, Power and the Transfer of Agricultural Knowledge

According to Andrew E. Barnes, formally educated Africans were most receptive to African-American ideas on education 'during the era when Booker T. Washington was most actively promoting Tuskegee as the bridge over which the African race could travel toward regeneration'. Thereafter, enthusiasm to replicate this path waned among this group, which comprised mainly African Christians.[29] The Tuskegee Institute in Alabama, a historically black college and land-grant institution that specialized in teaching the professional trades to African Americans while promoting group 'upliftment' and Christian morality, served as an inspiration to a slew of Liberian leaders at the turn of the twentieth century, even though state-led development was predictably low on the agenda at the time given financial restraints. The personal achievements and outlook of Tuskegee's founder and President, the influential African American educationist Booker T. Washington, who spent his entire life in the overwhelmingly rural and agriculture-dependent US South, became a guiding light for many in Liberia, a country that was at the time itself widely perceived among its own population as an agriculture-dependent state. Although President Arthur Barclay, who governed Liberia from 1904 to 1912, had been among his admirers, government records confirm the declining popularity of a trades-oriented (agricultural or industrial) education following Washington's death in 1915. His declining influence was at least partially tied to the appropriation of his life's work and philosophy by white US American-led organizations, which took it upon themselves to disseminate it across Africa.

The transfer of agricultural and industrial education – or a version thereof that had been originally geared towards African Americans in the rural US South at the turn of the twentieth century – to Africa during the interwar period has received increasing scholarly attention.[30] Historians have frequently associated it with 'subjugation', 'segregation' and 'separate development', although there have been notable exceptions.[31] Even scholars who do not subscribe to the theory posited by historian Donald Spivey, who condemned this form of training as essentially abetting a 'new slavery', have questioned the social stratification mechanisms underpinning it.[32] Prior to her death, Olivia Phelps-Stokes, a philanthropist and trustee of the Phelps-Stokes Fund whose endowment would be dedicated to furthering an industrial education agenda in Africa, did acknowledge that this form of agricultural and practical education was solidifying 'a bond of union between the coloured people [in the United States] and in the little state of Liberia'.[33] Echoing this sentiment in his 1922 report, Jones pronounced that the 'services of Booker Washington reveal the possibilities of men of African blood, the qualities of mind and soul they may attain, and the peculiar value of their contribution to human welfare'.[34] Contemporary observers in Liberia were not unaware of these and similar racist tropes tied to this form of education.

President King did not equivocate when expressing his discontent with the increasing prioritization of agricultural and industrial education in the 1920s. In 1922, he lamented that US religious and philanthropic organizations 'will no longer respond to appeals made to them for higher education among the Negroes in the States much less in Liberia. But for industrial education, yes'. Worse still, the type of industrial education that white US Americans 'experts' proselytized tended to pin Liberians to the same (racial) evolutionary plane as the downtrodden and supposedly naturally rural African Americans. Countering this narrative, Secretary Payne appealed for an environment-dependent approach instead of a racial approach to development in Liberia. In an article in the *Liberia Educational Outlook*, he explained that 'development (and the need for such) is not a racial trait, but [an] individual one due to other factors dependent on [geographical] location'.[35] He thereby sensibly implied that Liberia's development challenges had more to do with 'physical and climatic conditions' than with the biological make-up of its inhabitants, countering the explanatory framework invoked by powerful US educationists. For his readership, which would have included many foreign teachers working in the country, Payne distinguished 'the Liberian' as unique and facing specific local challenges:

> The Liberian, it is to be further noted, is also a triune being; that is, he is a body, a mind and a spirit. This fact, therefore, must necessarily suggest to him that he has his own life to live; his own battles to fight, problems of his life to solve, his own victories or successes to win or lose … He also cannot follow entirely those who would have him develop on his own racial lines, and confine his training to more Elementary or Secondary Courses of studies, with exclusive industrial or vocational background.[36]

These words, in full support of the government-sanctioned form of nationalism, were particularly impactful coming from an influential member of a local ethnic group. They were indicative of an era that the historian of Liberia C. Patrick Burrowes paints as marking a shift from Pan-Africanism to Liberian nationalism,[37] although Payne's problematic use of gendered language reveals his casual exclusion of approximately half the population from this political imaginary.

Additional geopolitical implications arose from Liberia's acceptance of foreign educational assistance that was provided on the premise of its recipients' limited intellectual capacity. With nationalist sentiment on the rise at home, the Liberian government was fighting for increased recognition within the international community. Liberian officials thus bristled at the notion of becoming a state considered useful exclusively for the reproduction of semi-skilled agricultural and manual labour – or, even worse, a state that was prepared to bow down to an extractive foreign-owned plantation. As Secretary Payne asserted, the hegemony of agricultural and industrial education would inevitably have an intellectually stunting effect upon a young state that was in dire need of 'modern advancement'. In his words, 'the Liberian's education must prepare and enable him to live completely in the world and to be able to endure or withstand the light of advancing civilisation, or [Liberians] will fall into psycho-physical decay and finally pass away'.[38] Payne's vision of a 'civilized' society could not be achieved with hoe or plough alone.

During the 1920s, there had in fact been two very distinct movements in Liberia pushing contrarian visions of 'civilization' underpinned by a regime of industrial and agricultural education. Opposite Phelps-Stokesism stood Garveyism, a 'back-to-Africa' movement led by the Jamaican Marcus

Garvey. Garvey's Christian, anticolonial, black nationalist Universal Negro Improvement Association (UNIA), with its Black Star Line of steamships that transported goods and people around Africa, operated on the presumption that persons of African descent in the Americas were now fully equipped with the tools and skills of 'industrial civilization' to enable them to return their wealth of knowledge to the African continent.[39] While some Africans were moved by Garvey's rhetoric of black pride, others felt wholly alienated by UNIA's chauvinistic attitudes towards them. As such, the arrival of both Phelps-Stokesism and Garveyism placed the Liberian government at an important, albeit unsatisfying, crossroads – although it is perhaps illusory to speak of government officials as having had a genuine choice in the first place.

Initially, representatives of UNIA announced that President King had given them permission to establish their organization's headquarters in Liberia, from where they aimed to operate and agitate throughout the continent.[40] However, this proposal drew the ire of Liberia's powerful colonial neighbours. Moreover, in Liberia itself, members of the Phelps-Stokes Fund-sponsored African Education Commission and other prominent figures who anticipated a reliance on US capital in the country's modernization plans joined the chorus of criticism directed at Garvey's supposed lack of virtue and business acumen. With the aim of avoiding retaliation from US private investors or philanthropists, on whom local public instruction had long depended, Liberia began deporting UNIA members. In 1926, no more than two years after their forced removal, the Firestone concession agreement was signed, according to which the US-based Firestone Rubber and Tire Company secured a ninety-nine-year lease for up to one million acres of land from the Liberian state for the purpose of establishing one of the world's largest rubber estates, thus giving the United States direct access to this vital cash crop during its automobile industry's boom years. The historian of science, medicine and the environment Gregg Mitman has described this deal, which was coupled with a mandatory US$5 million loan from the company to the Liberian state that served as a control mechanism for Firestone, as 'ushering in an era of transformational economic, environmental, and social change'.[41] In his 1922 report, Jones had contended that rural education would be futile without a corporate presence investing in Liberia in tandem. It was his belief that 'the loan will open up the country through more and better roads, will improve conditions of sanitation, and will stimulate economic development so that educational activities may be extended into the interior and the interest of the Natives [Africans] aroused in community improvements'.[42] With these processes underway, technical training became a major feature of Liberia's US-led economic development programme, which was centred on the plantation economy and on small-scale farmers producing rubber to sell to Firestone. The BWI, which US donors perceived as a cost-efficient alternative to sending Liberian students to study abroad, was entrusted with bringing this US vision of global integration into fruition. Indeed, given the acute fragility of the state, some scholars have suggested that government officials 'regarded the industrial [and agricultural] education plan as part of a larger [US] American attempt to gain control of Liberia'.[43]

Although tensions endured, Liberian leaders were somewhat successful in advocating for a more diverse educational landscape in which the liberal arts could survive. Meanwhile, the promise and eventual shortcomings of the BWI have been well documented. The institution continued to sell Phelps-Stokesism as a development and integration instrument for Liberia that would improve the condition of the Indigenous population through a curriculum centred around agriculture, homemaking, public health and the building trades. However, it is clear from the scholarship that the BWI's relationship with the Liberian government remained fraught for a variety of reasons, from the racial discrimination practiced by its New York-based board to the minimal political support offered to the Liberian government by its funders. Furthermore, Louise Johnson contends that government opposition was driven by bitterness on the part of 'Americo-Liberian settlers'[44] over the attention that wealthy philanthropic and religious organizations were giving to the rural population;[45] nevertheless, official records show that only certain segments of the Liberian ruling class stood in the way of rural development. Spivey has focused on the 'rudimentary education' initially offered by the BWI and the personal grievances of Indigenous students, who complained about having to perform 'rough work', including building roads for Firestone, without compensation.[46] BWI graduate numbers also remained dismal during its two decades of existence.[47]

The following section takes us to the BWI's inaugural ceremony, prior to all the aforementioned tensions that were to emerge at its board meetings (between Liberian government officials and the institution's administrators) and in its workshops, factories and fields (between students and staff). The analysis of speeches and reports from the BWI's inaugural ceremony, which were (re)printed in the *Liberia Educational Outlook*, shows how language was employed to rhetorically ignore, refine or wholly falsify local context to promote the transfer of knowledge. Even if much of this official rhetoric would never become reality, it gives us a sense of the extent to which US interests gave consideration to and negotiated with local pushback.

The BWI Inaugural Ceremony: Official Rhetoric and Practical Challenges

The BWI's inaugural ceremony began on the morning of 17 March 1929 at the school's newly constructed Council Hall, which reportedly could seat up to one

thousand visitors. To guarantee a large attendance, the ceremony was scheduled to coincide with the first-ever Great Council of Native [African] Chiefs,
which was taking place over a one-week period in the same location and was
being presided over by President King to discuss matters relating to the administration of the interior. With some sixty paramount chiefs and six hundred
town or village chiefs (as well as their respective spokespersons, interpreters
and attendants) present, the inaugural ceremony was described as an 'epoch-
making event'.[48] It comprised a full day of speeches, an official procession to
the school grounds as well as song and worship at regular intervals, including
a bandstand performance, the singing of the Liberian national anthem and the
recital of devotionals (including the benediction). A film demonstrating farming practices in the United States brought the day to a close. Representatives of
government as well as local businesses and educational organizations attended
the event. Participants from the United States included the African-American
United States Minister Resident, William T. Francis; Rebecca Davis, an adviser
to Jeanes Work, another US educational institution strictly serving African
Americans and Africans that gave primacy to vocational and manual labour-
related instruction; and Reverend Robert E. Campbell, Missionary Bishop of
the Protestant Episcopal Church in Liberia. Sibley represented the Advisory
Committee on Education.

Twelve Symbols

As a key part of this ceremony, and to give the BWI some local roots, twelve
rural chiefs, who were abruptly designated as cofounders of the school, each
presented a symbolic contribution at a large white 'altar of industry',[49] a table
that was intended to illustrate the institution's commitment to industry via
'training for the Head, the Hand, the Heart and the Home, and resting upon
a sound basis of Health', echoing the 4-H movement discussed by Corinne
A. Pernet elsewhere in this volume. The twelve offerings comprised a map of
Liberia, a Liberian flag, a US flag, a cutlass, a collection of agricultural commodities, a hammer, a piece of hand-spun Liberian country cloth, a needle and
thread, a textbook on health, a book on Liberia's natural resources, a copy of
the school charter and a Bible.

The BWI's school grounds occupied a rolling plateau on the banks of the
Du River, about half a mile from the centre of the town of Kakata (originally
Kakatown), which was located 41 kilometres north of the Liberian capital,
Monrovia. As part of the joint efforts between the Liberian government and
rural chiefs to extend roads into the interior to facilitate trade, among other
aims, the major 480-kilometre road connecting Monrovia on the coast with the
northern city of Sanniquellie, Nimba County, on the Guinean border reached
the city of Kakata in May 1924. The school covered an area of approximately

4 square kilometres (approximately 1,000 acres) at this site on the edge of the rural interior, providing access to farmland as well as some of the enticing aspects of city life. The anonymous author of the article 'Tuskegee Grounds Dedicated at Kakatown', who was likely Sibley himself, given the publication in which it appeared as well as the participants and events it depicted, described a 'new mushroom city'. While situated 'on the borders of the native [African] tribes',[50] it was swiftly developing a reputation as a cosmopolitan space – a meeting place for farmers, traders and businesspeople from all over the country. He went on to characterize this rapid transformation process bluntly: 'Three years ago [this] writer [himself] sat down in Kakatown for four days waiting on a wily old chief to get him 150 carriers to take him upon an expedition into the interior. Today a highway runs through the village'.[51] In the same edition of the newspaper, in a reprint of his Founder's Day Address, the US Minister Resident described Kakata as a city in transition that was giving rise to novel landscapes and lifestyles – 'novel', in this instance, implying a supposedly rare similarity for an African city to urban life in the United States and Europe 'with its up-to-date municipal buildings, its stores, churches, beautiful homes, modern playgrounds for the children, parks neatly kept, where the populace may gather at the close of the day and listen to Kakatown's Military Band or rest in the quiet of a glorious African sunset'.[52]

Kakata's own symbolism as a meeting place of 'the rural' and 'the urban' – and thus supposedly of 'tradition' and 'modernity' – was evoked during the inaugural ceremony when Chief Blackie, also known as Fahn Dahmi, the Paramount Chief of the Weaju-Gbolleh region of the northwestern Grand Cape Mount County, presented a Liberian flag at the altar, thereby emblematically demonstrating national unity and the loyalty of the country's various ethnic groups to the central government. The writer of the anonymous article in the *Liberia Educational Outlook* noted of this 'temporary capital of the Republic' that 'the native [Indigenous] people as well as the descendants of the early settlers are Liberians all, and there should be no distinction in treatment or of opportunity for either group'.[53] On this untainted terrain, sufficiently far removed from the central government's coastal headquarters in this highly unequal society, it thus seemed possible to imagine a shared national future that was rooted in the social amalgamation of the present.[54]

At the time, Kakata was simultaneously turning into a focal point for 'native [African] and European life', given both its proximity to Firestone's main Du plantation, some 10 miles away, as well as its location next to land that the company was eyeing for expansion.[55] The Firestone rubber plantation in Margibi County, which was now the country's largest employer, had sparked a proliferation of European and African merchant businesses along the lengthening highway. As a sign of gratitude for a corresponding rise in prosperity, Blamassi Kornah, the Paramount Chief of Gbaigbon in the Garbleh Section of the Dey/Senjeh District, delivered a US flag to the altar. In explaining the significance of this flag, the anonymous author perpetuated a convenient falsehood surrounding the United States' supposedly unceasing interest in the Republic of Liberia 'from its founding to the present', thereby erasing some eighty years of diplomatic cold-shouldering.[56] And yet, for some observers in the international community, this act of performative allyship may have actually improved the political standing of the Liberian government.

There were no representatives from the Tuskegee Institute present at the event, further demonstrating that the reins of power were overwhelmingly in the hands of white American educationists; indeed, Tuskegee never developed any formal ties with the BWI.[57] However, links to African-American culture and history still lent some legitimacy to the project. Booker T. Washington's biography was evoked in various speeches. The Jeanes Work supervisor, Rebecca Davis, an African-American woman, led the crowd in singing an 'American Negro spiritual'. Chosen for this occasion was 'Ain't Going to Study War No More', a song of renewal that told the story of African Americans' escape from slavery while still hailing the benefits of a pacifism fortified by (religious) education.[58] The song, which captured the hopes of a transforming United States, also potentially had something to say about Liberia's national ambitions at the time. In his speech, in line with the Phelps-Stokes Fund's own mission, Robert W. Patton, a white US American leader in the American Church Institute for Negroes, attempted to situate the BWI within his organization's long history of educating 'Negro people both at home and abroad'.[59]

During the ceremony, Reverend Robert E. Campbell of the Protestant Episcopal Church of Liberia was responsible for highlighting the crucial role of Christian training in the country's education system by placing a Bible within a box on top of the altar. As the anonymous author explained, the BWI was founded as 'an integrated school for children (boys and girls) from all sections of the country', who would grow up to advance the nation through their education rooted in the Christian faith.[60] Given Liberia's official status as a Christian country and its de facto legacy as an abolitionist state, this act would have likely garnered much approval among educated Liberian onlookers.

The Liberian government donated 1,000 acres of land to the BWI, although it remains unclear how this land had come into the possession of the state in the first place. To further emphasize its involvement in the institution's founding, Governor Daryu of Krutown in Montserrado brought a map of Liberia to the altar to distinguish the new school as 'a national institution',[61] albeit with the primary responsibility of educating Indigenous youth. This emphasis on the national significance of the school provides some explanation as to why representatives of the rural elite were incorporated into all aspects of the inaugural ceremony. President King, the master of ceremonies, asserted that 'they [the rural chiefs] had long asked for an institution that would enable their boys to be useful members of their village life, and that this school was being established for this purpose.'[62] Perhaps to underscore this paternalistic outlook in front of the audience, the otherwise towering presence of the Firestone plantations within the Liberian economy was conveniently overlooked. In reality, however, the location of the school meant that only some of its students could regularly return to their villages, while others adapted to life in a boarding school system that Harold R. Bare, an agriculturist hired by the Advisory Committee on Education, described as 'sever[ing] the child from the influence of undesirable customs and beliefs – an asset if a substitution for the old is made'.[63]

Certain objects presented at the altar evoked the BWI's curriculum: a hammer representing the skilled trades; a typical locally manufactured country cloth symbolizing Indigenous industries; a textbook on healthcare drawing attention to the desperate need for public health initiatives; and a needle and thread celebrating the training of girls in the art of homemaking. As the anonymous observer noted, there was a distinct desire on the part of educators at the BWI that the chiefs should 'send us their girls as well as their boys'. Girls, the institution purported, would be turned into 'good home-makers and housewives'.[64] In contrast, and in ignorance of the longstanding contributions of women and girls to local farming, Varfly Kolli, the Paramount Chief of Backemai delivered a cutlass, a tool typically handled by men and boys, to epitomize the centrality of agriculture to the curriculum of Africa's 'Little Tuskegee'.

US Minister in Resident William T. Francis, who like Sibley passed away from yellow fever later in 1929,[65] portrayed the training that would be offered by the BWI as being complementary (and certainly not fatal) to higher education – indeed, even equally 'scientific' in nature.[66] 'This industrial school and agricultural institute will furnish the skilled mechanics and the scientific farmers who are destined to become the backbone of the country', he declared, adopting a similar tone to the anonymous author, who was in all likelihood Sibley.[67] In a line that would have won over a particularly high number of government officials, the anonymous author wrote that agriculture should not be decoupled from the liberal arts. Summarizing the approach of the US educationists, both newspaper contributions went to great lengths to distinguish vocational education from the daily drudgery of the labour-intensive farm. The delivery of a book to the altar, the title of which received no mention in the *Liberia Educational Outlook*, emphasized the importance of 'intellectual training'.[68] Furthermore, foreign educationists saw several promising signs at the time of the ceremony that commercial agricultural pursuits were starting to be taken more seriously among educated Liberians. Even President King – as well as several members of his cabinet, including Payne – had taken up labour-intensive commercial farming.[69] Other forms of agricultural production, such as subsistence farming, that did not feed directly into local or global markets were not mentioned.

Finally, the ceremony also served to assuage government unease about the inherent racial prejudice of the educational scheme. Towards the end of the event, a large group of onlookers, including President King, gathered at the BWI's Cook Hall to watch a film selected by US educationists. This film, the showing of which was a welcome surprise given that many of the guests had apparently never seen a motion picture, documented 'boys and girls [perform-ing] agricultural work in America'. The audience 'followed the fortunes of an American boy and girl as they carried out the instructions give[n] [to] them by the Agricultural Agent'.[70] In a fundamental shift in rhetoric, the children cap-tured on the screen were not black but white. This was an intentional choice; as the anonymous author explained frankly, the motivation for showing a film with white protagonists was to lend farming some prestige. Moreover, in front of this largely black and understandably sceptical audience, the racial identity of the protagonists served the purpose of delinking agricultural labour from racial classification. It demonstrated to the audience 'that white boys and girls were not averse to working with their hands, and many commented upon this after the show was over, for most of them had acquired the idea that no white people in either America or Africa ever did manual work'.[71] Similarly, earlier in the day, a sanitized version of the Phelps-Stokes Fund's agenda was presented by the US Minister Resident, who claimed that Olivia Phelps-Stokes 'saw in Liberia men with the same internal propelling blood through the same intri-cate pipes and valves as other men'.[72] Such contributions serve to illustrate both the uneven terrain on which knowledge transfers occurred and the means by which resistance, negotiation and/or contestation – even if between highly unequal partners or only at the level of rhetoric or performance – could lead to new and unexpected outcomes. Lessons learned in the United States could not simply be imposed – even upon a struggling state like Liberia – without taking into consideration existing structures and concerns.

Conclusion

The twelfth and final object was a copy of the school charter, which was pre-sented by Boymah Quay, Paramount Chief of Sasstown, Tehr District, Kru Coast, marking the end to a ceremony that was purposefully choreographed to claim a formative place in Liberian history. In assessing the success of this aspiration, this chapter has viewed the BWI's history as a window into the expansion of state-led formal agricultural education in Africa during the inter-war period. Liberia, which was already seen as a case study for US-sponsored

African self-rule, represented an ideal platform and was meant to serve as a model for US-sponsored interracial cooperation in West Africa as part of the aforementioned process.

This chapter has demonstrated how unequal power dynamics as well as social prejudices informed global transfers of knowledge. Examining the adaptation of formal agricultural education from the US South to Liberia, it has shown how the pre-eminence of US religious and philanthropic leaders in Liberia's educational landscape in the 1920s paved the way for the speedy implementation of the recommendations made on African education by the Phelps-Stokes Fund-sponsored 1922 African Education Commission. At the time, members of the Commission were of the firm belief that agricultural and industrial education would improve economic conditions in Liberia and, in turn, the socioeconomic condition of the country's predominantly rural population as this form of instruction penetrated deeper into the interior. However, in practice, this was a process that would have mixed and contradictory outcomes.

Liberian government officials were not opposed to the prospect of educational transformation and expansion into the interior in the 1920s. However, they had originally anticipated commanding this process. In reality, they soon discovered that they had little room to act besides raising concerns on issues of racism and geopolitical ghettoization with the Advisory Committee on Education in Liberia. For instance, an environmental perspective that took ecological opportunities and limitations into consideration seemed largely absent from the US approach to agricultural development. Nevertheless, it appears as if US educationists were not entirely blind to the problematic paternalistic lens through which many of them viewed the challenges of Liberian development and education, with important rhetorical adjustments apparent in their contributions to the BWI's inaugural proceedings.

Ultimately, agricultural and industrial education in Liberia took its place alongside more academic forms of instruction. Whereas the latter overwhelmingly served urban dwellers in their efforts to become lawyers, politicians or other professionals, the BWI's inaugural ceremony made it clear that the former was designed to offer opportunities to the hitherto uneducated largely rural masses. However, in contrast to other parts of the continent and given the context of the arrival of the US-headquartered Firestone Company, BWI administrators and US donors at large did not tie this group's destiny to smallholder farming alone. Instead, large segments of the rural population were channelled into menial wage labour on the world's largest rubber plantation.

Cassandra Mark-Thiesen is the leader of the 'African Knowledges and the History Public*ation' junior research group at the Africa Multiple Cluster of Excellence, University of Bayreuth. She previously lectured in African and global history at the University of Basel. She was a 2016–18 Marie Heim-Vögtlin Research Fellow (Swiss National Science Foundation). She coedited the volume *The Politics of Historical Memory and Commemoration in Africa* (Degruyter, 2021) and is the author of *Mediators, Contract Men and Colonial Capital: Mechanized Gold Mining in the Gold Coast Colony, 1879–1909* (Rochester University Press, 2018). Her general research interests include the historical cultures of Africa as well as the history of work, education, inequality and globalization.

Notes

This work has been supported by the Swiss National Science Foundation under PMPDP1_164485.

1. Letter from Emory Ross to Members of the Executive Committee of the Phelps-Stokes Fund, 24 January 1949, Claude A. Barnett Papers, Correspondence with Channing H. Tobias 1949–50, Chicago History Society Archive.
2. Jones, *Education in Africa*, 57.
3. Ibid., 291.
4. Ibid., 290.
5. Ibid., 2, 29.
6. Ibid., 28–29.
7. A Board of Education had initially been constituted under the Arthur Barclay administration (1904–12).
8. Members of the Board of Education included ex-President Arthur Barclay, the Right Reverend Bishop T. Momolu Gardiner, the Rt Revd Bishop Matthew W. Clair, the Rt Revd Bishop Sampson Brooks, the Rt Revd Apostolic Father Ogee, Revd N.H.B. Cassell, Revd J.D. Curran, Revd W.H. Thomas and Mrs P.C. Parker. All were representatives of missionary or broader religious organizations conducting educational work in Liberia.
9. King's Annual Message to the Legislature, 14 December 1921, in Dunn, *Annual Messages,* 588.
10. European powers defined the principle of effective occupation in Article 35 of the General Act of the Berlin Conference. This set out the guidelines for the acquisition of territorial sovereignty over land along Africa's coast and, occasionally, into its interior, while also determining the limits of their respective colonial possessions. This principle completely transformed the nature of governance in Liberia, one of only two independent nation states on the African continent at the time, as it battled to keep British and French colonialists from taking control of its territory.
11. At the same time, a growing black electorate represented by figures such as Booker T. Washington helped to garner US support for Liberia as an independent black-led state.
12. McBride, *Missions for Science*, 2.
13. Sibley, *Education and Missions in Liberia*, 1.
14. Shoko, *Dignity of Labour*, 3, 6, 216; Clatworthy, *Formulation of British Colonial Education Policy*.
15. After graduating from Meharry Medical School in Nashville in 1904, Payne had served

as Secretary of the Interior before becoming Secretary of Public Instruction; Smyke, 'An Indigenous Liberian's Quest', 25, N7.

16. King, 22 December 1927, in Dunn, *Annual Messages*, 727. The exact number of conferences is not clear from President King's annual message.
17. Ibid.
18. Benjamin W. Payne, 'Mr. James L. Sibley Appointed Educational Advisor', *Liberia Educational Outlook,* April 1928, 2. Albert Porte Papers.
19. Ibid.
20. In 1928, President King announced that the Bureau of Agriculture, which had previously been attached to the Interior Department, was to be transferred to the control of the Department of Public Instruction. King, 18 October 1928, in Dunn, *Annual Messages*, 753
21. Sibley's official annual salary from the Liberian state was a symbolic one US dollar.
22. Sibley, *Education and Missions in Liberia*, 9.
23. The sisters Olivia and Caroline Phelps-Stokes had been generous donors to this institution at the beginning of the twentieth century; see Yellin, '(White) Search for (Black) Order'.
24. For most of the nineteenth century, the discussion around the United States' 'Negro Problem' neglected the impact of white supremacy and the history of slavery when assessing the social and economic conditions of African Americans, instead highlighting this group's supposed moral failings. After the 1880s, poverty research took a scientific – or empirical – turn as it put a spotlight on the capitalist system. 'Moreover', according to O'Connor, 'the new knowledge would be instrumental in other ways as well, serving the institution-building objectives of a burgeoning array of public and private organizations – social settlements, philanthropies, professional and civic groups, state and federal bureaus of research – that were beginning to look beyond the patchwork of local poor laws and private charities for ways of prevention rather than relief'; O'Connor, *Poverty Knowledge*, 26.
25. King, 22 December 1927, in Dunn, *Annual Messages*, 727.
26. King, 18 October 1928, in ibid., 751. The annual sum of US$150 enabled the publication of 150 copies of the newspaper each month.
27. King, 13 January 1921, in ibid., 576.
28. Hill, 'Intimate Relationships', 476.
29. Barnes, *Global Christianity*, 153.
30. See e.g. Zimmerman, *Alabama in Africa*; Yamada, 'Educational Borrowing', 21–37; Steiner-Khamsi and Quist, 'Politics of Educational Borrowing', 272–99; Berman, 'American Influence on African Education', 32–145.
31. For example, Andrew Barnes has demonstrated that African Christians also viewed industrial education as holding the potential for socio-economic upliftment; see Barnes, *Global Christianity*.
32. In the case of Britain's African colonies, the scholar of education and international development Shoko Yamada has highlighted that '[US] American models did not supersede what had been practiced already, but rather mixed with British notions about education for lower social ranks and local contexts'; Yamada, 'Educational Borrowing', 22.

33. Olivia Phelps-Stokes to Washington, 16 November 1909, cited in Moniba, 'Booker T. Washington', 99.
34. Jones, *Education in Africa*, 15.
35. Benjamin W. Payne, 'The Liberian and Education', *Liberia Educational Outlook*, February 1928, 4. Albert Porte Papers.
36. Ibid.
37. Burrowes, *Power and Press Freedom*, 135–38.
38. Payne, 'The Liberian and Education', 4.
39. Burrowes, *Power and Press Freedom*, 152.
40. Ibid., 137–38.
41. Mitman, *Empire of Rubber*, 75.
42. Jones, *Education in Africa*, 306.
43. Johnston, 'Tuskegee in Liberia', 66.
44. It has often gone unacknowledged that 'Americo-Liberian' is not a static category; its meaning has shifted as the country and its population have changed. Today, it is largely used as a derogatory term for members of the Liberian upper class, some of whom do not have any biological ties to the initial waves of black settlers from the Americas who helped to develop the early settler territory of Liberia.
45. Johnston, 'Tuskegee in Liberia', 66.
46. Spivey, *Politics of Miseducation*, 3, 39, 70; Johnston, 'Tuskegee in Liberia', 64.
47. Johnston, 'Tuskegee in Liberia', 61.
48. 'Tuskegee Grounds Dedicated at Kakatown', *Liberia Educational Outlook*, March 1929, 3. Albert Porte Papers.
49. It remains difficult to assess the chiefs' views on the new institution. According to President King, they had only gained knowledge of the 'aims and purposes' of the BWI on the day of the event; King, 30 October 1929, in Dunn, *Annual Messages*, 777.
50. 'Tuskegee Grounds Dedicated at Kakatown', 3.
51. Ibid.
52. William T. Francis, 'Founder's Day Address', *Liberia Educational Outlook*, March 1929, 4. Albert Porte Papers.
53. 'Tuskegee Grounds Dedicated at Kakatown', 3, 6.
54. Through his recent discovery of the handwritten agreement detailing the sale of land that would later become Liberia's capital, Burrowes has been able to reconstruct how different groups – namely repatriates, abolitionist Africans and African-American settlers – came together to found the country. See Ray Cavanaugh. 'Two Hundred Years Later, a Long-Lost Document Sheds Light on the Purchase of Liberia', *Washington Post*, 20 November 2021. Retrieved 27 October 2022 from https://www.washingtonpost.com/history/2021/11/20/liberia-purchase-agreement-1821-burrowes.
55. 'Tuskegee Grounds Dedicated at Kakatown', 3.
56. Ibid., 6.
57. According to Antoinette Brown-Sherman, 'no provisions were made to train Liberians to staff [the BWI] nor to hire African Americans experts until the 1940s'; Brown-Sherman, 'Review: The Politics of Miseducation', 88–94.
58. 'Tuskegee Grounds Dedicated at Kakatown', 4.
59. Ibid., 5.

60. Ibid., 4.
61. Ibid., 6.
62. Ibid., 4.
63. Harold R. Bare, 'Reaching the Multitudes with the Village School', *Liberia Educational Outlook*, October /November 1929, Albert Porte Papers.
64. 'Tuskegee Grounds Dedicated at Kakatown', 4.
65. Mitman, *Empire of Rubber*, 142.
66. Francis, 'Founder's Day Address', 6.
67. Ibid.
68. 'Tuskegee Grounds Dedicated at Kakatown', 6.
69. Francis, 'Founder's Day Address', 5.
70. 'Tuskegee Grounds Dedicated at Kakatown', 6.
71. Ibid.
72. Francis, 'Founder's Day Address', 5.

Bibliography

Barnes, Andrew E. *Global Christianity and the Black Atlantic: Tuskegee, Colonialism, and the Shaping of African Industrial Education*. Waco: Baylor University Press, 2017.

Berman, Edward H. 'American Influence on African Education: The Role of the Phelps-Stokes Fund's Education Commissions'. *Comparative Education Review* 15(2) (1971), 132–45.

Brown-Sherman, Mary Antoinette. 'Review: The Politics of Miseducation by Donald Spivey'. *Liberian Studies Journal* 7(1) (1987), 88–94.

Burrowes, C. Patrick. *Power and Press Freedom in Liberia, 1830–1970: The Impact of Globalization and Civil Society on Media-Government Relations*. Trenton: Africa World Press, 2004.

Cavanaugh, Ray, 'Two Hundred Years Later, a Long-Lost Document Sheds Light on the Purchase of Liberia', *Washington Post*, 20 November 2021. Retrieved 27 October 2022 from https://www.washingtonpost.com/history/2021/11/20/liberia-purchase-agreement-1821-burrowes.

Clatworthy, F. James. *The Formulation of British Colonial Education Policy, 1929–1961*. Washington DC: Office of Education (DREW), Bureau of Research, 1969.

Dunn, D. Elwood. *The Annual Messages of the Presidents of Liberia 1848–2010: State of the Nation Addresses to the National Legislature*. Berlin: De Gruyter Saur, 2011.

Hill, George J. 'Intimate Relationships: Secret Affairs of Church and State in the United States and Liberia, 1925–1947'. *Diplomatic History* 31(3) (2007), 465–503.

Johnston, Louise. 'Tuskegee in Liberia: The Politics of Industrial Education, 1927–1935'. *Liberian Studies Journal* 9(2) (1980), 61–68.

Jones, Thomas Jesse. *Education in Africa: A Study of West, South, and Equatorial Africa by the African Education Commission, under the Auspices of the Phelps-Stokes Fund and Foreign Mission Societies of North America and Europe*. New York: Phelps-Stokes Fund, 1922.

McBride, David. *Missions for Science: U.S. Technology and Medicine in America's African World*. New Brunswick, NJ: Rutgers University Press, 2002.

Mitman, Gregg. *Empire of Rubber: Firestone's Scramble for Land and Power in Liberia*. New York: The New Press, 2021.

Moniba, Harry F. 'Booker T. Washington, Tuskegee Institute, and Liberia: Institutional and Moral Assistance 1908–1969', Ph.D. dissertation. East Lansing: Michigan State University, 1975.

O'Connor, Alice. *Poverty Knowledge: Social Science, Social Policy and the Poor*. Princeton: Princeton University Press, 2001.

Sibley, James L. *Education and Missions in Liberia: A Preliminary Survey of the Filed for the American Advisory Committee on Education*. New York: Phelps-Stokes Fund, 1926.

Smyke, Raymond J. 'An Indigenous Liberian's Quest for the Presidency: Momolu Massaquoi and the 1931 Election'. *Liberian Studies Journal* 30(2) (2005), 1–28.

Spivey, Donald. *The Politics of Miseducation: The Booker Washington Institute of Liberia, 1929–1984*. Lexington: University Press of Kentucky, 1986.

Steiner-Khamsi, Gita, and Hubert O. Quist. 'The Politics of Educational Borrowing: Reopening the Case of Achimota in British Ghana'. *Comparative Education Review* 44(3) (2000), 272–99.

Yamada, Shoko. 'Educational Borrowing as Negotiation: Re-examining the Influence of the American Black Industrial Education Model on British Colonial Education in Africa'. *Comparative Education* 44(1) (2008), 21–37.

———. *Dignity of Labour for African Leaders: The Formation of Education Policy in the British Colonial Office and Achimota School*. Bamenda: Langaa RPCIG, 2018.

Yellin, Eric S. 'The (White) Search for (Black) Order: The Phelps-Stokes Fund's First Twenty Years, 1911–1931'. *Historian* 65(2) (2002), 319–52.

Zimmerman, Andrew. *Alabama in Africa: Booker T. Washington, the German Empire, and the Globalization of the New South*. Princeton: Princeton University Press, 2012.

 CHAPTER 3

'The Latest Developments in Agricultural Knowledge and Practice from the Outside World'

UNRRA's Agricultural Rehabilitation Work in Italy in the Aftermath of the Second World War

Amalia Ribi Forclaz

Various recent studies have focused on the interwar and immediate post-war years as a crucial period for understanding the agrarian transformations that occurred in Europe during the second half of the twentieth century.[1] In contrast to the rich literature on the history of colonial agricultural development, relatively little is known about the role played by wartime relief agencies and early postwar international organizations in the circulation of agricultural expertise, knowledge and technology in a European context.[2] As will be argued in this chapter, the archives of the United Nations Relief and Rehabilitation Administration (UNRRA) offer a rich platform for remedying this gap. They open a window into the rationale and implementation of UNRRA's short-lived but meaningful programme of 'agricultural rehabilitation', which was intended to re-establish agricultural production in war-damaged countries through the importation of farm machinery, cattle and breeding equipment, fertilizers, pesticides and seeds.

This chapter will first outline the creation and functioning of UNRRA's Agricultural Rehabilitation Division and look beyond the official rhetoric of 'reconstruction' to the long-term ideas of development and higher productivity that underpinned its work. The main part of the chapter then tries to unpack what agricultural rehabilitation meant in the case of Italy. A country that had seen major agricultural transformations during the interwar years, Italy offers a multifaceted lens through which to examine the logistical, political and social challenges encountered in the quest to induce agricultural transformation within specific localized contexts. In line with the focus of the present volume on the circulation, transfer and renegotiation of agricultural knowledge, UNRRA reports and reflections shed light on the complexity of agricultural aid, the range of different stakeholders – from government officials and agricultural experts to the farmers themselves – who had to be taken into account, and the unexpected resistance that emerged from different quarters.

Agricultural Rehabilitation and Postwar Reconstruction

UNRRA has in recent years emerged as a major actor in international and transnational histories of 'postwar reconstruction'.[3] The organization was established in November 1943 in Washington DC and began its work of managing the transition from war to peace in formerly occupied or soon-to-be liberated territories on 1 January 1944. It was conceived as a collective Allied enterprise, but was identified internationally as a North American organization. UNRRA's operations in Europe were scheduled to last for only three years, until the end of 1946, but continued because of delayed shipments until mid-1947.[4] Despite its short lifespan, as historians have shown, UNRRA was particularly active in providing relief to Eastern and Southern European countries such as Poland, the Soviet Union, Italy, Albania, Greece and Yugoslavia as well as Germany and China. These were all countries marked by destruction, food shortages, and the threat of epidemics and refugee streams, a multifaceted crisis that Ben Shephard has described as lasting until 1950.[5]

Whereas various scholars have stressed UNRRA's concern with postwar food security and its role in the provision of food aid, little research has yet looked into the goals, organization and implementation of UNRRA's agricultural programme.[6] This chapter focuses on the transfer of farming resources, such as tractors and seeds, but also of agricultural knowledge and techniques in the context of postwar reconstruction. As becomes clear when analysing archival records, UNRRA's aim when it came to agricultural rehabilitation was to assist in the 'resumption of urgently needed agricultural production' with a view to securing enough food for the populations of liberated countries.[7] Estimates of food and other supplies that would be needed after liberation had already been undertaken by the Allies since 1941.[8] With the formal commencement of UNRRA's activities in early 1944, a special expert committee, the Standing Technical Committee on Agriculture, began convening experts and making recommendations on 'the priorities attached to the delivery of different types of agricultural requirements'.[9] An administrative unit in charge of formulating, organizing and executing agricultural programmes, the Agricultural Rehabilitation Division, was immediately established. Based in Washington DC and headed by Edwin R. Henson, a former official in the United States Department of Agriculture (USDA), the Division's function was to estimate what supplies were needed by analysing reports and data, and then negotiating and organizing the purchase and delivery of these goods.[10]

During its first year, the Division was mostly concerned with collecting economic and statistical information on agricultural production and surveying the damage that the war had caused to farm machinery, livestock and fisheries, as well as seed, fertilizer and pesticide supplies.[11] Out of these studies emerged a bleak picture of the state of agriculture in Europe's war-torn countries. Tractors and other farm machinery had been requisitioned for military use, while animals had been slaughtered or stolen, leading to both a loss of draught power and an inability to plough land and cultivate crops. There was a shortage of fertilizer, tractors were standing idle because of missing replacement parts, and seeds had deteriorated because of poor soil conditions and a lack of imported planting equipment. Withdrawing armies had systematically destroyed crops, farms and essential equipment as well as agrarian education and research facilities.

Planning for agricultural aid that would help to remedy this situation raised complex questions about the potential transformation of land, farms and farming populations at a time of dramatic upheaval. Whereas there was a common understanding within UNRRA's bureaucracy that it was the aim of the organization to assist countries in rebuilding what had been destroyed or depleted by the war, the extent and meaning of UNRRA's role remained a matter of contestation within the organization. An UNRRA official in charge of analysing production needs maintained that 'it should be understood clearly that UNRRA is not writing agricultural production programs for any country, because this, obviously, must be the responsibility of the respective countries themselves'.[12] However, this assertion was not shared by all. Instead, it seemed evident to other UNRRA agricultural experts that some of the material supplied by UNRRA, especially 'modern farm equipment ... where it has not previously been extensively used ... could easily be the entering wedge to a complete over-haul of the industrial-agricultural pre-war balance in the country'.[13]

By the spring of 1945, the activities of the Agricultural Rehabilitation Division had moved from preparation into the action phase. Ships were loaded and large tonnages scheduled for shipment to liberated areas, with personnel beginning to move into several liberated countries.[14] UNRRA staff complained that it had taken the organization too long 'getting UNRRA operations actually under way'.[15] These delays were particularly problematic for agricultural undertakings. Seasonal planting and harvesting timetables required planning for the spring of 1946 to start a year earlier, and it became clear that it would be impossible to provide agricultural supplies in time. Another difficulty arose from the fact that many agricultural supplies were interdependent. For example, shipment of tractors needed to be followed up by the delivery of replacement parts and the arrival of trained mechanics who could demonstrate how to use imported machinery.[16]

Circumstances became even more complicated once the agricultural supplies arrived in the recipient countries. As the case of Italy illustrates, UNRRA's agricultural aid faced significant logistical, political and social challenges. As a former enemy country, Italy had not initially been considered for the UNRRA programme, but it ultimately became one of UNRRA's largest missions. Agriculture was an important sector in the Italian economy and a key ingredient of the country's social make-up. But while UNRRA's Italian mission shared some features with other UNRRA missions in the Mediterranean, particularly in Greece and Albania, the legacy of fascist ruralist policies and institutions made Italy a unique terrain for the reception and contestation of foreign supplies. The diverse interests of various stakeholders – including the Italian government, Italian experts working for domestic research institutions, local industrial manufacturers of machinery and, last but not least, Italian farmers – all had to be taken into consideration.

UNRRA and Italian Agriculture: The Meaning of Agricultural Rehabilitation

UNRRA aid to Italy was only one of many complex elements of Italy's postwar relationship with the United States and US-led aid programmes.[17] This is not the place to go into detail about the various domestic and foreign actors and political institutions or the internal disagreements and ideological divisions that shaped Italy's postwar agricultural recovery;[18] instead, the focus in this chapter is on outlining the general context of UNRRA's agricultural work in Italy. The Allies had started planning for the provision of postwar aid to Italy as early as 1943. In July 1944, an UNRRA observer mission arrived in the country to assess the need for relief and rehabilitation, and to issue recommendations in this regard. As Silvia Salvatici has shown, the mission first and foremost reported a need for the importation of food supplies, especially for children and nursing mothers, as well as medical supplies. Furthermore, assistance was also required with the resettlement and rehousing of internally displaced persons.[19] However, the political situation remained complex and the country was still militarily divided: Allied armies held the South and the islands, while the German military and Mussolini still ruled part of the North. Because of Italy's role within the Axis and the remaining fascist presence, opinion on helping Italy was contested among the Allies. In line with public opinion in Allied countries, some members of UNRRA's council did not think that an ex-enemy country should receive aid.[20]

Nevertheless, negotiations with the pro-Allied Italian government over the financial and administrative details of UNRRA's Italian mission, which had been placed under the leadership of Spurgeon Keeny, a US American with extensive experience of relief work, started in late 1944.[21] In line with the rapid succession of political and military developments in the first half of 1945, including Mussolini's death in April and Germany's surrender in May, attitudes towards Italy shifted in the country's favour. At the Potsdam Conference in July and August 1945, Italy officially joined the Allies in their unfinished war against Japan.[22] By the summer of 1945, UNRRA had therefore decided to treat Italy like any other liberated country. In terms of tonnage, UNRRA's Italian programme would become 'the largest to any receiving country', amounting to a total of 10 million tons of goods at a value of US$418 million and comprising a staff of approximately four thousand personnel.[23] Out of this massive aid programme, a relatively minor US$13 million was allocated to agricultural rehabilitation supplies, the largest proportion of which went to the importation of fertilizers and machinery (US$5 million). The rest of the programme included the shipment of pesticides, breeding equipment, veterinary and fisheries supplies, and seeds. According to UNRRA's official historian George Woodbridge, these supplies, together with the arrival of a group of agricultural experts, were meant 'to bring to Italy the latest developments in agricultural and veterinary knowledge and practice from the outside world from which it had been cut off throughout the years of war'.[24]

As with nonagricultural UNRRA supplies, the terms by which Italy was to receive this aid were carefully laid out in agreements between UNRRA and the Italian government. While UNRRA officials liked to point out that UNRRA goods were being given to Italy 'for free', the situation was more complex. In an agreement finalized in June 1946, the government was obliged to pay the net proceeds of sales of UNRRA imported goods into a special account, the so-called Lire Fund, which would then be used to fund agricultural rehabilitation projects that had been proposed by various Italian institutions or experts in agreement with UNRRA. In other words, there were two parts to UNRRA agricultural rehabilitation measures: the immediate importation of supplies and longer-term projects that were deemed worthy of financial assistance. For reasons of space, this chapter can only concentrate on the former, UNRRA's provision of supplies.

Agriculture and Agricultural Research in Italy

When UNRRA embarked on its agricultural rehabilitation mission in Italy, it was arriving in a country in which agriculture played a primary role and had undergone decades of government intervention, scientific development and socioeconomic reform. Regional variations in available land and labour resulted in important differences in production, farm size and tenancy patterns. These ranged from large-scale landownership (*latifundia*) in Lombardy and the South – a region that suffered from widespread emigration – to a preponderance of sharecroppers and small-scale tenants in Tuscany and Veneto. In 1945 about half of Italy's population was still engaged in agricultural production, which contributed roughly one-third of the national income. Most of Italy's agriculture centred on food production, particularly wheat, but also small grains and pulses, corn and potatoes as well as vegetables, citrus, wine and olives. Livestock farming was only a minor feature.

From the early twentieth century, agricultural education and research in Italy had undergone a process of institutionalization and professionalization that resulted in a well-established educational and scientific apparatus. Agricultural extension was based on the unique system of *cattedre ambulanti* (itinerant professorships), which involved agricultural scientists and economists travelling into the provinces to lecture peasants on practical techniques of modern farming and farm management.[25] Liberal, and later fascist, agricultural economists became internationally renowned experts, not least partly due to their role in the International Institute of Agriculture, which was headquartered in Rome. In the 1920s and 1930s, agriculture emerged as a pivotal element of the fascist modernization project. In an attempt to solve some of the issues relating to unproductive, marginal or malaria-infested land, the fascist regime invested in wide-reaching land reclamation schemes that intensified agricultural activity in the Pontine Marshes in Central Italy.[26] These were also accompanied by an internal colonization scheme that foresaw the movement of sharecroppers from Central Italy to the South in a bid to improve agricultural practices and increase production.[27] The so-called *battaglia del grano* (Battle for Wheat), which was launched in 1925, became emblematic of the regime's aim to achieve greater food self-sufficiency. This propagandistic and highly politicized campaign was accompanied by the establishment of agricultural science laboratories that undertook sustained experimentation with crop breeding, including the development of high-yielding seeds.[28]

However, state intervention and the development of industrial farming did not undermine common beliefs that had existed since the early twentieth century that landownership by small-scale farmers and the expansion of family farms would help to sustain a healthy agricultural sector. In fact, as Federico d'Onofrio has shown, 'technocratic tendencies and a scientifically legitimized discourse of modernization' coexisted during the fascist era with a 'localistic and anti-industrialist rhetoric' that centred on the peasant or the family farm as the economic and social bedrock of a productive and well-fed nation.[29]

During the Second World War, like in other European countries that were theatres of active combat, agriculture in Italy suffered from the dislocation of farming activities due to fighting on Italian soil, damage to agricultural build-ings, enemy plundering and loss of livestock.[30] Fertilizer shortages, an increase in fallow land and unfavourable weather conditions further reduced Italian agricultural production and weakened the agricultural sector, in turn lead-ing to food shortages, hunger and starvation.[31] In its report on the state of Italian agriculture, partly based on an economic survey by its observer mission and the input of Italian experts, UNRRA noted that 'serious food shortage[s]', which would be aggravated by distribution problems and the compulsory food requisitioning and rationing of the *Ammassi* system (state-owned grain stor-age centres), would likely become the 'most crucial problem' that Italy would face after liberation.[32] A shortage of wheat, production of which had fallen by one-third, as well as shortages of other staples such as olive oil and pasta were forcing the urban population in particular to resort to the black market.

The ongoing food shortages, UNRRA experts believed, could be averted by the importation of certain types of supplies, including fertilizers, the domestic production of which had declined during the war, and seeds, stocks of which were low due to the interruption in trade and scientific exchange. If 'putting farm production on its feet in the shortest practicable time' was UNRRA's main goal, there were also enduring weaknesses from the prewar era that required long-term solutions.[33] In the eyes of UNRRA officials from the United States in particular, Italian agriculture suffered from structural challenges, including the large proportion of mountainous sub-arid land, the small size of farms, underdeveloped animal husbandry and high reliance on manpower with 'little emphasis on labour-saving devices' or machinery.[34] Rehabilitation was there-fore a misleading term, as the aim of UNRRA was not to re-establish fascist agricultural programmes or pre-fascist conditions. On the contrary, UNNRA economic adviser William G. Welk professed that 'the ultimate goal of agri-cultural rehabilitation in Italy cannot be a return to pre-war conditions, partly because the economic orbit to which Italy belonged has been largely wrecked and partly because the whole self-sufficiency program must be discarded if Italy is to achieve social and economic progress'. Accordingly, UNRRA experts maintained, 'new programs and new goals must be established that will modify the structure of Italian agriculture'.[35]

Some of these goals could be seen as a reversion to pre-fascist land use, such as the 'partial shift from the production of grains for direct food con-sumption to a grain-livestock economy' that would boost meat production. But UNRRA's agricultural rehabilitation programme was also the start of a process of agricultural transformation that would range from resettlement programmes to 'an education program to increase and develop the skill of the peasants and make them able to handle modern machinery and raise improved types of livestock'.[36] However, what UNRRA officials seemed to have been less willing to consider was the likelihood that the transfer of aid would not go as smoothly as planned, because UNRRA did not directly distribute its agricultural supplies and had to rely entirely on local stakeholders. These actors, ranging from the government to agricultural cooperatives and farmers, held varying views on UNRRA's technical assistance. Whereas those in scientific circles seemed happy to cooperate, industrialists resented the importation of foreign machinery and farmers were sometimes reluctant to switch to using UNRRA seeds.

Livestock Shipping and US Ranging Experience

One of UNRRA's main concerns with regard to the prospects for agricultural rehabilitation in Europe was the loss of livestock and the implications thereof not only for draught power and breeding purposes but also dairy and meat production and consumption. The importation of cows, horses and mules was also related to the importation of veterinary supplies, the supply of animal feed and the availability of pasture. Even though livestock shipping was considered risky because of the complicated logistics involved and the potential outbreak of diseases, it became an essential feature of UNRRA's agricultural missions – albeit with somewhat limited success in Italy.[37]

Like elsewhere in Europe's war-damaged countries, livestock populations in Italy had suffered the effects of active warfare, dislocation, plunder, disease and increased slaughter due to food shortages.[38] UNRRA estimated that pig, sheep, goat and horse numbers had all dropped by 20–25 per cent during the war. With regard to the quality of livestock, UNRRA offered contradictory assessments. Italy could look back on a period of intensive scientific investment in breeding technologies during the interwar years, and UNRRA experts noted the 'worldwide reputation' of certain Italian scientists, such as those in the field of artificial insemination, which was predicted to become one of the major fields of postwar scientific development.[39] Some indigenous breeds were also admired.[40] But in comparison to the United States, UNRRA noted, Italian livestock numbers – and consequently per capita meat production – was 'extremely low'. Surprisingly, and to the disappointment of UNRRA experts, the demand for livestock remained limited; in comparison with other UNRRA agricultural missions, Italy was a relatively minor recipient.[41] All in all, about one thousand animals were imported, the majority of which were pedigreed bulls or heifers to improve existing herds or cows for distribution to poor families to cover their dairy needs.[42]

However, UNRRA's livestock assistance went beyond the mere supply of head of cattle. Surveying the Italian countryside, UNRRA experts found fault with the backward methods with which cattle were being ranged in mountainous areas. They claimed that such practices were leading to overgrazing on mountain pastures and soil erosion, a problem that US observers found to be typical of Mediterranean countries. Frederic G. Renner, a soil scientist experienced in surveying the western mountains of the United States, was sent to assess conditions in Central Italy. In his report, which was finalized in May 1946, Renner was particularly critical of the traditional movement of sheep farmers between lower and higher mountain pastures. Blaming this practice for soil depletion and erosion, he argued that it could be solved by the introduction of irrigation measures as well as a 'more enlightened' management of livestock that would incorporate fencing, supplemental feeding and rotational use of pastures.[43] As Renner put it, there was a need 'for an educational process in this regard'. He suggested sending Italians to study 'modern methods of range management in the US and Canada' by placing them on internships in organizations such as the Soil Conservation Service and the Forest Service of the USDA.[44]

Similarly, support for Italian exposure to US scientific expertise and knowledge also existed among veterinary experts, who proposed sending Italian veterinary scientists for short periods of study at US universities. This included, for example, Cornell, whose agricultural scientists were playing leading roles in contributing their expertise to US humanitarian ventures, such as the agricultural development work of the Near East Foundation.[45] Whereas UNRRA experts acknowledged the prewar excellence of certain Italian scientists and experiment stations, they also noted the 'intellectual isolation' from which Italian science had suffered after the outbreak of the war. Italian experts too complained about their lack of access to funding, research premises and international scientific literature. Most research institutions had seen their work interrupted during the war. Some, like the renowned wheat breeding station in Bologna (Istituto Allevamento Vegetale per la Cerealicoltura), had been evacuated during the German occupation, only to be requisitioned and occupied by British troops in 1945 – leaving no space, money or machinery for the resumption of research.[46] To remedy this situation, UNRRA identified a list of about twenty Italian experts, supposedly 'the most alert from the current research staff', to be sent to the United States, the United Kingdom or Canada to be brought up to date with the most recent research in fields ranging from general agronomy, soil studies, livestock nutrition and animal science to plant pathology and insecticide development.[47] As such, there was a clear intention on the part of UNRRA to draw Italian experts into a US and British imperial scientific orbit.

Tractors and Other Farm Machinery Supplies

One of the more emblematic yet controversial strands of UNRRA agricultural aid was the provision of agricultural machinery that was seen as lacking in Italy and the education of farmers in its use. From a US perspective, this would make Italian agriculture more productive and efficient, thereby reducing the need for manual labour. US experts noted that, despite the wide-reaching ruralization programmes of the fascist era, mechanization remained 'low', with 'little over 10% of the arable land ... ploughed with tractors and only 60% of the grain harvest ... threshed mechanically'.[48] Farm machinery was described as 'antiquated'. Moreover, as economic advisers had already noted during UNRRA's observer mission in 1944, 'tractors, binders, threshers, mowers, hay balers and other similar modern equipment' were all generally 'run down' or in the process of being 'cannibalized'. In other words, farmers were dismantling tractors into their basic parts, either in order to fix other machinery or to sell or exchange the parts that were fetching high prices on the domestic market.[49]

As UNRRA experts soon discovered, the importation of new farm machinery from the United States and the United Kingdom did not provide a straightforward solution to these problems. Instead, when a consignment of sixty-five UNRRA tractors arrived at the Consorzio Agrario (agricultural cooperative) in Arezzo in April 1946, UNRRA staff were dismayed to discover that the Italian government had priced them 'shockingly high' without consulting them. Thus, whereas UNRRA officials had anticipated the organization of tractor pools, effective distribution was hampered – most notably by the Federazione Consorzi Agrari (Federation of Agricultural Cooperatives), which was involved in maldistribution and corruption.[50] In some cases, such as in Veneto, UNRRA tractors were sold to farmers for double the UNRRA price.[51] Most typically, however, UNRRA was surprised to find that tractors that had been brought into Italy 'for immediate use' were standing 'idle' in warehouses.[52]

In fact, the views of the Italian government and UNRRA relief workers on the need for machinery imports differed. Whereas US observers noted that at least 4,000 tractors would need to be imported annually to sustain 'mechanization', the government only requested the importation of 1,400, stating that domestic production would provide the rest.[53] The situation was even more pronounced with regard to mowers, for which initial requests were reduced from 16,000 to just 1,000. As became clear, the Italian government, defending the interests of domestic machinery manufacturers, would have preferred UNRRA machinery supplies to be entirely scrapped in favour of less controversial and more urgent supplies of wheat and coal.[54] Not taking this preference into account, UNRRA officials insisted on a 'firm program' for the supply of foreign machinery.[55] They criticized the Italian government's 'tendency' to keep UNRRA imports of farm machinery low, claiming that this was being done 'in an attempt to protect [Italian] manufacturers' and to maintain an 'artificial scarcity' and 'high prices' with disastrous consequences for farmers and food production.[56] UNRRA officials repeatedly argued that Italian farmers were struggling due to a lack of imports and that it would be 'better to stop Italian manufacturing of tractors (the labour involved being negligible) and let the Italian farmer have the full benefit of farm motorization at prices within his reach'.[57]

It is difficult to judge from UNRRA sources whether such assessments were genuine or whether there was a portion of (long-term) economic self-interest on the part of US and Canadian machinery manufacturers such as Massey Harris that provided the tractors for UNRRA. However, what is striking is that UNRRA did not consider the possibility of providing financial aid and technical assistance to support the resumption of manufacturing in FIAT's war-damaged farm machinery factories. It is also not entirely clear how much of a demand for tractors there actually was among farmers. Whereas UNRRA noted that there were 'a lot of enquiries by farmers to [the] UNRRA office on the availability of farm machinery', very few made it into the archives.[58] An exception was a request that was submitted by the Italian farmer Alberico Brini from Rovigo Province for a US-made Caterpillar tractor 'at the price fixed by UNRRA' to help him circumvent commercial speculation and high prices.[59]

In addition to differing expectations, the intermediary role that local agencies were playing with the clear aim of undermining the use of UNRRA imported machinery also gave rise to logistical problems and disputes over supposedly exaggerated accounts and false facts. As was the case with many UNRRA supplies, tractors and ploughs arrived too late for spring planting, causing 'embarrassment' to the Italian mission.[60] Tests carried out by Italian experts using US-manufactured tractors reportedly showed that some of the equipment was unsuited to Italian soils.[61] UNRRA, pointing out that these were not UNRRA tractors but imports from other sources, denounced the publication of these supposedly false reports in the Italian press.[62]

Given the general reticence with which the government as well as local organizations and actors were making use of UNRRA aid, UNRRA deemed it necessary to directly stimulate the spirit of cooperation of Italian farmers. In May 1946, the regional director for UNRRA activities in Lombardy, Aldo L. Raffa, appealed to farmers in a speech that was broadcast on radio:

> May [Italian farmers] remember, now as well as in the future, that UNRRA's endeavors are not concentrated on an immediate but on a lasting result. In other words, UNRRA does not intend to help the Italian agriculturist to overcome the present critical stage only, but rather to create a sound basis for a substantial, long-range agricultural rehabilitation. All of UNRRA's activities are designed, as a matter of fact, to achieve this double purpose of giving immediate aid while at the same time providing for tangible, lasting benefits

which will remain after UNRRA is gone. This is particularly true of agriculture which has a double reconstructive value – to provide urgently needed food now, and to further the future well-being of the nation as a whole.[63]

Anticipating that this could be received angrily by Italian farmers, Raffa added:

Our experts and agricultural technicians … offer advice and help to Italian farmers … We do not intend thereby to teach agronomy to the Italian agriculturists, but only to bring them into line with the American and British farmer, acquainting them with the technical improvements applied during these last years. It is meant as an opportunity for an exchange of experiences, a sort of cordial and disinterested collaboration.[64]

While this spirit of exchange and cooperation could apply between certain interest groups, such as internationally minded Italian scientists and their British and US counterparts, UNRRA's relationship with Italian farmers remained complex.[65] A case in point is the wide range of reactions from the latter to the importation of UNRRA seed supplies, a process that – more than other aspects of UNRRA aid – depended on the goodwill and cooperation of farmers.

Reviving Cultivation through the Supply of Seeds?

From the very beginning of UNRRA's agricultural rehabilitation programme, its top priority was the supply of seeds, an intervention that the organization believed would boost the yields of certain crops, increase the land under cultivation with these crops and allow for the introduction of new crop varieties.[66] Seeds, much less bulky and seemingly easier to transport than other UNRRA supplies such as tractors or livestock, came with their own transportation difficulties because of their varying perishability as well as their packaging and storage requirements.[67] As such, the transfer of seeds demanded specialist scientific knowledge as well as a deep understanding of the local natural environment to which they were being transferred and the potential reactions of local farmers.[68] UNRRA officials who were responsible for procuring seeds took into account geological and climatic features of the recipient regions to make sure that they corresponded to each seed's indigenous climate and soil.[69] They were less aware, it seems, of social dimensions such as regional consumption values and patterns or food traditions that might have influenced whether the seed supplies would be fully accepted in a farming community.

UNRRA's seed unit had designed careful plans according to which recently liberated countries would receive seeds for planting, primarily as a means of overcoming the threat of starvation that was hanging over Europe but also for experimental purposes. In reality, control over seed allocations and enforcing the use of supplied seeds was beyond UNRRA. Especially with those crops that could be either eaten immediately by people or animals or planted later, such as pea and corn seeds, UNRRA directives were often ignored, with seeds entering the black market. To counter these problems, which were also prevalent in neighbouring countries such as Austria, UNRRA established a so-called Protective Service in early 1946. This body worked closely with local civil and military police in curbing black market activities and uncovering criminal misuse of UNRRA goods.[70]

The reports submitted by experts who followed up on the distribution of seeds in Italy tell a sobering story. Experts who visited farms in Tuscany to assess how UNRRA pea seeds had been used discovered that none had been planted in accordance with their original purpose. Upon visiting a farm called Fattoria Casabianca, which had received 1,500 kg of pea seeds, they found that all seeds had been milled and used as animal fodder. On another farm, where 2,000 kg had been received, the proprietor claimed that he had unsuccessfully tried to plant the seeds before going on to use them for animal feed. When asked to show where he had attempted the planting, he was unable to do so. On a third farm too, the seeds had not been sown and had instead been used to feed livestock. An UNRRA inspector came to the firm conclusion 'that practically no pea seeds had been sown in all Tuscany'.[71] In Ravenna, the sale of seeds was stopped to avoid them being used for unauthorized purposes. Farmers who were caught feeding seeds to pigs claimed they had not known that they should be used for sowing, but UNRRA argued firmly that its instructions had been clear.

Other reports on Italy also documented the sale of seeds on the black market. Farmers could apply for UNRRA seeds and, upon reception of a coupon, were supposed to collect them at the local rural cooperative. However, more often than not, the seeds were not collected by the farmers for whom they were intended, but by black marketeers, who falsely signed using the farmer's name and then sold them on to other traders. Furthermore, some of the Italian agents in charge of distribution sold the seeds on at higher prices.[72] Local UNRRA official Poggi Cavalletti, reported to the distribution unit that he had information from very reliable sources that made him suspect that a large quantity of UNRRA seeds in Modena Province were not ending up in the ground where they should have been planted. Out of ten examples of distribution that were investigated, it emerged that 'not one was carried out correctly' in compliance with UNRRA policy and procedures. Instead, 90 per cent of vetch seed had ended up 'on the black market or in the mouth of livestock'.[73]

There were likely multiple reasons for this outcome. First and foremost, UNRRA emerges as a rather weak actor in this dynamic, with no direct control over the distribution or use of seeds. Moreover, there was clearly an element of obstinacy on the part of farmers who preferred to use the seeds to feed their hungry animals, either because this was a more rational choice in their situation or because they did not have sufficient labour capacity or land on which to plant them. Along the lines of James Scott's seminal work on peasant resistance, the feigned ignorance and false compliance of Italian peasants could also be interpreted as acts of resistance.[74] Whereas there was no open confrontation, the response of farmers to UNRRA seeds undermined the organization's goals. However, this did not deter UNRRA officials from experimenting with longer-term seed projects. Indeed, towards the end of UNRRA's mandate, steps were taken to overhaul agricultural production by introducing hybrid corn strains, thus setting the stage for a European hybrid corn programme that would fully develop under the United States' Marshall Plan after 1947.[75]

Conclusion

This chapter has offered insights into the history of agricultural technical assistance and development in postwar Europe by examining the case of UNRRA's agricultural rehabilitation programme in Italy. While many aspects of this history require further research, this chapter has highlighted the gap that existed between expert planning and local implementation of agricultural aid. It shows how agricultural development in a postfascist country brought with it specific logistical, political and social challenges. The chapter points to the many nuances of UNRRA's agricultural rehabilitation measures, the hunger emergency that dictated how agricultural aid was organized, and the seeming contradictions that existed between ideas of Italian backwardness and isolation from innovative knowledge and technology, on the one hand, and admiration for Italy's existing structures and research institutions, on the other hand. What comes to the fore is a certain naivety on the part of UNRRA officials about the rehabilitative potential of agricultural supplies as well as a lack of knowledge about structural conditions on the ground and the needs and wants of the farmers themselves. Indeed, one of the shortcomings of UNRRA's agricultural mission in Italy was that it did not take into account the myriad regional or local agricultural institutions that had been inherited from the fascist regime or the various stakeholders who made up 'Italian agriculture' – from the scientific experts, tractor manufacturers and landowners to the farmers. The blunder that was UNRRA's Italian seed transfer programme is a telling example of the lack of control that the aid organization ultimately had over the process of agricultural development.

There is no doubt that UNRRA's agricultural rehabilitation programme – shaped by the military context of the Second World War – was a form of foreign intervention that bore similarities with colonial or interwar agricultural improvement and social engineering schemes. In the eyes of the architects of UNRRA's agricultural programmes, wartime relief and postwar rehabilitation called for transformation and modernization – often along the lines of a more globalized vision of postwar agricultural productivity and food security. UNRRA's short rehabilitation programme lived on in the massive postwar development machine; some UNRRA personnel and elements of the UNRRA missions were transferred to the United Nations' newly established Food and Agriculture Organization (FAO) in 1947. The shifts and continuities between the short-term UNRRA programmes and the more institutionalized FAO programmes that would unfold after 1947 remain to be studied by historians. However, the example of UNRRA in Italy does ultimately show that the success of any agricultural mission depended on in-depth knowledge of local institutions and actors as well as on the needs, preferences and acceptance of recipient farmers.

Amalia Ribi Forclaz is Associate Professor of International History and Politics at the Graduate Institute Geneva. She specializes in the history of humanitarian internationalism, international organizations, agriculture and development. Her recent publications include articles and chapters on agricultural expertise, education, rural movements, the International Labour Organization and the Food and Agriculture Organization. She is currently completing her second monograph, *Fields of Progress: The International Labour Organization and Agricultural Labour, 1920–1960* (under contract with Oxford University Press). Together with Liesbeth van de Grift, she coedited the volume *Governing the Rural in Interwar Europe* (Routledge, 2017).

Notes

Research for this chapter was carried out with the support of a Seed Money Grant from the Graduate Institute of International and Development Studies in Geneva. I thank Michele Sollai for his research assistance as well as his comments on an earlier version of this chapter. Thanks are also due to the editors and contributors of this volume for their valuable feedback and detailed critiques of multiple drafts of this chapter.

1. Martiin, Montojo and Brassley, *Agriculture in Capitalist Europe*; Staples, *Birth of Development*; Jachertz and Nützenadel, 'Coping with Hunger?'; Ribi Forclaz, 'From Reconstruction to Development'.
2. See, for example, van Beusekom, *Negotiating Development*; Hodge, *Triumph of the Expert*.
3. Reinisch, 'Introduction: Relief Work in the Aftermath of War'.
4. MacFarlane, 'The UNRRA Experience'.
5. Shephard, *The Long Road Home*. See also Shephard, 'Becoming Planning Minded';

Reinisch, 'Internationalism in Relief'; Salvatici, '"Help the People to Help Themselves"'; Williams, 'Reconstruction before the Marshall Plan'. Other recent studies, which for reasons of space cannot be cited here, have also provided insights into relief work in specific countries, including Poland, France, Greece, Germany, Italy, China and the Soviet Union.

6   For an exception, see McVety, *The Rinderpest Campaigns.*

7   Gerard A. Mahler, 'UNRRA's Agricultural Rehabilitation Activities: History and Economic Appraisal', United Nations Archives New York (UNA) S-1021-0008-06.

8. For an account of this preparation work, see Standing Technical Committee on Agriculture, 'Report on Status of the Agricultural Rehabilitation Program of UNRRA as of June 1945: Origins and Development of Plans of Agricultural Rehabilitation', 1, UNA S-1208-0000-0027.

9. 'UNRRA Technical Sub-Committee on Agricultural Priorities of Agricultural Requirements', 20 July 1944, UNA S-1208-0000-0005.

10. Mahler, 'UNRRA's Agricultural Rehabilitation Activities', 57, UNA S-1021-008-006.

11. Reports on these various resources exist in the form of a series of unpublished monographs in the UNRRA archives.

12. 'Considerations in the Analysis of Agricultural Data and Program Development for Liberated Areas', 2, UNA S-1208-0000-0001.

13. 'Basis for Distributing Agricultural Relief and Rehabilitation Equipment and Supplies into Eastern European Liberated Countries', n.d., unsigned, 1, UNA, S-1208-0000-0002.

14. E.R. Henson, Quarterly Report of the Agricultural Rehabilitation Division, 4 April 1945, UNA S-1211-0000-0087.

15. Henson to C.M. Bishop, confidential, 9 February 1945, UNA, S-1211-0000-0043.

16. Henson, Quarterly Report of the Agricultural Rehabilitation Division, 4 April 1945, 3, UNA, S-1211-0000-0087.

17. Belco, *War, Massacre and Recovery in Central Italy*; Rossi, 'L'UNRRA strumento di politica estera'; Romero, 'Gli Stati Uniti in Italia'.

18. On this topic, see the excellent study by Bernardi, *Il mais 'miracoloso'.*

19. The main contribution on UNRRA's work in Italy has thus far come from Silvia Salvatici, who examines UNRRA's assessment of Italian food needs in 1944–45 through the correspondence of its officials: Salvatici, '"Not Enough Food to Feed the People"'.

20. Woodbridge, *History*, vol. 2, 259.

21. Romero, 'Gli Stati Uniti in Italia'.

22. As quoted in Woodbridge, *History*, vol. 2, 266.

23. Ibid., 266 and 272.

24. Ibid., 280.

25. D'Onofrio, *Observing Agriculture in Early Twentieth-Century Italy*; Desideri, *L'amministrazione dell' Agricoltura (1910–1980).*

26. Longobardi, *Land-Reclamation in Italy*; Caprotti, *Mussolini's Cities.*

27. D'Antone, 'La Modernizzazione dell'agricoltura Italiana negli anni Trenta'.

28. Saraiva and Wise, 'Autarky/Autarchy'.

29. D'Onofrio, 'Microfoundations of Italian Agrarianism'.

30. William G. Welk to M.M. Menshikov, 'Notes on Italian Agriculture', 27 November 1944, 3, UNA S-1210-0000-0107.

31. UNRRA Italian mission, 'Economic Survey, Agriculture and Food', 26 July 1946, UNA S-1465-0000-0086; Daniele and Ghezzi, 'The Impact of World War II on Nutrition'.

32. Welk to Menshikov, 'Notes on Italian Agriculture', 27 November 1944, UNA S-1210-0000-0107.

33. 'Bases for Distribution of Agricultural Commodities among Countries', n.d., UNA S-1208-0000-0002.

34. UNRRA Italian mission, 'Economic Survey, Agriculture and Food', 26 July 1946, UNA S-1465-0000-0086.

35. Welk to Menshikov, 'Notes on Italian Agriculture', 27 November 1944, 1, UNA S-1210-0000-0107.

36. UNRRA Italian mission, 'Economic Survey, Agriculture and Food', 26 July 1946, UNA S-1465-0000-0086.

37. Robert Lintner, 'UNRRA Livestock Program; Historical Report', UNA S-1021-0009-03.

38. UNRRA Italian mission, Sub-Bureau of Relief Supply, Analysis Division, 'Italian Livestock Population in Peace and War', 10 May 1946, UNA S-1210-0000-0097.

39. C.S.M. Hopkirk to Hugh G. Calkins, 'Report on Veterinary Organisation and Production of Veterinary Biologics in Italy', 20 July 1946, UNA S-1210-0000-0105; Saraiva, *Fascist Pigs*.

40. Jean Malterre, 'Visite Zootechnique dans le Nord de l'Italie du 18 au 19 Novembre 1946', UNA S-1210-0000-0106.

41. Charles W Smith, 'Livestock and Meat Products in Italy', 14 June 1946, UNA S-1208-0000-0095.

42. Mahler, 'UNRRA's Agricultural Rehabilitation Activities', UNA S-1021-0008-08.

43. Hugh G. Calkins Col. J R.G. Sutherland, 'Report of F. G. Renner on Improvement of Grazing Lands of Central Italy', 25 May 1946, UNA S-1210-0000-0096.

44. Renner to Calkins, 'Improvement of Grazing Lands of Central Italy', 17 May 1946, UNA S-1210-0000-0096.

45. Dr M.M. Kaplan, 'Report of Field Trip in Italy', 18–29 November 1946, UNA S-1210-0000-0106.

46. P. Hudson, 'Agricultural Research in North Italy', 30 May 1946, UNA S-1465-0000-0085.

47. H. Cleveland to W.J. Legg, 27 April 1946, UNA S-1465-0000-0085.

48. UNRRA Italian mission, 'Economic Survey, Agriculture and Food', 26 July 1946, UNA S-1465-0000-0086.

49. Welk to Menshikov, Notes on Italian Agriculture, 4, UNA S-1210-0000-0107.

50. Cleveland to UNRRA Washington, 'Establishment of Tractor Pools', n.d., 38, UNA S-1465-0000-0085; Peter C. Borre to Mission Executive Officer, 'Farm Machinery', 2 September 1946, UNA S-1465-0000-0086.

51. F. Piva on 'irregular sale of 35 HP Minneapolis Tractor', Venice, 14 November 1946, UNA S-1465-0000-0087.

52. Keeny to Ministry of Agriculture, 'Disposal of UNRRA Tractors', 13 November 1946, UNA S-1465-0000-0087.

53. E.R. Henson, 'Memorandum', 11 December 1945, UNA S-1212-0000-0085.

54. Cesare Sacerdoti to UNRRA, 28 November 1945, UNA S-1212-0000-0085.

55. Henson to Edward Sard, 'Memorandum', 30 November 1945, UNA S-1212-0000-0085.
56. E.H. Bell to E.R. Henson, 'Report of Mr. Kovacs of Massey Harris Ltd. on the Farm Machinery Situation in Italy', 10 December 1945, UNA S-1212-0000-0085.
57. Kovacs to James M. Merritt, 11 October 1945, UNA S-1212-0000-0089.
58. Borre to Mission Executive Officer, 'Farm Machinery', 2 September 1946, UNA S-1465-0000-0086.
59. Alberico Brini (farmer, Rovigo Province) to Keeny, 12 January 1947, UNA S-1212-0000-0086.
60. Division of Agricultural Forestry and Fisheries, 'Procurement', 2 August 1946, UNA S-1212-0000-0086.
61. A.H. Baines (agricultural machinery specialist), 'Tractor and Plow Test at La Scuola di Meccanica Agraria alle Capannelle', 15 July 1946, UNA S-1465-0000-0086.
62. J. Imrie to Sub-Bureau of Relief Supply, 29 July 1946, S-1465-0000-0086.
63. Third Radio Conference by Regional Director A. L. Raffa, 29 May 1946, UNA S-1465-0000-0085.
64. Ibid.
65. Italo-American Association (Lombard Committee, Milan) to UNRRA Italian mission, 21 June 1946, UNA S-1465-0000-0085.
66. Standing Technical Committee Agriculture, 'Seeds for Liberated Countries', 24 August 1945, UNA S-1208-0000-0003.
67. G. Sutty, 'Report on Seed Potato Cultivation', 9 July 1946, UNA S-1465-0000-0089.
68. Glover, Venot and Maat, 'On the Movement of Agricultural Technologies'.
70. Standing Technical Committee Agriculture, 'Expert Panel on Crops', 25 May 1944, UNA S-1208-0000-0003.
69. 'Woodbridge, *History*, vol. 2, 47.
71. C.B. Foglietti (Regional Director, Emilia and Tuscany) to Keeny, 13 September 1946, UNA S-1465-0000-0098.
72. Foglietti to Keeny, 11 December 1946, UNA S-1465-0000-0098.
73. Ibid.
74. Scott, *Weapons of the Weak*.
75. Bernardi, *Il mais 'miracoloso'*.

Bibliography

Belco, Victoria. *War, Massacre and Recovery in Central Italy, 1943–1948*. Toronto: University of Toronto Press, 2010.
Bernardi, Emmanuele. *Il mais 'miracoloso': Storia di un'innovazione tra politica, economia e religione*. Rome: Carocci editore, 2014.
Caprotti, Federico. *Mussolini's Cities: Internal Colonialism in Italy, 1930–1939*. Youngstown: Cambria Press, 2007.
D'Antone, Lea. 'La Modernizzazione dell'agricoltura Italiana negli anni Trenta'. *Studi Storici* 22(3) (1981), 603–29.
Daniele, Vittorio, and Renato Ghezzi. 'The Impact of World War II on Nutrition and Children's Health in Italy'. *Investigaciones de Historia Económica/Economic History Research* (2017), 119–31.

Desideri, Carlo. *L'amministrazione dell' Agricoltura (1910–1980)*. Rome: Officina, 1981.

D'Onofrio, Federico. *Observing Agriculture in Early Twentieth-Century Italy: Agricultural Economists and Statistics*. Abingdon: Routledge, 2016.

———. 'Microfoundations of Italian Agrarianism: Italian Agricultural Economists and Fascism'. *Agricultural History Review* 92(3) (2017), 369–96.

Glover, Dominic, Jean-Philippe Venot and Harro Maat. 'On the Movement of Agricultural Technologies: Packaging, Unpacking and Situated Reconfiguration', in James Sumberg (ed.), *Agronomy for Development: The Politics of Knowledge in Agricultural Research* (Abingdon: Routledge, 2017), 14–30.

Hodge, Joseph M. *Triumph of the Expert: Agrarian Doctrines of Development and the Legacies of British Colonialism*. Athens, OH: Ohio University Press, 2007.

Jachertz, Ruth, and Alexander Nützenadel. 'Coping with Hunger? Visions of a Global Food System, 1930–1960'. *Journal of Global History* 6 (2011), 99–119.

Longobardi, Cesare. *Land-Reclamation in Italy*. London: King, 1936.

MacFarlane, David L. 'The UNRRA Experience in Relation to Development in Food and Agriculture'. *Journal of Farm Economics*, 30(1) (1948), 69–77.

Martiin, Carin, Juan Pan-Montojo and Paul Brassley (eds). *Agriculture in Capitalist Europe, 1945–1970: From Food Shortages to Food Surpluses*. Abingdon: Routledge, 2016.

McVety, Amanda. *The Rinderpest Campaigns: A Virus, Its Vaccines and Global Development in the Twentieth Century*. Cambridge: Cambridge University Press, 2018.

Reinisch, Jessica. 'Introduction: Relief Work in the Aftermath of War'. *Journal of Contemporary History* 43(3) (2008), 371–404.

———. 'Internationalism in Relief: The Birth (and Death) of UNRRA'. *Past and Present* 210(6) (2011), 258–89.

Ribi Forclaz, Amalia. 'From Reconstruction to Development: The Food and Agriculture Organization and the Conceptualization of Rural Welfare'. *International History Review*, 41 (2019), 351–71.

Romero, Federico. 'Gli Stati Uniti in Italia: il Piano Marshall e il Patto Atlantico', in Federico Barbagallo (ed.), *Storia dell'Italia repubblicana: La costruzione della democrazia. Dalla caduta del fascismo agli anni cinquanta*. Turin: Enaudi, 1994, 231–89.

Rossi, Luigi. 'L'UNRRA strumento di politica estera agli albori del bipolarismo', in Andrea Ciampani (ed.), *L'amministrazione per gli Aiuti Internazionali: La ricostruzione dell'Italia tra dinamiche internazionali e attività assitenziali*. Milan: Franco Angeli, 2002, 47–82.

Salvatici, Silvia. '"Not Enough Food to Feed the People": L'Unrra in Italia (1944–45)'. *Contemporanea*, 14(1) (2011), 83–99.

———. '"Help the People to Help Themselves": UNRRA Relief Workers and European Displaced Persons'. *Journal of Refugee Studies* 25 (2012), 452–73.

Saraiva, Tiago, and Matthew Norton Wise. 'Autarky/Autarchy: Genetics, Food Production, and the Building of Fascism'. *Historical Studies in the Natural Sciences* 40 (2010), 419–28.

———. *Fascist Pigs: Technoscientific Organisms and the History of Fascism*. Cambridge, MA: MIT Press, 2016.

Scott, James C. *Weapons of the Weak: Everyday Forms of Peasant Resistance*. New Haven: Yale University Press, 1985.

Shephard, Ben. 'Becoming Planning Minded: The Theory and Practice of Relief 1940–1945'. *Journal of Contemporary History* 43 (2008), 405–19.

———. *The Long Road Home: The Aftermath of the Second World War*. New York: Alfred A. Knopf, 2011.

Snowden, Frank. 'Latina Province, 1944–1950'. *Journal of Contemporary History* 43 (2008), 509–26.

Staples, Amy S. *The Birth of Development: How the World Bank, Food and Agriculture Organization, and World Health Organization Changed the World, 1945–1965*. Kent, OH: Kent State University Press, 2007.

Van Beusekom, Monica M. *Negotiating Development: African Farmers and Colonial Experts at the Office du Niger, 1920–1960*. Westport, CT: Heinemann, 2002.

Williams, Andrew J. 'Reconstruction before the Marshall Plan'. *Review of International Studies* 31 (2005), 541–58.

Woodbridge, George. *The History of the United Nations Relief and Rehabilitation Administration*, vols 1–3. New York: Columbia University, 1950.

CHAPTER 4

Building on Old Institutions

The Agricultural Extension Service and Village Institutes in Post-Second World War Rural Turkey

Heinrich Hartmann

Schools and vocational training programmes are indispensable educational institutions in rural areas across the world. Both have had an important role to play in processes of nation-building by fostering the link between modern statehood and the (rural) individual. Rural schools are typically the most accessible institution for broad sections of the rural population. Vocational training aims to boost the productivity of farmers by increasing their efficiency and output through instruction on the use of new agricultural technologies. In the case of Turkey, increasing agricultural productivity was the common aim of both forms of rural education. While the global historiography of education often neglects their connections, I will argue that spreading literacy via public schooling and vocational training, which was offered in Turkey by so-called village institutes, ultimately represented two sides of the same coin. I will use the context of early republican political reforms in Turkey in the period from the 1930s until the Marshall Plan-ignited productivity offensive after the Second World War to analyse this interrelatedness from a transnational perspective that highlights the role of international experts as well as local actors. Both educational pathways shared an understanding of how to create modern rural citizens who would be able to express themselves not only politically but also as independent economic actors. This involved making the individual conscious of her or his role in the fortunes of the national economy, with 'individual productivity' serving as the key indicator of economic development and the basis for a new entrepreneurial subjectivity. This overlapped with – but also partly contradicted – earlier attempts to enhance political and social cohesion in the Turkish countryside that were part of the Kemalist project to unify the Turkish nation on social and cultural grounds after the collapse of the culturally and ethnically diverse Ottoman Empire.[1]

I will first outline the history of Turkish village institutes against the backdrop of several attempts to reform Turkey's education system. Next, I will relate this to the history of the rural extension service in the country, which was established in the early postwar years in the context of the Marshall Plan and its productivity boost. Thereafter, I will explain how the Marshall Plan authorities in Turkey and the rural extension service began cooperating with the older village institutes. This incorporation of the national village institute programme into the transnational Marshall Plan fed into the enduring memory and legacy of these institutes after their closure in 1954.

A Unique Institution: Turkish Village Institutes

Village ideology was an outstanding feature of the late Ottoman reform movement that was advocated by many Ottoman intellectuals in the late nineteenth century.[2] Key figures such as the sociologist Prens Sabahattin adapted French sociological concepts and the progressivist notion of positivism – but also paternalistic, Catholic forms of community and family sociology – to the Turkish context, thereby preparing the ground for a new and engaged school of rural sociology that considered practical social reform as an eminent part of its understanding of social science.[3] Despite its practical ambitions, this science-based movement had long approached village life in a more theoretical manner during the late Ottoman and early republican periods of the early twentieth century, as reliable statistical data on Turkey's village populations were mostly absent or outdated as a result of the First World War, the Armenian genocide and the ongoing population exchanges with countries that had been part of the Ottoman Empire.[4]

The approach of the Young Turks and the Kemalist government was slightly more focused on national identity, as this followed the emblematic project of 'educating the rural masses' in an attempt to transform the disparate population of a faded empire into a unified Turkish republican nation that excluded many ethnic minorities. Movements like the so-called Towards the People movement (*halka doğru*), which followed the call to go 'towards the villages' (*köye doğru*),[5] became influential in the context of the Young Turks' takeover of power in 1908 and remained a powerful force in Turkish politics after the First World War. With the disintegration of the Ottoman Empire and the early Republic's quest for a new cultural basis, this cliché of a rural, village-based culture became a defining element of Turkish national identity, marking a clean break from the cosmopolitan and multiethnic Ottoman Empire.[6] With this nationalistic focus on the rural as the cradle of the nation, the Turkish government followed a similar approach to those of nation-building projects in other countries in the early twentieth century, reflecting a constant process of mutual observation and imitation, especially among Europe's authoritarian regimes.[7]

Protecting and developing 'the village' in a time of global economic crisis and amid political and ethnic turmoil became a primary national concern. Shortly after this agenda was incorporated into the Kemalist state modernization (*çagdaşlaşma*) ideology, the rural reformer and intellectual İsmail Hakkı Tonguç summarized the basic principles of this new form of Turkish village development:

> Contrary to what some people assume, the village issue does not merely entail the mechanical development of the village, but rather a meaningful and conscious resurgence of the village from within. The villagers must be revived and informed to the extent that no power can be able to exploit them ruthlessly for its own account and treat village dwellers as slaves or servants.[8]

The emblematic attempts of President Mustafa Kemal (known as Atatürk from 1935) to spread school education and literacy to remote villages were partially successful; after the establishment of the Schools of the Nation (Millet Mektepleri) programme in 1928, the literacy rate rose considerably in several regions.[9] However, its policies were undermined by the inaccessibility and lack of infrastructure in many rural areas as well as by regional conflicts and the resulting wilful neglect of some parts of the national territory. Even though the Kemalist government invested heavily in building schools, clear geographical disparities remained. Whereas the metropolitan regions of Istanbul and Ankara as well as the Aegean coastline enjoyed the benefits of state investment, large parts of Inner Anatolia and Kurdish-speaking southeastern Anatolia continued to be neglected.[10]

The notions of a uniform 'rural population' and an idealized Turkish 'village' did not mirror reality, especially in the remotest parts of rural Turkey. This elitist call for an inward-looking return to peasant culture was far removed from an institutional framework for genuine rural reform and failed to achieve more than a symbolic impact.

The subsequent turn towards pragmatism, which came towards the end of the Atatürk regime (1923–38), has a complex history. The attempt to create a nationwide rural social policy was among the early reform efforts of the republican government in the late 1920s and the 1930s. As the collection of statistics improved, the issue of rural poverty increasingly came under the focus of the government and compelled decision-makers to take an altogether different stand on the question of 'rural learning'. The 1935 Census revealed an alarming illiteracy rate, with approximately 76 per cent of men and 91 per cent of women unable to read or write. In remote villages, as many as 90 per cent of inhabitants were classified as illiterate.[11]

Atatürk's government invited numerous foreign scientists and scholars to assist with the development of a new social reform programme by offering them temporary government advisory roles. The diverse forms of expertise that emerged from this process can be divided into two contrasting types that are best illustrated by the respective work of two education experts: the US philosopher and education reformer John Dewey (1859–1952) and the Prussian educational administrator Gustav Oldenburg (1873–1948).

Dewey, who travelled to many countries in the 1920s and 1930s to advise their governments on education policy, came to Turkey in 1924. He recommended increasing the number of elementary schools across the country, especially in remote regions,[12] with the aim of strengthening the link between the individual and the new state and enhancing citizens' opportunities for direct political participation. Education in rural areas, he argued, should follow the national interest and be guided by a centralized schooling system while still relying on local initiative. The teacher, according to Dewey, would be a pivotal and emblematic figure, because it was through the work of individual teachers that national policies would ultimately be enacted and local needs articulated.

Oldenburg's vision was much more pragmatic and involved trying to introduce a new type of educational institution in 1920s rural Turkey to compensate for the fact that public schools were rare in most villages. With his own experiences in Germany in mind, Oldenburg travelled across Turkey and proposed establishing a hierarchical knowledge dissemination system that would be underpinned by the creation of new academic institutions (including what would become Ankara's famous High School of Agriculture [Yüksek Ziraat Okulu]), from where technical knowledge could be disseminated to remote village populations by travelling demonstration teams covering fields such as marketing, home economics, plant breeding and fertilizing.[13]

Both approaches failed to become an immediate reality in Turkey, but they nevertheless left their mark on the Turkish education system over the following three decades. Both Dewey and Oldenburg as well as other foreign experts came to the conclusion that there was a clear lack of formal education in the countryside. The traditional claim of Turkish elites that the peasant population was 'uneducated' (*cahil*, in the sense of being ignorant and uncivilized) was a widespread means of referring to the rural populace in paternalistic terms and became a basis for the state's exertion of authoritarian power over rural areas. Nevertheless, its ideological bias notwithstanding, there was an undeniable truth behind this claim: there was no institutional framework to facilitate the transmission of knowledge in rural contexts – whether by educating peasants at formal academic institutions or from one generation of rural dwellers to the next. Deficits in basic literacy, civic education and technical and technological knowledge transmission were all facets of the same problem.

The underlying problem was that the majority of Turkish teachers refused to take a job as a village teacher, especially in remoter parts of the country.[14] The existing centralized education programme for village teachers, which had been decreed by law in 1926, had produced an annual number of 600–650 trainee teacher graduates in the early republican period. However, given that about 800 teachers were retiring each year, this centralized system was unable to sustain itself. To counter this trend, trainee instructors were recruited from among the literate sections of village populations and admitted to special technical education programmes. The Village Law of 1937 defined a trainee instructor as:

> Someone [who was qualifying to be] employed to undertake the education and training of the inhabitants of villages whose population is too low for them to be assigned teachers. Their role is to guide villagers in conducting their agricultural affairs in a scientific manner and to instruct them in school or agricultural courses offered by the Ministries of Education or Agriculture.[15]

Recruitment for and implementation of this programme did not fall under the authority of the Ministry of Education, but was an initiative of the Ministry of Agriculture, whose chief concern was to promote modern agricultural techniques. This left a gap between a declining village school system and the ersatz education offered to aspiring farmers by special agricultural instructors.[16]

The 'new' approaches of scholars like Dewey or Oldenburg were, in reality, not so new to Turkey, as both concepts drew on earlier ideas that had been influential during the final years of the Ottoman Empire. However, recent scholarship has demonstrated the significant extent to which the new republican regime built the legitimacy of its own reform agenda on the employment of foreign experts. Especially in these early stages of the political reform process, the transmission of agricultural knowledge was a somewhat dialectic process: foreign advisers tended to draw on experiences from their home countries when offering their expertise, while Turkish officials and institutions often viewed foreign advice as one argument among many in an ongoing process of political negotiation.[17] As a result, neither a purely international perspective on rural education in Turkey nor the rather idiosyncratic attempts to identify a Turkish way, which have been widespread in Turkish historiography, do complete justice to the Turkish example. Instead, historians need to examine the transnational entanglements between the national path and its international influences.

The most influential reform idea was İsmail Hakkı Tonguç's creation of the village institutes (*köy enstitüleri*) in 1940.[18] Having studied in Germany and later in the United Kingdom and France, Tonguç had connections to scholars and practitioners of rural education across Europe and regularly travelled on Turkish government missions to Germany, Bulgaria, Yugoslavia, Hungary, Czechoslovakia, Austria, the Netherlands and Switzerland in order to study their rural schooling programmes.[19] In the mid-1930s, Tonguç was officially commissioned by the government to reform primary schooling and to study new practices of village development that would support easily accessible rural schooling. Instead of deploying teachers to the remotest parts of the country, Tonguç came up with the idea of providing local community members with a rudimentary education that would qualify them as village teachers or, in smaller villages, village instructors. This idea quickly became popular not only among Turkey's urban elites but also in rural areas.[20]

The 1937 Village Law was the basis for a programme that officially started three years later with the aim of institutionalizing the recruitment of instructors at the local level. Tonguç's plan was to establish a network of teacher training centres all over the country where trainee village instructors would receive a basic education from a relatively young age (starting at about fifteen) in Turkish, arithmetic and geometry, the social and education sciences, and arts and crafts. Trainees at each institute would come from the surrounding region. This proximity, it was hoped, would allow the institutes to remain in touch with the needs of local populations and promote regional traditions (such as textile crafts) as a means of community wealth creation while also benefiting from learners' familiarity with local soil and climate conditions as well as their families' connections to local trading networks. The village institute system was overseen by the Hasanoğlan-based Higher Village Institute (Yüksek Köy Enstitüsü), which was founded in 1943 with the responsibility for instructing the teacher trainers who would staff the village institutes. The teachers at this institute in Ankara Province came from various backgrounds, but many had studied abroad and were quite well known in pedagogical circles.

Turkish village institutes followed in the footsteps of well-established institutions of rural learning in several European countries. Daniel Rodgers has shown the extent to which Danish folk schools provided a model for other countries from the 1920s onwards. Elsewhere, especially in Central and Southeastern Europe, similar institutes for rural development were established in the early twentieth century, and it is probable that Tonguç learnt from these examples on his tours of the continent. However, there were other countries in which the emphasis of rural education institutions was more on enhancing the link between the individual and the nation state by spreading concepts of a national cultural identity among populations that were believed to be foreign to such forms of elite culture. The mission of these institutions was thus cultural – indeed, sometimes almost spiritual – and could be described as making a 'transcendent' nationalism apparent and popular in rural areas.[21]

In Turkey, by contrast, the mission of village institutes was much more pragmatic and local in scope.[22] Whereas spreading literacy and numeracy undoubtedly played an important role, there was less focus on training peasants within the bounds of a national-cultural educational repertoire. Instead, each village institute designed its curriculum around the needs and specificities of the local communities it served. Trainee village teachers received vocational training for five years. For male students, this included classes in agriculture, horticulture, cash cropping, animal husbandry and, eventually, fishery, as well as more complex forms of knowledge that were important for the development of self-sustaining farming businesses, such as engineering, construction and cooperative economics. Furthermore, village institutes tried to promote general culture by offering arts and crafts, music and theatre classes.[23] The curriculum for female students put much more emphasis on knitting, sewing and other aspects of home economics.[24] The vast spectrum of topics covered in the training of future village teachers came with an important side effect: students at the Higher Village Institute were overtrained. It would be the basic task of village teachers to instruct young rural children over a period of three to four years, which would hardly be sufficient time to transmit the detailed vocational knowledge that the trainee teachers were learning.[25] As such, the idea behind the village institutes went beyond ensuring that village teachers were sufficiently prepared for potential deployment to a village anywhere in Turkey. It sought to establish the school-teacher as an important village figure who would be able to transmit his (or, in a very few cases, her) knowledge to children, provide expert advice to the village headman and oversee the introduction of new technologies, while also being able to articulate the needs of the local population and being receptive to their wishes.

Ultimately, the history of the village institutes was not a very long one. They came under increasing pressure from right-wing parties, which gained power after the 1950 election, and especially from Prime Minister Adnan Menderes, who saw in their independence from the central government a communist threat. Furthermore, recent historiography has become more critical, high-lighting that their actual impact on Turkish modernization was restricted to only a few regions or even districts.

New Programmes: The Marshall Plan and Extension Services

After the Second World War, an increase in agriculture productivity seemed the only way for Turkey to cure the misery of its impoverished rural population and urban working classes as well as to define a new role for itself in Europe's postwar economy. Turkey envisioned its agriculture as filling the supply gap in the European market,[26] an aim that required a partial reorientation of Turkish production to meet the needs of European consumers, especially in cereals and wheat cultivation. As such, although this new agricultural emphasis was at the centre of the nationalist narrative behind Turkish rural education efforts, the village institutes had not only arisen out of a transnational context, but their role in the postwar recovery and their ideologically charged afterlife were also shaped by international developments.[27]

Turkey's important place in early postwar and Cold War geopolitics, including in the United States' containment policy as expressed in its 1947 Truman Doctrine, was mainly inspired by the country's strategic location between Southeastern Europe and the Middle East. Truman's Turkey strategy was built on the country's socioeconomic revival, especially of its rural areas, in order to prevent the rapid spread of communism among weakly governed peasant communities.[28] Turkey's foregrounding of agricultural and rural development policy can thus be understood as an important result of Truman's foreign policy. Together with Greece, Turkey became the first country to receive Marshall Plan aid and thus enjoyed rising investment in its agricultural sector, especially in wheat and cotton cultivation as well as the processing of raw cotton.[29]

But increased investment was only one of the Marshall Plan's impacts in rural Turkey. The Marshall Plan authorities relied heavily on the dissemination of knowledge and sought to address specific sections of the population. They started the *Village Hour* (*Köyün Saati*),[30] a weekly one-hour radio broadcast that was intended to inform the peasant population about relevant agricultural innovations and enhance economic and social cohesion in the villages. Infrastructural improvement, especially road building, accelerated in the Marshall Plan period from 1948 to 1952.[31] However, it is important to recognize that most villages remained untouched by these programmes due to their isolation from transportation infrastructure. Furthermore, a media revolution in the Turkish countryside could only be initiated by supplying villagers with the necessary equipment, but this task was complicated by widespread lack of access to the electricity grid or printing machines, while radio receivers remained costly and rare in villages.[32] Begüm Adalet has demonstrated how closely the politics of nudging peasant attitudes towards a 'modern' subjectivity was interwoven with issues of village accessibility to new infrastructure and technologies.[33] As a result, simpler and more readily available equipment like posters, billboards and film projectors were the most popular media for disseminating information on agricultural training or new machinery.[34]

It is noteworthy in this regard how officials in the Marshall Plan's Economic Cooperation Administration (ECA) reflected on the use of media. For ECA officials, different media forms represented more than mere instruments for expanding the sphere of expert influence into remote villages. Images were entrusted with creating an emotional attachment among peasants to the promises of modernity; in the words of US food and agriculture representative and ECA official Hugh K. Richwine, 'farmers must be impressed with these items and many others. To the extent that they believe and follow instructions more carefully'.[35]

In particular, the opportunity to project the latest ECA films encouraged experts to reflect on how new media technologies could be used to reach the 'mind of the peasant'. UNESCO experts like the Austrian-born professor of literary studies and filmography scholar Adolf Hübl insisted that it would be necessary not only to import more projection screens and projectors into Turkey, but also to find an adequate language with which to communicate with the local population. For him, this meant identifying topics that were relatable and understandable for Turkish peasants.[36] The sociologist Sigfried Kracauer, whom the ECA invited to observe its different programmes across the country, took the same line by emphasizing that only by addressing everyday problems could the rural inhabitants of Turkey be taught to understand the impact of a new technique.[37] Local norms and traditions also needed to be respected. As the Marshall Plan administrators were directing their media offensive from studios at the European Recovery Program headquarters in Paris, this was a more difficult task than was immediately apparent. Clips had to be filmed in Turkey, sent to Paris for cutting and sound montage, and then returned to Turkey for synchronization (dubbing the Turkish narration over the English original). Traditional music accompanied pivotal scenes, while the directors took special care to ensure that traditional rituals and greetings were respected in every depiction of encounters between young farmers and their elders.

The ECA reflected intensively on the question of how to reach as many farmers as possible through its information and outreach activities (which ECA officials termed Type E activities) as well as on the potential multiplying effects of each activity (a forecast based on the assumption that the audience would convey their newly acquired knowledge to their relatives and neighbours). According to these calculations, a poster, which was relatively easy to distribute, would reach an average audience of forty farmers, but demonstrations and film screenings would be seen by about one hundred farmers.[38] Because demonstrations and screenings required a better institutional distribution network than leaflets and posters, ECA experts readily turned to the existing village institutes.

Figure 4.1. Screen capture from *The Village Tractor* (1951), 6:08. Taken by Heinrich Hartmann

Converging Interests and Diverging Understandings of Knowledge Dissemination

One of the priorities shared by both the Kemalist reform movement of the early Turkish republic as well as diverse peasant movements was the question of land reform. There were widespread complaints among the rural population, but also among intellectuals, about an increasingly 'landless' peasant population who were being effectively forced to work as sharecroppers or day labourers and had little choice but to leave the impoverished east of the country in search of work in the more developed west. Despite the unanimity of these complaints among representatives from very different political backgrounds, the appeal to 'give land to the landless' revealed itself to be almost unachievable,[39] as the hierarchical structures of Turkish rural society, with its traditional elites,[40] were particularly robust and difficult to circumvent. From the late nineteenth century onwards, the role of large-scale local landholders became ever more important in rural areas, with the country's shifting orientation towards exports and cash crop cultivation having promoted a process of land concentration. Attempts to redistribute land, for which the republican regime depended on its ultimately unsuccessful co-option of local elites, failed – especially in light of persistent regional conflicts in restive Kurdish areas of Eastern Anatolia.[41]

Instead of the redistribution of land, it was new irrigation technologies, the increased use of fertilizer and newly introduced dry farming methods that raised hopes for the extension of arable land. Against this backdrop, attempts to endorse local efforts to make more land available for agriculture – an aim that guided the 1937 Village Law, the inauguration of the first village institutes and the 1944 land reform project – must also be understood as a bid to curb the revolutionary claims of the peasantry.

As early as 1943, the Ministry of Agriculture established a national extension service, the objective of which was to develop agricultural production as a basis for the self-reliance of rural populations. Initially centred in Southern Anatolia, Turkey's agricultural heartland, the service increased its coverage over the course of the following decade with the aim of serving the entire country by the mid-1950s.

The extension service made active use of the village institute infrastructure and relied on village teachers as the main foundation for its nationwide programme. The Ministry listed the responsibilities of the instructors:

1. He [the instructor] is responsible for providing the farmers with the information to encourage high production and quality, and [for] furnishing marketing news.
2. Teaching through showing, through doing, and how-to-do demonstrations showing the results of proved [sic] practices.

3. Provide local leadership by having some cooperators demonstrate proved [*sic*] practices for the neighbor[ing] farmers.
4. Keep some statistical records to know the complete inventories of the villages.
5. Study the agricultural and economical [*sic*] factors of his environment.
6. To prepare a monthly report.
He must travel 160 days of the year throughout his district [15–20 villages].[42]

Richard Robinson, who was sent to Gaziantep Province in Southern Anatolia first by the Institute of Current World Affairs, a US think tank, and later by the World Bank, observed how the demonstrators gained authority in local communities. According to Robinson, knowledge dissemination was the only possible basis for the Turkish state to intervene in local settings. Starting in the Ottoman era, he explained, distrust in state institutions had undermined villagers' attitudes towards the state. The fact that the instructors possessed certain technical qualifications helped locals to establish a relationship built on trust in, or at least respect towards, them.[43]

After the arrival of ECA officials in Turkey, the bottom-up logics of the village institutes blended with the country's new form of Marshall Plan-funded, state-led developmentalism, as embodied by the central role played therein by experts. ECA officials paid particular attention to traditional institutions in Turkey, as these offered a unique means of addressing smallholders and peasant communities. By contrast, to target equivalent groups in other countries, the Marshall Plan missions had been forced to establish entirely new structures. In Turkey, Russell H. Dorr, the director of the local ECA mission, was able to write to Fevzi Lütfi Karaosmanoğlu, the Minister of Agriculture, to praise the country's existing system of agricultural training, especially the village institutes: 'The use of village teachers as local leaders to assist the county agents during the summer is unique and should prove to be of great value in obtaining results from improved farming methods and other practices which may be demonstrated.'[44]

In the early postwar period, international enthusiasm for Turkey's approach to rural education reached a peak. The newly established UNESCO in Paris, which developed a particular interest in the village institutes in its quest to identify an educational model for predominantly rural countries in a decolonizing world, chose to conduct a survey on Turkish rural education initiatives in 1948.[45] In particular, the emphasis on problem-solving in village institute teaching attracted the attention of international experts. Village institute representatives were also invited to the United States as part of exchange programmes[46] to discuss their experiences in the context of what appeared to be the dawn of a new era of agri-capitalism.[47]

However, in part, this also demonstrates the hindrances to closer integration between international training programmes and the older Turkish village institutes. The latter had long been based on a somewhat leftist vision that promoted a strong sense of agrarian collectivism in which the village served as a social and political countermodel to capitalist society. This ideological basis of the village institute movement was barely compatible with the capitalist principles that the Marshall Plan sought to inculcate in Turkey's agricultural sector. As a consequence, early optimism among international experts about the prospects for merging existing Turkish institutions with their new international counterparts quickly turned to disillusion. US experts in particular were left dissatisfied that the village institutes did not promote individual initiative and responsibility and were not following the attempts of Marshall Plan programmes to encourage rural entrepreneurship by transforming peasants into commercial farmers.[48]

Part of the problem was the target audience of the international programmes. It turned out that many of the peasants who had an active interest in benefiting from Marshall Plan education initiatives came from an elevated social background and saw individual training as a step towards boosting their income. Consequently, this form of education served to accelerate the concentration of land rather than to counteract pauperization among the Turkish peasantry.[49]

It is difficult to fully assess the impact on the ground of a knowledge dissemination process mediated by schools and village institutes because we have a rather limited and opaque understanding of the social dynamics in Turkish villages in this period due to a lack of historical records. Typically, we can only appraise the local context from experts' reactions. However, their conception of a politically informed and rational democratic citizenry was not reflected in the social realities of Turkey at the time and has come under considerable attack from various sides.[50] When Richard Robinson reported from Gaziantep in 1949 for the *Journal for Current World Affairs*, he described a situation in which Kemalist and international reforms were failing because of the distrust between Anatolian peasants and government institutions, which were smothering the initiative of individual villagers:

> The Village Law is a perfect example of this tendency of the ascendency of the philosophy of force over that of persuasion and encouragement. The duties of the village government are itemized down to the most minute detail (i.e. the contraction of a guest house, prohibition against sleeping in the same room with animals). The motive is perhaps admirable, but the psychology is questionable. Little is left to the initiative of the villager.[51]

Meanwhile, Turkish government officials did not agree with the transformation of old institutions into new ones that propagated a form of individualistic modernity based on self-promotion. Instead, the government chose to shut down the village institutes in 1954 as part of its fight against the communist threat and despite their popularity among international organizations and experts.

It was precisely their transnational potential that kept alive the idea of the village institutes, as US and other foreign experts repeatedly referred to this erstwhile institution as a global model for rural self-determination and community-based education and learning. Indeed, the fact that the village institutes remain a topic that is regularly addressed in Turkish political discourse is undoubtedly partly due to international observers in the 1960s and 1970s who continued to discuss their legacy.

Conclusion

In the early post-Second World War period, the various myths and narratives proclaiming 'the village' as the cradle of national culture – an idea that was circulating not only in Western and Eastern Europe but also in many other parts of the world – blended into a new tale of the village as the heterotopy of Cold War modernization in the West. Modernization was a process that would be characterized by the integrated development of new roads and other infrastructure, social hygiene, mechanized production and efficient division of labour. It was accompanied by a new conceptualization of individual subjectivity based on educating peasants to become farming entrepreneurs and informed citizens.[52] New forms of vocational training and schooling played a vital role in this narrative. However, village models were built on the legacies of earlier national, regional and local village development strategies, which the agents of Cold War modernization actively sought to instrumentalize. As such, 'the Cold War village' not only inherited its respective national, regional and local traditions, but was also a far from homogeneous concept.

In the Turkish example, this not only led to certain overlaps between national and international logics of development, but also to significant discrepancies between national and local interests as national policies shifted dramatically from the relatively authoritarian foundations of the rural education system, particularly of the village institutes, to the capitalist policies of the Menderes government in the 1950s. Although the Marshall Plan authorities, especially the ECA special mission to Turkey, were very intrigued by Turkey's existing system of village teachers and local demonstrators, they were seemingly unaware that the days of the village institutes were already numbered. Indeed, the fact that Marshall Plan officials were attracted to the idea of an institution that had been accused of communist leanings points to the multiple misunderstandings between the local, national and international levels.

Whether this high-level policy confusion did have a genuine impact on teachers, students, villagers and local authorities on the ground remains an open question. On the one hand, many of the teachers who had received their education in the republican village institutes in the 1940s and early 1950s continued teaching for decades thereafter. However, as more academic-centred institutions took the place of the village institutes, one of the latter's key benefits was lost: their strong emphasis on community-based learning and other grassroots initiatives. US experts had regarded community-based learning as crucial for integrating village trainers and teachers from all over Turkey into a nationwide network of rural education. As this model broke down, a more top-down dissemination of the latest knowledge was the only viable alternative.

Heinrich Hartmann is Professor for Social and Economic History and the History of Technology at the Helmut Schmidt University in Hamburg. He has written a monograph, *Eigensinnige Musterschüler* (Campus, 2020), on expert knowledge in Turkish rural development in the twentieth century and has a broader research focus on European development programmes in the Mediterranean.

Notes

1. Yıldırmaz, *Politics and the Peasantry in Turkey*.
2. Dumont, 'Les origines'.
3. Öğün Boyacıoğlu and Boyacıoğlu, "Prens/Sultanzâde Mehmed Sabahaddin Bey", 261–319. On Leplaysian traditions in Turkey and the Mediterranean, see Kalaora and Savoye, *Les inventeurs oubliés*; Rabinow, *French Modern*; Burke III, *Ethnographic State*; Saada, 'Nation and Empire in the French Context'.
4. See a series of articles in *European Journal of Turkish Studies* 7 (2008) and 12 (2011).
5. Çetin, 'Cumhuriyet'.
6. Karaömerlioğlu, *Orada bir Köy*; Karaömerlioğlu, 'The Peoples' Houses'.
7. Ahmad, 'Agrarian Policy of the Young Turks'; Ahmad, 'Search for Ideology'; Plaggenborg, *Ordnung und Gewalt*.
8. İsmail Hakkı Tonguç, as cited in Yakut, 'Çifteler Köy Enstitüsü', 8.
9. Caymaz and Szurek, 'La révolution au pied de la lettre'.
10. Ibid.; Yılmaz, 'Learning to Read (Again)'.
11. Evered, *Empire and Education*; Fortna, *Learning to Read*.
12. Dewey, *The Middle Works*; Bilgi and Özsoy, 'John Dewey's Travelings'.
13. Oldenburg, 'Das landwirtschaftliche Unterrichtswesen'.
14. Tanyer, 'Bir Eğitimine Devrimcisi'.
15. Law on Village Instructors, No. 3238, 26 April 1937, cited in Altunya, 'Türkiye'de "Köy Eğitmeni Yetiştirme" Deneyimi', 61.
16. Altunya, 'Türkiye'de "Köy Eğitmeni Yetiştirme" Deneyimi'.
17. Bilgi and Özsoy, 'John Dewey's Travelings'.
18. Tonguç outlined his basic ideas in his classic *Canlandırılacak Köy*. See also Türkoğlu, *Tonguç ve enstitüleri*; Işın, *Düşünen Tohum*; Kirby, *Türkiye'de Köy Enstitüleri*; Karaömerlioğlu, 'The Village Institutes'.

19. Tanyer, 'Bir Eğitimine Devrimcisi', 18–36, 43–49.
20. Gümüşoğlu, 'Kars Cılavuz Köy Enstitüsü', 74–76.
21. Rodgers writes of a 'spiritual adjunct, if not a spiritual motor for the day-to-day business of practical cooperation'; Rodgers, *Atlantic Crossings*, 357.
22. Karaömerlioğlu, 'The Village Institutes', 58.
23. Türkoğlu, *Tonguç ve enstitüleri*', 209–12.
24. Ibid., 246–58.
25. Şimşek, *Köy Enstitüsünden*, 131–35.
26. 'World Cereals Position for 1947/48, prepared by the IEFC Secretariat', 5 July 1947, in NARA Truman Library, International Emergency Food Council File, C.P. Anderson Papers.
27. Karaömerlioğlu, 'The Village Institutes Experience in Turkey', 50. However, the author overemphasizes the importance attached to the goal of increasing production and the role of cultural pessimism while ignoring the aim of improving rural governance.
28. Christofis, 'Turkey and the Cold War'; Hale, 'Turkey'.
29. Tören, *Yeniden Yapılanan Dünya*.
30. The *Village Hour*, which had begun as the *Marshall Hour*, was an integral part of the radio broadcasting schedule under the government of Prime Minister Adnan Menderes; Ersarı, 'Ellili Yıllarda Radyo ve Siyaset', 409–13.
31. Adalet, *Hotels and Highways*.
32. Brockett argues that media use in rural areas started to increase from the mid-1950s; Brockett, *How Happy*, 83–88.
33. Adalet, *Hotels and Highways*; Adalet, 'Questions of Modernization'.
34. McGlade, 'From Business Reform Programme to Production Drive'.
35. Letter, Richwine to Undersecretary of State Genca, 5 April 1950; NARA Washington, RG 469, Entry 1399, Box 22.
36. Correspondence between Hübl and the Ministry of Agriculture in Ankara, January 1951; UNESCO Archives Film – Mission 1951 307: 778.5 (560) A 57 '51'; Bischof, *Images of the Marshall Plan*.
37. Fritsche, *American Marshall Plan Film*.
38. All numbers are from the Starch Report, NARA College Park, RG 469, Entry 1399, Box 62.
39. Hatipoğlu, 'Toprak Reformu Tarihçesi', 21–22; Şahin, 'Toprak Reformunu Gerekli Kılan Sebepleri', 31–36; Kaya, *Land Use, Peasants and the Republic*.
40. Especially the *ağas* (large landowners), who constituted both the landed elite and the political leadership in many small communities and villages.
41. Parvin and Hiç, 'Land Reform versus Agricultural Reform?', 207–34.
42. Ministry of Agriculture, General Directory of Agriculture, Education Section, 1952; 'Technical Agricultural Organization of Turkey', NARA Washington, RG 469, Entry 1399, Box 4.
43. 'In order to hold down the post of district director, one must be at least a high school graduate. To be a county governor, one must be a college graduate. But, the village headmen are elected by their fellow villagers and very frequently are elderly men who neither read nor write. The relationship, then, is often one of teacher and student – but not without considerable friction. I would venture to say that this is one of the most

critical points in the organization of government in Turkey, for here are elected officials being closely controlled by non-elected, administrative officials.' Letter, 31 January 1949, as cited in Robinson, *Letters from Turkey*.

44. Letter, Russell H. Dorr to Minister of Agriculture, Fevzi Lütfi Karaosmanoğlu, 18 September 1950; NARA Washington, RG 469, Entry 1399, Box 4.

45. Letter, UNESCO Director-General, Jean Thomas, to Turkish Minister of Education, Tahsin Banguoğlu, 28 June 1948; UNESCO Archives, Fundamental Education Centre – Turkey 375 A 031 (560). UNESCO, which desired closer collaboration with the Rockefeller Foundation and the Institute of Current World Affairs when conducting the survey, proposed Richard Robinson as the survey leader. However, Robinson declined to participate, with UNESCO ultimately deciding to hire the Turkish rural sociologist Yıldız Sertel in his place; see letter, J.B. Browers (Fundamental Education Division, UNESCO) to President of the Rockefeller Foundation, John Marshall, 27 November 1948; UNESCO Archives, Fundamental Education Centre – Turkey 375 A 031 (560).

46. Wofford, *Teaching in Small Schools*. This book was translated into Turkish by the Turkish Ministry of Education in 1951; RAC, Rockefeller Foundation, RG 1.2, Series 805 – Turkey, Box 1. See also Kirby, *Türkiye'de Köy Enstitüleri*, 495–98.

47. Wofford wrote another book on one such exchange programme, which was published posthumously in 1954; Wofford, *The Workshop Way*.

48. 'My final conclusion after this brief study of provincial government in Turkey is that the gravest fault that can be lodged against the government is the discouraging of private enterprise. … He is told what he must do; little is left to his own volition.' Ibid., 37.

49. This was argued by Richwine in his response to a request to participate in an international youth exchange organized under the auspices of the Marshall Plan, 12 January 1951; see also letter, Richwine to the Ministry of Foreign Affairs, 18 September 1950; NARA Washington, RG 469, Entry 1399, Box 4; Report on the US Mission to Turkey for the Foreign Operations Administration, Washington, 27 January 1955; NARA Washington, RG 469, Entry 1399, Box 62. See also letter, Norman L. Smith to President of the 4-H International Farm Youth Exchange, Clinton G. Gaylord, 22 September 1954; NARA Washington, RG 469, Entry 1399, Box 62.

50. This critique was also characteristic of the broader Middle East context; Coon, 'Point Four and the Middle East', 83–94.

51. Letter, 7 January 1949, as cited in Robinson, *Letters from Turkey*, 35. Robinson's extensive reports were informed by a multitude of interviews that he had conducted with villagers, muhtars and regional administrators.

52. Sackley, 'Village Models', 749–78.

Bibliography

Adalet, Begüm. 'Questions of Modernization: Coding Speech, Regulating Attitude in Survey Research'. *Comparative Studies in Society and History* 57(4) (2015), 912–41.
———. *Hotels and Highways: The Construction of Modernization Theory in Cold War Turkey*. Stanford: Stanford University Press, 2018.

Ahmad, Feroz. 'The Agrarian Policy of the Young Turks 1908-1918', in Feroz Ahmad (ed.), *From Empire to Republic: Essays on the Late Ottoman Empire and Modern Turkey, Vol. 1* (Istanbul: Istanbul Bilgi University Press, 2008), 63–88.

———. 'The Search for Ideology in Kemalist Turkey, 1919–1939', in Feroz Ahmad (ed.), *From Empire to Republic: Essays on the Late Ottoman Empire and Modern Turkey, Vol. 1* (Istanbul: Istanbul University Press, 2008), 174–94.

Altunya, Hüseyin. 'Türkiye'de "Köy Eğitmeni Yetiştirme" Deneyimi (1936–1948)', in Ekrem Işın (ed.), *Düşünen Tohum, Konuşan Toprak: Cumhuriyet'in Köy Enstitüleri 1940–1954, Vol. 1* (Istanbul: Istanbul Araştırmaları Enstitüsü, 2012), 60–80.

Bilgi, Sabhia, and Seçkin Özsoy. 'John Dewey's Travelings into the Project of Turkish Modernity', in Thomas S. Popkewitz (ed.), *Inventing the Modern Self and John Dewey* (London: Palgrave Macmillan, 2005), 153–177.

Bischof, Günter, and Dieter Stiefel (eds). *Images of the Marshall Plan in Europe: Films, Photographs, Exhibits, Posters*. Innsbruck: StudienVerlag, 2009.

Brockett, Gavin D. *How Happy to Call Oneself a Turk: Provincial Newspapers and the Negotiation of a Muslim National Identity*. Austin: University of Texas Press, 2011.

Burke III, Edmund. *The Ethnographic State: France and the Invention of Moroccan Islam*. Berkeley: University of California Press, 2014.

Caymaz, Birol, and Emmanuel Szurek. 'La révolution au pied de la lettre: L'invention de "l'alphabet turc"'. *European Journal of Turkish Studies* 6 (2007). Retrieved 25 July 2022 from https://doi.org/10.4000/ejts.1363.

Çetin, Türkân. 'Cumhuriyet Döneminde Köycülük Politikaları: Köye Doğru Hareketi', in Metin Celâl (ed.), *75 yılda Köylerden Şehirlere* (Istanbul: Tarih Vakfı Yurt Yayınları, 1998), 213–30.

Christofis, Nikos. 'Turkey and the Cold War', in Frank Jacob (ed.), *Peripheries of the Cold War* (Würzburg: Königshausen und Neumann, 2015), 255–81.

Coon, Carlton S. 'Point Four and the Middle East'. *Annals of the American Academy of Political and Social Science* 270(1) (1950), 83–94.

Dewey, John. *The Middle Works, 1899–1924. Vol. 15: 1923–1924*. Carbondale: Southern Illinois University Press, 1983.

Dumont, Paul. 'Les origines de littérature villageoise en Turquie'. *Journal Asiatique* 266(1) (1978), 67–95.

Ersarı, Nevra. 'Ellili Yıllarda Radyo ve Siyaset', in Mete Kaan Kaynar (ed.), *Türkiye'nin 1950'li yılları* (Istanbul: İletişim, 2015), 393–422.

Evered, Emine Ö. *Empire and Education under the Ottomans: Politics, Reform and Resistance from the Tanzimat to the Young Turks*. London: I.B. Tauris, 2012.

Fortna, Benjamin. *Learning to Read in the Late Ottoman Empire and the Early Turkish Republic*. Basingstoke: Palgrave Macmillan, 2010.

Fritsche, Maria. *American Marshall Plan Film Campaign and the Europeans: A Captivated Audience?* London: Bloomsbury, 2018.

Gümüşoğlu, Firdevs. 'Kars Cılavuz Köy Enstitüsü', in Ekrem Işın (ed.), *Düşünen Tohum, Konuşan Toprak: Cumhuriyet'in Köy Enstitüleri 1940–1954, Vol. 2* (Istanbul: Istanbul Araştırmaları Enstitüsü, 2012), 70–94.

Hale, William. 'Turkey', in Yezid Sayigh and Avi Shlaim (eds), *The Cold War and the Middle East* (Oxford: Oxford University Press, 1997), 250–278.

Hatipoğlu, Şevket Raşit. 'Toprak Reformu Tarihçesi', in T.M.M.O. Birliği Ziraat Mühendisleri Odası (ed.), *Toprak Reformu Semineri* (Ankara: no publisher 1964), 21–22.

Işın, Ekrem (ed.). *Düşünen Tohum, konuşan Toprak: Cumhuriyet'in Köy Enstitüleri*. Istanbul: Istanbul Araştırmaları Enstitüsü, 2012.

Kalaora, Bernard, and Antoine Savoye. *Les inventeurs oubliés: Le Play et ses continuateurs aux origines des sciences sociales*. Paris: Seyssel, 1989.

Karaömerlioğlu, Asım. 'The Peoples' Houses and the Cult of the Peasant in Turkey'. *Middle Eastern Studies* 34(4) (1998), 67–91.

———. 'The Village Institutes Experience in Turkey'. *British Journal of Middle Eastern Studies* 25(1) (1998), 47–73.

———. *Orada bir Köy var uzakta: Erken Cumhuriyet Döneminde Köycü Söylem*. Istanbul: İletişim Yayinlari, 2006.

Kaya, Safiye Yelda. *Land Use, Peasants and the Republic: Debates on Land Reform in Turkey, 1923-1945*. Ankara: Middle Eastern Technical University, 2014.

Kirby, Fay. *Türkiye'de Köy Enstitüleri*. İstanbul: Tarihçi Kitabevi, 1962.

McGlade, Jacqueline. 'From Business Reform Programme to Production Drive: The Transformation of US Technical Assistance to Western Europe', in Matthias Kipping and Ove Bjarnar (eds), *The Americanisation of European Business: The Marshall Plan and the Transfer of US Management Models* (London: Routledge, 1998), 18–34.

Öğün Boyacıoğlu, Aslıhan, and Levent Boyacıoğlu. 'Prens/Sultanzâde Mehmed Sabahaddin Bey (1879-1948)', in Cağatay Özdeir (ed.), *Türkiye'de Sosyoloji, Vol. 1* (Ankara: Phoenix, 2008), 261–319.

Oldenburg, Gustav. 'Das landwirtschaftliche Unterrichtswesen in der Türkei und seine Zukunftsaufgaben'. *Berichte über Landwirtschaft* 7(3) (1927), 393–425.

Parvin, Manoucher, and Mükkerem Hiç. 'Land Reform versus Agricultural Reform? Turkish Miracle or Catastrophe Delayed?' *International Journal of Middle East Studies* 16(2) (1984), 207–234.

Plaggenborg, Stefan. *Ordnung und Gewalt: Kemalismus – Faschismus – Sozialismus*. Munich: Oldenbourg Verlag, 2012.

Rabinow, Paul. *French Modern: Norms and Forms of the Social Environment*. Cambridge, MA: MIT Press, 1989.

Robinson, Richard D. *Letters from Turkey*. Istanbul: Robert College, 1965.

Rodgers, Daniel T. *Atlantic Crossings: Social Politics in a Progressive Age*. Cambridge, MA: Belknap Press of Harvard University Press, 1998.

Saada, Emmanuelle. 'Nation and Empire in the French Context', in George Steinmetz (ed.), *Sociology and Empire: The Imperial Entanglements of a Discipline* (Durham, NC: Duke University Press, 2013), 321–39.

Sackley, Nicole. 'Village Models: Etawah, India, and the Making and Remaking of Development in the Early Cold War'. *Diplomatic History* 37(4) (2013), 749–78.

Şahin, Turan. 'Toprak Reformunu Gerekli Kılan Sebepleri', in T.M.M.O. Birliği Ziraat Mühendisleri Odası (ed.), *Toprak Reformu Semineri* (Ankara: no publisher, 1964), 31–36.

Şimşek, İbrahim. *Köy Enstitüsünden öğretmenliğe öğretmenden öğrenciye*. Istanbul: Türkiye İş Bankası Kültür Yayınları, 2016.

Tanyer, Turan. 'Bir Eğitimine Devrimcisi: İsmail Hakkı Tonguç', in Ekrem Işın (ed.), *Düşünen Tohum, Konuşan Toprak: Cumhuriyet'in Köy Enstitüleri 1940-1954, Vol. 1* (Istanbul: Istanbul Araştırmaları Enstitüsü, 2012),38-51.

Tonguç, İsmail Hakkı. *Canlandırılacak Köy*. Istanbul: Remzi Kitabevi, 1939.

Tören, Tolga. *Yeniden Yapılanan Dünya Ekonomisinde Marshall Planı ve Türkiye Uygulaması*. Istanbul: Sosyal Araştırma Vakfı, 2007.

Türkoğlu, Pakize. *Tonguç ve enstitüleri*. Istanbul: Türkiye İş Bankası Kültür Yayınları, 2000.

Wofford, Kate S. *Teaching in Small Schools*. New York: Macmillan, 1946.

———. *The Workshop Way with Foreign Students: A Report of a Turkish Project in Rural Education at the College of Education, University of Florida, October 23, 1952 to September 1, 1953*. Gainesville: University of Florida Press, 1954.

Yakut, Kemal. 'Çifteler Köy Enstitüsü', in Ekrem Işın (ed.), *Düşünen Tohum: Konuşan Toprak: Cumhuriyet'in Köy Enstitüleri 1940-1954, Vol. 2* (Istanbul: Istanbul Araştırmaları Enstitüsü, 2012), 6-26.

Yıldırmaz, Sinan. *Politics and the Peasantry in Turkey: Social History, Culture and Modernization*. London: I.B. Tauris, 2017.

Yılmaz, Hale. 'Learning to Read (Again): The Social Experiences of Turkey's 1928 Alphabet Reform'. *International Journal of Middle East Studies* 43(4) (2011), 677-97.

 PART II

Across Borders

Transnational Expertise and Entangled Bodies of Knowledge

 CHAPTER 5

Models for the Village

Prototypes for Rural Modernization in Poland and Yugoslavia, 1910–40

Heiner Grunert

Models and prototypes played a central role in rural modernization from the late eighteenth century. Model or demonstration farms, model farmhouses, model rural schools and agricultural experiment stations were increasingly established in various rural peripheries in Europe, North America and other parts of the world. Using concrete models, urban intellectuals and scholars as well as rural elites aimed to develop and disseminate scientific concepts as well as to regulate and improve agriculture and rural life in general. City dwellers and educated professionals, as well as the rural population itself demanded catch-up development in rural areas. Governing elites saw model facilities as a means of increasing control and exploitation of peripheral regions or colonized land. Model, demonstration and experimentation facilities in the countryside therefore also illustrated the extent to which urban elites regarded rural contexts as fields of experimentation for potential social and technological improvements.[1]

Although demonstration and model facilities have been common in rural and agricultural contexts since the eighteenth century, their number and scope seemed to reach a peak in the first decades of the twentieth century. At least until the 1930s, most experts were convinced that ideal, science-based and rational solutions for almost every social problem existed and only needed to be correctly implemented – a common conviction that Ulrich Herbert or Lutz Raphael see as a central feature of 'high modernity'.[2]

Ideas of an ideal (rural) society in the future were partly based on an idealized past. From the nineteenth century, antimodernists emphasized notions of ideal, largely symbiotic agrarian societies, which had presumably existed in the past and needed to be restored in the present. In this way, model institutions were meant to correct the supposed mistakes of the past, reflecting romanticized and orientalist perspectives of rural society and 'the peasant', in which 'the rural' served as a symbol of 'tradition', 'emotion' and 'concreteness'. Here, concrete demonstration, illustration and imitation were intended to meet this supposedly 'reality-based' and 'visual thinking of the peasant', as many intellectuals put it, including German Nazi theorists of the 1930s, reflecting their *völkische* views on community.[3]

In this chapter, I understand the desired, anticipated and perceived accelerated social changes that could be observed in many rural areas of Europe from the eighteenth century as 'rural modernization'. These changes were based on the conviction that whole societies *should* and *could* be transformed using new kinds of knowledge, technology and reason.[4] In order to change individual and social life, rural dwellers and urban experts sought out, followed and adopted pre-existing models. The diversity of models that were used reflects the many ways in which individuals and groups, experts and laypersons created, selected, adopted and/or appropriated paths towards and goals of fundamental change, a process that Shmuel Eisenstadt convincingly described as the emergence of 'multiple modernities' and Christopher Bayly called 'a process of emulation and borrowing'.[5]

Within ideas of 'being modern',[6] rationality played a central role. As one of the core concepts of the Enlightenment, rationality placed the emotionless scientific consideration of the meaningful connection between cause and effect at the centre of decision-making. Acting in a 'rational' manner implied a supposedly future-oriented rationale (*zweckrational*) as opposed to adherence to emotion-led traditions. 'Rational' was thus a central term in scientific works on rural areas from the late eighteenth century onwards, being invoked in pursuit of permanent yet sustainable profit maximization and thus an optimum degree of positive development.[7] From about 1900, rural and agrarian discourses used the term 'modern' alongside 'rational' increasingly frequently, with the two terms often defining each other in circular ways. In European and North American rural discourses of the early twentieth century, the attribute 'rational' valorized ideas on key topics ranging from production methods to living and working conditions. Until the 1920s, both left- and right-wing political actors considered rationalization a desirable means and goal.[8] Only from the mid-1920s did critical voices emerge, linking rationalization with mass unemployment and social inequality.[9]

Recent research on rural modernization, especially in and on Eastern Europe, mostly focuses on social or political movements (such as agricultural societies and agrarian political parties, which gave rise to 'agrarianism' as a sociopolitical philosophy) or on huge visionary transformation projects for rural areas and natural spaces (such as irrigation and drainage of entire regions or large infrastructure projects).[10] However, far less frequently is attention paid to the widespread, everyday modernization of rural living and working environments from 1850 to 1950, efforts that from their outset were conceived of as step-by-step processes. These include the establishment of elementary, women's, professional and medical education in rural areas, the improvement of rural medical care and nutrition services, and the promotion of healthier rural living and working conditions.[11]

Taking this into account, this chapter investigates how elites – whether urban or rural, academics or supposedly uneducated peasants – developed and disseminated prototypes for rural modernization using and reusing globally entangled concepts, expertise and methods. The focus lies on the enormously diverse territories that in 1918 were unified to form Poland and Yugoslavia (1918–29: officially the Kingdom of Serbs, Croats and Slovenes; 1929–41: the Kingdom of Yugoslavia) respectively. Until the 1910s, these regions had been part of other territories, including the German, Russian, Habsburg or Ottoman Empires, or, in the case of Yugoslavia, Serbia or Montenegro. Thus, until 1918, Poland and Yugoslavia existed only as utopias for a few elites. I address questions regarding the role of models in creating, developing and spreading knowledge on rural areas and agriculture. Who contributed in which ways to such processes? Where did models for rural development originate? What was the relationship between the adoption and the adaption of these models? Which effects of model development and dissemination can be observed? To this end, I will investigate several models for rural life – relating to housing, education, healthcare and agrarian work – by examining models that were built as well as those that never made it beyond the planning stage.

At the beginning of the twentieth century, the predominantly agrarian societies of Eastern Central and Southeastern Europe were characterized by a stark urban-rural contrast. Rural modernization was intended to overcome the deep split between their huge, mostly illiterate rural populations and emerging urban elites, who were typically oriented towards Western Europe. For this reason, both in Polish and South Slavic regions, urban as well as peasant emancipatory organizations and political parties gained ground after 1900. Additionally, Polish intellectuals and politicians considered the sharp divide between the nobility, city dwellers and the rural population to have been a principal reason for Poland's political weakness in the eighteenth century, which eventually led to the country's partition between Russia, the Habsburg Empire and Prussia. As a result, rural modernization became an important political imperative in re-established Poland after 1918.

Most of the nation states that succeeded the empires of the Habsburgs, Ottomans and Romanovs after the First World War formulated powerful ambitions to integrate their populations, equalize social and regional differences, and dissolve their urban-rural divides. Poland and Yugoslavia, which emerged from the war as large and heterogeneous nation states with respective populations that were three-quarters and four-fifths rural,[12] were home to widely disparate social structures and traditions, religions, languages and ethnicities. Again, unequal legal and economic systems, and divergent ways of living and working were considerably more prevalent within rural populations than in urban environments, where people lived under much more homogeneous sociopolitical structures. Rural modernization therefore aimed at the political, legal, economic and psychological integration of the rural social space into the new nation state as well as the harmonization and improvement of living conditions across the countryside. In both Poland and Yugoslavia, agricultural land was divided into large estates cultivated by small-scale farmers or landless agricultural labourers and medium- or small-sized family farms. Regionally distinct national or religious groups dominated specific parts of the country-side, which made agricultural policy also a field of religious and minorities policy.[13] As such, rural modernization efforts tended to reflect the social and political divisions of both countries while revealing the broad social efforts from above and below to integrate and emancipate their rural populations.

Model Farms and Agricultural Experiment Stations

Model farms were the first institutions established in Europe with the aim of instigating a broad modernization effect in agriculture. They were supposedly progressive, efficiently managed farms that were run by respected farmers and supported by the state, private individuals and/or civil society organizations. They were founded partly out of the desire of educated experts and/or rural elites to recreate the successes of other farmers and partly because educated experts sought to spread modern production methods among the rural popu-lation by means of imitation.

The first so-called model farms (German: *Musterbauernhöfe*; French: *fermes modèles*) emerged in Europe at the end of the eighteenth century. They were the result of reform efforts dating back to the sixteenth century that had spread via so-called paterfamilias literature.[14] In Poland, a number of noble-men founded model farms (*ferme wzorowe*) in the eighteenth century. One, for example, imported cattle from the Netherlands, showcased a new type of stable and cultivated newly introduced crops such as red clover or potatoes. In other European countries, like Switzerland, urban enlightenment societ-ies sought to popularize scientific knowledge in the countryside. With state support, these societies encouraged innovative farmers and promoted their successes within their own country and throughout Europe. The best-known example was Jakob Guyer, also known as Kleinjogg, a farmer from outside Zurich. Guyer became a minor celebrity among enlightened intellectuals across Europe at the end of the eighteenth century – on the one hand for devel-oping new techniques of soil cultivation and animal husbandry, and on the other for devising a supposedly new reason-based form of thinking in and about rural areas.[15] Based on the above trends, the model farm became one of the most important instruments in agricultural education in the nineteenth century. From the 1850s, more and more states provided material and structural support for individual model farms. Prussia and the Habsburg Empire supported such farms especially in their eastern and southeastern provinces – often in regions that were considered backward, such as those with low agricultural yields, high illiteracy rates and/or large-scale emigration.

Especially in Eastern Central Europe, a comparatively high number of agricultural publications made use of the term and concept of the model farm. Agriculture textbooks that were translated from German, English or French often already bore the model concept in their titles. One example was the successful *Textbook of Agriculture* (original: *Lehrbuch der Landwirthschaft*) by the Bohemian agricultural teacher Anton Rudolf Schneider. This book, which was first published in 1880 on behalf of the Viennese Ministry of Agriculture, became a standard agricultural textbook that was published until 1957. Already in 1887 it had appeared in a Polish translation with a revised title *The Model Farmer: Rational Textbook of Agriculture*.[16] Readers in the countryside – mostly teachers, priests or educated farmers – demanded concrete examples of success, preferably from Western countries. As such, from 1870 to 1910, dozens of books about exemplary agriculture or model farms were published in Polish alone.[17]

After the First World War, model farms continued to be regarded as an important means of concrete education and renewal in agriculture. The governments and administrations of the newly founded states in Eastern Central and Southeastern Europe typically continued to support existing model farms that had been established before the war. Following trends elsewhere in Europe and North America from the 1910s,[18] the Kingdom of Serbs, Croats and Slovenes set up a central government programme in the 1920s, according to which two 'respected model farmers' (*uzor ratari*) per county – adding up to a total of hundreds of model farms throughout the country – were to be financially supported and have their farms developed. The provincial administrations selected supposedly progressive, wealthy and respected farmers, who were then provided with modern equipment, seeds, artificial fertilizers and cheap loans by the Ministry of Agriculture.[19] Additionally, cooperatives and agricultural associations increasingly devoted themselves to practical education by demonstration. In the early 1920s, for example, the Association of Serbian Agricultural Cooperatives in Zagreb provided financial and moral support – especially in predominantly Serbian-inhabited, 'backward' regions such as the Krajina – calling model farmers the 'main bearers of knowledge and enlightenment in our villages'.[20] In the following years, regional and national agricultural administrations as well as experts from agricultural associations attempted to achieve an astonishingly broad spectrum of supposedly modern goals via these model farms: to promote and implement new production methods while also strengthening rural areas in wider economic and cultural aspects.

From the end of the nineteenth century, experts within ministries of agriculture and education, agricultural schools and cooperatives planned to strengthen and decentralize fruit and vegetable cultivation using allotments, vegetable gardens and school gardens. Furthermore, it was thought that this would minimize the supposed alienation of modern societies from nature and aid their moral development through down-to-earth horticulture. Allotments and vegetable gardens were important objects of rural and suburban modernization in Europe. With its focus on change, rural modernization also meant what Hobsbawm called the 'invention of tradition'.[21] In this process, modernizers clearly distinguished between misguided traditions, which had to be combated, and traditions worth preserving, which had to be maintained and protected from accelerated change. Model facilities were therefore intended either to preserve or to counter cultural traditions. One of many relevant examples in this regard was horticulture. A horticultural society in Warsaw planned to establish ornamental model gardens (*wzorowe ferme ogrodnicze*) throughout Poland from 1919. The organization aimed to preserve the decorative garden culture that was said to be typical of Polish noble estates and national culture, especially in eastern Poland. The Warsaw-based society argued that increasing economic pressure was forcing people to utilize their garden space more and more efficiently, which would soon signify the end of classical ornamental gardens. The society thus appealed to the government to preserve these traditions of rural culture for future generations by means of state-supported model gardens.[22]

Agricultural experiment stations, which were often developed in combination with agricultural schools, institutes or academies, were another model institution of rural modernization. They were established in Northern and Western Europe as well as North America from the beginning of the nineteenth century. In contrast to the typically profit-oriented model farms, experimental stations and agricultural institutes were aimed at developing and disseminating applied knowledge on specific areas of agriculture. Depending on local agricultural needs and practices, they conducted applied research on livestock breeds, plant varieties or fertilizers while also developing new methods of livestock husbandry or crop cultivation. Often first established at the initiative of individual experts or private agricultural organizations, they were later frequently taken over by the state.

In Marymont near Warsaw, noblemen, intellectuals and a priest initiated the founding of an Agronomic and Forestry Institute in 1816 – one of the first of its kind in Europe. It was deliberately modelled on agricultural training institutes and model farms in Switzerland (Hofwyl, near Bern) and Prussia (Möglin), which had been founded only a few years earlier. In 1861–62, the

Russian government moved this important agricultural institute to Nowa Aleksandria/Puławy on the Middle Vistula River, where it continued to grow in importance. At about the same time, the Habsburg Empire also pushed for the foundation of agricultural institutes in the provinces, such as Dublany in Galicia (founded in 1853 near Lviv/Lwów) or Križevci in Croatia-Slavonia (founded in 1860 to the northeast of Zagreb). Both institutes quickly became known far beyond their home regions. Especially from the 1860s onwards, the number of experimental stations and agricultural schools, institutes and academies increased considerably in many European countries.[23]

Governments were pushing for the establishment of more and more decentralized agricultural experimental stations that would assume greater supervisory duties. In 1897, the Kingdom of Serbia, for instance, passed a law according to which 'fruit or wine growing stations' were to be created in all districts.[24] In 1919 and 1921, Yugoslavia reorganized the advisory, teaching and research tasks of agricultural experiment and control stations (*poljoprivredne ogledne i kontrolne stanice*), of which there were soon dozens throughout the country.[25]

In several spheres of rural life, such as housing, hygiene, work or nutrition, practical education via demonstration by experts and lay imitation was considered to be the most promising means of developing rural societies. As a result, the number of model farms as well as experimental and demonstration facilities grew steadily in countries like Poland and Yugoslavia from the 1910s to the 1930s. The increased involvement of intergovernmental and private international organizations, such as the International Institute of Agriculture (IIA) in Rome, the International Labour Office/Organization (ILO) in Geneva and its Mixed Advisory Agricultural Committee (MAAC), or the Rockefeller Foundation, contributed to this trend after 1918. Moreover, the Rockefeller Foundation promoted the US model of rural youth clubs – especially the 4-H clubs and the Young Men's Christian Association (YMCA) – and financed scholarships for Eastern Europeans to attend demonstrations of 'scientific agriculture' in the United States from the 1920s.[26]

From the early 1930s, the Great Depression caused mass impoverishment in rural areas across Europe, especially in the agriculture-dominated economies of Eastern Europe. Consequently, scepticism towards previously propagated development models grew rapidly among rural populations and academics. In the mid-1930s, the Polish agronomist Anatol Listowski considered it one of the most important postulates of rural development not to blindly adopt foreign models. Imposing systems developed in relation to different social structures, he wrote, would be doctrinaire, one-sided and ultimately wrong. In addition, the Croatian anthropologist Vera Erlich noted on the basis of questionnaires from Yugoslav villages in the 1930s that:

[I]t was striking how much better farms were managed by German, Czech, Slovak, and Hungarian colonists, settled in the neighbourhood of the old residents of some South Slav regions ... But [these colonists] were in no way envied or imitated, but rather ridiculed by their South Slav neighbours. The values of the 'bourgeois' period – frugality, rational working methods and viewpoints – were never fully accepted by the South Slav peasants.[27]

Model Farmhouses and Model Villages

In parallel to new farming concepts, new building concepts for rural houses and farmhouses also emerged in Europe, especially in England, from the eighteenth century.[28] Ideas about social reform or nationhood as well as the sociomedical debates at the end of the nineteenth century promoted these newly conceptualized designs for 'rational' and 'healthy' farmhouses. Numerous pamphlets and guidebooks appeared in Europe and North America from 1900. From the 1910s, books on model farmhouses were published in Eastern Central and Southeastern Europe that combined 'foreign' models from elsewhere in Europe and North America with local inventions and traditions. All of these texts claimed to provide concrete proposals for houses and farmsteads that were fireproof, easier to heat and more conducive to efficient work, while offering superior general living conditions.

One of the first publications of this kind in Eastern Europe appeared on the western edge of the Russian Empire. The bourgeois Polish Society for Housing (Towarzystwo urządzeń mieszkań) in Vilnius aimed to improve the living conditions of the middle class as well as industrial and agricultural workers and farmers. In 1910, it published several brochures with designs for model houses, including urban dwellings, farmhouses and houses for farmworkers.[29] The type plans for the farms were the result of a public tender process for designing three standard farm sizes. Together with representatives from several agricultural societies, the Society for Housing selected successful designs, which were subsequently 'corrected and completed', as the Society explained, with ideas from England, France, Sweden and Canada that had been provided by the Russian Ministry of Agriculture.[30] Civil society planning and the international exchange of ideas for improving rural areas were certainly in the interests of empires like Russia. Although some houses would be built in a Western style (with a raised ground floor, large roof overhang and half-hip roof), all the proposed farmhouses would be wooden constructions in traditional cubature with regionally typical decorative elements. In their sample plans, the editors emphasized the arrangement of the buildings and the division of the interiors, both of which were based on hygienic and rational considerations. The Polish urban milieu saw an improvement in living conditions in the countryside as a

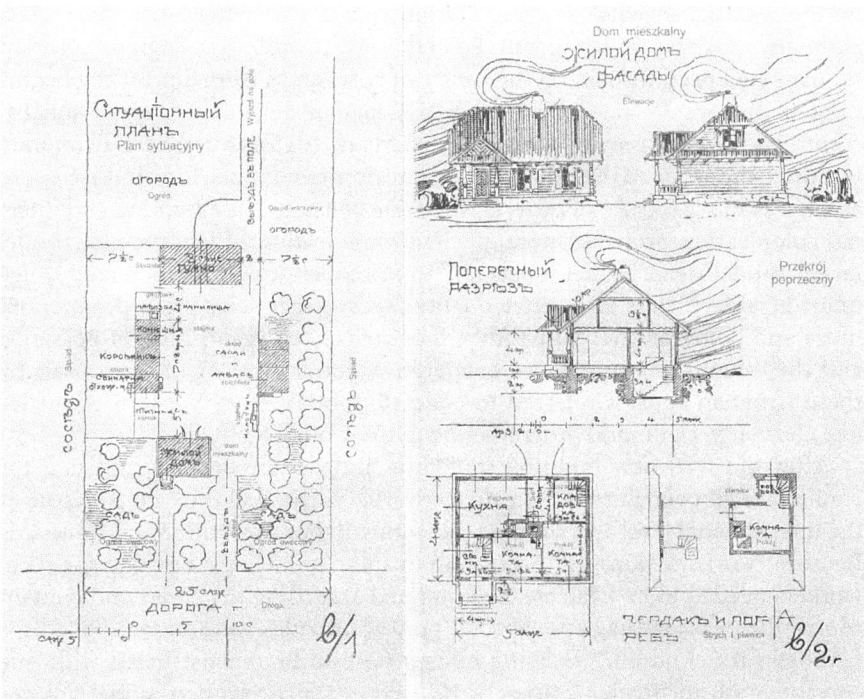

Figure 5.1. Bilingual Polish-Russian situation plans, perspectives and sections for a middle-size type of model farmstead in the Vilnius region, 1910. Wileńskie Towarzystwo Urządzeń mieszkań, *Typy wzorowych zagród włościańskich*. Vilnius: Zawadzki, 1910, attachments

prerequisite for modernizing society as a whole (while simultaneously raising national consciousness among the rural population). Dark, damp and unhygienic housing in towns and villages was seen as the cause of widespread social apathy and Polish society's supposed corresponding lack of progress.[31]

During the First World War, societal planning efforts for rural areas in Europe increased and agricultural topics gained in importance across the continent; urban spaces, by contrast, suffered considerable decay.[32] As a result, agriculture and rural areas increasingly became objects of an imagined or planned modernization. Polish and South Slavic intellectuals alike were already discussing models for future transformations during the war – mostly with dreams of their own independent nation states in mind. One striking approach towards future models could be seen in a large photographic exhibition in Warsaw in 1915 that displayed images of farmhouses, village churches and small-town markets from all over a still-divided Poland. In these examples of rural and small-town architecture that had already been partially destroyed by the war, urban elites saw ideal prototypes for a soon-to-be-resurrected, authentic postwar independent Poland.[33] Meanwhile, in Zagreb, agrarian scholars had been discussing the future of rural areas from almost the beginning of the war.[34] Vladimir Šteiner, a Croatian agronomist and publicist, commissioned a survey of economic experts in 1915 entitled 'Our Economic Future'.[35] The scope of their demands and recommendations for rural areas was as wide as the spectrum of experts who were consulted: melioration and internal colonization projects; more efficient organization of labour; new model farms, model wells, model toilets and even model dunghills; increased usage of artificial fertilizers and better-quality seeds; larger-scale grain production; more and better animal husbandry; more effective organization of peasants; and the establishment of more cooperatives. Still, most of the proposals by these Croatian experts referred to concrete models from Western countries like Germany, Denmark, Switzerland and the United States.

After the war, new building standards and designs were formulated for rural areas all over Europe.[36] In the early 1920s, the ILO took up the issue at the international level and adopted recommendations for minimum standards for rural workers' housing. According to these guidelines, housing for rural workers needed to be heatable, be separated according to gender and contain rooms for personal hygiene. Special protection rules were to be applied for families with children.[37] Existing houses were to be reconstructed with due consideration for hygienic aspects. ILO experts also planned model villages and model colonies that were to be copied in rural areas. They were convinced that the housing conditions of the rural population would improve simply by spreading the benefits of industrialization.[38]

Both in Poland and Yugoslavia, state-sanctioned model designs for improving life and work in rural areas were developed in the early 1920s. One such project in Yugoslavia was a booklet published by the regional office of the Yugoslav Ministry of Public Health in Bosnia-Herzegovina in 1924, which contained construction plans for and descriptions of 'healthy rural houses' for all regions of Bosnia.[39] Similar to the projects initiated in Vilnius, these plans had been drawn up after a call for tenders and then discussed with civil society actors and 'some more respected and intelligent farmers'.[40] To ensure their widest possible distribution and application, the publishers assured interested parties that the plans would be available free of charge throughout Bosnia .

An imagined healthy and clean future in the countryside was contrasted with the lingering unhealthy presence of the past. According to the booklet, Bosnian peasants were generally 'extremely backward for the present day' and were still building houses that 'did not even deserve that name'. Indeed, half of Bosnian farmhouses were actually sheds; consisting of one room with an open fireplace, two doors and tiny window openings, they were full of smoky and dirty air with heat in one corner and damp cold in the other. In the words of

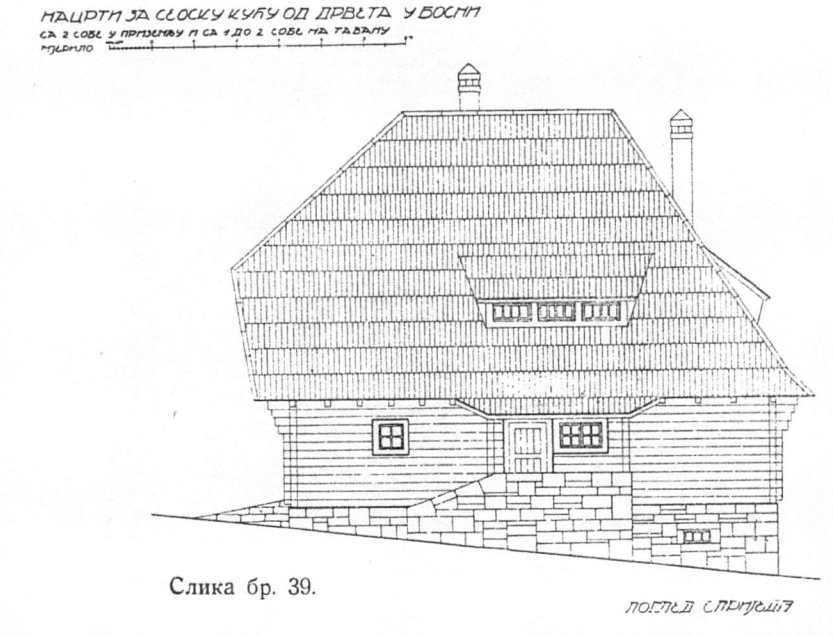

Figure 5.2. View of a model wooden farmhouse for central Bosnia. Zdravstveni odsek za BiH u Sarajevu (ed.), *Zdrave seoske kuće za Bosnu i Hercegovinu*. Sarajevo: Državna štamparija, 1924, 84

the authors, such houses were 'a veritable breeding ground for all kinds of illnesses.'[41] As alternatives, the booklet recommended three regional farmhouse types: a 'Central European' brick house for northern Bosnia, a wooden house for central Bosnia and a 'Mediterranean' stone house for Herzegovina. All three farmhouse types had several rooms, including a spacious kitchen with an 'efficient stove' that was explicitly designed with the intention of protecting forests from the wastage of wood while also allowing for a continuation of the tradition of baking bread 'on an open fire'. There were also specifications for room layout, room height and the window area to living space ratio. The farmhouse would be functionally separate in the centre of the farmyard. Moreover, it was recommended that it should be oriented towards the cardinal points of the compass: the living rooms facing southwards, and the kitchen and storeroom northwards. The farm buildings were to be arranged in a concentric pattern around the house. Accordingly, the booklet proposed the building of a sheepfold to the left of the street entrance, a stable and cowshed to the right, and a vegetable and fruit garden at the back. For reasons of efficiency and hygiene, the authors demanded to build the well as far away as possible from

Figure 5.3. Perspective view of the model brick farmhouse for northern Bosnia.
Zdravstveni odsek za BiH u Sarajevu (ed.), *Zdrave seoske kuće za Bosnu i Hercegovinu*.
Sarajevo: Državna štamparija, 1924, 58

the livestock and toilet facilities, and close to the kitchen. The publication was
richly illustrated with plans and images of houses. It presented ideal types of
'healthy houses' that were adapted to the realities of the Bosnian countryside
and easy to copy, but nevertheless rationally structured and progressive.

Plans for model villages – realized or not – had existed in Central and
Eastern Europe at least since the 1900s. In partitioned Poland, there were
several examples of conceptualized or partially realized model villages that
had been initiated by local priests, teachers, cooperatives and/or agricultural
(youth) organizations. The model village projects in Pilica (near Kielce),
Zanęcin (near Warsaw) or Lisków (near Kalisz) were directed against individ-
ualism and capitalism, and focused on collective living and working, education
and the promotion of a lively national village culture while at the same time
making use of state-of-the-art technology and infrastructure. The individual
projects differed in the extent of their collective living and working arrangements and the way in which they approached religion. After 1918, ideas for
ideal or model villages proliferated parallel to broad discussions on agricultural reform that were omnipresent across the societies of Eastern Europe.[42]
Existing model villages were typically growing in size and national importance
and often received state support. Organizers tried to set up model facilities
across a wide range of sectors: schools, farms (as well as farmers) and cooperatives were all to serve as models. One of the best examples of model village
development was the village of Lisków in the Prussian partition of divided

Poland. Here, the Catholic priest Wacław Bliziński initiated numerous social, educational, cultural and economic reforms in the early 1900s. From 1902, he established a cooperative shop followed by cooperative facilities such as a dairy, a mill, a bakery and a slaughterhouse as well as a cultural centre, public baths, a fire brigade and an orphanage. From their very beginning, the local cooperatives promoted the use of artificial fertilizers and new cereal seeds, purchased breeding cattle and sent members on training courses in locations as far away as Warsaw. Even before the First World War, Lisków had already become known as a model village. After 1918, agri-political elites developed it into the best-known model village in Poland. From the early 1920s, Lisków possessed a primary and a secondary school, modern sporting facilities, an infirmary with thirty beds, a dental surgery and a brick factory.[43] In 1925 and 1937, when national exhibitions imagining the future of Polish rural life were held in Lisków, state propaganda declared that 'every enlightened Polish farmer' should visit the village.[44] Documentaries were made for the newsreel, essays and reviews about the exhibition were published, and numerous international experts as well as thousands of Poles visited the village on special trains.[45]

However, there were also critical voices. Many experts considered the state-supported model villages to be clearly out of touch with reality. Others engaged in an abstract debate on the ideal size and form of farms in cooperatively organized model villages. Several voices were raised in favour of either small- or large-scale farms, although a majority of experts in Europe agreed that individual land ownership was more progressive.[46]

Ideas for model villages were also circulating and being debated in interwar Yugoslavia. In Croatian contexts, such ideas often reflected the divide between clerical and anticlerical yet religious actors, such as the enormously influential Croatian Peasant Party (Hrvatska [Pučka/Republikanska] Seljačka Stranka). In 1924, for example, a clerical Catholic society based in Zagreb propagated a concept for a Croatian model village based on the orderly, clean and healthy family as the seat of religion, morality and progress.[47] In his book *The Croatian Model Village*, the Catholic priest and philologist Josip Andrić (1894–1967) presented his visions for improving rural life by means of social and cultural reforms. The key for him was church-centred religiosity and socialization (in the sense of Catholic Action),[48] which together with education and technological progress would lead to order and concord, beauty, prosperity, health and good nutrition. With reference to the Bavarian village of Oberammergau and its centuries-old Catholic Passion Play tradition, he promoted a lively Christian village culture as a means of uniting, educating and mobilizing villagers in an antimodernist manner that was nevertheless still modern. Andrić also called for the establishment of anticapitalist associations in the form of Catholic cooperatives and regarded autonomous Croatian village municipalities as the foundation of state and society. Only an autonomous village municipality, he was certain, could become a true model municipality – with good roads, streets and bridges as well as a fire brigade, a network of doctors and an infirmary.[49]

In parallel to rising nationalism across Europe, international discussions about village modernization intensified in the 1930s. At the first European Conference on Rural Hygiene, which was held under the auspices of the League of Nations Health Organisation in Geneva in 1931, representatives of twenty-three European and eight non-European observer countries discussed a broad spectrum of topics. The Conference formulated recommendations for village development in the public health sector and the broad category of sanitation, which concerned the disposal of sewage and refuse, the supply of water and housing, and the improvement of land.[50] Eight years later, the League of Nations Health Organisation declared 'that the rational planning of houses and villages and area-planning in the countryside were questions of prime importance'.[51] It established a Housing Commission for this purpose, which sent out questionnaires to experts in numerous countries. Based on the results, the Commission organized an exhibition on village planning at the International Exposition of Art and Technology in Paris in 1937.[52] In preparation for a second European Conference on Rural Hygiene, planned for the autumn of 1939, an international Housing Commission led by M.M. Vignerot, an engineer from the French Ministry of Agriculture, travelled for eight weeks through seven European countries in 1938, including Poland and Yugoslavia. The Commission compiled a report on 'Rural Housing and Planning' covering a vast number of topics relating to rural infrastructure development and house building, which was to be included as an annex to the conference proceedings.[53] According to the Commission's report, the poor living conditions in the countryside were mainly a product of poor-quality housing, which experts saw as one of the key reasons for the rural exodus of the younger generation. Although the report was open to considering regional differences and diverse development pathways, it nevertheless recommended detailed specifications for village buildings, such as the structural separation of living and farming premises. It considered at least three separate bedrooms desirable, namely for the adults, boys and girls respectively. It also recommended minimum dimensions for living spaces, ceiling heights and windows that were strongly reminiscent of Ernst Neufert's building design theory published three years earlier, which had formulated universal building standards.[54] The report was remarkable not only for its construction-related recommendations, but also for its demands for the development of municipal facilities in rural areas. In addition to schools, administrative buildings and infirmaries, the report recommended that rural municipalities should establish and maintain markets and slaughterhouses as well as washhouses, museums and libraries, sporting facilities, promenades and public parks 'for the leisure and recreation of the inhabitants' – facilities that, just a few decades earlier, were conceivable only as urban social spaces.[55] According to the report, rural municipalities should draw up development plans like Dutch municipalities had already successfully done. The conference for which the report was prepared did not take place due to the outbreak of the Second World War, but its ideas would have an impact on village planning in Europe after 1945.

Model Orphan Farms

'Village' and 'nature' played a central role in progressive education around the turn of the twentieth century. The Polish pedagogue Kazimierz Jeżewski (1877–1948) was one of the first in Eastern Europe to formulate the idea of raising orphans with families instead of in children's homes. Jeżewski clearly developed his ideas based on his studies in Denmark and Switzerland, where he encountered, among others, J.H. Pestalozzi's (1746–1827) educational concepts. Pestalozzi had in turn been influenced by French physiocracy as well as ideas of reformed agriculture – not least those of Jakob Guyer (Kleinjogg), the aforementioned Swiss model farmer.[56] From 1905, Jeżewski had attempted to organize the placement of orphans in select rural families and to combine this with the concept of model farms and model villages. He was convinced that the principle of example and imitation – thus of emulating (role) models – was the most important motor for social change. With the support of Polish industrialists (such as Stanisław Glezmer) and influential intellectuals (including the author Maria Konopnicka as well as the Nobel laureates in Literature Henryk Sienkiewicz and Władysław Reymont), his Society for Orphan Nests (Towarzystwo Gniazd Sierocych) opened the first model farm for orphans in Stanisławczyk (near Przemyśl) in 1909. By 1914, the organization was managing eight such model farms for orphans in Habsburg Galicia. On these farms, five to ten orphans lived with a family, where they were to have a Catholic upbringing surrounded by familial warmth, sun and nature, and to be guided by 'practical, rational teaching'. In return, the host families were given additional land, from which they were to provide for themselves as far as possible. Jeżewski's plan was that the family farms would also function as models in agricultural terms.[57] In his model orphan farms, Jeżewski saw 'people of reason and culture' at work, who in stable and barn, field and garden, kitchen and living room would do their best to promote a conservative, Christian enlightenment. If the intelligent educator and farmer, Jeżewski wrote, managed to pass on his understanding of family, culture and work to the children, then the second goal would also be achieved: 'the orphan's nest would become a centre of economic and moral culture for its neighbouring farmers' and would eventually create a 'brand new [type of] human being'.[58]

After the First World War, there were countless orphans in Poland as well as numerous visions for the newly independent Polish state. Jeżewski could thus succeed in convincing decisive members of the Polish Parliament to establish a state-run foundation for orphan villages – the Kościuszki Village Foundation (Wieś Kościuszkowska) – in 1919.[59] The Foundation planned to merge twenty new model orphan farms to form cooperative village colonies. These model villages were to be self-governing and would operate their own schools. Despite significant political support in the 1920s, which almost resulted in one such village being founded in Pomerania in 1927, Jeżewski's plans were ultimately never realized due to the high levels of funding that they required and the developing global economic crisis. Still, he continued to campaign for the implementation of his plans until the 1930s and launched another initiative after the Second World War that was once again unsuccessful.[60]

The project of model orphan farms was only one example of the progressive educational movements in Europe that had started to spread at the turn of the twentieth century and gained traction in the 1920s. Like the Waldorf educational model based on the methods of Rudolf Steiner, progressive education emphasized the importance of 'natural' surroundings, fresh air and practical work. In the firm belief that life in nature and with family and religion would transform the whole of society, Jeżewski's model orphan farms combined religious worldviews, progressive educational approaches and the ideal of modern small-scale farming with the conviction that change in society had to begin with example and imitation in rural contexts.

Models for Rural Health and Hygiene

Following the enormous progress in the natural science of medicine in the nineteenth century, social and cultural determinants of health increasingly came into focus around 1900. This social turn in medicine found its expression in the new concepts of hygiene and public health. Hygiene – understood as the application of scientific knowledge for the purposes of maintaining and improving collective health – was, from the outset, a core concept of rural modernization, especially in the first half of the twentieth century.

Since the Romantic era, narratives about rural health have oscillated between extreme positions and incorporated open contradictions. On the one hand, an entire village, or certain parts thereof, would be considered 'sick' and in need of healing – both from the aberrations of the traditional past and the deformities of Capitalist modernity. At the same time, and often without addressing the contradiction, rural areas promised 'naturalness' and thus a harmonious refuge offering health, originality, order and purity. In this context, rural societies were seen as presenting a wholesale means of healing supposedly sick modern societies. At this point, there was a *grosso modo* East-West divide in Europe: in industrialized Western Europe (as in North America), the countryside was seen as healthier than urban areas; in Eastern Europe (and in large parts of the rest of the world) it was claimed that an urban lifestyle promised good health.[61] Indeed, large areas of rural Eastern Europe suffered from comparatively poor health and education outcomes and a much lower doctor-patient ratio.[62] Eastern Europe was thus a significant resonance chamber for concepts of hygiene. This allowed social medicine specialists from Paris, Vienna, Prague or Berlin to have a lasting influence on future doctors from the region – also because the application of public health concepts seemed comparatively simple and promising in rural areas.[63]

Following the founding of new nation states in Eastern Europe in 1918, sociomedical improvement became a high priority in the region. Along with the United Kingdom and Germany, several of the new states in Eastern Europe, such as Yugoslavia, Poland, Czechoslovakia and Hungary, were pioneers in establishing schools of public health and institutes of hygiene. Once again, the US school of hygiene model and massive financial support from the Rockefeller Foundation were decisive in this pan-European development after 1918.[64] In May 1919, Yugoslavia was one of the first countries in Eastern Europe to establish a Ministry of Public Health. The country's need and political will to catch up in healthcare was also reflected in the founding of the first medical faculty in the capital, Belgrade, in 1918. The establishment of these two new institutions was largely attributed to Milan Jovanović Batut (1847–1940), a Serbian physician and hygiene specialist who had been educated in Vienna. It was mostly at Jovanović Batut's instigation that Andrija Štampar (1888–1958), likewise a Vienna-educated, committed social physician, was appointed head of the newly established Department of Racial, Public and Social Medicine within the Ministry of Public Health. Due to his intensive work in support of health improvement in rural areas, Štampar soon became a highly sought-after expert on rural social medicine within Yugoslavia as well as in China, the United States and Canada.[65]

Poland, too, founded a Central Epidemiological Institute (Państwowy Centralny Zakład Epidemiologiczny) a few days after the country's re-establishment that was soon renamed the State Institute of Hygiene (Państwowy Zakład Higieny). In the wake of various epidemics and pandemics such as the 1915 typhoid fever outbreak in Eastern Europe or the so-called Spanish flu of 1918–19, the Rockefeller Foundation supported the opening of hygiene institutes and schools in Zagreb and Warsaw.[66] But it was also internationally well-connected young sociomedical professionals who pushed for the establishment of national institutes of hygiene. In Poland, the bacteriologist Ludwik Rajchman (1881–1965), who had trained in Krakow and Paris and had professional experience in London, played a decisive role in the establishment of the Institute. Rajchman was soon considered an international expert due to his commitment and pioneering methods in the fight against epidemics. In as early as 1921, the League of Nations entrusted him with the task of establishing an International Health Organization, the predecessor of the World Health Organization (WHO). Until 1938, Rajchman, like Štampar, travelled across the world as an adviser to the League of Nations. Rajchman also became an adviser to the governments of several countries, including his native Poland as well as China, and in 1946 was one of the cofounders of UNICEF.

In Yugoslavia, health politicians, scientists and hygiene experts such as Jovanović Batut and Štampar relied on their broad education and a decentralized state healthcare system to leave their mark. Štampar was responsible for the establishment of more than six hundred medical institutions all over the country by 1931, including polyclinics, bacteriological stations, anti-rabies stations, outpatient clinics for various diseases, health stations, public baths and sanatoria.

In addition to treating the sick and publishing textbooks and public awareness material, Yugoslav health centres organized dozens of courses every year, mainly for the rural population but also for teachers and scholars. There were hygiene and veterinary courses for farmers, infant courses for young mothers and various domestic courses for rural women. In Poland too, there had been

Figure 5.4. A newly built health station in an unknown Yugoslav (Bosnian?) village in the 1920s. Courtesy of the Croatian State Archives (HDA), 831 Štampar Andrija, 12.3.2

Figure 5.5. Completed model well in an unknown location in the Kingdom of Serbs, Croats and Slovenes in the 1920s. Courtesy of the HDA, 831/18 Štampar Andrija, 12.3.2.

nationwide hygiene courses since the early 1920s, including special courses for primary school teachers, priests or general medical practitioners. Other courses were organized by women's associations or agricultural cooperatives, while rural hygiene competitions were also popular.[67] Several programmes, such as winter courses or farmers' universities, were based on Danish, German, Swiss or Austrian models, but they also developed their own curricula that were partly endorsed by international experts such as those working for the Rockefeller Foundation.

From its beginning as a field of rural modernization, sociomedical education (often referred to as medical enlightenment) made use of various models and examples as a means of disseminating knowledge. Its educational narratives also incorporated cautionary examples and contrasting before-and-after images. Local health centres in Yugoslavia built dozens of model facilities to demonstrate how life could be improved through better hygiene. Here again, the Rockefeller Foundation partly funded several of these model facilities. Supported by the Zagreb School for Public Health (Škola narodnog zdravlja), local health centres built model sewers, cisterns, septic tanks and toilets as well as model wells and walkways in villages throughout the country. As in Bosnia in the early 1920s, public health officers throughout Yugoslavia initiated the planning and construction of model farmhouses. In several cases (such as in Mraclin, Donji Kraljevec and Kolarec) in the 1920s and 1930s, the School for Public Health supervised the reconstruction of destroyed villages and their conversion into model villages adhering to modern hygienic and aesthetic standards.[68]

The courses and model facilities served to demonstrate concrete technological improvements, but they were also an instrument for the comprehensive, aesthetic and moral education of the rural population. The courses were
intended to aid the dissemination of educational content from the fields of
agriculture, human and veterinary medicine, and business administration
while also addressing moral issues of individual and family life. Following the
examples showcased in the courses and by the model sanitary facilities, trained
and mobilized rural inhabitants were expected to take responsibility for 'sani-
tizing' their homes and villages, thereby improving their medical, technological and living circumstances.[69] Already in the early 1930s, the immense range
of activities offered by the relatively quickly established network of Yugoslav
health centres was considered exemplary across Europe. In 1930, for instance,
an international panel of experts recommended that Greece should adopt at
least some elements from the Yugoslav system of health centres.[70]

Health cooperatives established from the early 1920s predominantly in
Serbian regions were another remarkable development in the Yugoslav healthcare system. These cooperatives operated health centres in rural areas and
small towns, employing doctors, nurses and even veterinarians. By the end
of the 1930s, their membership figures had grown to several hundred thousand.[71] In the 1930s, these institutions, known internationally as Yugoslav
health cooperatives, were regarded among experts at the League of Nations as
a promising model for village healthcare that could be copied globally.[72] For
example, health cooperatives founded in India before the Second World War
were reportedly based on the Yugoslav model.[73] Today, health cooperatives
continue to be considered by the United Nations as 'a reliable enterprise model
for health and wellbeing'.[74]

The new nation states in Eastern Central and Southeastern Europe made
considerable progress in the field of social medicine in the 1920s and 1930s.
This was due to the high priority attached to this field by their governments,
but it was also a result of the internationally trained and well-connected professionals who promoted innovative model programmes, especially in rural
areas. These programmes adopted concepts from countries that were regarded
as progressive in specific areas of public health. Last but not least, funding from
the Rockefeller Foundation took on a steering function. However, Poland and
Yugoslavia also developed their own rural modernization concepts that were
considered worthy of imitation internationally.

Conclusions

There was a broad spectrum of models used in rural modernization initiatives
in Eastern Europe in the first half of the twentieth century. Some models orig-

inated in the Global West. Others were the product of diverse templates that were combined and adapted to local needs to create models for agriculture, construction and infrastructure as well as culture, education and socialization. Both urban educated and partially uneducated village elites planned and used models as a means of disseminating what they understood as modern knowledge. These models were meant to promote comprehensive progress in the countryside. Some models were even planned to help preserve traditions.

Due to simultaneous sociopolitical uncertainties and a firm belief in the power of rational decisions, the interwar period was, as Kiran Patel states, characterized by its 'hype around planning and intervention'.[75] These plans and interventions were increasingly to be found in proposed or completed models in rural areas. Their extensive use was in turn based on the conviction that an ideal solution existed for every socioeconomic problem. Still, model facilities and demonstration sites in rural areas also reflected orientalist devaluations of rural societies, with academic experts often understanding tangible models as the only means of educating, mobilizing and transforming supposedly simple, lethargic and unimaginative rural populations. A largely illiterate rural population, as in Poland and Yugoslavia, was usually regarded in educated circles as incapable of understanding rational relationships of cause and effect. According to this perception, such villagers learnt only through demonstration and believed only what they saw. However, contrary to this view, rural inhabitants were actively and extensively searching for prototypes of 'modern' change. Consequently, tangible facilities for experimentation and demonstration in rural areas represented valued opportunities for practical, applied and easily accessible education. Model wells, toilets and sewage channels as well as model farms and agricultural experiment stations were therefore often welcomed in rural areas and regarded locally as signs of progress.

Facilities that were constructed according to prototype plans were never identical copies of pre-existing structures or objects, nor did serious experts ever demand this. In each case, experts were convinced of the necessity of local adaptation. Models followed global developments, yet created their own national, regional and/or local impulses in order to solve specific problems. State-run or state-funded model programmes were also an example of the central 'state's 'advancement' into its peripheries.[76] In the first four decades of the twentieth century, agrarian and rural experts placed astonishingly high expectations on model institutions. Devising concrete models, they planned and predicted the mobilization and holistic education of rural society for the intended benefit of both the individual and the collective.

The expectation of creating examples, even beacons, of rural development, was rarely fulfilled, but sometimes such efforts did lead to innovative, pioneering initiatives. For example, the rural health cooperatives that were created in

Yugoslavia in the 1920s succeeded in establishing efficient and self-governing healthcare structures in rural areas that repeatedly attracted international attention and praise. Another example was the model orphan farms project initiated by the Polish pedagogue Kazimierz Jeżewski, whose decentralized family education system for orphans was in some respects far ahead of contemporary pedagogical developments in Europe.

Heiner Grunert is a research assistant for the Chair of Eastern European History at the Ludwig Maximilian University of Munich and a lecturer in the Department of History at the University of Basel. His work focuses on the modern religious and rural history of Eastern Central and Southeastern Europe. He is currently working on conceptualizations of the future of rural areas in early twentieth-century Poland and Yugoslavia. His publications include *Glauben im Hinterland: Die Serbisch-Orthodoxen in der habsburgischen Herzegowina 1878–1918* (V&R, 2016).

Notes

1. Cf. Couperus et al., 'Experimental Spaces'.
2. Herbert, 'Europe in High Modernity'; Raphael, 'Ordnungsmuster der "Hochmoderne"?'; cf. Couperus et al., 'Experimental Spaces'.
3. See e.g. the Nazi philologist and 'race theorist': Günther, *Das Bauerntum*, 451–53.
4. For the concept of rural modernization, cf. Bruisch and Gestwa, 'Introduction', 7–8.
5. Bayly, *The Birth of the Modern World*, 10; Eisenstadt, 'Multiple Modernities'.
6. Bayly, *The Birth of the Modern World*, 10.
7. Already in 1809, the term 'rational' had appeared in the title of an important scientific work on agriculture: Thaer, *Grundsätze der rationellen Landwirthschaft*.
8. Cf. e.g. the statements on 'rationalization' in the German left-wing *Deutsche Gewerkschaftszeitung* or the Polish national-conservative *Dzien Polski* in the 1920s.
9. Cf. *pars pro toto*: 'The Chairman of the American Delegation to the International Economic Conference (Robinson) to the Secretary of State, Washington 10.6.1927 (550.M1/319): Papers Relating to the Foreign Relations of the United States, 1927, Volume I.' Retrieved 5 November 2022 from https://history.state.gov/historicaldocuments/frus1927v01/d203.
10. Bruisch and Gestwa, 'Introduction'; Wendland et al., 'Polesia'; Toshkov, *Agrarianism as Modernity*; Chałasiński, *Młode pokolenie chłopów, passim*.
11. Jones, *Gender and Rural Modernity*.
12. In 1931, two-thirds of the working population in Poland worked in agriculture and fisheries. In Yugoslavia, this figure was around 80 per cent. Of the countries of Central and Southeastern Europe, only Czechoslovakia had a majority of the working population *not* working in agriculture. See Teichova, *Kleinstaaten im Spannungsfeld*, 24–25.
13. Cf. Müller, *Bodeneigentum und Nation*.
14. On *paterfamilias* literature, cf. Kruse, 'Hausväterliteratur'.

15. On Jakob Guyer, see Hirzel, *Die Wirthschaft*; Phillips, 'Socrates on the Farm'. On Polish model farms in the eighteenth century, see Marszewski, 'Warszawski związek hodowlany'; Pawlik, *Hodowla bydła rogatego*.

16. Schneider, *Lehrbuch der Landwirthschaft*; Schneider, *Rolnik wzorowy*.

17. Cf. e.g. Jaroszewski, *Gospodarstwo wzorowe. Uprawa*; Dmochowski, *Nasze wzorowe gospodarstwa*; Chełchowski, *Nasze wzorowe gospodarstwa*; Miczyński, *Rolnik wzorowy czyli*; Hempel, *Nasze wzorowe gospodarstwa*.

18. Fitzgerald, *Every Farm a Factory*, 53.

19. Naredba Ministarstva za poljoprivredu i voda, 17 May 1926, as well as the questionnaires completed by district authorities on model farmers (*uzorni ratari*); Archives of Yugoslavia, Belgrade [AJ] 67, 11/71, 12/79 and 13/84.

20. Report by the Supervisory Board of the Union of Serbian Agricultural Co-operatives in Zagreb on the work and circumstances of model farmers in 1921: Serbian Archives Belgrade [Arhiv SrbijeBeograd – AS], D-1, f. 4.

21. Hobsbawm, *The Invention of Tradition*.

22. Warsaw Horticultural Society [Towarzystwo ogrodnicze Warszawskie] to Ministry of Agriculture and State Property [MRiDP], 15 September 1919; Central Archives of Modern Records [Archiwum Akt Nowych Warszawa – AAN], Ministry of Agriculture and Agrarian Reform [MRiRR] 5599.

23. Cf. e.g. Klemm, 'Die Agrarwissenschaften'; Delegacja Doświadczalna, *Stacje doświadczalne*.

24. *Zakon o unapređenju*; *Pravilnik za izvršenje*.

25. *Zakon o poljoprivrednim*; *Zakon o obnavljanju*. Banovina Hrvatska, a province that existed from 1939 to 1941 within the Kingdom of Yugoslavia, alone operated agricultural stations in about ten localities as well as fruit and vine-growing stations in at least fourteen other localities. Croatian State Archives Zagreb [Hrvatski Državni Arhiv Zagreb – HDA] 161–46.

26. International Labour Office, *Vocational Education*, 8.

27. Erlich, *Family in Transition*, 402.

28. Robinson, 'Model Farm Buildings'.

29. *Typ wzorowego mieszkania*; *Typy wzorowych zagród*.

30. *Typy wzorowych zagród*, 1.

31. *Księga pamiątkowa wystawy*.

32. Couperus et al., 'Experimental Spaces', 476; cf. Borodziej and Górny, *Der vergessene Weltkrieg*, 213–18.

33. Kalinowski, *Materyały do architektury*.

34. Šteiner, *Naša gospodarska budućnost*.

35. Ibid.

36. In some European countries, legal standards for housing and workplaces in rural areas had already been in place since the 1880s. In 1886, the German Reich was one of the first countries in Europe to adopt statutory minimum standards for the accommodation of agricultural workers as part of its social legislation. This was followed before the First World War by countries such as the Netherlands, the United Kingdom and France. League of Nations – Health Organisation, ''European Conference on Rural Hygiene. Vol. I, 50–52.

37. League of Nations – International Labour Office, *International Labour Conference*, 406, 805–6.
38. League of Nations – Health Organisation, 'European Conference on Rural Hygiene. Vol. I', 53.
39. Zdravstveni odsek za BiH u Sarajevu, *Zdrave seoske kuće.*
40. Živanović, 'Kako su nastali', 14.
41. Ibid., 7.
42. Chętnik, *Wieś wzorowa*; Kwieciński, *Wieś idealna źródłem*; Chmielińska, *Wieś polska Lisków*; for discussions on agrarian reforms, cf. Müller, *Bodeneigentum und Nation.*
43. Bliziński, *Działalność spółdzielni*, 28; Koło Koleżeńskiej Uczniów Szkoły Hodowlanej w Liskowie, *Jednodniówka.*
44. Liga Popierania Turystyki and Spółdzielnia Turystyczno-Wypoczynkowa, 'Gromada', *Praca i kultura wsi.*
45. Piątkowski, *Łódzka izba rolnicza*; Chałasiński, *Młode pokolenie chłopów*; Karczewski, *Lisków.*
46. For criticism of Polish model villages, see Chętnik, *Wieś wzorowa*; Piątkowski, *Łódzka izba rolnicza.*
47. Andrić, *Hrvatsko uzor-selo.*
48. Catholic Action is a global lay movement that has existed since the turn of the twentieth century. Its goal is to increase the influence of religion in everyday society by means of Catholic civic associations.
49. Andrić, *Hrvatsko uzor-selo*, 31–35.
50. League of Nations – Health Organisation, 'European Conference on Rural Hygiene. Vol. I'; League of Nations – Health Organisation, 'European Conference on Rural Hygiene. Vol. II'.
51. League of Nations, 'European Conference on Rural Life', 5.
52. Ibid., 6.
53. Ibid.
54. Ibid., 8–18; Neufert, *Bau-Entwurfslehre.*
55. League of Nations, 'European Conference on Rural Life', 24.
56. Kuźma, 'Wiedza propedeutyczna'; Łuczyński, 'Rodzinne domy dziecka'.
57. Jeżewski, *Wioski Kościuszkowskie.*
58. 'Odezwa z roku', 3–10.
59. Jeżewski, *Wioski Kościuszkowskie*, 3–4. The foundation was named after Tadeusz Kościuszko (1746–1817), an enlightened Polish military and leader of the battles for Poland's independence in the 1780s and 1790s who also became known as the 'peasants' liberator'.
60. Jeżewski, *Wioski i ogniska*; cf. Jamrożek, 'Wkład ruchu ludowego'.
61. In 1905, in his global bestseller *Retour à la terre*, the former French Prime Minister Jules Méline expressed his Romantic contempt for the urban in his formulation that cities were 'the abyss for humanity'. In his 1922 *Rural Sociology*, the US sociologist John Gillette assessed living conditions in rural areas to be clearly better than those in cities when it came to matters of health. Quoted according to the German edition: Méline, *Die Rückkehr*, 183; Gillette, *Rural Sociology*, 96.

62. Cf. *pars pro toto*: Štampar, *Socijalna medicina*; Štampar, *Zdravlje i društvo*.
63. Promitzer, *Health, Hygiene, and Eugenics*.
64. Litsios, 'Selskar "Mike" Gunn'.
65. On Andrija Štampar, see Dugac, 'Andrija Stampar (1888–1958)'; Dugac et al., 'Care for Health'.
66. Ciechański, 'Ludwik Rajchman', 210.
67. League of Nations – Health Organisation, 'European Conference on Rural Hygiene. Vol. II', 52.
68. Kranjčević, 'Jedinstven primjer sveobuhvatnog'; Kranjčević, *Zanemarena baština*, 41–70.
69. Štampar, 'Deset godina unapređivanja', 108.
70. League of Nations – Health Committee, 'Minutes of the Sixteenth Session', 35.
71. Stamenović, Milorad. 'Zdravstvene zadruge za pomoć sela'. In: *Politika* (27.05.2019).
72. Štampar, 'Deset godina unapređivanja'; Müller, 'Zdravstene zadruge'; League of Nations – Health Organisation, 'European Conference on Rural Hygiene. Vol. II', 183; League of Nations, 'European Conference on Rural Life', 36.
73. Nayar and Razum, 'Health Co-operatives', 569.
74. United Nations, 'Healthcare Cooperatives: A Reliable Enterprise Model for Health and Wellbeing'. Nairobi, March 26, 2018'. Retrieved 5 November 2022 from https://www .un.org/development/desa/cooperatives/wp-content/uploads/sites/25/2019/03/1903 26_ihco_EGM-nairobi.pdf.
75. Patel, 'The Green Heart', 15.
76. Ganzenmüller and Tönsmeyer, *Vom Vorrücken*.

Bibliography

Andrić, Josip. *Hrvatsko uzor-selo: Pouka o prosvjeti i napretku seoskog života*. Zagreb: Druš. sv. Jeronima, 1924.

Bayly, Christopher A. *The Birth of the Modern World, 1780–1914: Global Connections and Comparisons*. Oxford: Blackwell, 2004.

Bliziński, Wacław. *Działalność spółdzielni i organizacyj rolniczych w Liskowie: Referat, wygłoszony na zjeździe spółdzielni w Wilnie, w dniu 18 grudnia 1927 roku*. Warsaw: Związek Rewizyjny Polskich Spółdzielni Rolniczych, 1928.

Borodziej, Włodzimierz, and Maciej Górny. *Der vergessene Weltkrieg: Europas Osten 1912– 1923. Bd. 1: Imperien 1912–1916*. Darmstadt: wbg Theiss, 2018.

Bruisch, Katja, and Klaus Gestwa. 'Introduction: Expertise and the Quest for Rural Modernization in the Russian Empire and the Soviet Union'. *Cahiers du monde russe: Russie – Empire russe – Union soviétique et États indépendants* 57(1) (2016), 7–30.

Chałasiński, Józef. *Młode pokolenie chłopów: Procesy i zagadnienia kształtowania się warstwy chłopskiej w Polsce. Tom II: Świat życia, pracy i dążeń kół młodziez wiejskiej*. Warsaw: Spółdzielnia Wydawnicza 'Pomoc Oświatowa', 1938.

Chełchowski, Stanisław. *Nasze wzorowe gospodarstwa włościańskie*. Warsaw: Druk 'Gazety Rolniczej', 1899.

Chętnik, Adam. *Wieś wzorowa: Projekty młodzieży ludowej skupiającej się przy 'Drużynie'*. Warsaw: Drużyna/Księgarnia Ludowa, 1917.

Chmielińska, Aniela. *Wieś polska Lisków w ziemi kaliskiej.* Lisków: Komitet Wystawy w Liskowie, 1925.

Ciechański, Jerzy. 'Ludwik Rajchman – (współ)twórca wspólnoty epistemicznej biomedycyny i higieny publicznej oraz międzynarodowego reżimu ochrony zdrowia po I wojnie światowej', in Edward Haliżak, Teresa Łoś-Nowak, Anna Potyrała and Joanna Starzyk-Sulejewska (eds), *Polska w instytucjach międzynarodowych w latach 1918–2018* (Warsaw: Narodowe Centrum Kultury/Polskie Towarzystwo Studiów Międzynarodowych, 2019), 201–32.

Couperus, Stefan, Liesbeth van de Grift, and Vincent Lagendijk. 'Experimental Spaces: A Decentred Approach to Planning in High Modernity. Introduction'. *Journal of Modern European History* 13(4) (2015), 475–88.

Delegacja Doświadczalna przy sekcji rolnej w Warszawie. *Stacje doświadczalne w Królestwie Polskiem, ich zadanie i urządzenie.* Warsaw: Gazeta Rolnicza, 1904.

Dmochowski, Leon. *Nasze wzorowe gospodarstwa: Ze sprawozdań urzędowych komisyi wystawowej.* Warsaw: Gazeta Rolnicza, 1886.

Dugac, Željko. '"Like Yeast in Fermentation": Public Health in Interwar Yugoslavia', in Christian Promitzer, Sevasti Trubeta and Marius Turda (eds), *Health, Hygiene, and Eugenics in Southeastern Europe to 1945.* Budapest: Central European University Press, 2011, 193–232.

———. 'Andrija Stampar (1888–1958): Resolute Fighter for Health and Social Justice', in Iris Borowy and Anne Hardy (eds), *Of Medicine and Men: Biographies and Ideas in European Social Medicine between the World Wars* (Frankfurt: Peter Lang, 2014), 73–101.

Dugac, Željko, Stella Fatović-Ferenčić, Luka Kovačić, and Tomislav Kovačević. '"Care for Health Cannot Be Limited to One Country or One Town Only, It Must Extend to Entire World": Role of Andrija Štampar in Building the World Health Organization'. *Croatian Medical Journal* 49(6) (2008), 697–708.

Eisenstadt, Shmuel N. 'Multiple Modernities'. *Daedalus* (2009), 1–29.

Erlich, Vera. *Family in Transition: A Study of 300 Yugoslav Villages* [orig. Croatian: *Porodica u transformaciji.* Zagreb: Naprijed, 1964]. Princeton: Princeton University Press, 1966.

Fitzgerald, Deborah. *Every Farm a Factory: The Industrial Ideal in American Agriculture.* New Haven: Yale University Press, 2010.

Ganzenmüller, Jörg, and Tatjana Tönsmeyer (eds). *Vom Vorrücken des Staates in die Fläche: Ein europäisches Phänomen des langen 19. Jahrhunderts.* Cologne: Böhlau, 2016.

Gillette, John M. *Rural Sociology.* New York: Macmillan, 1922.

Günther, Hans F.K. *Das Bauerntum als Lebens- und Gemeinschaftsform.* Leipzig: Teubner, 1939.

Hempel, Antoni. *Nasze wzorowe gospodarstwa włościańskie. Cz. 2.* Warsaw: Nakładem autora, 1906.

Herbert, Ulrich. 'Europe in High Modernity: Reflections on a Theory of the 20th Century'. *Journal of Modern European History* 5(1) (2007), 5–21.

Hirzel, Hans C. *Die Wirthschaft eines philosophischen Bauers.* Zurich: Orell, Gessner, Füesslin und Comp., 1774.

Hobsbawm, Eric. *The Invention of Tradition.* Cambridge: Cambridge University Press, 1983.

International Labour Office. *Vocational Education in Agriculture*. Geneva, 1929.

Jamrożek, Wiesław. 'Wkład ruchu ludowego w kształtowanie się koncepcji systemu edukacji narodowej w Drugiej Rzeczypospolitej'. *Neodidagmata* 21 (1992), 55–64.

Jaroszewski, Zygmunt. *Gospodarstwo wzorowe: Uprawa roślin zbożowych i pastewnych, groszkowych, koniczynnych i traw*. Krakow: Nakładem autora, 1880.

Jeżewski, Kazimierz. *Wioski Kościuszkowskie: Gospodarczy i społeczno-wychowawczy program działalności towarzystwa wiosek kościuszkowskich*. Warsaw: Zakłady Graficzne 'Polska Zjednoczona', 1930.

———. *Wioski i ogniska Kościuszkowskie: Gospodarczy i społeczno-wychowawczy program działalności towarzystwa gniazd sierocych i wiosek kościuszkowskich*. Warsaw: Spółdzielnia Wydawnicza 'Cyztelnik', 1946.

Jones, Elizabeth B. *Gender and Rural Modernity: Farm Women and the Politics of Labor in Germany, 1871–1933*. Farnham: Ashgate, 2009.

Kalinowski, Zdzisław (ed.). *Materyały do architektury polskiej. Tom 1: Wieś i miasteczko*. Warsaw: Gebethner i Wolff, 1916.

Karczewski, Wacław. *Lisków: Dzieje jednej polskiej wsi*. Krakow: Wystawa 'Praca i Kultura Wsi' w Liskowie, 1937.

Klemm, Volker. 'Die Agrarwissenschaften und die Modernisierung der Gutsbetriebe in Ost- und Mitteldeutschland (Ende des 19./Beginn des 20. Jahrhunderts)', in Heinz Reif (ed.), *Ostelbische Agrargesellschaft im Kaiserreich und in der Weimarer Republik: Agrarkrise – junkerliche Interessenpolitik – Modernisierungsstrategien* (Berlin: Akademie Verlag, 1994), 173–90.

Koło Koleżeńskiej Uczniów Szkoły Hodowlanej w Liskowie (ed.). *Jednodniówka uczniów Szkoły Hodowlanej Łódzkiej Izby Rolniczej w Liskowie*. Lisków, 1937.

Kranjčević, Jasenka. 'Jedinstven primjer sveobuhvatnog dizajna ruralnih naselja u Hrvatskoj. Obnova izgorjelog sela Kolarec'. *Sociologija sela* 32(3–4) (1994), 149–63.

———. *Zanemarena baština: Prostorne strukture sela u Hrvatskoj*. Zagreb: Srednja Europa, 2018.

Kruse, Ulrike. 'Hausväterliteratur: Praktische Ratgeber für eine imaginierte Landwirtschaft'. *Traverse* 21(2) (2014), 40–52.

Kuźma, Józef. 'Wiedza propedeutyczna o opiece nad sierotami i dziećmi opuszczonymi przez rodziców', in Józef Kuźma (ed.), *Opieka i wychowanie dzieci sierocych w Polsce* (Krakow: Krakowskie Towarzystwo Edukacyjne, 2007), 11–43.

Kwieciński, Jan. *Wieś idealna źródłem bogactwa narodowego*. Szamotuły: Nakładem autora, 1921.

League of Nations. 'European Conference on Rural Life 1939. General Technical Documentation: Rural Housing and Planning. Report Prepared under the Auspices of the Health Committee'. Geneva, 1939.

League of Nations – Health Committee. 'Minutes of the Sixteenth Session. Held at Geneva from September 29th to October 7th, 1930'. Geneva, 1930.

League of Nations – Health Organisation. 'European Conference on Rural Hygiene (29.6.–7.7.1931): Vol. I: Recommendations on the Principles Governing the Organisation of Medical Assistance, the Public Health Services and Sanitation in Rural Districts'. Geneva, 1931.

———. 'European Conference on Rural Hygiene (29.6.–7.7.1931): Vol. II: Minutes'. Geneva, 1931.

League of Nations – International Labour Office. 'International Labour Conference: Third Session. Vol. I. First and Second Parts'. Geneva, 1921.

Liga Popierania Turystyki, and Spółdzielnia Turystyczno-Wypoczynkowa 'Gromada', *"Praca i kultura wsi" w Liskowie: Od 8.6. do 4.7.1937 r.* Warsaw: Tymieniecka, 1937.

Litsios, Socrates. 'Selskar "Mike" Gunn and Public Health Reform in Europe', in Iris Borowy and Anne Hardy (eds), *Of Medicine and Men: Biographies and Ideas in European Social Medicine between the World Wars* (Frankfurt: Peter Lang, 2014), 23–44.

Łuczyński, Andrzej. 'Rodzinne domy dziecka jako efektywna forma opieki całkowitej nad dziećmi osieroconymi', in Józef Kuźma (ed.), *Opieka i wychowanie dzieci sierocych w Polsce* (Krakow: Krakowskie Towarzystwo Edukacyjne, 2007), 121–36.

Marszewski, Antoni. 'Warszawski związek hodowlany: (Szkice rozwoju hodowli bydła nizinnego czarno-białego)', in Jan Lutosławski (ed.), *Księga Pamiątkowa na 75-lecie 'Gazety Rolniczej', 1861–1935: Księga wsi polskiej – źródła, dzieje i kierunki jej kultury. Tom I* (Warsaw: Wydaw. Zakładu Narodowego im. Ossolińskich, 1938), 417–24.

Méline, Jules. *Die Rückkehr zur Scholle und die industrielle Überproduktion: Übers. v. Konrad zu Putlitz-Gross-Pankow.* Berlin: Parey, 1906.

Miczyński, Kazimierz. *Rolnik wzorowy czyli Przypomnienie co, kiedy i jak w gospodarstwie czynić należy.* Lviv: Macierz Polska, 1906.

Müller, Dietmar. *Bodeneigentum und Nation: Rumänien, Jugoslawien und Polen im europäischen Vergleich. 1918–1948.* Göttingen: Wallstein, 2020.

Müller, Vendelin. 'Zdravstene zadruge i budućnost našega staleža'. *Glasnik za staleška i zdravstvena pitanja* 4 (1932), 99–100.

Nayar, K. Rajasekharan, and Oliver Razum. 'Health Co-operatives: Review of International Experiences'. *Croatian Medical Journal* 44(5) (2003), 568–75.

Neufert, Ernst. *Bau-Entwurfslehre: Grundlagen, Normen und Vorschriften über Anlage, Bau, Gestaltung, Raumbedarf, Raumbeziehungen, Maße für Gebäude, Räume, Einrichtungen und Geräte mit dem Menschen als Maß und Ziel: Handbuch für den Baufachmann, Bauherrn, Lehrenden und Lernenden.* Berlin: Bauwelt-Verlag, 1936.

'Odezwa z roku 1911', in Towarzystwo Gniazd Sierocych (ed.), *Wzorowe zagrody jako program działalności towarzystwa gniazd sierocych* (Warsaw: Zakłady Graficzne A. Hurkiewicz, 1918), 3–11.

Patel, Kiran K. 'The Green Heart of Governance: Rural Europe during the Interwar Years in a Global Perspective', in Liesbeth van de Grift and Amalia Ribi Forclaz (eds), *Governing the Rural in Interwar Europe* (Abingdon: Routledge, 2018), 1–23.

Pawlik, Stefan. *Hodowla bydła rogatego w Polsce w zarysie.* Lviv: Księgarnia Gubrynowicza i Syna, 1925.

Phillips, Denise. 'Socrates on the Farm: Agricultural Improvement and Rural Knowledge in Eighteenth-Century Germany and Switzerland'. *Berichte zur Wissenschaftsgeschichte* 44(2) (2021), 159–79.

Piątkowski, Antoni. *Łódzka izba rolnicza i ministerstwo rolnicta i reform rolnych, a wystawa 'Praca i kultura wsi' w Liskowie: Uwagi krytyczne.* Warsaw: Zakłady Drukarskie W. Piekarniaka, 1937.

'Pravilnik za izvršenje zakona o obnavljanju i unapređenju vinogradarstva (1900)'. *Glasnik Ministarstva poljoprivrede i voda* 1(3) (1923), 340–69.

Promitzer, Christian. *Health, Hygiene, and Eugenics in Southeastern Europe to 1945.* Budapest: Central European University Press, 2011.

Raphael, Lutz. 'Ordnungsmuster der "Hochmoderne"? Die Theorie der Moderne und die Geschichte der europäischen Gesellschaften im 20. Jahrhundert', in Ute Schneider and Lutz Raphael (eds), *Dimensionen der Moderne: Festschrift für Christof Dipper* (Frankfurt: Peter Lang, 2008), 73–91.

Robinson, John M. 'Model Farm Buildings of the Age of Improvement'. *Architectural History* 19 (1976), 17–31, 89–92.

Schneider, Anton R. *Lehrbuch der Landwirthschaft für Ackerbauschulen: Im Auftrage des hohen k.k. Ackerbau-Ministeriums verfaßt.* Kadaň: Vincenz Uhl's Buchhandlung, 1880.

———. *Rolnik wzorowy: Podręcznik racyonalny gospodarstwa wiejskiego dla użytku praktycznych gospodarzy.* Warsaw: Nakład Maurycego Orgelbranda, 1887.

Štampar, Andrija. *Socijalna medicina: Uz saradnju jugoslovenskih socijalnih lekara.* Zagreb: Izdanje instituta za socijalńu medicinu, 1925.

———. 'Deset godina unapređivanja narodnog zdravlja', in Mirko Dražen Grmek (ed.), *U borbi za narodno zdravlje. Izabrani članci Andrije Štampara: Sv. 3* (Zagreb: Izdavački Zavod Jugoslovenske Akademije, 1966), 102–16.

———. *Zdravlje i društvo.* Zagreb: Hrvatska naklada, 1939.

Šteiner, Vladimir (ed.). *Naša gospodarska budućnost: Stručna anketa.* Zagreb: Vlastita naklada, 1915.

Teichova, Alice. *Kleinstaaten im Spannungsfeld der Großmächte: Wirtschaft und Politik in Mittel- und Südosteuropa in der Zwischenkriegszeit.* Munich: Oldenbourg, 1988.

Thaer, Albrecht D. *Grundsätze der rationellen Landwirthschaft: Bd. 1.* Berlin: Realschulbuchhandlung, 1809.

Toshkov, Alex. *Agrarianism as Modernity in 20th-Century Europe: The Golden Age of the Peasantry.* London: Bloomsbury Academic, 2019.

Wendland, Anna V., Diana Siebert, and Thomas Bohn. 'Polesia. Modernity in the Marshlands: Interventions and Transformations at the European Periphery from the Nineteenth to the Twenty-First Century'. *Zeitschrift für Ostmitteleuropa-Forschung/ Journal of East Central European Studies* 68(3) (2019), 319–43.

Wileńskie Towarzystwo urządzeń mieszkań (ed.). *Księga pamiątkowa wystawy urządzeń mieszkań i ogrodniczej: Wilno 16.8.–15.9.1909.* Vilnius: Zawadzki, 1909.

———. *Typ wzorowego mieszkania dla robotników wiejskich.* Vilnius: Zawadzki, 1910.

———. *Typy wzorowych zagród włościańskich.* Vilnius: Zawadzki, 1910.

'Zakon o obnavljanju i unapređenju vinogradarstva (1921)'. *Glasnik Ministarstva poljoprivrede i voda* 1(1) (1923), 113–20.

'Zakon o poljoprivrednim oglednim i kontrolnim stanicama (1921)'. *Glasnik Ministarstva poljoprivrede i voda* 1(1) (1923), 78–84.

'Zakon o unapređenju voćarstva (1897)'. *Glasnik Ministarstva poljoprivrede i voda* 1(1) (1923), 107–12.

Zdravstveni odsek za BiH u Sarajevu (ed.). *Zdrave seoske kuće za Bosnu i Hercegovinu.* Sarajevo: Državna štamparija, 1924.

Živanović, Todor. 'Kako su nastali ovi planovi?' in Zdravstveni odsek za BiH u Sarajevu (ed.). *Zdrave seoske kuće za Bosnu i Hercegovinu* (Sarajevo: Državna štamparija, 1924), 7–16.

CHAPTER 6

Shifting Priorities

Dutch Agricultural Education and Local Knowledge Circulation, c. 1890–1970

Ronald Plantinga and Harm Zwarts

National and regional knowledge infrastructures play a pivotal role in the dissemination and adaptation of transnational forms of knowledge. This chapter studies the main changes in the agricultural knowledge infrastructure in the Netherlands from 1890 to 1970. By 1890, a knowledge infrastructure was still largely absent, which meant that it was left to Dutch farmers themselves to adapt knowledge to local conditions. However, by the 1930s, an agricultural education and extension system had been set up with the aim of adapting knowledge imported from abroad to local conditions. These changes in the Dutch agricultural knowledge infrastructure occurred against the backdrop of accelerating specialization – a shift from bulk production to the production of higher-value products, such as vegetables, flowers and dairy products – and land scarcity. Specialization and land scarcity combined to demand a more intensive usage of fertilizer, cattle feed and other inputs, consequently making Dutch agriculture more knowledge-intensive.

Studies narrating the development of the Dutch agricultural knowledge infrastructure have hitherto focused on the national level without problematizing the importance of connections with the local and regional levels.[1] This is unfortunate given the wide variety of soil types and farming practices within the Netherlands. Dutch agronomists have divided the country into multiple agricultural zones, which can be classified into six categories based on soil type, farming methods and agricultural specialization. The first category consists of areas in the west and the north of the country that are known as pasture regions or former peat areas and have a strong specialization in dairy farming. The second comprises the sea clay areas, which specialize in cash crop cultivation and are located in the southwest and the northeast. Zones covering a smaller area are the sandy dunes along the western coastline (known since the late nineteenth century for greenhouse horticulture and flower production), the river clay areas along the country's major rivers (characterized by their many orchards) and the small set of regions in the north known as the 'peat colonies', where from the mid-nineteenth century peat bogs were turned into farmland on which crops could only be cultivated with intensive fertilizing. However, constituting the largest category of agricultural land are the sandy regions in the south and the east. Farming in these inland regions remained small in scale until the mid-twentieth century, while specialization in dairy, pig or poultry husbandry or arable farming only occurred gradually in the early twentieth century.[2]

Due to the wide variations in soil conditions and farming methods between these agricultural zones, the local level has been highly significant for knowledge intensification in Dutch agriculture. But how was transnational knowledge disseminated locally and adapted to the ecological conditions of the various Dutch agricultural zones? To answer these questions, we first provide a short overview of the historical development of Dutch agricultural education. We then discuss two examples of knowledge adaptation and dissemination. First, we examine the ways in which Dutch local agricultural education and consultancy services were organized during the interbellum in order to diffuse and adapt specific chemical knowledge on artificial fertilizers. Second, we discuss the manner in which business economics and scientific management (Taylorism) was diffused and adapted regionally via agricultural extension services and agricultural education.

This chapter shows that from the 1890s to the 1940s, the Dutch agricultural knowledge infrastructure was organized in such a way that variations in soil conditions and farming methods between the country's distinct agricultural zones were taken into account. An infrastructure consisting of local agricultural schools, agricultural consultants and local agricultural organizations was geared towards improving land productivity, which was mainly achieved through intensive fertilizing and adaptation to local conditions. After the Second World War, when labour productivity growth became the central government's main objective, this knowledge infrastructure was rearranged, with less consideration being given to local variations. As such, the development of the country's agricultural knowledge infrastructure since 1890 has mirrored the shifting priorities in Dutch agricultural policy.

Dutch Agriculture and Its Knowledge Infrastructure, c. 1890–1945

Nineteenth-century Dutch agricultural education had been characterized by its limited scale. Furthermore, in the blunt summary of one scholar, its development was a 'long sequence of failures'.[3] Because the central government was dominated by politicians adhering to laissez-faire liberalism who were unwilling to expand government expenditure or increase national taxation, it did not allocate funding for agricultural education. Nineteenth-century Dutch agricultural education was thus dependent on the private initiative of agricultural societies, which were often small, poorly organized and lacking the necessary resources. In short, without government support, Dutch agricultural education could not expand.[4]

A major watershed was the Agrarian Depression of the 1870s and the 1880s. The rapid collapse in prices led to an accelerating specialization in higher-value products, mostly vegetables, dairy products and processed foodstuffs, such as sugar and starch extracted from sugar beets and potatoes respectively.[5] This shift towards higher-value products required more intensive fertilizing.[6] Until the late nineteenth century, Dutch farmers had used organic fertilizers, such as manure, animal bones, compost and human waste, to maintain the fertility of their plots. However, from the 1880s, Dutch farmers rapidly increased their use of saltpetre, sulphate, potassium and other artificial fertilizers. By the start of the First World War, the Netherlands had become the largest per hectare user of artificial fertilizers in Europe.[7]

The rapidly growing use of artificial fertilizers and other inputs posed problems that the Dutch agricultural sector had been unable to solve. Because individual farmers could not check the quality of the artificial fertilizers, feed and seeds that they purchased, they were in a weak bargaining position in relation to their (international) suppliers. As had been the case in various German states, where the need for quality control was one of the main reasons behind the establishment of publicly funded agricultural experiment stations from the mid-nineteenth century onwards, the Dutch government decided to take on a more central role in fostering agronomic research and agricultural education.[8] Improving the standard of agricultural education and subjecting inputs to agricultural experiments to evaluate their performance was expected to improve the bargaining position of individual farmers vis-à-vis their suppliers. When this issue was discussed in the Dutch Parliament in 1887, one liberal politician argued that although he resented the imposition of protectionism via tariff barriers, he saw 'protectionism of knowledge' as the most effective way to increase the international competitiveness of Dutch farmers.[9]

Once the central government became involved in agricultural education, the Dutch agricultural knowledge infrastructure expanded swiftly. The small agricultural school in Wageningen, which had been established in 1873, was elevated to the nation's sole college for higher agricultural education in 1876 and was further expanded in the 1890s. Although it initially concentrated on educating agronomists to work in the plantation economy of the Dutch East Indies, from the 1890s its focus shifted to training agronomists who could establish agricultural schools throughout the Netherlands, an objective whose progress had hitherto been partially hindered by the lack of trained experts.[10] The Wageningen agricultural college was modelled after the German agricultural colleges established in earlier decades, most famously those in Weihenstephan (Bavaria) and Hohenheim (Württemberg), which had become blueprints for public agricultural colleges across Europe.[11]

Another major development in the Dutch agricultural knowledge infrastructure that was based on the German example was the introduction of agricultural consultants. Starting in the 1870s, Dutch agricultural societies hired private teachers to give lectures on agronomy, as had been done in the German states. During the Agrarian Depression, Dutch agricultural consultancy services came under the auspices of the state. The first *rijkslandbouwleraar* or *rijkslandbouwconsulent* (state agricultural teacher or state agricultural consultant) was employed in 1890. In the following decades, the Dutch agricultural consultancy system expanded rapidly. The consultants hired during the 1890s were assigned to large geographical areas, usually one of the eleven provinces, which often incorporated different agricultural zones with varying soil conditions and farming methods. Gradually, however, the districts to which consultants were deployed became smaller in size and usually corresponded to specific agricultural zones. Moreover, some consultants were assigned the task of specializing in a particular farming method. By 1935, there were thirty-five consultants, of which eighteen were specializing in horticulture, twelve in livestock farming, three in poultry farming and two in beekeeping. During the Great Depression in the 1930s, the agricultural consultants, who had previously focused primarily on agronomic issues, were also tasked with advising on production costs and other financial matters. In order to facilitate this change, the consultancy system was again restructured. Besides expanding the number of agricultural consultants, their districts were split into smaller subdivisions, responsibility for each of which was then delegated to assistants. Shortly after the Second World War, there were eighty-one agricultural consultants working in twenty-three different districts and overseeing a network of no less than 760 'assistant consultants'.[12]

Following the German example, the Dutch agricultural consultants' role was to convey expert knowledge to farmers. Within their districts, they helped to establish platforms for communication among farmers, typically in the form of local agricultural periodicals, and took the initiative in setting up local agricultural organizations, usually supply cooperatives that gave farmers easy access to key inputs. Unsurprisingly, the involvement of agricultural consultants was sometimes met with opposition. Although historical documentation of resistance is very rare, agricultural periodicals occasionally contain hints of criticism. Apart from the warning that agricultural education and consultancy was too theoretical and detached from practice, a discussion in one agricultural periodical during the Great Depression reveals that some experts believed that agricultural education and consultancy had become too strongly focused on agronomic and technological facets of farming, and had thus neglected to train farmers in business aspects, especially on how to lower production costs.[13] Another writer argued that farmers had lost a degree of independence and initiative: consultancy had become 'regency', forgetting that its role should be merely advisory.[14] Whether or not these voices represented a broader sentiment, the expansion of the Dutch agricultural consultancy system continued unchallenged and strengthened by government support throughout the 1930s.

Besides consultancy work, the agricultural consultants were also responsible for local agricultural education. Unlike the situation in most German states, where agricultural consultants were teachers and had to confine their consultancy work to the summer months, the Dutch agricultural consultants did not teach at schools.[15] Instead, a system was created in which the consultants prepared local schoolteachers for an official teachers' qualification in agronomy. The qualified schoolteachers could then add agronomy to the standard curriculum of their local school or establish local agricultural schools that fully specialized in agricultural training. Moreover, these schoolteachers were seen as an extra layer in the agricultural consultancy system: they were expected to become the resident experts on farming in their villages and were thus to serve as the link between local farming communities and the assistant consultants or the agricultural consultants themselves.[16]

Over the years, the number of agricultural courses organized by the agricultural consultants as well as the number of agricultural schools increased steadily. The number of winter courses, for instance, grew from a mere seven with a total of 231 students in 1890 to 1,320 courses with 23,515 students in 1920.[17] Some of these courses were amalgamated into winter schools. After the first winter school opened in 1893, by 1920 there were thirty located across the country. In 1921, the agricultural education system was restructured into different school types. While some schools remained standard schools that offered their students supplementary practical farm training during the winter months, others became year-round preparatory schools for the agricultural college in Wageningen. Shortly after the Second World War, there were 145 'lower' agricultural schools with 11,904 students and 71 'middle' agricultural schools with 5,106 students.[18] Although it is difficult to quantify the impact of these schools, it has been estimated that by the mid-twentieth century, at least half of all Dutch farmers had received some form of agricultural education.[19]

The Netherlands' agricultural knowledge infrastructure expanded throughout the first half of the twentieth century. With agricultural consultants assigned to small geographical districts, assistant consultants deployed to even smaller subdivisions, and schoolteachers active at the village level, the agricultural knowledge infrastructure was structured to take local variations in soil conditions and farming methods into account. To explore how this functioned in practice, the following section examines how chemical knowledge on artificial fertilizers was locally adapted.

Adapting Chemical Knowledge to Local Circumstances during the Interbellum

Since the late nineteenth century, as mentioned above, Dutch agriculture had been characterized by the growing use of artificial fertilizers. Guano (bird excrement with a high content of nitrogen, phosphate and potassium) and nitrogen-rich saltpetre were imported in increasing quantities from Latin America, while the German states were the main source for potash salt, phosphates, Thomas slag (a phosphate-rich by-product of steel production) and ammonium sulphate (a nitrogen-rich byproduct of gas and coke production).[20] Dutch agriculture also became heavily dependent on chemically produced fertilizers after the discovery of the Haber-Bosch process in 1909, which introduced methods of chemically converting nitrogen into ammonia. The Netherlands rapidly became the largest user of nitrogen fertilizers in Europe: by 1928, Dutch farmers applied an average of 26.3 kilograms of nitrogen per hectare, considerably more than their counterparts in Belgium (19.3 kilograms) and Germany (13.9 kilograms).[21]

This high usage of artificial fertilizers can be explained by various changes in demand and supply. With artificial fertilizers, Dutch farmers could boost the productivity of their land, cease the labour-intensive task of collecting and spreading manure, and – most importantly – specialize in cash crop cultivation.[22] Important changes in supply were the emergence of supply cooperatives, which granted farmers access to international markets, and the infiltration of the Dutch fertilizer market by foreign fertilizer companies from the late nineteenth century, followed by the Dutch companies Hoogovens (a steel producer) and Dutch State Mines (DSM), which also marketed chemically produced nitrogen fertilizers from the 1930s.[23]

The increase in artificial fertilizer usage rapidly made Dutch agriculture more knowledge-intensive. In addition to the aforementioned fact that Dutch farmers had initial difficulties assessing the quality of their inputs, the application of artificial fertilizers required them to learn how to take a wide range of variables into account. An individual farmer needed to be familiar with, among other considerations, the chemical structure of the soil (its nutrient and acid content) and the groundwater level. Furthermore, an individual farmer also needed to have theoretical knowledge on the properties of different artificial fertilizers and awareness of the short- and long-term effects each artificial fertilizer could have. Although there is little available evidence, the historiography suggests that there were instances in which Dutch farmers, when unfamiliar with imported artificial fertilizers, applied the wrong type of fertilizer, used too much fertilizer on a given plot of land or accidentally let fertilizer wash away into the groundwater.[24]

Knowledge was disseminated by supply cooperatives and fertilizer companies. The German company Kalisyndikat was the first to open an information agency in the Netherlands (in Utrecht in 1904) and was soon followed by other fertilizer companies, which organized lectures, distributed brochures, set up experimental fields and published the results of their experiments in agricultural periodicals. However, these efforts proved inadequate.[25] The fertilizer companies lacked location-specific knowledge on soil types and other local characteristics, and the supply cooperatives were often too small in scale and unprofessionally organized to establish effective knowledge networks.[26] Nevertheless, the collaboration between fertilizer companies, supply cooperatives and agricultural consultants does suggest that agricultural consultants were expected to play an important role in the diffusion of knowledge on artificial fertilizers.[27] We will use the example of one agricultural consultant to examine how this was achieved in practice.

The excellent recordkeeping of Jacob Elema, the main agricultural consultant in the province of Drenthe from 1895 to 1936, allows us to closely track his day-to-day work. Most of Drenthe is located in the eastern sandy regions, which were characterized by small-scale farming until at least the mid-twentieth century.[28] Elema's time in Drenthe coincided with the integration of the province's agriculture into international markets (through infrastructural improvements) and its increasing specialization, particularly in potato production. For the small-scale farmers of Drenthe, this usually meant the intensified use of inputs, especially artificial fertilizers.[29]

In the early years after his arrival in Drenthe in 1895, Elema was received with scepticism. He wrote in his notebook that although some of his interlocutors were 'developed', 'awake', 'ambitious' or had 'started to accept new ideas', others were 'distrustful', 'underdeveloped', 'conservative' or 'had the wrong spirit'.[30] In particular, older farmers saw no need to apply artificial fertilizers and deemed Elema's lectures on chemistry too theoretical.[31]

In order to gain the trust of the local farming population, Elema organized lectures, assisted with the establishment of agricultural organizations and set up stands at village markets to initiate closer contact with local farmers. The aim of his lectures, Elema wrote to his superiors, was to acquaint his audiences with 'rational fertilizing', with the exact content of each lecture depending on the local 'characteristics of the soil and the farm'.[32] Although his lectures initially concerned general aspects of fertilizing, in later years he focused on nitrogen, phosphorus, potassium or chalk more specifically.[33]

Elema also set up a network of experimental fields all over his district to study a variety of soil types. Special 'demonstration' fields (*demonstratievelden*) provided visual evidence of the effects of artificial fertilizers, while 'observation' experiments (*observatieproeven*) were conducted to evaluate the effects of imported fertilizers on the soils of Drenthe and to assess if they were locally suitable.[34] Even foreign companies, most notably IG Farben, wrote to Elema to ask him to test their products on Drenthe's soils.[35]

Elema's experimental fields were managed by a network of local schoolteachers whom he had trained to become certified agronomy teachers and experts on farming conditions in their respective villages.[36] Their training curriculum was concentrated on the application of artificial fertilizers. Out of a total of 231 teaching hours, 99 hours were spent on chemistry, 30 hours on fertilizing and another 30 hours on 'soil knowledge', a course intended to familiarize the schoolteachers with local soil conditions.[37]

With his network of agronomy teachers, Elema was able to expand agricultural education in Drenthe. By 1918, there were twenty-three winter courses for adult farmers with a total of 390 students, twenty-one winter courses for children with 285 learners, five courses (concentrating on home economics) for women with ninety-seven students, and one course for new agronomy teachers with ten students.[38] Drenthe's first winter school opened in 1907 and was followed by others, culminating in a total of twenty-five agricultural schools in the province by the early 1950s. Although it is difficult to assess the impact of agricultural education, a 1955 survey found that approximately 70 per cent of Drenthe farmers below the age of thirty-five had attended some form of agricultural education.[39]

Elema's work in Drenthe illustrates how agricultural consultants established connections between local farmers and the wider agricultural knowledge infrastructure. It also exemplifies the role of consultants in the expansion of agricultural education, as well as the intersection between agricultural intensification, knowledge demand and the expansion of agricultural knowledge infrastructure at the local level. As a consequence of the province's integration into international markets, farmers in Drenthe were pushed towards specialization and intensification. For the many farmers who owned small plots of land with relatively unfertile, sandy soil, increasing land productivity was the main aim, but this required the application of large quantities of artificial fertilizer. The agricultural knowledge infrastructure within Drenthe during Elema's consultancy was organized in such a way that local conditions, which were of particular importance for fertilizing, could be taken into account, especially the ecological constraints faced by local farmers. In the decade after the Second World War, by contrast, Dutch agriculture underwent nationwide structural change that was directed towards increasing labour productivity growth and upscaling the sector. As the following section will show, this had a profound impact on the country's agricultural knowledge infrastructure.

Dutch Agriculture and the Postwar Agricultural Knowledge Infrastructure, 1945–70

During the postwar boom, the Dutch economy grew rapidly, corresponding with the general trend in Western Europe. Especially in the industrial sector, wages and employment rose swiftly. With wage growth and labour productivity in the agricultural sector not keeping pace with the industrial sector, agricultural producers were faced with labour shortages. Agricultural workers sought employment in the industrial sector, where they could obtain higher wages and enjoy more favourable working conditions.[40] Government agricultural policy tried to maintain the income of farmers by awarding producer price subsidies while also targeting improved productivity. However, in order to remain competitive with other sectors of the economy, farmers had to produce more, despite the decreasing labour power at their disposal. After extensive discussions, Dutch policy-makers and politicians reached a consensus in the late 1950s that 'structural change' (*structuurverandering*) needed to be the aim of agricultural policy. In addition to producer price policies, which from 1963 onwards were enacted at the European level through the framework of the Common Agricultural Policy (CAP), 'structural change policy' (*structuurbeleid*) became one of the two pillars of agricultural policy in the Netherlands. Compared with other European Community (EC) countries, structural change in agriculture was more urgent in the Netherlands, with the corresponding result that scale expansion and capital intensification also became more pronounced.

The introduction of the structural change policy marked a sea change in Dutch agricultural policy. During the interbellum, the government had supported small-scale farms; now, it went in the opposite direction by stimulating scale expansion and capital intensification.[41] Especially in the Dutch collective memory, Sicco Mansholt, the Netherlands' first postwar Minister of Agriculture (1945–58) and a future President of the European Commission (1972–73), is considered the symbol of this structural change policy. Its long-term goals were higher incomes for farmers, low food prices for consumers and a strong export position.[42] However, given that many farmers were effectively forced to quit farming due to the rationalization that it entailed, it is remarkable that there was only limited opposition to the structural change policy. One explanation is that Dutch neocorporatist institutions facilitated close coordination between representatives from the agricultural sector and the government; it is illustrative that, from 1948 onwards, representatives from farmers' organizations held monthly meetings with Mansholt. Although a minority of small-scale farmers organized in opposition as 'Free Farmers' and subsequently founded the Farmers' Party (Boerenpartij), this had little impact on the neocorporatist style of decision-making.[43]

Implementing structural change on the ground demanded new knowledge and skills from farmers. As agriculture is bound to regional and local environmental, cultural and economic conditions, knowledge on farming methods needed to be adapted to these specific circumstances. Moreover, operating traditional small-scale farms was a fundamentally different responsibility in comparison to running larger and more capital-intensive farms. A combination of agricultural education and the work of the Dutch Agricultural Extension Service (Rijkslandbouwvoorlichtingsdienst [RLVD]) was intended to equip Dutch farmers with the tools for knowledge-driven adaptation. This expansion of the regional knowledge infrastructure was visible in the growth in the number of RLVD employees from 500 in 1946 to 1,420 in 1950 and 1,580 in 1956.[44] Similarly, a rising number of students were enrolling at agricultural schools, which offered more extensive programmes in comparison to the prewar years.[45]

As was underscored in the introduction to this chapter, earlier studies focused in particular on the role of national institutions and neglected the contribution of regional organizations to agricultural innovation. However, the importance of the regional level can be observed in the large number of regionally organized agricultural organizations and cooperatives that were active from the second half of the nineteenth century onwards.[46] Private agricultural societies, which functioned independently across the length and breadth of the country, were active in developing and disseminating knowledge. A similar role was played by the regional branches of national agricultural organizations, such as the Protestant Christelijke Boeren en Tuinders Bond (Christian Farmers' and Horticulturalists' Union [CBTB]) or the Roman Catholic Aartsdiocesane Boeren- en Tuinders Bond (Roman Catholic Archdiocesan Farmers' and Horticulturalists' Union [ABTB]). Apart from acting as lobby groups for farmers, these organizations developed their own education, research and extension services.[47] There were also strong links between farmers and food processing cooperatives, constituting dense regional networks in which knowledge on the production and processing of specific products was exchanged. In the dairy sector, for instance, cooperative dairy factories were united under regional organizations that conducted research and development, marketing, lobbying and employee training.[48] These regional organizations supported the structural change policy. They also contributed to the development and introduction of new technologies, thereby facilitating scale expansion and rationalization of farms. In general, resistance to structural change and new technologies was limited in scope. Indeed, there was more resistance from representatives of the agricultural sector to the government's producer price policies, which affected the short-term income of farmers.[49]

The importance of the regional level was also recognized by the central government, which divided the RLVD into multiple regional branches. This allowed for the adaptation of its activities to regional and local needs. Moreover, it enabled agricultural educators to develop close relationships with farmers within a specific area. However, despite the RLVD's regional structure, knowledge transfer continued in a predominantly top-down manner: consultants shared their insights with individual farmers during regular visits to farms and gave lectures to groups of farmers. Interestingly, contemporary research into Dutch agricultural extension methods pointed to the limitations of top-down education, advising consultants instead to be modest, build personal relationships with farmers and listen to their ideas.[50] Bottom-up methods of disseminating knowledge were also being increasingly institutionalized. In the late 1940s and the 1950s, the RLVD promoted the foundation of agricultural extension societies (*verenigingen voor bedrijfsvoorlichting* [VVBs]), which constituted an additional institutional layer for the exchange of knowledge between farmers and consultants. Farmers within a small, designated area – often a subarea of a regional RLVD branch – could become members of their local district societies. The goal of these societies was to disseminate knowledge on topics such as farming methods and to distribute new technologies.[51] During regular meetings, members could address their questions on various aspects of agricultural modernization to the RLVD agricultural consultants as well as discuss these issues with their colleagues. Meanwhile, the consultants could reach multiple farmers at the same time without needing to visit their farms individually.[52] As this section has shown, the structural change policy was thus accompanied by a profound expansion and intensification of the agricultural knowledge infrastructure.

Tools of Rationalization (1): Business Economics

From the perspective of a Dutch farmer in the 1950s or 1960s, adaptation to exogenous factors (such as changes in the labour market or price policies or the introduction of the structural change policy) demanded strategic decision-making. A farmer's ability to adapt was constrained by, among other factors, the opportunities that a farm offered for scale expansion or the availability of new technologies.[53] The biggest constraint for adaptation was that, at least until the 1960s, most farms were too small for extensive mechanization. In contrast to larger farms, their low profit margins simply could not support large-scale investment in new technologies.[54] Although scale expansion was considered the most viable option for achieving mechanization by policymakers, this could not be realized overnight. Unlike in the industrial sector, mergers were not a realistic option in the primary sector, in which family-owned and family-operated farms predominated. As available land is scarce in the Netherlands, the creation of larger production units required a significant share of Dutch farmers to sell their farms, forcing them either to find another job or go into retirement. From 1964 onwards, the structural change policy subsidized farmers who were willing to sell their farms.[55] However, as the impact of government subsidies was limited, the outflow of farmers largely depended on there being sufficient willing sellers with other reasons for wanting to leave the farming sector.

Despite the obstacles to realizing scale expansion, the need for productivity growth became more urgent in the 1950s as the cost of labour increased and the government's price support policies guaranteed progressively lower prices each year. With structural change not immediately realizable, productivity growth – whether in the form of land or labour productivity – initially had to be achieved on relatively small-sized farms. At first, agricultural consultants and educators proposed a combination of limited farm mechanization and rationalization. It was at this point that knowledge – in the form of business economics and scientific management – that had originally been developed and applied abroad, especially in Germany and the United States, was introduced in the Netherlands. Before analysing the body of knowledge associated with scientific management in the following section, we first focus on the application of business economics in postwar Dutch agriculture.

In the postwar period, rational and quantitative analysis of farming became increasingly common in the Netherlands. The application of business economics in agricultural accounting, in which a farm's individual revenues and expenses were meticulously recorded, was seen by agricultural extension officers as an important tool for increasing farm efficiency.[56] Whereas farmers had traditionally spent most of their time working on the land and with their livestock, office work was now becoming more and more important. Often encouraged and supported by agricultural extension workers and agricultural organizations, a growing group of farmers were analysing the performance of their farms through the lens of business economics. Business economics, whose application had been widespread in the US industrial sector since the nineteenth century, was increasingly applied in US agriculture from the beginning of the twentieth century.[57] However, in the Netherlands, its introduction was delayed. It was only with the application of business economic analysis in the dairy industry in the 1950s that business economics received significant attention in agriculture. The Agricultural Economic Institute (Landbouw Economisch Instituut [LEI]), a national institute focused on economic analysis for the agricultural sector that was founded in 1940, contributed to the dissemination of business economics, initially by importing knowledge that had been produced in other countries. Annual LEI reports reference visits by foreign experts to the organization's headquarters as well as multiple study trips by its employees to, among other countries, Denmark, the United States and Germany.[58]

The function of business economics was twofold. On the one hand, it enabled the implementation of economies of scale. Like the managers of the Netherlands' increasingly large factories, Dutch farmers had to deal with the growing complexity of their businesses. James R. Beniger has described the increasing complexity of companies as a result of ever-denser information flows. According to Beniger, a large company can be better managed through more efficient information processing – first by its bureaucracy and later by computers – and by reducing the amount of information to complete a given task (rationalization).[59] The development and application of business economics and scientific management corresponded to both improvement in the management of companies and the successful completion of rationalization processes, thereby setting the conditions for subsequent scale expansion. Until at least the end of the 1960s, rationalization on relatively small-scale farms offered an alternative to the more difficult task of achieving economies of scale. During this period, business accounting and analysis were promoted by the central government with the aim of achieving higher productivity within existing company structures.

The application of business economics to improve the performance of farms meant that analytical methods were needed to interpret raw data from individual farms. Most attention was paid to methods that could provide insights into income generation and farm management. During the 1940s, a sophisticated method for calculating costs in the agricultural sector was developed by the LEI. In 1948, this research was published in a dissertation by its director, Jan Horring. Inspired by methods developed in the United States, he devised a method for estimating the cost of various aspects of agricultural production processes. His aim was to estimate potential profit, an insight that could be used to guide the selection of the most profitable business operations.[60] A method for comparing profits was also developed at the Central Accounting Cooperative (Centrale Coöperatieve Landbouwboekhouding [CCLB]), which was based in the northern province of Friesland. This research resulted in a dissertation by its director, Anne Vondeling, a future Dutch Minister of Agriculture (1958), who like Horring obtained his doctorate in 1948. His underlying idea was that the performance of individual farms could only be evaluated properly in relation to reliable data on the performance of comparable businesses. After all, a farm's commercial performance largely depended on variables such as specialization (dairy, mixed or arable farming) and soil type (such as clay or sand).[61]

However, the main challenge in the application of business economics was that only a small proportion of farmers maintained business accounts in the 1940s. Reliable business economic data were thus not widely available. This problem was solved in two ways. First, agricultural consultants developed new methods for estimating the commercial performance of companies. This effectively circumvented the original problem: even without detailed accounts, advice could still be given on more efficient farm management.[62] A second, more accurate method was to analyse the accounts required for taxation, which were already maintained by a majority of farmers. In 1955, a national advisory committee drew up guidelines to ensure that sufficient data for conducting business economic analyses were generated in the accounting process.[63]

When considering the dissemination of knowledge to farmers, the regional and local levels become more relevant. Unfortunately, few written sources offer the perspective of farmers. The written sources produced by (semi-)government organizations nevertheless provide insights into networks connecting the global and national with the regional and local levels. RLVD advisers visited farms regularly, often at the request of farmers, to evaluate the results of their business economic analyses, frequently helping to design multiyear business plans on the basis thereof.[64] The RLVD also organized courses on business economics. Nevertheless, due to the limited number of extension workers, the RLVD and similar organizations were unable to provide advice to each farmer individually. Agricultural extension societies and business study groups, which were established from the late 1940s onwards, contributed to the dissemination of business economic knowledge at the local level. The RLVD used the VVBs to disseminate knowledge on different subjects, of which business economics was one of the most prominent, in the late 1950s and early 1960s. In southwestern Friesland, for instance, local VVBs organized their own programmes for farmers wishing to improve the management of their farms through the application of business economics.[65] Farmers also founded their own study groups across the Netherlands in which they shared, analysed and discussed their account books in an informal way with the aim of improving the profitability of their farms.[66]

Tools of Rationalization (2): Business Organizational Knowledge

In relation to the rationalization of work techniques, the Netherlands' agricultural sector lagged behind both the Dutch industrial sector and other European countries' agricultural sectors.[67] Fitzgerald has shown for the United States that the scientific analysis of working methods, which was first developed by Frederick Taylor, was first applied in agriculture during the 1920s and 1930s.[68] Auderset (in this volume) details how an extensive research field into agricultural methods developed in Germany during the interbellum. In the Netherlands, research on and attention to 'work organization' (*arbeidsorganisatie*) was limited during the interwar years. Although Taylorism was linked to agriculture for the first time in 1919, it was only in 1931 that the first extensive report was published by A.P. van den Ban. As a prominent agricultural consultant and professor at Wageningen University, he had visited Germany in the late 1920s to obtain the latest knowledge. However, in the Netherlands, detailed research into work organization was only initiated directly after the Second World War.[69]

In the autumn of 1946, H.T. Tjallema, the director of arable and pasture farming at the Ministry of Agriculture, ordered an explanatory study into the 'extent [to which] the industry's method of studying the working method in agriculture could be applied'. Conducted in collaboration with the Amsterdam-based consultancy firm Bosboom and Hegener, which had extensive experience in organizational research, the study initially concentrated on the harvesting of potatoes. By measuring the duration of individual tasks in order to calculate standard times for each task, it was observed that weather conditions, the composition of the soil and the size of the potato tubers were all factors that impacted on the results. The study's authors therefore struggled to identify a general list of the most efficient agricultural working methods, but professed their hope that the results could be used to simplify the production process, thereby making it more efficient. However, the exploratory study's ultimate conclusion was that Taylorism could not be applied to agriculture 'because it involves completely different activities, involving a very large number of variable factors'.[70]

Although the Netherlands' first experiences with business organizational research in agriculture were not entirely positive, the central government decided that further research was required. A more extensive government-funded study was thus launched in 1948. After six researchers completed a course offered by Bosboom and Hegener, they recorded time observations at various locations across the country. Their long-term strategy was to collect results over a period of several years that would allow for general recommendations on the most efficient working methods. This research was soon concentrated at the Institute for Agricultural Technology and Rationalization (Instituut voor Landbouwtechniek en Rationalisatie [ILR]), which had been founded in 1949. Although the ILR was based in Wageningen – and was thus located at the heart of the national agricultural knowledge infrastructure – most of this research was conducted at the Oostwaardhoeve experimental farm in the Wieringermeerpolder region. As one of the most recent and largest *polders* (areas of reclaimed land), the Wieringermeerpolder constituted an example of a rationally planned agricultural area. Unlike for most business organizational research studies in agriculture, which are typically conducted within a small area, the wide extent of this data collection area produced generalizable results.[71] Apart from relying on the expertise of Dutch consultancy firms, representatives from participating agricultural research institutes and Tjallema, who was representing the Ministry of Agriculture, embarked on a three-month stay in the United States in 1950. They visited ten Eastern and

Midwestern states, collecting an extensive amount of information on farm rationalization methods.[72]

Over the course of the 1950s, knowledge on business organizational research was concentrated at the ILR, from where a total of six thousand work studies were conducted from 1947 to 1957. Aspects of farming with the greatest potential for labour saving were prioritized, such as the milking of cows, the feeding and caretaking of livestock, and the harvesting of potatoes and grains.[73] A. Moens became the Netherlands' foremost expert in the field of business organizational research in the agricultural sector. He conducted his studies in Wageningen and joined the ILR in the early 1950s as head of its labour research department.[74] During the 1940s and 1950s, he published regularly on the subject of labour rationalization and was clearly inspired by the methods introduced by Frederick Taylor and his adherents in the industrial sector. 'In agriculture, what can we adopt from the principles of the modern industrial business organization?', Moens asked rhetorically in 1955. 'Our answer is: *everything*.'[75]

The ILR became part of an international knowledge network focused on the mechanization and rationalization of the agricultural sector. On the one hand, the ILR's researchers contributed to the global dissemination of knowledge on labour rationalization in the agricultural sector by sharing their insights with foreign colleagues. As is apparent from Table 6.1, foreign visitors were received regularly, both at the ILR headquarters in Wageningen and on the Oostwaardhoeve experimental farm.[76] On the other hand, the ILR functioned as an intermediary by serving as a conduit for knowledge originating from abroad that would be of benefit to Dutch farmers. Its employees regularly

Table 6.1. Incoming visitors to the ILR and outgoing study trips by ILR employees. Source: Annual Reports, ILR

Year	Wageningen Institute: Total Visitors	Wageningen Institute: Foreign Visitors	Oostwaard-hoeve: Total Visitors	Oostwaard-hoeve: Foreign Visitors	International 'Study Trips' by ILR Employees
1954	4,791		1,884		
1955	4,076		1,558	277	
1956	3,850		1,316	95	
1957	3,855		1,460	341	
1958	3,074		1,831	241	
1959	2,877	243	1,745	186	12
1960	2,357	499	1,105	164	21
1961	1,928	380	1,001	96	23
1962					24
1963					
1964		553			29

participated in international conferences and visited foreign research institutes and companies. Most visits were to other European countries, initially to Germany, but later also to France, the United Kingdom or Denmark. In 1963, two ILR employees travelled to the United States in order to obtain an impression of the state of the art in mechanization and rationalization. They produced an extensive report that was published in the Netherlands in 1964.[77] By this point, unlike in the late 1940s and early 1950s, methods of business organizational research had become popular in the Netherlands, which had become both a beneficiary and a source of transnational knowledge on this discipline globally.

From the second half of the 1950s, most research on working methods was conducted at the regional level. This claim is supported by evidence from the province of Friesland, for which extensive archival records from the regional agricultural extension services are available. Already in 1946–47, working hours on thirty-one farms had been recorded and analysed;[78] however, this did not yet constitute a business organizational study as per the ILR's method. Ten years later, the ILR established programmes for research focusing on a specific region, whether or not in collaboration with an RLVD regional department. The advantages of such regional research were, according to Moens, the wider dissemination of research methods and a further opportunity to test the ILR's conclusions.[79] In May 1956, a more extensive investigation was started on twelve Frisian pasture farms in which the RLVD and the ILR worked closely together 'to gain a clear understanding of the structure of the various organizational forms, in this case of the pasture farm and its consequences on the level of labour needs, costs, revenues and required labour effort', as the ILR declared in a 1962 report. Based on those companies that tracked time measurements for three years – the report boasted that 'about 200,000 working hours were recorded and determined'[80] – a multitude of tasks performed on Dutch farms were analysed and the impact of different forms of business organization on costs calculated.[81]

The regional studies made knowledge accessible to interested farmers and extension workers. Whereas information on working methods had often been confined to individual farms, where it spread as tacit knowledge by word of mouth, it was now being recorded and codified in written research. This meant that results became easier to transfer to other contexts, thereby contributing to their wider dissemination. According to extension workers, the sharing of knowledge on working methods ultimately contributed to an increase in productivity without the need for scale expansion or capital intensification. One report argued that the rationalization of working methods in dairy farming was an important objective that could contribute to boosting a farm's cattle herd or generating more time for other activities. In turn, this could lead to higher profits or the opportunity to operate a larger business with a smaller workforce.[82]

Conclusion

This chapter has analysed how transnational knowledge was adapted to specific local circumstances across the Netherlands from the late nineteenth century until the 1960s. This period witnessed a constant expansion of the Dutch knowledge infrastructure in the agricultural sector. Before the 1890s, there had been little state support for agricultural education or consultancy services. However, in the following decades, the need to support and sustain small farms drove the central government to create a knowledge infrastructure. Although this initially consisted of national organizations, which played a particularly important role in higher education as well as in research and development, there was subsequently a consistent focus on the local level until the 1960s. In this period, the production and top-down diffusion of knowledge by national organizations, such as the agricultural college in Wageningen, was no longer seen as efficient or desirable. The increasing number of local agricultural schools and the ever-smaller geographical districts to which agricultural consultants were assigned allowed for the consideration of local variations in farming practices and soil conditions. Moreover, local farmers' organizations, such as agricultural societies and the RLVD-initiated agricultural extension societies, further contributed to the wider dissemination of agricultural knowledge and its adaptation to local conditions.

This focus on the local production, dissemination and adaptation of knowledge in Dutch agriculture changed from the late 1960s as farming became increasingly detached from its erstwhile environmental constraints. Agricultural education and extension thus became structured in a way that minimized environmental differences between the Netherlands' various agricultural zones. The regional dimensions of the country's knowledge infrastructure gradually disappeared as agricultural extension services were reorganized (1970s–1980s) and privatized (1980s–1990s). Moreover, local farmers' organizations and regional branches of national organizations were merged under centralized national bodies.

There was another noteworthy shift after the Second World War, as the orientation of international knowledge transfers in Dutch agriculture broadened from a narrow focus on Germany to a European and transatlantic orientation. This can be partly explained by the new geopolitical world order of the Cold War, during which the Netherlands received Marshall Plan aid and became politically and culturally oriented towards the United States. However, there were also gradual changes in the demand for agricultural knowledge itself. Before and directly after the Second World War, Dutch agricultural policy had been directed towards the intensification of small-scale farming through the increased application of fertilizer. However, in the postwar period, improving labour productivity by means of scale expansion and mechanization became the main goal. Because these goals could not be realized in the short term, the Dutch knowledge infrastructure was initially focused on improving efficiency by applying business economics and scientific management techniques. This saw the knowledge infrastructure being expanded once more in an attempt to make small-scale farms viable through the introduction of new working methods. However, as the number of farms declined and capital intensification became a more important driver of productivity growth, the type of knowledge that was in demand shifted again with profound effects on the agricultural knowledge infrastructure.

In conclusion, the development of the Netherlands' agricultural knowledge infrastructure was the result of shifting priorities in Dutch agricultural policy. Until the 1940s, the country's knowledge infrastructure was aimed at enhancing land productivity through intensive fertilizing, which required a careful consideration of local conditions. After the Second World War, by contrast, productivity growth via scale expansion and mechanization became the main goal, an aim that was less dependent on the local context.

Ronald Plantinga was a lecturer and researcher at the University of Groningen and currently works at the Netherlands Environmental Assessment Agency. He wrote his doctoral thesis, which he defended in 2021, on post-Second World War transitions in Frisian dairy production. In his research, he focuses on rural history, environmental history and business history, with a special interest in Dutch regional and national policy.

Harm Zwarts is an assistant professor in economic and social history at the University of Groningen. He is interested in the intersection of economic and environmental history, with a special focus on energy transitions and agricultural development. In his doctoral thesis, defended at Wageningen University in 2021, Dr Harm Zwarts studied the historical development of Dutch agricultural innovation from 1870 to 1960.

Notes

1. On the Dutch context, see Faber, 'Het Nederlandse innovatiesysteem', 208–32; Davids, Lintsen and van Rooij, *Innovatie en kennisinfrastructuur*; Maat, 'Het innovatiesysteem', 233–62; Maat, 'Science Cultivating Practice'.
2. For a more detailed description of the various Dutch agricultural zones, see Zwarts, 'Knowledge, Networks, and Niches', 19–21.
3. Van der Poel, *Het landbouwonderwijs*, 13.
4. Ibid., 35–44.
5. From the 1880s to the beginning of the First World War, Dutch exports of vegetables, potato starch and beet sugar increased fivefold; see Zwarts, 'Knowledge, Networks, and Niches', 40–41.

6. As has been shown for neighbouring Belgium, which experienced a comparable specialization. See Blomme, *Economic Development*, 248.
7. We refer to artificial fertilizers as those produced via a chemical process or through extraction from mines. This does not include fertilizers originating from organic sources, such as manure or compost. Van Zanden, 'First Green Revolution', 216.
8. Grantham, 'Shifting Locus of Agricultural Innovation', 191–214. Jonathan Harwood has also argued that the fear of political upheaval among impoverished peasants was a motivation for some German states to improve agronomic research and agricultural education; see Harwood, 'Why Did Nineteenth-Century States Establish Agricultural Research Stations?', 246.
9. From 'Handelingen Tweede Kamer 1887–1888, 40e zitting, zitting van donderdag 22 december 1887', 627, Dutch Government website. Retrieved 5 November 2022 from re pository.overheid.nl/frbr/sgd/18871888/000039381/1/pdf/SGD_18871888_0000138 .pdf.
10. Van der Haar, *Landbouwuniversiteit Wageningen*, 43–45, 54–57.
11. Porceddu and Rabbinge, 'Role of Research and Education', 1–13. For an overview of the many agricultural colleges in the German states, see the chapter 'Mapping the Institutional Landscape' in Harwood, *Technology's Dilemma*.
12. This paragraph is based on Zwarts, 'Knowledge, Networks, and Niches', 102–5.
13. 'Imkrimping van den Veestapel', *Nieuwsblad van Friesland*, 3 May 1933.
14. 'Op en om de boerderij', *Nieuwsblad van Friesland*, 13 May 1936.
15. On the situation in the German states, see Uekötter, *Die Wahrheit ist auf dem Feld*, 72–78, 334, 411.
16. Zuurbier, 'De besturing', 30–32.
17. Centraal Bureau voor de Statistiek, *De ontwikkeling van het onderwijs in Nederland*, 217.
18. Goudswaard, *Agrarisch onderwijs*, 171, 225, 246.
19. Van den Ban, 'Hoeveel boeren', 314–17.
20. Bieleman, *Boeren in Nederland*, 282; Smil, *Enriching the Earth*, 43–60.
21. Homburg, *Groeien door kunstmest*, 39–44.
22. Knibbe, 'Feed, Fertilizer and Agricultural Productivity', 55.
23. Homburg, *Groeien door kunstmest*, 30–32, 86.
24. Van Zanden, 'Mest en ploeg', 59–60.
25. Homburg, *Groeien door kunstmest*, 30–32, 86.
26. Zwarts, 'Knowledge, Networks, and Niches', 99–101.
27. On the importance of agricultural consultants for the spread of knowledge on artificial fertilizers, see Bieleman, *Boeren in Nederland*, 284; van Zanden, *De economische ontwikkeling*, 262.
28. In the 1910 Census, 52 per cent of farmers in Drenthe were categorized in the smallest property class, with a mere 1–5 hectares of land. See Bieleman, *Boeren op het Drentse zand*, 542–47.
29. Bieleman, 'De landbouw', 547–90.
30. Drents Archief (DA), Rijkslandbouwleraar/Rijkslandbouwconsulent voor Drenthe (RvD), access number 0154, inventory number 44, 'Boekjes en schriftjes met verzichten van door J. Elema gehouden landbouwlezingen, 1896–1937'.
31. Boekholt, 'De nieuwste tijd', 624–25.

32. Citations from DA, Rijkslandbouwleraar/Rijkslandbouwconsulent voor Drenthe (RvD), access number 0154, inventory number 9, Correspondence 1989, 'Verslag van de landbouwlezingen gehouden in den winter 1897/98 door den Rijkslandbouwleeraar voor Drenthe', 1.

33. Elema mentioned the topics of his lectures in his annual reports.

34. DA, Rijkslandbouwleraar/Rijkslandbouwconsulent voor Drenthe (RvD), access number 0154, inventory number 28, Correspondence 1931–33, 'Overzicht van de ant-woorden der landbouwconsulenten op de circulaire dd 9 September 1932 van den Inspecteur van den Landbouw' and 'Overzicht van de onderwerpen, waarvoor de con-sulenten veldonderzoek wenschelijk achten'.

35. DA, Rijkslandbouwleraar/Rijkslandbouwconsulent voor Drenthe (RvD), access number 0154, inventory number 27, 'Ingekomen stukken en kopieën van verzonden stukken 1927–1930'.

36. Boekholt, 'De nieuwste tijd', 624–25.

37. The remaining hours were spent on learning about botany, dairy production, cattle breeding and cattle feed. DA, Rijkslandbouwleraar/Rijkslandbouwconsulent voor Drenthe (RvD), access number 0154, inventory number 21, Correspondence 1914–17, 'Verslag over de opleidingscursus voor landbouwonderwijzers, 17 March 1915'.

38. DA, Rijkslandbouwleraar/Rijkslandbouwconsulent voor Drenthe (RvD), access number 0154, inventory number 21, Correspondence 1914–17, 'no. 581, untitled letter, 18 April 1917'.

39. Dekker, *Landbouwonderwijs in Drenthe*, 61.

40. Bieleman, *Boeren in Nederland*, 462–64; Brassley, Martiin and Pan-Montojo, 'Similar Means', 267–74.

41. Karel, *De maakbare boer*, 85–88.

42. Van Merriënboer, *Mansholt*.

43. De Groot and Bauwens, 'Vijftig jaar landbouwbeleid', 146–69; Krajenbrink, 'Het Landbouwschap'.

44. Zuurbier, 'De besturing', 51, 55.

45. Goudswaard, *Agrarisch Onderwijs*, 219, 319.

46. On the Netherlands, see Karel, *De maakbare boer*; Maat, 'Het innovatiesysteem', 233–62; Zuurbier, 'De besturing'. On international trends, see Flückiger, 'Mediators between the Industrial State and Agriculture', 267–88; Henke, *Cultivating Science*.

47. Apart from in numerous memorial books, the history of these organizations has been documented by van der Woude, *Op goede gronden*; Duffhues, *Voor een betere toekomst*; Smits, *Boeren met beleid*.

48. On the activities of these associations, see the Yearly Reports of the Koninklijke Nederlandse Zuivelbond (FNZ).

49. Krajenbrink, 'Het Landbouwschap', 146–50.

50. Van den Ban, *Boer en landbouwvoorlichting*, 135–38; Ministerie van Landbouw, 'Agrarische voorlichting'.

51. Tresoar, Leeuwarden (hereinafter T), Rijkslandbouwconsulentschap voor Zuid-Oost Friesland te Drachten, access number 56-05, inventory number 351, 'Het ontstaan en ontwikkeling van de Verenigingen voor Bedrijfsvoorlichting'.

52. Broekhuis, 'Verenigingen voor Bedrijfsvoorlichting', 112–14.

53. Landbouw Economisch Instituut, 'De Nederlandse landbouw', 51.

54. Rijssenbeek, 'De ballade van den boer', 155.
55. Van den Brink, 'Structuur in beweging', 115–53.
56. *Tien jaren Landbouw-Economisch Instituut*, 108.
57. Fitzgerald, *Every Farm*, 33–74; Auderset and Moser, *Die Agrarfrage*, 49–102.
58. Landbouw Economisch Instituut, Yearly Report, 1950; Landbouw Economisch Instituut, Yearly Report, 1952.
59. Beniger, *The Control Revolution*, 15.
60. Horring, *Methode van kostprijsberekening*.
61. Vondeling, *Bedrijfsvergelijking*, 32–34.
62. Appelhof, 'Technische voorlichting', 457–62; T, Rijkslandbouwconsulentschap voor Noord-Friesland te Leeuwarden 1936–69, access number 56-01, inv. 91, Circulaire bedrijfsvoorlichters, 1 September 1964; 'Eenvoudig benaderen van het bedrijfsresultaat: gemakkelijke methode van RLVD te Sneek'. *Friesch Landbouwblad* 58 (1961), 1340; 'Methode voor benaderen bedrijfsresultaten op weidebedrijven', *Friese Koerier*, 14 November 1961.
63. T, Rijkslandbouwconsulentschap voor Zuid-West Friesland te Sneek 1943–69, access number 56-02, inv. 356, 'Rapport No. I van de landelijke adviescommissie voor bedrijfseconomische analyse. De mogelijkheid om fiscale boekhoudingen van agrarische bedrijven dienstbaar te maken aan de bedrijfsvoorlichting'.
64. See the following Dutch handbook on agricultural extension: Ministerie van Landbouw, 'Agrarische voorlichting', 127–40.
65. T, toegang 56-05, inv. 2, 'Jaarverslag van de Dienst 1959'; T, toegang 56-05, inv. 3, 'Jaarverslag van de dienst 1962.
66. Vondeling, *Bedrijfsvergelijking*, 38, 157. On the specific example of Groningen, see Groninger Maatschappij van Landbouw and Rijkslandbouwconsulent voor Noordelijk-Groningen, *Verslagen van de Landbouw-Bedrijfsstudiegroepen*.
67. Vermij, 'Schaalvergroting', 114.
68. Fitzgerald, *Every Farm*, 88–93.
69. Burgers, 'Vakonderwijs aan den landarbeider', 106–11; van den Ban, *De beteekenis*.
70. Huisman, 'De bestudering van arbeidsmethoden', 369–72.
71. Moens, 'Onderzoek en voorlichting', 76; Corstiaensen and Moens, 'Het onderzoek van arbeidsmethoden', 457–61.
72. Corstiaensen et al., *Farm Management*.
73. Moens, 'Onderzoek en voorlichting', 76.
74. 'Prof. Dr. ir. A. Moens (1922–2003)', *Reformatorisch Dagblad*, 6 May 2003.
75. Moens, 'Arbeidsmethoden en de organisatie van het werk', 543–48.
76. Yearly Reports ILR 1954–64.
77. Postuma and Coolman, *Aspekten van de mechanisatie*.
78. Directie van Landbouw, 'Onderzoekingen, waarnemingen en berekeningen', 26–27.
79. Moens, 'Onderzoek en voorlichting', 80.
80. Postma, *De arbeidsorganisatie*, 7.
81. In addition to its extensive research conducted in collaboration with the ILR, the RLVD also initiated a study on thirteen farms in southwestern Friesland in May 1959 (RLVD Z.W.Friesland, 'Samenvattend verslag van de L.E.I. tijdschrijfbedrijven over de zomer 1959' [T, access number 56-02, inv. 358]).
82. Postma, *De Arbeidsorganisatie*, 13.

Bibliography

Appelhof, G.J. 'Technische voorlichting + economische voorlichting = bedrijfsvoorlichting'. *Landbouwvoorlichting* (1957), 457–62.

Auderset, Juri, and Peter Moser. *Die Agrarfrage in der Industriegesellschaft: Wissenskulturen, Machtverhältnisse und Natürliche Ressourcen in der Agrarisch-Industriellen Wissensgesellschaft (1850–1950)*. Göttingen: Vandenhoeck & Ruprecht, 2018.

Beniger, James. *The Control Revolution: Technological and Economic Origins of the Information Society*. Cambridge, MA: Harvard University Press, 1986.

Bieleman, Jan. 'De landbouw in de periode 1850–1945', in J. Heringa et al. (eds), *Geschiedenis van Drenthe*, 2nd edn (Meppel: Boom, 1986), 547–90.

——. *Boeren op het Drentse zand, 1600–1910: Een nieuwe visie op de 'oude' landbouw*. Wageningen: Afdeling Agrarische Geschiedenis, Landbouwuniversiteit, 1987.

——. *Boeren in Nederland: Geschiedenis van de landbouw 1500–2000*. Amsterdam: Boom, 2008.

Blomme, Jan. *The Economic Development of Belgian Agriculture 1880–1980: A Quantitative and Qualitative Analysis*. Leuven: Leuven University Press, 1992.

Boekholt, P.T.F.M. 'De nieuwste tijd 1850–1945', in J. Heringa et al. (eds), *Geschiedenis van Drenthe*, 2nd edn (Meppel: Boom, 1986), 591–678.

Brassley, Paul, Carin Martiin and Juan Pan-Montojo. 'Similar Means to Secure Food Supplies across Western Europe: A Conclusion', in Paul Brassley, Carin Martiin and Juan Pan-Montojo (eds), *Agriculture in Capitalist Europe, 1945–1960* (Abingdon: Routledge, 2016), 267–74.

Broekhuis, E. 'Verenigingen voor bedrijfsvoorlichting'. *Maandblad voor de Landbouwvoorlichtingsdienst* 4 (1947), 665–67.

Burgers, P.H. 'Vakonderwijs aan den landarbeider'. *Cultura* 31 (1919), 106–11.

Centraal Bureau voor de Statistiek. 'De ontwikkeling van het onderwijs in Nederland'. The Hague: 1966.

Corstiaensen W.P.M., and A. Moens, 'Het onderzoek van arbeidsmethoden in de landbouw'. *Maandblad voor de Landbouwvoorlichtingsdienst* 6 (1949), 457–61.

Corstiaensen W.P.M. et al. *Farm management en work simplification in de Verenigde Staten van Amerika: Verslag van een Studiereis in het N.O. Deel van de Verenigde Staten*. The Hague: Landbouw-Economisch Instituut, 1950.

Davids, Mila, Harry Lintsen and Arjan van Rooij. *Innovatie en Kennisinfrastructuur: Vele Wegen naar Vernieuwing*. Amsterdam: Boom, 2013.

De Groot, M.N., and A.L.G.M. Bauwens. 'Vijftig jaar landbouwbeleid in Nederland: consensus en conflict', in A.L.G.M. Bauwens, M.N. de Groot and K.J. Poppe (eds), *Agrarisch bestaan: beschouwingen bij vijftig jaar Landbouw-Economisch Instituut* (Assen: Van Gorcum, 1990), 146–69.

Dekker, H. *Landbouwonderwijs in Drenthe: kwantitatieve en kwalitatieve analyse van de belangstelling van de boerenzoons voor het landbouwonderwijs*. The Hague: Landbouw-Economisch Instituut, 1961.

Directie van Landbouw. 'Onderzoekingen, waarnemingen en berekeningen betreffende het heidebedrijf in Z.W. Friesland'. The Hague: 1947.

Duffhues, Ton. *Voor een betere toekomst: het werk van de Noordbrabantse Christelijke Boerenbond voor Bedrijf en Gezin, 1896–1996*. Nijmegen: Valkhof Pers, 1996.

Faber, Jasper. 'Het Nederlandse innovatiesysteem, 1870–1990'. *NEHA Jaarboek* 66 (2003), 208–32.

Fitzgerald, Deborah. *Every Farm a Factory: The Industrial Ideal in American Agriculture.* New Haven: Yale University Press, 2003.

Flückiger, Daniël. 'Mediators between the Industrial State and Agriculture: The Social Profile and Professional Activities of Agronomists in Switzerland, 1871–2007', in Peter Moser and Tony Varley (eds), *Integration through Subordination: The Politics of Agricultural Modernisation in Industrial Europe* (Turnhout: Brepols, 2013), 267–88.

Goudswaard, N.B. *Agrarisch onderwijs in Nederland, 1783–1983.* Culemborg: Educaboek, 1986.

Grantham, George. 'The Shifting Locus of Agricultural Innovation in Nineteenth-Century Europe: The Case of Agricultural Experiment Stations', in Gary Saxonhouse and Gavin Wright (eds), *Technique, Spirit and Form in the Making of the Modern Economies: Essays in Honor of William N. Parker* (Greenwich, CT: Jai Press, 1984), 191–214.

Groninger Maatschappij van Landbouw and Rijkslandbouwconsulent voor Noordelijk-Groningen. *Verslagen van de Landbouw-Bedrijfsstudiegroepen in het gebied der Groninger Maatschappij van Landbouw.*

Harwood, Johnathan. *Technology's Dilemma: Agricultural Colleges between Science and Practice in Germany, 1860–1934.* Oxford: Peter Lang, 2005.

———. 'Why Did Nineteenth-Century States Establish Agricultural Research Stations? The Origins of the South German Plant-Breeding Stations, c. 1900', in Peter Moser and Tony Varley (eds), *Integration through Subordination: The Politics of Agricultural Modernisation in Industrial Europe* (Turnhout: Brepols, 2013), 245–66.

Henke, Christopher. *Cultivating Science, Harvesting Power: Science and Industrial Agriculture in California: Inside Technology.* Cambridge, MA: MIT Press, 2008.

Homburg, Ernst. *Groeien door kunstmest: DSM Agro 1929–2004.* Hilversum: Verloren, 2004.

Horring, J. *Methode van kostprijsberekening in de landbouw.* Emmen: Ten Kate, 1948.

Huisman, L.H. 'De bestudering van arbeidsmethoden in de landbouw'. *Maandblad voor de Landbouwvoorlichtingsdienst* 4 (1947), 369–72.

Karel, Erwin. *De maakbare boer: streekverbetering als instrument van het Nederlandse landbouwbeleid 1953–1970.* Groningen and Wageningen: Nederlands Agronomisch Historisch Instituut, 2005.

Knibbe, Merijn. 'Feed, Fertilizer and Agricultural Productivity in the Netherlands, 1880–1930'. *Agricultural History* 74(1) (2000), 39–57.

Krajenbrink, E.J. 'Het Landbouwschap: "zelfgedragen verantwoordelijkheid" in de land- en tuinbouw 1945–2001', Ph.D. dissertation. Groningen: University of Groningen, 2005.

Landbouw-Economisch Instituut. 'De Nederlandse landbouw in een groeiende econo-mie: uitgave ter gelegenheid van het 25-jarig bestaan van het Landbouw-Economisch Instituut'. The Hague: 1965.

Maat, Harro. 'Science Cultivating Practice: A History of Agricultural Science in the Netherlands and Its Colonies, 1863–1986', Ph.D. dissertation. Wageningen: Wageningen University, 2001.

———. 'Het innovatiesysteem voor de Nederlandse landbouw'. *NEHA Jaarboek* 66 (2003), 233–62.

Ministerie van Landbouw en Visserij – Directie van de Landbouw. 'Agrarische voorlichting'. The Hague: 1961.

Moens, A. 'Arbeidsmethoden en de organisatie van het werk'. *Landbouwvoorlichting* 12 (1955), 543–48.

———. 'Onderzoek en voorlichting op het gebied van arbeidstechniek en arbeidsorganisatie III'. *Landbouwvoorlichting* 15(2) (1958), 75–82.

Porceddu, Enrico, and Rudy Rabbinge. 'Role of Research and Education in the Development of Agriculture in Europe'. *European Journal of Agronomy* 7 (1997), 1–13.

Postma, G. *De arbeidsorganisatie in het weidebedrijf: resultaten van een driejarig organisatie-onderzoek op 10 klei-weidebedrijven in Friesland*. Wageningen: Instituut voor Landbouwtechniek en Rationalisatie, 1962.

Postuma, H.H., and F. Coolman. *Aspekten van de mechanisatie en rationalisatie van de landbouw in de V.S. Verslag van een studiereis naar de Verenigde Staten van Amerika*. Wageningen: Instituut voor Landbouwtechniek en Rationalisatie, 1964.

Rijssenbeek, T.C.J.M. 'De ballade van den boer'. *Veeteelt en Zuivelberichten* 8 (1965), 155–64.

Smil, Vaclav. *Enriching the Earth: Fritz Haber, Carl Bosch, and the Transformation of World Food Production*. Cambridge, MA: MIT Press, 2001.

Smits, Mari. *Boeren met beleid: honderd jaar Katholieke Nederlandse Boeren- en Tuindersbond, 1896–1996*. Nijmegen: Valkhof Pers, 1996.

Tien jaren Landbouw-Economisch Instituut: opbouw van het economisch onderzoek in landbouw, tuinbouw en visserij. Assen: Van Gorcum & Comp. N.V., 1950.

Uekötter, Frank. *Die Wahrheit ist auf dem Feld: Eine Wissensgeschichte der Deutschen Landwirtschaft*, 3rd edn. Göttingen: Vandenhoeck & Ruprecht, 2012.

Van den Ban, Anne Willem. 'Hoeveel boeren hebben landbouwonderwijs gevolgd?'. *Landbouwvoorlichting* (1956), 314–17.

———. *Boer en landbouwvoorlichting: de communicatie van nieuwe landbouwmethoden*. Assen: Van Gorkum & Comp. N.V., 1963.

Van den Ban, P.A. *De beteekenis van de landbouwarbeidsleer*. Wageningen: LEB Fonds, 1931.

Van den Brink, A. 'Structuur in beweging: Het landbouwstructuurbeleid in Nederland 1945–1985', Ph.D. dissertation. Wageningen: Wageningen University, 1990.

Van der Haar, Jan. *De geschiedenis van de Landbouwuniversiteit Wageningen. Deel I: van school naar hogeschool, 1873–1945*. Wageningen: Landbouwuniversiteit Wageningen, 1993.

Van der Poel, J.M.G. *Het landbouwonderwijs in Nederland tot 1918*. Wageningen: Centrum voor Landbouwpublikaties en Landbouwdocumentatie, 1976.

Van der Woude, Rolf. *Op goede gronden: geschiedenis van de Christelijke Boeren- en Tuindersbond (1918–1995)*. Hilversum: Verloren, 2001.

Van Merriënboer, Johan. *Mansholt: een biografie*. Gorredijk: Uitgeverij Noordboek, 2019.

Van Zanden, Jan Luiten. *De economische ontwikkeling van de Nederlandse landbouw in de negentiende eeuw, 1800–1914*. Wageningen: Afdeling Agrarische Geschiedenis, Landbouwhogeschool, 1985.

———. 'The First Green Revolution: The Growth of Production and Productivity in European Agriculture, 1870–1914'. *Economic History Review* 44(2) (1991), 215–39.

———. 'Mest en ploeg', in Harry Lintsen (ed.), *Geschiedenis van de techniek in Nederland: de wording van een moderne samenleving 1800–1890. Deel I: techniek en modernisering. landbouw en voeding* (Zutphen: Walburg Pers, 1992), 53–69.

Vermij, R. 'Schaalvergroting en haar edealen', in J.W. Schot, H.W. Lintsen, A. Rip and A.A. Albert de la Bruhèze (eds), *Techniek in Nederland in de twintigste eeuw. Deel VII* (Zutphen: Walburg Pers, 2003), 105–39.

Vondeling, Anne. *Bedrijfsvergelijking in de landbouw.* Wageningen: Veerman en Zonen, 1948.

Zuurbier, P.J. 'De besturing en organisatie van de Landbouwvoorlichtingsdienst', Ph.D. dissertation. Wageningen: Landbouwhogeschool Wageningen, 1984.

Zwarts, Harm. 'Knowledge, Networks, and Niches: Dutch Agricultural Innovation in an International Perspective, c. 1880–1970', Ph.D. dissertation. Wageningen: Wageningen University, 2021.

 CHAPTER 7

Missed Encounters and Unexpected Connections

*Transatlantic Crossings in the Study of Agricultural Work,
1920–60*

Juri Auderset

In 1927, Georg Derlitzki, the founding director of the Experiment Station for the Study of Agricultural Work in Pommritz, Saxony, addressed the audience at the International Congress of Scientific Management in Rome with a lecture on the significance of the recently proclaimed science of agricultural work.[1] 'It is incomprehensible', Derlitzki exclaimed, 'why so many institutions struggle to increase the efficiency of steam engines, internal combustion engines, while the scientific study of 'the most valuable motor' in farming, 'the human motor', had been wrongfully neglected. In Derlitzki's view, only the 'rationalization of agricultural work based on physiological principles' and an orchestrated attempt to study and improve farm work in order to 'raise the efficiency of the human motor' would help to tackle the multiple crises that were haunting European agriculture during the interwar years. These challenges included meeting the food security expectations of the growing nonagricultural, urban-industrial population by increasing agricultural labour productivity, coping with the pressing rural labour shortages, and raising the living standards and social welfare of destitute farming families and the rural working classes.[2] While many of his contemporaries associated the concept of 'work rationalization' with 'Americanism', Taylorism and scientific management,[3] Derlitzki remained sceptical towards the Taylor system on the grounds that it was tailored for the industrial workshop. Furthermore, in his eyes, it was above all a method to reduce costs and maximize output and profits on the back of workers. Instead, Derlitzki called for a science of agricultural work that was based on both physiological laboratory research and a thorough investigation of the specific and varying conditions and practices of this form of labour. Along these lines, the science of agricultural work not only promised to ease the physically demanding work of farm labourers, but also explicitly claimed to be of relevance for smallholders and peasant-owned family farms, where the divide between managing and working on a farm was extremely porous.

As Derlitzki's intervention indicates, agricultural work became a subject of intense scientific debate in the interwar years that brought together North American and European visions of work efficiency and agricultural labour. In Western and Central Europe, the recent experiences of food scarcity during the global agricultural crisis in the 1920s, the continuing shortages of agricultural labour and the increasing significance of the movement for the rationalization of work all contributed to the creation of new scientific institutions that focused on the study of agricultural work. The scientific optimization of agricultural working techniques was an integral part of broader attempts to shape the rural world in the age of 'industrialism' and 'high modernity'.[4] Inspired by the enthusiasm that spread throughout the Western world for Taylorism, scientific management, psychotechnics and work physiology,[5] a growing number of agricultural scientists, farmers, engineers and economists began to apply these industrially inspired epistemic models to agriculture and disseminated their findings via agricultural colleges and schools to a broader rural public.[6] However, at the same time, Derlitzki's critique of Taylorism also demonstrates that the study of agricultural work was far from a homogeneous body of scientific research; instead, it exhibited what Anson Rabinbach has aptly termed 'a field of contestation between different approaches to social knowledge'.[7]

Whereas the various endeavours to shape agricultural working practices using scientific knowledge eventually left their mark on European and North American farming alike, a closer look at the emergence, development and transnational entanglements of these visions of efficient agricultural labour also reveals a story of the missed encounters, unfulfilled expectations, asynchronous trajectories and unexpected connections on which this chapter will focus. As I will argue, the epistemic power and the practical significance of knowledge in agriculture does not grow out of scientific insights themselves, as tenacious as their claims to universal validity may be, but are instead highly dependent on the social, economic and cultural contexts into which such knowledge is introduced and in which it interacts and competes with other forms of knowledge. This approach emphasizes the social and economic importance of contested forms of knowledge in shaping agriculture's transformation in industrial-capitalist societies in the nineteenth and twentieth centuries.[8] It takes seriously the knowledge and experience of those who actually worked with animals, plants and the soil without understating the cultural and material force of what the farmer and writer Wendell Berry has called the 'industrial ideal' that had begun to shape the expectations of agricultural progress and modernity in the Western world from the mid-nineteenth century.[9]

By focusing on the circulation of knowledge relating to the study of farm labour, this chapter investigates the transnational entanglements that have shaped key debates on the science of agricultural work. The transnational circulation of knowledge and practices is mirrored not only in the intense travelling of agriculturalists and the myriad accounts that they wrote in their attempts to understand the impacts of capitalist industrialization on agriculture in different societies around the world,[10] but also in the proliferation of international research institutes and initiatives. As Daniel T. Rodgers has shown in his book *Atlantic Crossings*, the historical exploration of the connections between the industrializing countries of the late nineteenth and early twentieth centuries provides insights into 'a largely forgotten world of transnational borrowings and imitation, adaptation and transformation' in which rural reform and agricultural restructuring enjoyed a prominent place.[11]

As I will argue in this chapter, the scientific investigation of agricultural work was one of the threads – albeit frayed and twisted in its ambiguity – that made up this web of transnational connections. The question of whether the knowledge emerging from the scientific study of farm work actually had an impact on agricultural debates and practices was a highly contested and contingent issue. Unquestionably, scientific knowledge on agricultural work circulated widely and zigzagged across the Atlantic; however, as the transatlantic history of farm labour studies shows, this field of knowledge could also be ignored or deemed irrelevant in one particular context, only to become significant under different social and economic circumstances in another. Accordingly, as knowledge claims about the improvement of agricultural work circulated in time and space, they were constantly reinterpreted, redesigned and re-embedded within specific patterns of agricultural thought and practice. As such, every transfer of knowledge also implied a transformation of knowledge.[12] Moreover, scientific knowledge claims relating to agricultural work also faced highly variable, heterogeneous localized conditions that were somewhat at odds with the attempts to model agricultural work along industrial lines.[13] The embeddedness of agricultural work in specific and dynamic ecological systems contrasted sharply with the potential for standardizing working conditions and production processes on the industrial shop floor. While the determination to model agricultural labour on the paradigm of the factory was one of the driving forces shaping the transatlantic crossings that this chapter examines, some of the most interesting discussions in this transnational dialogue arose out of the tensions and frictions that were provoked by attempts to industrialize farm labour.

The first section of this chapter discusses the emergence of a science of agricultural work in interwar Europe and outlines some of the most pertinent epistemic problems that structured discourse on agricultural work in this context. The following section then switches across the Atlantic Ocean to elaborate on the Work Simplification Program, which was initiated in the United States in 1942. On the one hand, this programme drew on the investigations that had occupied European scholars in the field of farm work studies in the interwar years; on the other hand, it also remodelled and redesigned this knowledge according to the specific circumstances of the labour shortages that bedevilled US agriculture during the Second World War. The third section crosses the Atlantic once again to focus on the attempts to introduce the concept of farm work simplification to the reconstruction of postwar European agriculture.

From the 'Taylorization of Agriculture' to the 'Science of Agricultural Work' in Interwar Europe

In September 1919, Wilhelm Seedorf, a German agricultural economist and soon-to-be professor of agricultural economy at the University of Göttingen, gave a lecture before the German Agricultural Society (Deutsche Landwirtschafts-Gesellschaft) entitled 'The Perfection of Agricultural Labour and the Better Education of Agricultural Laborers with Special Consideration of the Taylor-System'. While the scientific study of agricultural chemistry and animal husbandry, the improvement of plants and the development of agricultural machinery had been thriving since the middle of the nineteenth century, Seedorf argued, research into agricultural work had not yet attracted the attention it deserved. Agricultural economists had investigated labour conditions on farms from time to time, he explained, but their surveys were primarily directed at 'counting the workforce' rather than actually analysing and improving working conditions and practices on farms. To raise the efficiency of agricultural labour, he urged, a transfer of ideas from North America to Europe and from the industrial shop floor to the farm was needed, and it was Frederick W. Taylor's scientific management that he suggested as the prime source of inspiration. 'Serious attempts to apply Taylor's ideas to American agriculture have so far not been undertaken', he reported, '[but] Taylor's thoughts contain such a wealth of inspiration that we have every reason to make ourselves familiar with them.'[14]

Seedorf's lecture was only one of many contributions that proposed the application of Taylorist principles to agriculture in the late 1910s and early 1920s. In fact, Taylorism and the vision of a factory-like organized farm had captured the imagination of numerous agricultural economists who were struggling to find remedies for the dislocations caused by the First World War in the sphere of agricultural production. Moreover, a shortage of farm labour had been addressed as a serious challenge for Western and Central European agriculture ever since the beginning of the rural exodus and the 'flight from the land' that accompanied the process of industrialization from the mid-nineteenth century onwards.[15] Agricultural associations, farmers' organizations and representatives of the early social sciences, such as the Verein für

Socialpolitik (German Economic Association), regularly pointed to the problem of the 'rural labour question', with Max Weber being only the most prominent contributor to these debates.[16] Taylorism seemed to offer at least a partial
solution to such concerns. Konrad von Meyenburg, a Swiss engineer who had
visited Taylor several times in the early 1890s, began to call for the application
of Taylorist principles to agriculture in as early as 1905.[17] In 1916, Ernst Laur
used his reputation as one of the leading agricultural economists of the time
to introduce Taylor's ideas on scientific management to agricultural circles in
Switzerland. While Laur was somewhat sceptical of this endeavour and pon-
dered that agricultural work could hardly be 'organized like in a factory', he
nevertheless saw Taylor's writings as an important inspiration for farmers and
agricultural reformers who were seeking to 'render numerous tasks more productive'.[18] A few years later, in 1921, Georg Derlitzki wrote an important article
on 'The Taylor System and its Application to Agriculture'. In the same vein as
Laur, Derlitzki argued that although Taylorism offered suggestions for rendering agricultural work more productive, the localized specificities of agricultural work demanded far-reaching changes in the theory before it could be
applied to farming operations. As Derlitzki contended, various obstacles stood
in the way of those who were interested in applying Taylorism to agriculture:

> The working conditions in industry are much more invariant than in agri-
> culture, where we are facing permanently changing working conditions and
> challenges, even in one and the same task. Think of the hoeing of beets, for
> instance: how differently this task must be handled depending on whether
> the hoeing takes place on heavy, crusted and rocky soil or on light ground,
> whether it takes place on a damp or a weedy piece of the acre; it even depends
> on the kind of weeds, furthermore on the size of the plants, on the exposure
> to sunlight, etc. etc. Every moment the working conditions can be different
> and therefore require a different handling of the hoe.[19]

As Derlitzki's reflections indicate, the distinctive challenges of improving
agricultural work made it difficult, if not outright impossible, to transfer the
industrial model wholesale to farming. The realization of improvements in
agricultural working methods therefore required new institutions, experimental arrangements and knowledge networks to be constructed. At the same
time, Derlitzki's subtle considerations on the idiosyncrasies of agricultural
work already signalled a departure from the early gospel of efficiency and the
calls for an outright 'Taylorization of agriculture' and a 'Taylorist reform of
the working processes of men, animals and machines' that had spread among
some early enthusiasts of scientific management.[20]

   As scholars dedicated to the study of agricultural work began to recognize the
variable and dynamic ecological and sociocultural factors that left their mark on

the world of agriculture, the scope of interests that they claimed to cover increasingly expanded. The early enthusiasm for Taylor and the application of his methods to agriculture soon began to wane, and a more sophisticated and empirically grounded 'science of agricultural work' took its place in the mid-1920s. Beyond the narrow search for methods to increase the productivity, efficiency and maximum output of the labour force that was associated with the 'Taylorization of agriculture', this new approach advocated a more all-encompassing interest in the complexities of agricultural work. It called for a more exhaustive consideration of the variable and dynamic conditions of agricultural work, and aimed to achieve the physiological and psychological rationalization of the labouring bodies of farmers and farm labourers, targeting the elimination of fatigue, overwork and wasteful movements, while at the same time enhancing what Derlitzki described as the 'efficiency of the human motor'.[21]

Thus, as the complexities of the scientific study of agricultural work came to the fore, Seedorf's early call for the establishment of specialized research institutes gained ground. The founding of the pioneering Pommritz Experimental Station for the Study of Agricultural Work in 1919, which was funded by the German state of Saxony, only marked the beginning of a wave of institution-building in the field of farm labour studies during the interwar years.[22] While Pommritz became a frequently visited site for international scholars interested in agricultural work, a series of similar research institutes and experiment stations were founded across Europe in the second half of the 1920s. Moreover, many existing institutes began to discover agricultural work as a new field of research.

These manifold and geographically widespread attempts to research agricultural work were increasingly bound together as international organizations developed an interest in the new discipline, creating forums for transnational exchanges and thus acting, in the words of Kiran Klaus Patel, as 'clearinghouses of global expertise'.[23] In 1927, the International Management Congress in Rome hosted an intense and contested discussion on the prospects for the science of agricultural work.[24] In the same year, the International Labour Organization started cooperating with the International Institute of Agriculture and the International Management Institute for the further investigation of scientific management in agriculture.[25] In 1929, in the context of this concentrated scholarly preoccupation with farm work, Frédéric Etienne Tapernoux observed a 'wave of enthusiasm' surrounding the new discipline.[26] When the International Institute of Agriculture published the book *L'organisation scientifique du travail agricole en Europe* in 1931, its author, the Russian agronomist Morduch Tcherkinsky, drew an overall picture of a Europe-wide network of scientific institutions, experiment stations and university institutes that were dedicating their intellectual and financial energies first and foremost to the study of agricultural work.[27]

Figure 7.1. Measuring the energy metabolism of agricultural workers with a respiratory apparatus during a field experiment conducted by the work physiologist Géza Farkas near Budapest, 1929. Courtesy of Harvard Medical Library collection, Center for the History of Medicine in the Francis A. Countway Library, Harvard University

While these endeavours certainly created forums for discussing problems related to agricultural work in different geographical contexts, they also revealed that the new science of agricultural work was driven by heterogeneous motivations and was shaped by a variety of methodological approaches. Moreover, the enthusiasm that the work scientists observed among their peers was not always shared by farming populations. Time and again, they reported that while some farmers and farm labourers welcomed their advice, others were reluctant to change their working habits and techniques.[28] While some work scientists explained these reservations with reference to the stereotypically 'conservative' character of 'the farmer', others were prepared to examine the different conceptions of work among farming communities. What the latter group discovered was what Louise Howard has aptly called a 'social kaleidoscope of agricultural labour'.[29] Farmers and their families as well as farm labourers usually associated their work with a diverse set of cultural values and motivations that went well beyond the search for more efficiency and profitability, which more conventional work scientists put at the centre of their investigations. Undoubtedly, alleviation from hard physical labour as well as a desire to render their own, their families' and their workers' labour more profitable were purposes shared by most farmers, but their individual conceptualizations of work were seldom reducible to these goals heralded by most proponents of the science of agricultural work. Franz Ineichen, a Swiss farmer who eagerly applied the findings of the science of agricultural work on his farm, reported that some of his colleagues saw themselves as having been degraded to 'machines' or 'working animals' in the conceptual schemes advocated by work scientists.[30] In contrast to this 'productivist' perspective, farmers and farmworkers often articulated a more all-encompassing meaning of work that emphasized virtue, skill, diligence, autonomy, education, cultural uplift and knowledge about nature through work as inherent features of the performance of agricultural labour[31] – a vision of work that was deeply rooted in peasant, artisanal and craftsmanship culture.[32] Unsurprisingly, elements of this understanding of work continued to prevail under industrial-capitalist conditions and became a regular source of misunderstandings and dissent when it came to applying the results of farm labour studies in practice.

However, such tensions and conflicts did not impede knowledge on the scientific study of agricultural work from circulating among farming communities. Indeed, such sobering experiences encouraged scientists to develop even more elaborate procedures to disseminate knowledge via journals, farmers' meetings and agricultural schools, and to seek closer contact with farmers. Given this expanding circulation of knowledge about agricultural work and the improvement thereof, it was only a question of time before North American observers noticed this development. Notably, however, the flowering of the science of agricultural work in the networks of European agronomists and the intense rationalizing fervour that accompanied it still provoked amazement among US agricultural experts who were observing the evolution of European agriculture in the interwar years. US agriculturalists had thus far predominantly refrained from efforts to apply Taylorism to agriculture, C.R. Jones' short contribution on 'Scientific Management as Applied to the Farm, Home and Manufacturing Plant' in 1916 being the exception that would seem to prove the rule.[33] Accordingly, when some of them observed the proliferation of scientific investigations into farm work along the lines that Taylor had proposed for studies on industrial plants, they reacted with astonishment. For instance, Asher Hobson, the US delegate at the International Institute of Agriculture in Rome, observed in 1927 how: 'In America the Taylor System is accorded little importance in its application to agriculture. It is exclusively of interest to industry.' But among European agronomists and agricultural economists, Hobson noted with surprise, there were 'enthusiastic followers of Taylor'.[34]

Conversely, when European agriculturalists visited the United States in search of the heartland of scientific management, they found surprisingly few traces in agriculture. Wilhelm Seedorf, for instance, used his study trip to the United States in 1930 to investigate working practices on US farms. Before travelling through the country, he spent six weeks at the United States Department of Agriculture (USDA) in Washington DC, where he conducted research at the USDA's library and hoped to engage with US experts in the field of farm labour research. But, to his disappointment, there were only a few scholars with whom he could discuss his ideas. Only Rollin H. Barrett, an assistant professor of farm management at the Massachusetts Agricultural College in Amherst, worked with methods that reminded Seedorf of the ones that were developed and applied in European agriculture. Drawing on cinematographic methods to analyse farm operations and applying time and motion studies, Barrett's aim was that of 'getting farmers to think of the efficiency of their own practices'.[35] When Seedorf turned to the Taylor Society with the hope of gaining insights into labour studies on US agriculture, he had a revealing experience: instead of receiving information on scientific management in agriculture in the United States, he was asked to give a speech on his views on the relevance of Taylorism and the science of agricultural work in Europe, because none of the attendees at the meeting had ever heard about Taylor's scientific management being applied to farming.[36] Despite these rather disillusioning experiences in the United States, Seedorf was aware of the symbolic meaning attached to Taylor's name, and he never ceased to emphasize the importance of 'meeting immediate pupils of Taylor in order to discuss questions regarding the science of work' in his reports back to the Ministry of Science, Arts and Education in Berlin.[37] Towards the end of his visit to the United States, Seedorf used the opportunity of the International Congress of Agricultural Economists, which took place in Ithaca, New York in August 1930, to spread his ideas on the science of agricultural labour. As I will outline below, this talk would come to be remembered by some of his US colleagues, who only seem to have captured the relevance of Seedorf's suggestions a decade later, when the state of farm labour in the United States had shifted decisively.[38] However, for the time being, there were very few experts who shared the view of Walter J. Roth, an agricultural economist and specialist for European agriculture at the USDA, who cautioned his colleagues in the early 1930s that it was 'quite possible that we in the United States shall later find ourselves definitely interested in farm labor studies in the United States. In this case the pioneer work done by the German research workers in this field should be of considerable value to us'.[39]

Americanizing Farm Labour Studies: The Farm Work Simplification Program

Indeed, Roth's prediction was soon to become true, and the longlasting reservations towards the scientific investigation of agricultural working practices among US scholars would ultimately transform themselves into a serious interest. Crucial in this regard was the fear of severe labour shortages on US farms that spread as the United States prepared to enter the Second World War. The perception of a transition from labour abundance to labour shortages on

US farms came with unexpected speed. Whereas the agricultural economist William T. Ham of the USDA spoke in 1940 of a 'superabundance of labor power on American farms',[40] the situation had changed dramatically only one year later. Although federal officials at the USDA and the Department of Labor remained sceptical that the rumours of a farm labour scarcity that began to circulate in early 1941 were accurate, they started to collect evidence on the labour situation on US farms. Based on a nationwide farm labour survey, a USDA study estimated that from September 1941 to August 1942, the remarkable number of 1.6 million farmworkers and farmers had left the agricultural sector to work in industry or to join the armed forces.[41] Alarmed by such a drain of the agricultural workforce, federal officials concluded that they had to create a farm labour supply programme to meet the real or imagined needs of US agriculture.[42]

The Federal Farm Labor Supply Program encompassed a wide array of measures, ranging from recruiting migrant farmworkers from Mexico, the Bahama Islands and Jamaica or the mobilization of high school students to join the agricultural labour force to the creation of a so-called Women's Land Army, a programme that recruited, trained and placed millions of women on farms during the war.[43] But the Farm Labor Supply Program not only aimed to increase the number of workers on farms, it also sought to improve working techniques and make agricultural labour more productive. As the director of the Bureau of Agricultural Economics at the USDA, the economist Howard R. Tolley, who together with M.L. Wilson, Henry A. Wallace and Carl Taylor had been one of the leading 'agrarian intellectuals' who had shaped the New Deal's agricultural policies in the 1930s,[44] described in late 1942:

> We have in the United States the land, we have the know-how ... we have the technological knowledge and ability among the farmers ... we have a reasonably good supply of farm machinery ... we will do fairly well on fertilizer, but labor, that is, the manpower, will have to be used more effectively, will have to be mobilized more effectively and will have to be more efficient.

Tolley detected a 'real need for a training program, developing the technology of hand labor on the farm', which he believed would prevent the farming population from falling short of the agricultural war production goals that had been set by the government.[45] This perception and the urgency with which leading representatives of the federal agencies in the USDA called attention to the farm labour problem eventually led to an unexpected reappraisal of the insights that the science of agricultural work had carved out in Europe during the interwar years.

The decisive moment that provided the opportunity to inject this knowledge into the US discourse was a debate in December 1942 on the 'manpower crisis of agriculture' during a hearing of the Congressional Subcommittee on Technological Mobilization, which was part of a far-reaching initiative to mobilize scientific and technological research and resources for the US war effort as well as for 'peacetime progress and prosperity'.[46] The Subcommittee had invited several experts from the fields of agricultural economics and industrial engineering to discuss the potential benefits of farm work efficiency studies with representatives of the USDA, including Howard Tolley and the director of the Labor Division at the Farm Security Administration, Nathan Gregory Silvermaster. One of the invited experts was David B. Porter, a professor of industrial engineering at New York University who had studied with one of Taylor's collaborators, Henry L. Gantt. Invited to give an overview of the progress of industrial labour research, Porter declared himself confident that this approach 'will work universally' and was thus 'applicable to agriculture', estimating that agricultural labour productivity might be increased from 25 to 50 per cent if work simplification methods were systematically introduced.[47] Interestingly, Tolley reminded the members of the Subcommittee, who had reacted rather enthusiastically to Porter's calculations, that there could be 'some complications' regarding the application of such techniques to agriculture. 'After all, a farmer cannot be exactly put on the assembly line', he insisted. Suggestions arising from the analysis of working procedures in industrial plants might be helpful for the 'repetitive type of work' that also occurs in farming, he maintained, but many other types of agricultural work seemed to be at odds with factory conditions.[48] Silvermaster reminded the efficiency experts that their task was not solely to teach labourers how to work more efficiently; they were also expected to record and evaluate the tacit knowledge that shaped the working techniques of farm labourers. There 'exists a lot of skill among workers themselves which has gone to waste', he complained, because efficiency experts were accustomed to instructing when instead they should be observing and listening.[49]

While Tolley's caveat to some extent echoed the reservations that Georg Derlitzki and Ernst Laur had expressed during the interwar years, Daniel M. Braum made these European connections more explicit. Braum, who worked at the USDA's Division of Training, compared the impressive European research in the field of agricultural labour studies with 'the very meager work that [had] been done' in the United States. Quoting from the lectures that Wilhelm Seedorf had given in the 1930s at multiple editions of the International Congress of Agricultural Economists and reminding the members of the Congressional Subcommittee of the wide-ranging research that the Experiment Station in Pommritz had conducted in the 1920s and 1930s (but mistakenly thinking that Seedorf rather than Derlitzki was its director), Braum painted a picture of US backwardness in the field of farm labour research. Facing a 'crisis of manpower' in agriculture, confidence in technological innovation and in replacing human and animal labour with machinery and motor-powered tools had reached its limits. In Braum's view, it was thus high time for an orchestrated attempt to make scientific progress in farm labour studies and to render the performance of US farmers and farm labourers more efficient.[50]

Already three months before the hearing in Congress, Braum had contacted Lillian Moller Gilbreth, the wife of Frank Gilbreth and a pioneering scholar in time and motion studies as well as the doyenne of industrial management techniques in the United States.[51] While asking her for advice regarding his upcoming statement at the Technological Mobilization hearing, Braum also attempted to involve Lilian Gilbreth in his plans to establish a programme for applying scientific management techniques to agriculture. Gilbreth had written extensively on motion and fatigue studies in industrial settings and the service sector, had introduced applied psychology to industrial management and had experimented with the application of scientific management to household work.[52] A professor since 1935 at Purdue University in Lafayette, Indiana, a land-grant college and an academic stronghold for the agricultural sciences, Gilbreth recalled how she had been drawn ever 'closer to agricultural problems' at this time.[53] Hence, Braum's offer seemed like an opportunity to continue her life's work, namely to adapt scientific management techniques to a wide variety of tasks and jobs. 'The subject of the application of elementary principles of scientific management to agriculture', wrote Gilbreth, 'is one to which I have divided much attention and a tremendous amount of interest.'[54]

Together with Braum and the industrial engineer Marvin E. Mundel, who led the Time and Motion Study Laboratory at Purdue University, Gilbreth established a programme called Farm Work Simplification at Purdue. They organized several training sessions in farm work simplification in late 1942 and early 1943, introducing agricultural researchers to time and motion studies techniques, and assisting them in developing their research. With the financial support of the General Education Board of the Rockefeller Foundation and under the general direction of E.C. Young and Lowell S. Hardin, farm work simplification laboratories were set up at twelve land-grant colleges across the United States. A myriad of scholars began to apply time and motion studies to farming operations in order to render 'the farmer motion-minded' and to develop more 'time consciousness' in farm work.[55] There were at least some farmers and farmworkers who appear to have taken this advice seriously. Braum quoted a letter from a Midwestern farmer: 'We are so busy just doing our work that we fail to stand back and watch ourselves make unnecessary labour. Most of us need a little thought stimulation and since your letter I have noted many ways of simpler movement. They are just simple ideas but previously lacked "inoculation" [*sic*].'[56]

As the different research projects progressed, the second half of the 1940s witnessed intense debates on the achievements of the Farm Work Simplification

Figure 7.2. Studying the farm layout and analysing movements and walking distances in the context of a Farm Work Simplification Program in West Lafayette, Indiana, c. mid-1940s. J.C. Allen and Son, Farm Work Simplification Study. Courtesy of Rockefeller Archive Center, General Education Board Records, Series 13, Box 44, Folder 473

Program. The American Farm Economics Association hosted regular sessions on farm work simplification at its annual meetings, while the flagship journal for US agricultural economists, the *Journal of Farm Economics*, as well as the USDA's *Yearbook of Agriculture* welcomed contributions on this research.[57] Moreover, one of the most widely used textbooks on farm management incorporated chapters on scientific management in agriculture and farm work simplification in its 1947 edition, while several state agricultural colleges began to include farm work simplification courses in their curriculum from 1948 onwards.[58] The various studies conducted under the auspices of the Farm Work Simplification Program were synthesized in 1949 in the form of an influential book by Lawrence M. Vaughan and Lowell S. Hardin.[59]

While debates on farm work simplification in the United States mirrored in part the same problems with which European researchers had wrestled during the interwar years, they also departed to some extent from this lineage. The challenges of applying techniques devised for factory labour to farm work constituted a common reference point for scholars on both sides of the Atlantic. However, as the Farm Work Simplification Program progressed, the way in which US experts perceived these problems and their potential solutions changed markedly. On the one hand, scholars like Howard Tolley and Lester Blum argued for a differentiated perspective that was open to adopting industrially inspired techniques, but that would also account for the unique nature of agricultural work by placing certain limitations on the wholesale application of industrial scientific management techniques to agriculture.[60]

By contrast, the trend among some of the leading scholars in the Farm Work Simplification Program was moving in another direction. Instead of accounting for the peculiarities of agricultural work and reflecting on the differences between agricultural and industrial labour, the leading voices in farm work simplification increasingly favoured an approach that downplayed these complexities and instead opted for a homogeneous perspective on work in factories and on farms. For instance, Lowell S. Hardin, the assistant director of the Farm Work Simplification Program, noted in 1949 that 'differences between urban industry and farming are frequently more apparent than real',[61] and Braum called for 'a common language between the leaders in agriculture and industry' when it came to analysing working practices and applying scientific management techniques.[62] J.E. Wills from the Illinois College of Agriculture epitomized this shift in perspective when he wrote in 1954:

> The crux of the problem is the extent to which industrial work and farm work can be reduced to common elements and common terms, and the extent to which management problems arise under essentially similar conditions. And it is evident that, with recent technological advances, the organization and the operational problems of farms are taking on more and more the characteristics of business or industrial units.[63]

This interpretative trend among some of the leading representatives of farm work simplification in the United States foreshadowed a tendency that came to dominate discourse on agricultural work in the postwar era in North America and Western Europe alike: in order to integrate agriculture into the patterns of a capitalist industrialization that was on the verge of its 'great acceleration',[64] farming had to be interpreted as if it were similar to industry. This required abstraction from its biotic conditions, from its embeddedness in diverse ecological and sociocultural systems and, therefore, from the idiosyncrasies of agricultural work.[65]

The Productivity Drive in Postwar Europe and the Appropriation of Farm Work Simplification

The year 1947 witnessed two major endeavours to introduce the conceptualizations of agricultural work that had been derived from the United States' Farm Work Simplification Program into the transnational networks of agricultural experts that were slowly being restored after their collapse during the Second World War. In early July 1947, Daniel M. Braum gave a speech on 'Progress in Scientific Farm Management' at the eighth International Management Congress in Stockholm; two months later, Lowell S. Hardin spoke on the evolution of the Farm Work Simplification Program at the sixth International Conference of Agricultural Economists in Dartington Hall, England. Both emphasized the achievements of farm work simplification in the United States in the context of the war effort and underscored its relevance for the postwar reconstruction of European agriculture. According to Braum, when 'the farmer' began to see himself as 'his own production engineer', he would be able 'to better plan and control the sequence of his operations and flow of work, thus reducing lost time and unprofitable operations'.[66] Using a similar rhetoric of industrial effectiveness and rational progress, Hardin argued that the time and motion studies developed by industrial engineers would turn the 'trial and error' of conventional farming into a more systematic and scientific approach that would reduce 'the labour and cost of doing a job' by eliminating 'unnecessary work', identifying the 'easiest, most effective methods' and standardizing these 'improved work methods'.[67]

With their faith in scientific progress and technological advancement along the lines of industrial manufacturing and in their determination to overcome the challenges posed by the idiosyncrasies of agricultural work, Hardin and Braum spearheaded a version of agricultural development that James C. Scott has labelled 'high modernist agriculture'.[68] As we have seen, such visions have a long history and have fuelled attempts to transform working practices on farms for decades – although they have often resulted in a complex process of cultural accommodation as farmers have sought to find ways to make industrially inspired schemes work for them rather than simply accepting them directly from the shop floor. However, in the 1950s, these ventures fell on more fertile terrain as changes in agricultural technology, broadening access to fossil fuel resources, the replacement of working animals with motorized machinery, the lavish use of fertilizers and pesticides, and the rise of capital intensity had brought a level of uniformity and standardization to farming that was without historical precedent.[69]

Apart from their far-reaching environmental and social consequences, these fundamental changes also altered the perceptions of work and research agendas within the scientific study of agricultural work. In particular, the 1950s witnessed an epistemic shift away from an intellectual preoccupation with the temporal and spatial logics of organic resources that agricultural work still had to take into account towards a 'voice of decontextualized rationality',[70] which saw in farming little more than the management of an 'industrial unit' that was detached from its specific ecological, social and cultural contexts. This epistemic shift also stemmed from rapid technological changes, which led more than one contemporary observer of agriculture to see the mid-1950s as a 'turning point' in the history of farm work.[71] With motorization becoming more advanced in this decade and multipurpose and more versatile tractors and agricultural machinery entering the farm gates,[72] the imperative to improve human labour lost its erstwhile urgency. Instead of transforming agricultural working methods, industrially minded agricultural economists now called for the wholesale shift of labour from human and animal bodies to motorized machines. As Vaughan and Hardin declared bluntly: 'Only as man directs rather than provides power does he become a true manager.'[73] Hence, although this tendency had already been observable among some representatives of the Farm Work Simplification Program in the late 1940s, such conceptualizations of agricultural work that emphasized efficiency, output and progress by turning the farmer into a manager, by overcoming drudgery through the use of motor-powered technology, and by promoting the 'industrialization' of agriculture gained currency on both sides of the Atlantic in the 1950s and 1960s – even though they were sometimes concealed behind a veiled rhetoric that celebrated the peasantry and rural life as an anchor of stability and tradition in a world of rapid change. Seen in this light, Braum's and Hardin's contributions were only forerunners of a much broader tendency that came to dominate debates on the scientific investigation of agricultural work in the postwar era.

This renewed tendency to model agricultural work along the lines of industrial scientific management with the principal goal of 'saving' labour was strengthened during the course of what some historians have called the postwar 'productivity drive' in Europe.[74] An instructive example of how the European desire to 'catch up with America' led to a reappraisal of the concepts and approaches developed in US farm work simplification is provided by the agricultural programmes that were established by the European Productivity Agency (EPA) in the mid-1950s. In 1953, under the auspices of the Marshall Plan's technical assistance programme, the EPA was founded with the goal of promoting productivity in its member countries.[75] As one of the institutional embodiments of what Charles S. Maier has called the 'politics of productivity',[76] the EPA soon targeted agriculture, an economic sector that was regarded as especially 'backward' and in need of 'development' and 'technical progress'.[77] In 1956, it launched a survey to collect data on ongoing research projects in the field of farm labour studies, which was followed by an international conference in Wageningen in the Netherlands in July of the same year.[78] The EPA saw its role as integrating and orchestrating the various research projects on farm labour studies conducted by research institutes across Western Europe. This aptly fitted the EPA's self-fashioned image as a motor for turning the supposedly backward agricultural sector into one that was more in tune with the organization's own vision of industrial efficiency and productivity.[79]

Revealingly, the EPA buttressed these claims by comparing the situation in mid-1950s Europe with the conditions with which US agriculture had wrestled in the early 1940s. Just as agriculture in the United States had faced a shortage of farm labour accompanied by far-reaching changes in agricultural technology in the early 1940s, European societies were confronted with a similar interplay between 'manpower shortage' and a 'chain reaction of change in agricultural technology'. It was this constellation, an EPA report stated in 1957, 'that resulted in the setting up of the Farm Work Simplification Laboratory at Purdue University in the United States in 1942 and also resulted in a new emphasis on labour management in Europe'.[80] Hence, according to the EPA, the concept that was destined to integrate the various research on farm work and to capture the problems of farm labour in Western Europe in the mid-1950s was the very one that Lillian Gilbreth had devised almost fifteen years earlier: work simplification.

The transatlantic links between the United States' Farm Work Simplification Program and the productivity mission of the EPA were instrumental in fostering a vision of agriculture geared to industrial expectations. Indeed, this vision was by no means restricted to experts at the EPA. In fact, European agronomists displayed a remarkable degree of enthusiasm for US ideas on work simplification, because they were themselves steeped in a process of institutional restructuring, rapid technological change and epistemic reorientation with its own repercussions for the science of agricultural work. In a certain sense, as such, transnational debates on the study of agricultural work had come full circle: the language of leading representatives of the study of agricultural work in the 1950s echoed the hopes and aspirations that the early enthusiasts of Taylorism in agriculture had formulated some thirty years earlier. However, voices that called for more attention to be paid to the specific characteristics of the biotic resources that continued to shape agricultural work – even in an age of industrializing agriculture – were increasingly pushed to the margins. As the botanist and pioneer of organic agriculture Sir Albert Howard wrote with a mixture of scorn and regret on the threshold of this transition: 'Farming has come to be looked at as if it were a factory'. This, he warned, went hand in hand with a disregard for 'the observant farmer and labourer, who have spent their lives in close contact with Nature' and who could, if they were listened to, be 'of the greatest help to the investigator'.[81]

Conclusion

This chapter has assessed several key historical moments in the history of the scientific study of agricultural work and has unshackled them from the national frameworks into which historical investigations are frequently pressed. It has explored the entangled history of the science of agricultural work in Western Europe and North America, detailing how the problematization of agricultural work was shaped by reciprocal observations and attempts to look at other societies' experiences with similar problems and corresponding coping strategies. Agricultural work thus became a field of interdisciplinary scientific inquiry on which North American and European visions of agricultural work and the scientific investigation thereof intermingled and competed. The history of these entanglements is rewarding because it shows that agriculturalists in the period from the 1920s until the 1950s were part of a transnational dialogue on the problems of agricultural work in modern industrial societies and that their search for remedies was informed by mutual observations, selective borrowings and local appropriations. These endeavours reflected and relied on transnational social networks and intellectual connections through which an epistemic space of expertise on agricultural work was unlocked, thereby fostering an evolving and contested dialogue on the methods and aims of studying agricultural work. Thus, as knowledge circulated in time and space, the concepts that permeated discourses relating to the study of farm work increasingly became cultural hybrids. Just as the emergence of a science of agricultural work in interwar Europe is unthinkable without the influence of US scientific management, so too were the United States' Work Simplification Program and the European tailoring of the science of work to the productivity drive in the postwar era entrenched in traditions that reached across the Atlantic. Following these transatlantic currents reveals that the rural histories of Europe and the United States share much more in common than is often imagined.

However, at the same time, the transatlantic connections that enabled and sustained the circulation of knowledge on farm work far from approximated a tightly interwoven web; instead, they resembled a rather frayed and patchy tangle of ideas. The transnational history of farm work research is also a history of uneven, fragmentary and contingent processes – of voices unheard, expectations unfulfilled and reunions missed. That agricultural work was a problem to be addressed first and foremost by scientific methods was by no means self-evident. In general, a collective perception of crisis was required to transform agricultural work into an object of scientific investigation and intervention, and to vivify processes of selective transnational borrowing. Moments of intense transnational circulation of knowledge on farm work emerged from contexts of crisis – whether the dislocations caused by the First World War and the Great Depression, the perception of labour shortages in the context of the United States' war effort in the early 1940s or the challenges associated with the reconstruction of European agriculture after the Second World War. Seen in this light, the transnational history of farm labour research and the metamorphosis of its conceptual frameworks underscore Sanjay Subrahmanyam's argument that 'modernity is historically a global and *conjunctural* phenomenon, not a virus that spreads from one place to another'.[82] Indeed, as the accrual of knowledge on agricultural work and the search to render it more efficient became part of the gospel of modernity and fostered attempts to model agriculture on industrial manufacturing, the scientific study of agricultural work became a contested meeting ground that brought together hitherto unconnected actors in a transnational discursive community. However, the occurrence of these encounters remained highly contingent, while the encounters themselves were marked by an ambivalent fusion of different patterns of thought on agricultural work in the age of industrial modernity that were often ultimately tailored to specific local needs and aims. Agricultural work thus provides an interesting paradox: there are few other forms of work that are shaped more thoroughly by local environment than farming, and yet the 'knowing of nature through labor'[83] that farming inspires and that the early science of agricultural work attempted to objectivate also moved through currents that took it far beyond the local.

Juri Auderset is Assistant Professor for the History of the Nineteenth and Twentieth Centuries at the Institute of History at the University of Bern and a researcher at the Archives of Rural History in Bern. He earned his BA, MA and Ph.D. from the University of Fribourg. His research and teaching interests include the history of agriculture and industrialization, the history of work and capitalism in the nineteenth and twentieth centuries, the history of the Age of Revolutions, conceptual history and historical semantics.

Notes

1. Derlitzki, 'Bedeutung der Landarbeitsforschung', 136. All translations from German- or French-language sources are the author's own.
2. Patel, 'Green Heart of Governance'; Brassley, Segers and van Molle, *War, Agriculture and Food*.
3. Nolan, *Visions of Modernity*; de Grazia, *Irresistible Empire*.
4. Herbert, 'Europe in High Modernity', 19.
5. Rabinbach, *Human Motor*; Vatin, *Le travail*.
6. Auderset, 'Manufacturing'.
7. Rabinbach, *Eclipse*, 101.
8. Auderset and Moser, *Agrarfrage in der Industriegesellschaft*, 20–26.
9. Berry, 'Whose Head Is the Farmer Using?', 21. On this issue, see also Fitzgerald, *Every Farm a Factory*, 10–32.
10. Auderset and Moser, 'Exploring Agriculture'.
11. Rodgers, *Atlantic Crossings*, 7 and 318–66.
12. Krige, 'Introduction', 5.
13. Goodman, Sorj and Wilkinson, *From Farming to Biotechnology*, 6–14; Mann and Dickinson, 'Obstacles'.
14. Seedorf, *Vervollkommnung der Landarbeit*, 2–3 and 9. On Seedorf's research, see also Oberkrome, *Ordnung und Autarkie*, 82–83.
15. Flemming, 'Landarbeit', 245.

16. Weber, *Verhältnisse*. On the transnational links of this scholarship, see Zimmerman, *Alabama in Africa*, 73–80.
17. Von Meyenburg, Konrad. 'Alte und neue Arbeitsziele. Vortrag an der Jahrestagung des Schweizerischen Werkbundes in Bern, 9. September 1928', Archivbestand Konrad von Meyenburg (AfA Nr. 764), Archives of Rural History, Bern.
18. Laur, *Landwirtschaftliche Arbeiterfrage*, 171.
19. Derlitzki, *Taylorsystem*, 8.
20. Winter, *Taylorismus*, 153–55.
21. Derlitzki, 'Bedeutung der Landarbeitsforschung', 139.
22. Auderset, 'Manufacturing', 235–37.
23. Patel, *The New Deal*, 39. On other areas of transnational cooperation in food and agriculture during the interwar years, see Knab and Ribi Forclaz, 'Transnational Co-operation'.
24. *Atti del III Congresso Internazionale*. See also Karns Alexander, 'Rationalization'.
25. ILO Archives, AG 803/1/3: Mixed Advisory Agricultural Committee, 3rd session, January 1927: New Questions Laid before the ILO, 8–10.
26. Tapernoux, 'L'Organisation scientifique', 379.
27. Institut International d'Agriculture, *L'organisation scientifique du travail agricole*, 5–8 and 22–34.
28. See e.g. Seedorf, 'Methods and Results', 961; Tapernoux, 'Organisation du travail agricole', 8.
29. Howard, *Labour in Agriculture*, 63.
30. Ineichen, 'Arbeitsorganisation', 22.
31. 'Betrachtung über die Rationalisierung', 844.
32. Sewell, *Work and Revolution in France*, 280–81.
33. Jones, 'Scientific Management'.
34. Hobson, 'Agricultural Economics', 423.
35. Nachlass Wilhelm Seedorf, Niedersächsische Staats- und Universitätsbibliothek Göttingen (NSUG), COD. MS. W. SEEDORF C 56: Briefwechsel zur Vorbereitung einer Reise in die USA; Barrett, 'Study of Labor Saving Methods', 352.
36. Nachlass Wilhelm Seedorf, NSUG, COD. MS. W. SEEDORF H 4: Tagebuch: Studienreise durch die Vereinigten Staaten 1930. – Abschrift nach dem plattdeutschen Tagebuch, 20 and 160.
37. Seedorf to the Ministerium für Wissenschaft, Kunst und Volksbildung, 18 April 1930, Nachlass Wilhelm Seedorf, NSUG, COD. MS. W. SEEDORF H 3: Tagebuch, Studienreise durch die Vereinigten Staaten 1930.
38. Seedorf, 'Methods and Results'.
39. Roth, 'Review', 659.
40. Ham, 'Farm Labor in an Era of Change', 908 and 915.
41. *Technological Mobilization*, Vol. 3, 717.
42. Rasmussen, *History of the Emergency Farm Labor Program*; Tucker, 'Agricultural Workers'; Hahamovitch, *Fruits of Their Labor*, 151–81.
43. Hahamovitch, *No Man's Land*, 22–49; Carpenter, '"Regular Farm Girl"'.
44. Gilbert, *Planning Democracy*, 47–48.
45. *Technological Mobilization*, vol. 3, 713 and 715.

46. Ibid., vol. 1, 1.
47. Ibid., vol. 3, 732–33 and 736.
48. Ibid., vol. 3, 740.
49. Ibid., vol. 3, 756.
50. Ibid., vol. 3, 742 and 746.
51. Daniel M. Braum to Lillian Gilbreth, 25 September 1942, Daniel M. Braum Papers, Kansas State University Archives and Manuscripts, P 2005.07, Box 2, Folder 7.
52. Lancaster, *Making Time*, 312; Graham, 'Domesticating Efficiency'.
53. Lillian Gilbreth to Roy Read, 21 September 1942, Daniel M. Braum Papers, Kansas State University Archives and Manuscripts, P 2005.07, Box 2, Folder 7.
54. Ibid.
55. Mundel, 'Farm Work Simplification', 565; Young, 'Farm Work Simplification Studies', 239.
56. *Eighth International Management Congress*, vol. 3, 497.
57. Young and Hardin, 'Simplifying Farm Work'; *Journal of Farm Economics* 28(1) (1946), 314–40; *Journal of Farm Economics* 29(1) (1947), 209–32.
58. Black et al., *Farm Management*, 549–59.
59. Vaughan and Hardin, *Farm Work Simplification*.
60. Blum, 'Job Analysis in Agriculture', 202.
61. Hardin, 'Functional Approach', 384.
62. Braum, 'Progress in Scientific Farm Management', 326.
63. Wills, 'Industrial Management Techniques', 566.
64. Bonneuil and Fressoz, *Shock of the Anthropocene*, 51.
65. Moser and Varley, 'State and Agricultural Modernisation', 20–24.
66. Braum, 'Progress in Scientific Farm Management', 324 and 326. Although experts like Braum usually addressed 'the farmer' in the form of a masculine stereotype, the research by work scientists also encompassed labour usually associated with female farmers and workers; see Jones, *Gender and Rural Modernity*, 127–59.
67. Hardin, 'Work Simplification in Agriculture', 384–85.
68. Scott, *Seeing Like a State*, 262.
69. Pfister, '1950s Syndrome'; Pessis, Topçu and Bonneuil, *Une autre histoire des 'Trente Glorieuses'*.
70. Kloppenburg Jr., 'Social Theory', 248.
71. Priebe, *Landarbeit Heute und Morgen*, 15.
72. Auderset and Moser, 'Mechanisation and Motorisation', 156–158.
73. Vaughan and Hardin, *Farm Work Simplification*, 12.
74. Barjot, 'Introduction', 13.
75. Boel, *The European Productivity Agency*. On the transnational links of European postwar reconstruction and the Marshall Plan, see Speich Chassé, 'Towards a Global History of the Marshall Plan'.
76. Maier, 'Politics of Productivity'.
77. Patel, 'History of European Integration and the Common Agricultural Policy', 17–19.
78. European Productivity Agency, *Labour Management on the Farm*, 7.
79. Biebuyck, 'Calories, Tractors and "Technical Agriculture"'.
80. European Productivity Agency, *Labour Management on the Farm*, 15.

81. Howard, *Mein landwirtschaftliches Testament*, 194 and 216.
82. Subrahmanyam, 'Hearing Voices', 99–100.
83. White, *Organic Machine*, 3.

Bibliography

Atti del III Congresso Internazionale di Organizzazione Scientifica del Lavoro, 3 vols. Rome: L'Universale, 1927.

Auderset, Juri. 'Manufacturing Agricultural Working Knowledge: The Scientific Study of Agricultural Work in Industrial Europe, 1920s–1960s'. *Rural History* 32(3) (2021), 233–48.

Auderset, Juri, and Peter Moser. 'Mechanisation and Motorisation: Natural Resources, Knowledge, Politics and Technological Change in 19th- and 20th-Century Agriculture', in Carin Martiin, Juan Pan-Montojo and Paul Brassley (eds), *Agriculture in Capitalist Europe, 1945–1960: From Food Shortages to Food Surpluses* (Abingdon: Routledge, 2016), 145–64.

———. *Die Agrarfrage in der Industriegesellschaft: Wissenskulturen, Machtverhältnisse und natürliche Ressourcen in der agrarisch-industriellen Wissensgesellschaft (1850–1950)*. Vienna: Böhlau, 2018.

———. 'Exploring Agriculture in the Age of Industrial Capitalism: Swiss Farmers and Agronomists in North America and the Transnational Entanglements of Agricultural Knowledge, 1870s to 1950s'. *Agricultural History* 96(1–2) (2022), 91–127.

Barjot, Dominique. 'Introduction', in Dominique Barjot (ed.), *Catching up with America: Productivity Missions and the Diffusion of American Economic and Technological Influence after the Second World War* (Paris: Presses Paris Sorbonne, 2002), 13–52.

Barrett, Rollin H. 'Study of Labor Saving Methods and Technique on Vegetable Farms in Massachusetts'. *American Journal of Agricultural Economics* 14(2) (1932), 351–52.

Berry, Wendell. 'Whose Head Is the Farmer Using? Whose Head Is Using the Farmer?', in Wes Jackson, Wendell Berry and Bruce Colman (eds), *Meeting the Expectations of the Land: Essays in Sustainable Agriculture and Stewardship* (San Francisco: North Point Press, 1984), 19–30.

'Betrachtung über die Rationalisierung der Landwirtschaft', *Die Grüne* 60 (1932), 843–45.

Biebuyck, William. 'Calories, Tractors and "Technical Agriculture": Manufacturing Agrarian Cooperation within the OEEC (1947–1954)', in Mark Bevir and Ryan Phillips (eds), *Decentring European Governance* (Abingdon: Routledge, 2019), 17–43.

Black, John D. et al. *Farm Management*. New York: Macmillan, 1947.

Blum, Lester. 'Job Analysis in Agriculture'. *Journal of Farm Economics* 27(1) (1945), 195–204.

Boel, Bent. *The European Productivity Agency and Transatlantic Relations, 1953–1961*. Copenhagen: Museum Tusculanum Press, 2003.

Bonneuil, Christophe, and Jean-Baptiste Fressoz. *The Shock of the Anthropocene: The Earth, History and Us*. London: Verso, 2017.

Brassley, Paul, Yves Segers and Leen van Molle (eds). *War, Agriculture and Food: Rural Europe from the 1930s to the 1950s*. New York: Routledge, 2012.

Braum, Daniel M. 'Progress in Scientific Farm Management', in *Eighth International*

Management Congress, Stockholm 1947: Papers Submitted to the Sectional Meetings, Vol. 1 (Stockholm: Esselte Aktiebolag, 1947), 319–29.

Carpenter, Stephanie Ann. '"Regular Farm Girl": The Women's Land Army in World War II'. *Agricultural History* 71(2) (1997), 162–85.

De Grazia, Victoria. *Irresistible Empire: America's Advance through 20th-Century Europe*. Cambridge, MA: Belknap Press, 2005.

Derlitzki, Georg. *Das Taylorsystem und seine Anwendung auf die Landwirtschaft, Schriften der Ökonomischen Gesellschaft*. Leipzig: Reichenbach, 1921.

———. 'Die Bedeutung der Landarbeitsforschung in Deutschland', in *Atti del III Congresso Internazionale di Organizzazione Scientifica del Lavoro, Parte II: Memorie, Vol. 1* (Rome: L'Universale, 1927), 135–39.

Eighth International Management Congress, Stockholm 1947: Papers Submitted to the Sectional Meetings, 3 vols. Stockholm: Esselte Aktiebolag, 1947.

European Productivity Agency. *Labour Management on the Farm*. Paris: European Productivity Agency of the Organisation for European Economic Cooperation, 1957.

Fitzgerald, Deborah. *Every Farm a Factory: The Industrial Ideal in American Agriculture*. New Haven: Yale University Press, 2003.

Flemming, Jens. 'Die Landarbeit in der Zeit der Industrialisierung: Der "preußische Weg"', in Arne Eggebrecht et al. (eds), *Geschichte der Arbeit: Vom Alten Ägypten bis zur Gegenwart* (Zurich: Buchclub Ex Libris, 1982), 243–302.

Gilbert, Jess. *Planning Democracy: Agrarian Intellectuals and the Intended New Deal*. New Haven: Yale University Press, 2015.

Goodman, David, Bernardo Sorj and John Wilkinson. *From Farming to Biotechnology: A Theory of Agro-industrial Development*. Oxford: Blackwell, 1987.

Graham, Laurel D. 'Domesticating Efficiency: Lillian Gilbreth's Scientific Management of Homemakers, 1924–1930'. *Signs* 24(3) (1999), 633–75.

Hahamovitch, Cindy. *The Fruits of Their Labor: Atlantic Coast Farmworkers and the Making of Migrant Poverty, 1870–1945*. Chapel Hill: University of North Carolina Press, 1997.

———. *No Man's Land: Jamaican Guestworkers in America and the Global History of Deportable Labor*. Princeton: Princeton University Press, 2011.

Ham, William T. 'Farm Labor in an Era of Change', in *Yearbook of Agriculture 1940: Farmers in a Changing World* (Washington DC: US Government Printing Office, 1940), 907–921.

Hardin, Lowell S. 'Work Simplification in Agriculture', in *Proceedings of the Sixth International Conference of Agricultural Economists* (London: Oxford University Press, 1948), 384–401.

———. 'The Functional Approach to Effective Farm Labor Utilization'. *Journal of Farm Economics* 31(1) (1949), 382–84.

Herbert, Ulrich. 'Europe in High Modernity: Reflections on a Theory of the 20th Century'. *Journal of Modern European History* 5(1) (2007), 5–21.

Hobson, Asher. 'Agricultural Economics in Europe'. *Journal of Farm Economics* 9(4) (1927), 421–32.

Howard, Albert. *Mein landwirtschaftliches Testament*. Berlin: Siebeneicher, 1948.

Howard, Louise Ernestine. *Labour in Agriculture: An International Survey*. London: Oxford University Press, 1935.

Ineichen, Franz. 'Die Arbeitsorganisation in der Landwirtschaft'. *Schweizerische Land-wirtschaftliche Monatshefte* 22 (1944), 1–27.

Institut International d'Agriculture, *L'organisation scientifique du travail agricole en Europe*. Rome: Bestetti & Tumminelli, 1931.

Jones, Clement Ross. 'Scientific Management as Applied to the Farm, Home and Manufacturing Plant', in *Proceedings of the 30th Annual Convention of the Association of American Agricultural Colleges and Experiment Stations* (Burlington: Free Press Printing Company, 1916), 108–15.

Jones, Elizabeth Blight. *Gender and Rural Modernity: Farm Women and the Politics of Labor in Germany, 1871–1933*. Abingdon: Routledge, 2009.

Karns Alexander, Jennifer. 'Rationalization Comes to Rome: Expertise in Labour Management at the Third International Congress, 1927', in Joris Vandendriessche et al. (eds), *Scientists' Expertise as Performance: Between State and Society, 1860–1960* (Abingdon: Routledge: 2015), 147–60.

Kloppenburg, Jack Jr. 'Social Theory and the De/Reconstruction of Agricultural Science: Local Knowledge for an Alternative Agriculture', in George Henderson and Marvin Waterstone (eds), *Geographic Thought: A Praxis Perspective* (Abingdon: Routledge, 2009), 248–65.

Knab, Cornelia, and Amalia Ribi Forclaz, 'Transnational Co-operation in Food, Agriculture, Environment and Health in Historical Perspective'. *Contemporary European History* 20(3) (2011), 247–55.

Krige, John. 'Introduction: Writing the Transnational History of Science and Technology', in John Krige (ed.), *How Knowledge Moves: Writing the Transnational History of Science and Technology* (Chicago: University of Chicago Press, 2019), 1–31.

Lancaster, Jane. *Making Time: Lillian Moller Gilbreth – A Life beyond 'Cheaper by the Dozen'*. Boston, MA: Northeastern University Press, 2004.

Laur, Ernst. *Die landwirtschaftliche Arbeiterfrage in der Schweiz: Vierter Teil: Vorschläge zur Lösung des Problems*. Brugg: Verlag des Schweizerischen Bauernsekretariats, 1916.

Maier, Charles S. 'The Politics of Productivity: Foundations of American International Economic Policy after World War II'. *International Organization* 31(4) (1977), 607–33.

Mann, Susan A., and James M. Dickinson. 'Obstacles to the Development of a Capitalist Agriculture'. *Journal of Peasant Studies* 5(4) (1978), 466–81.

Moser, Peter, and Tony Varley. 'The State and Agricultural Modernisation in the Nineteenth and Twentieth Centuries in Europe', in Peter Moser and Tony Varley (eds), *Integration through Subordination: The Politics of Agricultural Modernisation in Industrial Europe* (Turnhout: Brepols, 2013), 13–40.

Mundel, Marvin E. 'Farm Work Simplification'. *Mechanical Engineering* 65(8) (1943), 565–66.

Nolan, Mary. *Visions of Modernity: American Business and the Modernization of Germany*. New York: Oxford University Press, 1994.

Oberkrome, Willi. *Ordnung und Autarkie: Die Geschichte der deutschen Landbauforschung, Agrarökonomie und ländlichen Sozialwissenschaft im Spiegel von Forschungsdienst und DFG (1920–1970)*. Stuttgart, Steiner 2009.

Patel, Kiran Klaus. 'The History of European Integration and the Common Agricultural Policy: An Introduction', in Kiran Klaus Patel (ed.), *Fertile Ground for Europe? The*

History of European Integration and the Common Agricultural Policy since 1945 (Baden-Baden: Nomos, 2009), 7–23.

———. *The New Deal: A Global History*. Princeton: Princeton University Press, 2016.

———. 'The Green Heart of Governance: Rural Europe during the Interwar Years in Global Perspective', in Liesbeth van de Grift and Amalia Ribi Forclaz (eds), *Governing the Rural in Interwar Europe* (Abingdon: Routledge, 2018), 1–23.

Pessis, Céline, Sezin Topçu, and Christophe Bonneuil (eds), *Une autre histoire des 'Trente Glorieuses': Modernisation, contestations et pollutions dans la France d'après-guerre.* Paris: La Découverte, 2013.

Pfister, Christian. 'The "1950s Syndrome" and the Transition from a Slow-Going to a Rapid Loss of Global Sustainability', in Frank Uekötter (ed.), *The Turning Points of Environmental History* (Pittsburgh: University of Pittsburgh Press, 2010), 90–118.

Priebe, Hermann. *Landarbeit Heute und Morgen: Grundfragen und praktische Hilfen.* Hamburg: Paul Parey, 1953.

Rabinbach, Anson. *The Human Motor: Energy, Fatigue, and the Origins of Modernity.* Berkeley: University of California Press, 1992.

———. *The Eclipse of the Utopias of Labor.* New York: Fordham University Press, 2018.

Rasmussen, Wayne D. *A History of the Emergency Farm Labor Program, 1943–47.* Washington DC: US Government Printing Office, 1951.

Rodgers, Daniel T. *Atlantic Crossings: Social Politics in a Progressive Age.* Cambridge, MA: Harvard University Press, 1998.

Roth, Walter J. 'Review of *Arbeitsverfahren und Arbeitsleistungen in der Landwirtschaft*'. *Journal of Farm Economics* 13(4) (1931), 658–60.

Scott, James C. *Seeing Like a State: How Certain Schemes to Improve the Human Condition Have Failed.* New Haven: Yale University Press, 1998.

Seedorf, Wilhelm. *Die Vervollkommnung der Landarbeit und die bessere Ausbildung der Landarbeiter und besonderer Berücksichtigung des Taylor-Systems.* Berlin: Deutsche Landbuchhandlung, 1919.

———. 'Methods and Results of Research Work on the Efficiency of Human Labor on German Farms', in *Proceedings of the Second International Conference of Agricultural Economists* (Menasha: George Banta, 1930), 952–66.

Sewell, William H. Jr. *Work and Revolution in France: The Language of Labor from the Old Regime to 1848.* Cambridge: Cambridge University Press, 1980.

Speich Chassé, Daniel. 'Towards a Global History of the Marshall Plan: European Post-war Reconstruction and the Rise of Development Economic Expertise', in Christian Grabas and Alexander Nützenadel (eds), *Industrial Policy in Europe after 1945: Wealth, Power and Economic Development in the Cold War* (Basingstoke: Palgrave Macmillan, 2014), 187–212.

Subrahmanyam, Sanjay. 'Hearing Voices: Vignettes of Early Modernity in South Asia, 1400–1750'. *Daedalus* 127(3) (1998), 75–104.

Tapernoux, Frédéric Etienne. 'Organisation du travail agricole'. *Bulletin de la Classe d'Agriculture de la Société des Arts de Genève* 5(3) (1930), 1–16.

———. 'L'Organisation scientifique du travail agricole', in *Actes: XIVe Congrès international d'agriculture, Bucarest, 7, 8 et 10 juin 1929, Vol. 2* (Bucharest: Cultura Nationala, 1930–1932), 379–451.

Technological Mobilization: Hearings before a Subcommittee of the Committee on Military Affairs, United States Senate, 3 vols. Washington DC: US Government Printing Office, 1943.

Tucker, Barbara M. 'Agricultural Workers in World War II: The Reserve Army of Children, Black Americans, and Jamaicans'. *Agricultural History* 68(1) (1994), 54–73.

Vatin, François. *Le travail, sciences et société: Essais d'épistemologie et de sociologie du travail.* Brussels: Éditions de l'Université de Bruxelles, 1999.

Vaughan, Lawrence M., and Lowell S. Hardin. *Farm Work Simplification.* New York: Wiley, 1949.

Weber, Max. *Die Verhältnisse der Landarbeiter im ostelbischen Deutschland: Dargestellt auf Grund der vom Verein für Socialpolitik veranstalteten Erhebungen.* Leipzig: Duncker & Humblot, 1892.

White, Richard. *The Organic Machine.* New York: Hill & Wang, 1996.

Wills, John Elliot. 'Industrial Management Techniques in Agriculture'. *Journal of Farm Economics* 36(4) (1954), 565–74.

Winter, Gustav. *Der Taylorismus: Handbuch der wissenschaftlichen Betriebs- und Arbeitsweise für die Arbeitenden aller Klassen, Stände und Berufe.* Leipzig: Hirzel, 1920.

Young, Ernest Charles. 'Farm Work Simplification Studies'. *Journal of Farm Economics* 26(1) (1944), 232–39.

Young, Ernest Charles, and Lowell S. Hardin. 'Simplifying Farm Work', in *Yearbook of Agriculture 1943–1947: Science in Farming* (Washington DC: US Government Printing Office, 1947), 817–23.

Zimmerman, Andrew. *Alabama in Africa: Booker T. Washington, the German Empire, and the Globalization of the New South.* Princeton: Princeton University Press, 2010.

 CHAPTER 8

Putting Down Roots

Rural Youth Clubs in Costa Rica and Inter-American Development Cooperation, 1940–75

Corinne A. Pernet

Superar lo mejor was the somewhat ambiguous slogan of the 1966 Inter-American Rural Youth Congress for young rural leaders that was hosted in Rio de Janeiro, Brazil. The slogan was an allusion to the motto of the US 4-H youth clubs, 'To make the best better'. However, *superar* literally means to overcome an obstacle, challenge or opponent, so that the slogan could also be read as 'to overcome the best', emphasizing effort and competition under difficult conditions. The conference was organized by the Inter-American Program for Rural Youth, better known by its Spanish-language abbreviation PIJR (Programa Interamericano para la Juventud Rural). Headquartered in Costa Rica, the PIJR was established in 1960 as an attempt to federate and give visibility to rural youth movements in Latin America that sought to instil modern agricultural methods and turn the countryside into a productive asset and source of wealth. The conference welcomed high-level speakers, including the Brazilian Minister of Agriculture, representatives from the Organization of American States (OAS) and agricultural supply companies, specialists in agricultural extension work and, most importantly, delegations from rural youth clubs, most of which were modelled on the US 4-H clubs.[1]

Having first spread in the United States at the beginning of the twentieth century, the 4-H clubs for rural children and young adults were quintessentially structured as a private-public partnership. Founded and run by land-grant colleges in partnership with the United States Department of Agriculture (USDA), they also relied on close ties with the private sector for financial support and expertise. The pledge undertaken by the young club members explained what 4-H represented: 'I pledge my **h**ead to clearer thinking, my **h**eart to greater loyalty, my **h**ands to larger service, and my **h**ealth to better living, for my club, my community, my country.' Head, heart and hands were thus to work together in the acquisition und utilization of technological prowess in agriculture (for the boys) and homemaking (for the girls), all in pursuit of 'better living'. The four Hs were also symbolized in the four-leaf clover that served as the logo for the clubs. Apart from its focus on individual (material and personal) improvement, 4-H community life would prepare the youthful club members for democratic citizenship. According to the 4-H vision, the path to better living and loyal service lay not in dry instruction, but in 'learning by doing'. A US club typically had its own clubhouse situated next to several stables for small-scale animal husbandry and surrounded by vegetable gardens.[2] This was the rural youth club model that US agricultural extension experts aspired to transplant to other parts of the world – and that rural reformers in many countries, including across Latin America, were eager to emulate. Cuban 4-H clubs had started to emerge during the 1930s,[3] while the first clubs in Venezuela were established in 1940 after government officials visited 4-H clubs in Puerto Rico. The Venezuelan clubs operated under the name '5-V clubs', the five Vs standing for Venezuela, valour, vigour, truth (*verdad*) and modesty (*verguenza*).[4]

This chapter explores how the 4-H movement and the PIJR took hold in Central America, with a focus on Costa Rica. This rural youth movement has generally received scant historical attention, and its Latin American manifestations even less. However, the excellent work of Wilson Picado does mention the clubs as part of the US-sponsored agricultural advisory programmes established after the Second World War in Central America. According to Picado, the clubs were intended to jumpstart the Green Revolution through the introduction of new seeds, breeds, fertilizers and pesticides.[5] The few works on the PIJR have examined it as a US agent in the global Cold War[6] or as an instrument of capitalist expansion.[7] From the late 1940s onwards, the US government, the inter-American organizations as well as key Costa Rican actors all viewed the 4-H youth clubs (and later the PIJR) as part of the solution to one of the great socioeconomic problems in the region: millions of agricultural smallholders attempting to eke out a meagre living on limited land while more lucrative export goods (such as bananas, cotton and sugar) were produced on large plantations. The promise of the 4-H clubs was to provide rural girls and boys as well as young women and men with tools and knowhow that would have a positive impact on their lives and help them to overcome these challenging circumstances.

The dominant narrative concerning development policies in Latin America holds that projects that empowered disenfranchised rural inhabitants emerged with the Alliance for Progress after 1961.[8] However, certain notions of community development in rural areas have always coexisted with high-modernist approaches.[9] In Mexico, for instance, varieties of community development have been practised since the 1920s, and the country took on a pioneering role in the training of rural extension experts from the 1950s.[10] The development approaches of Latin American modernizers could coincide and interlink with

US models even while being embedded in quite different ideological contexts. This chapter thus offers a more fine-grained analysis of why, how and for whom the 4-H clubs functioned in local contexts in Central America, their beginnings as a top-down venture imposed by external actors notwithstanding.

The Institutional Context of Rural Youth Clubs in Costa Rica

The efforts to establish 4-H clubs in Latin America received a strong boost in the early 1940s, when President Franklin D. Roosevelt's Good Neighbor policy gained urgency due to the war in Europe and the disruption of global commodity supply chains. One key figure in fostering agricultural extension in Central America was Roosevelt's then Secretary of Agriculture, Henry A. Wallace, 'the most renowned agrarian New Dealer' with strong internationalist tendencies.[11] Wallace was keenly aware of the strategic importance of Central America and brokered several cooperation agreements at the beginning of the Second World War to secure foodstuffs and rubber from the region. Moreover, he pushed for the deployment of US extension workers to increase production there.

In 1940, Wallace sought direct cooperation with Latin American agricultural specialists by proposing the establishment of an Inter-American Institute for Agricultural Sciences (Instituto Interamericano de Ciencias Agrícolas [IICA]) under the auspices of the Pan-American Union (PAU), the predecessor of the OAS. The PAU welcomed Wallace's proposal and decided that Costa Rica would offer the most suitable location for the project. Costa Rica's President, Rafael Calderón García, was willing to set aside a sizeable area of land and declared himself enthusiastic about 'technical progress for an expanded and flourishing agriculture'.[12] With cooperation in agriculture important to the Roosevelt administration, Wallace took it upon himself to travel to the small town of Turrialba, some 60 kilometres east of the capital, San José, to officially open the IICA in May 1943. Given the wartime emphasis on the productivity of tropical agriculture, which provided important crops such as coffee, bananas and sugar, the IICA began by establishing divisions for agricultural engineering, entomology, crop production, soil science and livestock production.

After the war, the IICA began its extension work by establishing a Division of Economics and Rural Welfare in 1948. This was initially headed by Spencer Hatch, who had practice in community development approaches as a YMCA missionary in rural India.[13] The Division offered programmes to train the agricultural advisers who would staff the expanding number of extension stations in Latin America. There were also six-week intensive programmes for select rural teachers who were to become 'agents of change'. Their role would be to establish and then guide – either independently or in tandem with an extension agent – 4-H-inspired rural youth clubs.[14] Moreover, there were ten-hour *cursillos* (short courses) for rural teachers geared towards boosting them in their role as community leaders. While the IICA contributed to the training of *extensionistas* (agricultural extension workers) and offered important support for the 4-H clubs, the responsibility for financing and running the clubs lay elsewhere.

After the Second World War, the United States reorganized the work of its agricultural experts in Latin America and created the Inter-American Technical Service for Cooperation in Agriculture (Servicio Técnico Interamericano de Cooperación en Agricultura [STICA]), which was financed by President Truman's Point IV foreign aid legislation. This enabled governments interested in modernizing their agricultural sector to negotiate technical cooperation agreements with STICA, for which the United States would carry a part of the costs – typically, one-third to one-half of the proposed budget. Costa Rica's government was very interested in such opportunities; as of 1950, more than half of the country's labour force was working on farms and two-thirds of its population of 945,000 lived in the countryside. While Costa Rica was less poor than its Central American neighbours, its average life expectancy was still only approximately forty-six years (as had been the case in the United States in the late nineteenth century).[15]

Given this context, establishing an agricultural extension service, including youth clubs, was a crucial part of STICA's engagement in Costa Rica, the main aim of which was to improve living standards in the countryside. Even if experts brought new technologies and the necessary knowhow to rural areas, they still required farmers who were willing and able to use new technologies.[16] The 4-H youth clubs offered an attractive vehicle with which to spread modern agricultural techniques, because children and young adults were considered 'a pliable mass' who could be influenced more easily than supposedly recalcitrant adult farmers.[17] After the first 4-H youth clubs in Costa Rica had been established by the Ministry of Education in 1947 as part of a programme to promote school gardens and lunches, STICA established its own programmes and began training advisers for the clubs in 1949. The motto and slogans for the Costa Rican clubs were translated almost literally from their US 4-H equivalents. For example, the US motto 'Head, Heart, Hands, Health' became 'Saber [Knowledge], Sentimiento [Feeling], Servicio [as in "Using one's hands in service to the community"] and Salud [Health]'.

Work among the rural youth was an early priority for the Costa Rican agricultural extension service. In 1955, for instance, extension agents held 323 meetings with farmers, but over 3,000 meetings with 4-S clubs.[18] Because attempts to create organized groups of farmers with whom the extension agents could work on a regular basis towards the goal of modernizing agriculture had not been very successful,[19] considerable care was taken to socialize the rural youth into regular close contact with the extension stations and agents, as the reports of the Ministry of Agriculture and Industry show. The 1950 census indicated that 125,000 children between the ages of ten and nineteen lived in the countryside. Only 25 per cent were still attending school, as many children started to work from around the age of fourteen.[20]

The new 4-S clubs quickly attracted interest among children and young adults. From a modest start of 19 clubs with a total of 451 members in 1949, there were 178 clubs with 3,115 members by 1953. Further growth was limited by the low number of extension workers available to assist and guide the new clubs. The number of STICA extension workers had grown from five in 1948 to only eleven by 1950 (including one lone woman, who taught home economics). The Ministry's reports noted the great personal sacrifices of the extension agents, who spent a considerable proportion of their leisure hours working on 4-S issues.[21] Still, the 4-S clubs also had to rely on volunteer leaders to support their activities.

In 1955, STICA shifted its priorities to agricultural research and withdrew from the Costa Rican 4-S programme. Responsibility for the 4-S clubs now lay solely with the country's Ministry of Agriculture.[22] Although resources became scarcer as a result, the 4-S club movement continued to grow and reached a membership of between 4,500 and 5,000 during the early 1960s. However, given these numbers, 4-S clubs were enrolling a mere 3–4 per cent of rural children in Costa Rica. Yet, hopes remained high that these aspiring farmers would be able to ignite future progress in Costa Rican agriculture.

In the early 1950s, the Ministry described the 4-S clubs as key for 'communal progress and dignification of rural life'. Especially considering that so many rural teenagers were leaving school early, 4-S clubs were to serve as a conduit for informal education.[23] The clubs were tasked with providing their members with practical knowledge and involving them in projects that would make them 'look towards the future with more confidence'. The rural youth, it was hoped, would thereby be empowered to contribute to the economic well-being of their families. Moreover, participation in the clubs would help these children and young adults to become good citizens who would respect democratic processes and shoulder responsibility within their communities. In an attempt to circumvent any tensions with the Catholic Church, the Ministry declared that the 4-S clubs respected 'Christian morals' and offered no competition to communal religious life.[24] While these ambitions represented the government's vision for the 4-S clubs, most of the young club members would have had different reasons for joining. Indeed, it was the activities and social aspects that attracted potential members and accounted for the success of the clubs.

Learning by Doing: The 4-S Clubs in Action

The activities of the Costa Rican 4-S clubs varied from location to location, but most commenced with the young members establishing or reorganizing a family vegetable garden. Supplied with seeds by the extension agents, the boys and girls were then taught how to plant, weed and fertilize their plots. Their gardens contributed produce to the family dinner table and improved nutrition, as Costa Rica's starch-based main staples of rice, beans and corn tortillas were typically only infrequently supplemented with leafy greens or proteins.[25] The girls also learnt how to turn garden produce into appetizing meals and, after abundant harvests, into conserves to be stored for later family consumption or sale. Seeing that children's participation in 4-S clubs came with benefits for the whole family, parents became less reluctant to let their own children join a club. Many parents had been decidedly sceptical about the clubs because they believed that their children should be under parental supervision and were afraid that membership would be expensive, cause problems and distract their children from more important activities.

Once a club was established and functioning, the club members typically decided on projects that they wanted to undertake with the support of the adult club leaders, namely agricultural extension workers or teachers who had undergone the appropriate training. Besides vegetable plot 'starter projects', popular activities included the raising of rabbits or chickens for family consumption or sale. Other clubs taught their members how to keep bees.[26] Occasionally, the extension service donated large livestock like breeding pigs or cattle from demonstration farms to a 4-S club with the idea that any offspring could be distributed among the club members.[27] In 1960, over two hundred children and young adults were learning how to care for large farm animals, including how to present them at agricultural exhibitions.[28] Members also attended demonstrations by extension officers on topics such as how to use fertilizers or pesticides to increase crop yields or how to vaccinate chickens, with demonstration equipment provided by the local extension office. All in all, such projects provided a platform for extension agents to introduce the young club members to 'modern' methods of agriculture. While the extension service thus taught and embraced the use of fertilizers and pesticides, the 4-S clubs were also engaged in soil conservation and reforestation projects. They participated in the annual Conservation of Natural Resources Weeks that were celebrated in Costa Rica in the 1950s. Promoting better irrigation practices was also part of the 4-S programme.

At times, 4-S clubs were run like small-scale enterprises. This involved, for example, a club taking out a small loan with which to invest in tomato plants, repaying the loan with the proceeds from the sale of the tomatoes, and using any profit to invest in new projects.[29] Although such projects fell under the financial responsibility of the clubs and were run with the assistance of the club leaders, their example was intended to inspire the young club members to be enterprising as individuals. The 4-H clubs also organized small fairs in nearby communities to show off – and sell – their produce and manufactured products (such as preserves and handicrafts). These events had a positive effect by encouraging attendees to appreciate the benefits of the 4-S movement, which made it easier for the clubs to gain access to the resources in their communities that they needed for their work (such as a barn or abandoned house for use as a clubhouse, building materials, seeds or livestock).[30] The clubs also participated in larger agricultural shows and competitions. For example, at the National Dairy Cattle Exhibition that took place in Cartago in March 1955, twenty-five 4-S club members proudly displayed their calves, but they also strolled through the exhibition, taking in the 'magnificent' stands of the participating ministries and the many private companies that were displaying their modern machinery, feed or vaccination equipment.[31]

Although they learned much about 'modern' agriculture, boys from the poorest families appreciated receiving basic tools through their 4-S clubs, including hoes, picks, rakes, shovels or hammers, while girls were given sewing kits or preserving jars. Many of these implements were donated by third parties, such as the humanitarian organization CARE.[32] The 4-S programme was not only concerned with making the rural youth more productive; if young persons were to be encouraged to stay in the countryside, rural homes needed to be made 'more pleasant' and 'dignified'.[33] Girls and young women were taught how to sew clothes, tablecloths and curtains, and were encouraged to use flowers and inexpensive decorations to make their homes more appealing. For a girl who slept in a single room along with twelve other family members, sewing clothes was probably more relevant than home decoration, but all of these activities were popular. The boys also engaged in home improvement, learning how to build simple furniture, install sinks and construct hygienic outhouses, and whitewash their houses. Most 4-S club members would receive home visits from extension agents several times per year, which were an opportunity for the agents to assess how families were doing in general and to offer advice.[34]

The 4-S clubs also functioned as important venues of rural sociability. Club meetings typically took place every other week, and there were regular additional offerings, such as day-long training sessions, excursions to nearby demonstration plots, or opportunities to participate in community events or agricultural fairs. Although these activities took place under adult supervision, they offered members the opportunity to be around persons of their own age, which was particularly important for those who had already left school. Members could enjoy an autonomous space away from their families in which their personal preferences counted to at least a certain degree. For young persons with little access to urban amenities, even the educational films about rural life that 4-S clubs would show once or twice a year could offer a welcome change of scene.[35] Some 4-S clubs also provided opportunities to engage in community work. In the Orosi region, for instance, local clubs came together to raise funds and organize the construction of a Stations of the Cross for a local church, an initiative that caught the attention of the Archbishop of San José. At its inauguration, the Minister of Agriculture as well as the US Ambassador were also present.[36]

The Costa Rican extension service, supported by STICA, supplemented its work on the ground with public relations activities. In the early 1950s, it produced a monthly magazine, *La Carreta*, which took its name from the typical brightly painted Costa Rican oxcart. Members of 4-S clubs received the magazine free of charge, while it was distributed more widely through the extension offices. In Costa Rica, the country with the highest literacy rate in Central America (ca. 68 per cent), the magazine had a large potential audience. It contained articles on agricultural knowhow, which were always tied to an in-season crop or product, as well as on inexpensive and simple but nutritious recipes. *La Carreta* also reported on 4-S activities. Seeing their club's achievements covered in a national magazine would have offered a feeling of pride for the young participants. By 1955, 72,000 copies of *La Carreta* had been distributed.[37] The agricultural extension service also broadcast its own weekly radio programme that regularly featured the activities of 4-S clubs.[38]

Even after STICA withdrew from the 4-H club programme in 1955, the Costa Rican Ministry of Agriculture was able to increase the number of clubs and boost their membership into the 1960s. It introduced an annual National Week of 4-S Clubs and offered considerable public recognition for the clubs and their leaders. In 1960, the Costa Rican Parliament passed a law to create a National 4-S Foundation (Fundación Nacional de Clubes 4-S), whose role it would be to support the extension service in its work, and to receive and distribute funds and material support donated by the private sector.[39] Moreover, the 4-S clubs also continued to receive material support from the IICA. These developments occurred at a time when the 1959 Cuban Revolution was underlining the strategic importance of democratic rural youth movements in Latin America, as the next section explores.

Taking Stock before Scaling up: Rural Youth Programme Surveys

From 1959, Latin American elites, the United States and commercial actors with ties in the region were all rocked by the Cuban Revolution and the anticapitalist direction it was taking. Preventing the spread of revolutionary turmoil became the order of the day, with the countryside a major target of reformist policies that were intended to quell any potential unrest. In 1960, the Organization of American States joined a private foundation, the American International Association for Economic and Social Development (AIA), in bringing rural youth clubs from across the Western Hemisphere together under the banner of the progressive yet decidedly nonrevolutionary PIJR, which was headquartered within the IICA in Turrialba.

The AIA was a foundation established by Nelson A. Rockefeller, a scion of one of the richest families in the United States who had a longstanding interest in Latin America. For decades, Rockefeller had been arguing that it was in the best interests of US businesses to support social reforms in Latin America. Beginning in the 1940s, the AIA had engaged in a basic version of rural extension described as 'A man, a girl, and a jeep' in reference to extension workers, home economists and transportation being considered the main ingredients for jumpstarting rural economies.[40] The AIA supported youth clubs in Venezuela and Brazil, and ran several projects on small budgets.[41] The AIA's then chief rural extension officer, Howard E. Law, was impressed with the work of the Venezuelan 5-V clubs, but he argued that they were hampered by their dependence on government funding and their small budgets. In 1957, Law started lobbying the AIA with the idea of scaling up 5-V operations by raising money from the private sector to finance the clubs' activities. However, it took the spectre of the Cuban Revolution for Law to obtain funds from the AIA to bolster these 4-H-inspired youth clubs. As AIA Vice President John Camp stated, the rural masses had become frustrated by their harsh circumstances and were 'demanding a better way of living'. 'If they don't get it', he warned, 'they may resort to political means to attain their needs.'[42] The newly established PIJR tried to pre-empt such political radicalism by raising the standard of living in the countryside and offering a 'productive' outlet for youthful energy by bringing together 4-H clubs from across Latin America to form an internationally visible reformist rural youth movement.

However, before engaging in major programmes, the PIJR leadership decided to take stock of 4-H-style clubs and their activities in Central America. Earl Jones, a US agricultural extensionist who had already undertaken research at the IICA in the late 1950s, was tasked with compiling this study. Jones completed considerable desk research on rural living conditions and conducted surveys of diverse stakeholders to assess the state of rural advancement. Importantly, he also sent questionnaires to a representative selection of clubs from across the region and supplemented these with in-person interviews with club members. The 115 members' survey responses provide valuable glimpses into the 4-H clubs.[43]

An important question Jones sought to answer was why young Central Americans joined 4-S clubs. Pressure from parents did not seem play any role;

instead, the most frequent answer to this question was 'to learn something useful for the farm and home', which was, after all, the raison d'être of the clubs. However, only forty-five respondents (thirty-four between ten and thirteen years of age, and eleven between the ages of fourteen and twenty-one) mentioned this as their main reason for joining. For twenty-four respondents in the younger age category, social activities and companionship were also important motivations for joining.[44] Similarly, the career plans of the respondents showed that farming was not perceived as an attractive occupation. Of the fifty-three boys surveyed, only eighteen (seventeen of whom came from a single club) wanted to become farmers, whereas twenty-two aspired to be mechanics or engineers, and eleven aimed to become teachers. Similarly, of the sixty-two girls surveyed, thirty-seven and nineteen aspired to be seamstresses and teachers respectively, while a mere four girls wanted to be rural homemakers.[45] The female respondents probably knew from personal experience what being a 'homemaker' entailed in rural Central America, but had little idea of the long hours and poor pay faced by seamstresses. The fact that members of both genders mentioned teaching as a desirable career indicates that there was a widely held aspiration to climb the social ladder. Ironically, eight boys and twelve girls stated that they joined a club specifically to boost their chances of moving away from the countryside.[46]

While the respondents might not have preferred rural life, most considered the 4-S programme to be beneficial, although their judgement in this regard varied according to age and gender. Almost all of the club members under fourteen years of age (seventy-seven out of eighty-one) thought that 4-S activities were 'very' or 'quite useful', with only four boys (and no girls) saying that they offered 'little usefulness'. The thirty-four members between the ages of fourteen and twenty-one were slightly more critical: five young men and two young women saw 'little usefulness' in the programme, nine young men and seven young women saw 'some usefulness', but only two young men and five young women considered the 4-S clubs to be 'very useful'.[47] With growing age and experience came the realization that the 4-S clubs could not change socio-economic structures and that improvement of rural living conditions would be a long and difficult journey.

Enthusiasm was greatest among respondents whose club activities had led to an increase in their family's food supply or home comfort. In one club, the children came from exceedingly small farms (below 3 acres), lived in rough wooden or cane houses and owned no shoes. In such circumstances, a vegetable garden or a rabbit-raising or food preservation project could make a significant contribution to family welfare. Overall, most of the 115 surveyed youth (ninety-two) declared themselves to 'like' such 'individual projects' 'very much'. Collective projects fared decidedly less well ('liked very much' by only 23 respondents). Recreation opportunities and club meetings were the other features of 4-S clubs that were appreciated by the vast majority of respondents (100 and 97 respectively). However, a sizeable group of respondents were less enthusiastic about other key features of 4-S clubs: Only thirty-seven respondents 'liked' the regular competitions 'very much', while twenty-nine 'liked' them 'somewhat', another sixteen 'liked' them 'little' and thirteen did not participate in competitions at all. Interestingly, achievement day itself, a club's annual prize-giving celebration, was viewed rather more positively despite the general dislike of competitions ('liked very much' by sixty-six respondents and 'liked somewhat' by thirty).[48] Questions about the desired qualities of volunteer leaders and extension agents elicited revealing answers. Among all the respondents, the qualities most frequently mentioned were (in this order): 'good teacher', 'knows the subject', 'nice person', 'wants to help' and 'patient'.[49]

This was consistent with a previous study by Jones, a 1959 survey of rural teenage boys in Costa Rica. The respondents' ideal extension worker had been one who 'knows coffee, hard worker, good teacher, intelligent, honourable, knows the people', is 'patient and pragmatic' and is a 'good guy' who 'wants to help'. However, as much as the respondents wanted 'intelligent leaders', they did not want them to 'act superior', but rather to 'keep his word'.[50] Together with the emphasis on the importance of hands-on, hardworking demonstrators, this can be interpreted as criticism of urban experts who preferred talking to getting their hands dirty.[51] Moreover, the insistence that extension agents needed to 'keep their word' evokes past experiences of broken promises. In the pursuit of rural development, there was perhaps only a thin line between encouragement and optimism, on the one hand, and 'broken promises', on the other.

The IICA distributed approximately two thousand copies of a summarized version of Jones' research[52] and integrated his findings into its training programmes. In 1961, for instance, the IICA organized a workshop for 4-S volunteer club leaders in Puriscal, Costa Rica. The accompanying handbook emphasized that club leaders needed to be well qualified, but nothing was more important than for them to have 'amicable respect' for the rural youth and to attempt to understand the problems of the club members. Club leaders also needed to have the ability to devise projects according to local needs and (economic) capacities.[53] Jones was very clear that the 4-S clubs should first and foremost be 'devoted to improvement of the economic situation' and to eliminating 'dangers and inconveniences' in rural homes. Another of his recommendations was to soften the competitive aspects of club life, which did 'more harm than good' for the many 'who cannot compete in any group'. For Jones, offering members personal attention and helping to improve their skills would be a better approach.[54]

By the beginning of the 1960s, a rising level of expertise on working with the rural youth had developed around the IICA in Turrialba. Agricultural advisers and experts were evolving their own approaches that were adapted to Central American conditions and focused squarely on the needs of the membership of each club. However, the trajectory that the 4-S movement subsequently took under the auspices of the PIJR marked a directional shift in its priorities.

Scaling up and Widening the Gap: the IICA and the PIJR

When the PIJR set to work in 1960, it aimed to give more visibility to the 4-S clubs, also with a view to attracting more funding from the private sector. The PIJR sought to turn itself into a beacon for the rural youth, an organization that would bring together young people from all over rural Latin America, irrespective of nationality, politics or ethnicity. Because government training of extension workers through the different national ministries of agriculture never seemed to keep up with demand, the PIJR stepped up its own efforts to promote 'volunteer leaders' for the 4-S clubs. Until the late 1960s, the PIJR's programme emphasized the transnational character of the 4-S youth movement and promoted training opportunities in many different locations. However, requiring extension workers as well as volunteer leaders to travel extensively had the paradoxical effect of widening the gap between them and the club members whom they were supposed to serve in the countryside.

Jones' study also surveyed the opinions of 47 4-H programme officials on how best to attract and support volunteer youth leaders. The top two entries were 'recognition' (twenty-six mentions) and 'training' (twenty-six), both of which were considered crucial to maintain the volunteers' motivation and commitment. Only six respondents cited international exchanges as an incentive in this regard. Similar views were expressed on how to strengthen the commitment of programme officials, with 'training' (twenty-five), 'recognition' (seventeen) and 'technical assistance' (thirteen) being the three most cited prerequisites for successfully mentoring a club. Once again, with only three mentions, 'international exchanges' were not considered important.[55] On the other hand, the respondents' insistence on the importance of technical assistance pointed to one of the major problems facing 4-H clubs: their funding shortfall.[56]

To durably boost club membership, the respondents cited the importance of offering incentives for club members. To appeal to members below fourteen years of age, clubs needed to offer 'economic help' (twenty-two mentions) and be based on their members' interests (twenty-one). Recognition (seventeen mentions) and recreation (eleven) were also recognized as motivating factors for this younger group. The picture changed slightly for those older than fourteen. For this group, programmes based on 'member interest' were paramount (forty mentions), while 'economic help' (the supply of seeds, livestock or basic equipment) ranked second (twenty-four). Providing recognition (seventeen mentions) or training (eleven) were also deemed important.[57] When asked what form of support the 4-S clubs should receive from donors and international organizations, the club leaders were clear that recognition for hard work and achievement in the form of prizes, equipment or jobs would be helpful. International exchanges were not considered attractive and received only four mentions from the younger group and a single mention from the older members.[58]

In the heady days of the early 1960s, the PIJR attempted to chart a course that satisfied these diverse demands. Nevertheless, despite the survey finding that attitudes towards travel and exchanges were cool, the PIJR pressed on with a considerable programme of international workshops, conferences and exchanges that brought together youth leaders from across the Americas.[59] In so doing, the PIJR privileged what it perceived as a political necessity over the club leaders' and programme officials' day-to-day grassroots work with their rural constituents.

The PIJR increased its offering of international training courses for volunteer leaders and club officials. The 1961 Seminar for Rural Youth Leaders in Turrialba, for instance, brought together participants from Argentina, Brazil, Colombia, Costa Rica, Ecuador, Honduras, Peru, Uruguay, Venezuela and the United States.[60] In 1963, training courses for volunteer leaders were held in Jamaica and El Salvador.[61] Linking training to international travel limited the circle of possible participants. Travel was not easy to organize for volunteer leaders who had responsibilities on their family farms, especially if long distances were involved. This also meant that girls and women would become increasingly marginalized in PIJR activities.[62] In Costa Rica, for instance, there were ninety-eight female 4-S volunteer leaders in 1961, thirty of whom were housewives, twenty of whom were teachers and ten of whom were farmers. It is doubtful whether these women could have easily engaged in long-distance travel or international exchanges.[63]

The PIJR deemed a stay in the United States as 'the most important' aspect of its six-month training programme for club leaders.[64] Fostering relations between the United States and Latin American youth leaders clearly represented a political agenda rather than the most effective means through which to improve their leadership skills. While creating a mobile network of experts in rural youth work undoubtedly had its advantages, these came at the risk of widening their distance to the field. It remains unclear whether international exchanges resulted in improved extension work or even served as motivation for 4-S leaders. Nevertheless, the PIJR went even further by considering it necessary to bring all youth leaders who had been on exchanges together in a seminar to discuss their experiences.[65]

Much energy and money were expended on hosting high-level conferences in different countries, where young leaders could be showcased and have the opportunity to interact with bureaucrats and national elites. Indeed, ministers and even presidents appeared at these conferences to give inspirational speeches at elaborate banquets. In 1964, seventy-two youth leaders travelled to the United States for two weeks, first to attend the Inter-American Rural Youth Congress and then to participate in a tour of 4-H clubs and state fairs. This trip was financed in part by the Alliance for Progress and the US 4-H Foundation.[66] The lavish banquet at the 1966 Congress in Rio de Janeiro, during which winners of major prizes such as training fellowships or travel stipends for further conferences were announced, was sponsored by the Brazilian subsidiary of the US department store giant Sears Roebuck. Photographs from the event show several 4-S club members who appear quite uncomfortable in these surroundings. The Congress' work group meetings, during which 4-S clubs' successes and challenges were discussed, could be similarly intimidating,[67] but a visit to a local 4-H club was likely less stressful. The Congress's final large-scale edition was held in Panama in 1967 and included delegates from twelve countries. Not all actors within the 4-H movement in Latin America were happy with such extravaganzas. Unlike officials stationed at IICA headquarters, many

Figure 8.1. A Sears Roebuck-sponsored banquet during the first Inter-American Congress of the Inter-American Program for Rural Youth. Orton Memorial Library, Turrialba, Costa Rica

extension agents – who worked throughout the year with club members in the field – thought that too much money was being spent on conferences and public relations activities even as the clubs had to scramble for the most basic supplies.[68]

In 1967, the PIJR suffered a severe blow when Nelson Rockefeller, frustrated by the unwillingness of the private sector to contribute money to his foundation, dissolved the AIA. The loss of AIA funding left the PIJR directors in Costa Rica with severely limited means. From 1968, 'administration and supervision' of the PIJR was transferred to the 4-H Foundation in the United States, while its South American offices were closed and its activities reduced.[69] The next large injection of funding into the PIJR (over US$600,000) was a four-year grant from the US-based Kellogg Foundation starting in 1971. But the Kellogg Foundation's interests did not lie in personal development, leadership or contributions to democracy. Instead, it sought to evaluate whether 4-S club youth work had a positive impact on food production and economic development. Guatemala, Costa Rica, Paraguay and Venezuela were chosen to implement pilot projects to increase food production.[70] The Costa Rican project, for instance, was supposed to boost the production of corn and pork by 450 per cent.[71] This was a far cry from the beginnings of the 4-S movement in Costa Rica, when the needs of the local youth had determined the clubs' programmes. Personal growth and capacity building among the rural youth thus took a backseat to a singular focus on raising productivity. However, the engagement of the Kellogg Foundation was short-lived and no further grants were forthcoming. When the 4-H Foundation also refused to provide further financial support, the PIJR was discontinued in 1975.

Reflecting on the implications of the collapse of the PIJR, Gabriel Rosenberg has claimed that the Latin American 4-H clubs 'fell into disarray and dissolved'.[72] However, this was clearly not the case in Costa Rica. Throughout the 1960s and 1970s, Costa Rican 4-S clubs continued their work with personnel and supplies from the Ministry of Agriculture as well as additional technical support from the IICA and other international organizations such as the Food and Agriculture Organization of the United Nations. By 1976, there were over eight hundred 4-S clubs in Costa Rica with a combined membership of over 15,000. Their activities remained much the same as before: meetings, projects and demonstrations as well as field trips. Even rabbits were still promoted as an inexpensive source of nutritious meat.[73] Although they had become less visible at an international level, 4-S clubs in Costa Rica were there to stay.

Conclusion

Agricultural extension in Central America was initially promoted by the United States as a means of ensuring regional food security at a time of global crisis. In postwar Central America, reformist forces were keen to encourage the rural youth to become community organizers who would promote the 4-H club model. While the ideological underpinnings of 4-H did not have strong roots in the Central American countryside, the youth clubs proved successful in their own right. When given the opportunity, many rural children and young adults in Central America – who were disadvantaged in every sense – flocked to the 4-H clubs because they offered a space for sociability as well as a chance to acquire practical skills and contribute to household production.

This extension work with the rural youth was based on cooperation between a large number of international and domestic actors, a context that created its own challenges. Especially in the years following the Cuban Revolution, the anticommunist agendas of many Western hemisphere governments bolstered their interest in the rural youth. For the 4-H movement in Latin America, the influx of money from the AIA, a private foundation, permitted a scale-up of the 4-H clubs. However, above all, it contributed to the professionalization of youth programme leaders and volunteers, thereby creating a visible elite of rural youth specialists with international connections. The PIJR considered this professionalization process wholly desirable as an avenue for social mobility and seemed oblivious to its paradoxical effect. Few of the volunteer club leaders had the capacity or desire to participate in or organize conferences and other large-scale events; by expending so many resources on the few who did wish to operate on an international level, the PIJR contributed to widening the gap between the 'leaders' of youth extension work and the rural communities whom they served.

After the grandiose dreams of a reformist, transnational rural youth movement centred in Costa Rica disintegrated, the country's 4-S clubs nevertheless continued with their work and even expanded their membership. Of course, Costa Rica has been in a privileged position. Other countries in the region – Nicaragua, Guatemala, El Salvador and Honduras – all had to contend with military juntas, revolutions and protracted civil wars. In Nicaragua, the 1979 Sandinista revolution put an end to the country's 4-H clubs, but they re-emerged gradually after 1996.[74] Costa Rica, by contrast, has maintained stability under governments that have expanded the state's presence and services in the countryside year after year. This stability, in turn, has also contributed to the country's higher standards of living.

Unquestionably, Costa Rica's 4-S clubs began in the 1940s as a transplant: a top-down, outside-in intervention in rural community life. By catering – for the most part – to the needs of Costa Rica's disadvantaged rural youth for decades, this transplant has nevertheless found fertile ground. The 4-S clubs were able to grow sufficiently deep roots in the Costa Rican countryside to foster a continuing demand for their services from the rural population. Successive Costa Rican governments, in turn, have considered the 'learning by doing' approach of the 4-S clubs to be beneficial for agriculture as well as for social welfare, as evidenced by the Ministry of Agriculture's continuing financial support even after foreign funding dwindled and the international visibility of the 4-H movement waned.

Today, there are around 280 4-S clubs with close to 5,000 members in Costa Rica, more than half of them children and young adults. Recent research has found that among students enrolled at professional (agricultural) colleges in Costa Rica, former or active members of 4-S clubs 'exhibited significantly higher levels of positive youth development' (namely 'competence, confidence, character, caring and connection') than their peers who had not been 4-S members.[75] After a partial shift in target groups, 4-S clubs for women of all ages have been established in recent decades; today, women account for approximately 40 per cent of all 4-S members.[76] A detailed examination of the evolution of the 4-S clubs lies beyond the scope of this chapter, but their principle of 'learning by doing' as well as the small incentives and technical training offered to their members remain much the same. A cursory browse of the Facebook pages of present-day Costa Rican 4-S clubs shows that they still proudly display the four-leaf clover symbol and that their manifold activities continue to appeal to the country's rural youth.

Corinne A. Pernet is a historian who has worked extensively on Latin American countries' entanglements with international organizations (the Pan-American Union, the League of Nations, the International Labour Organization, the Food and Agriculture Organization and the United Nations Educational, Scientific and Cultural Organization), addressing themes such as food and nutrition policy, education and development. From 2010 to 2016, she worked as a Swiss National Science foundation (SNF) research professor at the University of St Gallen and the University of Basel before switching to the University of Geneva. Since 2020, she has been head of the Department of International Educational Development at the Zurich University of Teacher Training (PHZH). With Corinna R. Unger and Iris Borowy, she recently coedited the *Routledge Handbook on the History of Development* (Routledge, 2022).

Notes

1. Programa Interamericano para la Juventud Rural (PIJR), 'Make the Best Better', ix, x.
2. Rosenberg, *4-H Harvest*, 2–8.

3. Rosenberg, 'Programa Interamericano', 3.
4. The inclusion of 'modesty' in the slogan might have had to do with the large female membership of the 5-V clubs and the fact that the propriety of girls and women was a major societal concern. '4-H Clubs Speak Spanish', 37; Warren, '4-H Clubs', 190–91.
5. Picado, 'Genética Guerrera', 126.
6. Rosenberg, *4-H Harvest*, 186–222.
7. Marin and Andreu, 'Juventud Rural', 619–22, 643–50.
8. The Alliance for Progress was an aid programme of the John F. Kennedy administration to promote social reforms and democracy in Latin America. Latham, *Right Kind of Revolution*, 111, 124–33; Streeter, 'Nation Building', 61–62.
9. Immerwahr, *Lure of Community Development*, 4–14; cf. Ekbladh, *Great American Mission*.
10. Langrod, 'Community Development', 122–39.
11. Olsson, *Agrarian Crossings*, 120.
12. Instituto Interamericano de Ciencias Agrícolas (IICA), *IICA – Fifty Years*, 24.
13. Fischer-Tiné, 'Low-Modernist', 193–200.
14. IICA, 'Annual Report 1950', 88–89.
15. Fox, 'Real Progress', 6.
16. IICA, 'Agricultural Extension', 3–10.
17. Rosenberg, *4-H Harvest*, 183.
18. Ministerio de Agricultura e Industrias (MAI), 'Memoria 1955', 89–90.
19. MAI, 'Memoria 1951', 191; MAI, 'Memoria 1953', 254.
20. MAI, 'Memoria 1953', 245.
21. Ibid., 247.
22. Fox, *U.S. Aid*, 5.
23. Jones, 'Study of Rural Youth Programs', 90.
24. MAI, 'Memoria 1953', 245–46.
25. Coto, 'Alimento Bendito', 13–16; cf. Pernet, 'Entanglements and Dependencies', 110–115.
26. Ministerio de Agricultura y Ganadería (MAG), 'Memoria 1960', 58.
27. MAG, 'Memoria 1957', 49.
28. MAG, 'Memoria 1960', 62.
29. MAI, 'Memoria 1951', 192.
30. Ibid., 193.
31. MAI, 'Memoria 1955', 33.
32. MAG, 'Memoria 1959', 45–46; MAG, 'Memoria 1960', 66, 100; MAG, 'Memoria 1964', 87; see also Wieters, *Showered with Kindness?*
33. MAI, 'Memoria 1951', 196; MAI, 'Memoria 1955', 249.
34. MAG, 'Memoria 1960', 62.
35. MAI, 'Memoria 1955', 88.
36. MAI, 'Memoria 1953', 248.
37. MAI, 'Memoria 1955', 87.
38. MAI, 'Memoria 1951', 253.
39. MAI, 'Memoria 1960', 56.
40. Boardman, *AIA*, n.p.; Vessuri, 'Foreign Scientists', 267–70.

41. Dalrymple, *AIA Story*, 63; Rivas, *Missionary Capitalist*.
42. '12 Americans Staff AIA in Costa Rica', *Gettysburg Times*, 8 November 1962, 6.
43. Jones, 'Rural Youth Programs', 73–74, 86.
44. Ibid., 62.
45. Ibid., 59.
46. Ibid., 62.
47. Ibid., 64.
48. Ibid., 63.
49. Ibid., 67.
50. Jones, 'Study of a Costa Rican Rural Education Center', 51.
51. Harwood, 'Peasant Friendly Plant Breeding', 398–400.
52. Jones, *Summary*.
53. Jones, 'Liderazgo', n.p. (23–24, my pagination).
54. Jones, *Summary*, 5–6.
55. Jones, 'Rural Youth Programs', 50.
56. In Costa Rica, the cost of the whole programme amounted to US$78,000 US per year, approximately 8 per cent of the Ministry's budget. See ibid., 49.
57. Ibid., 50.
58. Ibid.
59. Fundación Nacional 4-H de los Estados Unidos, 'Seminario Interamericano', Table 27 (n.p.).
60. Ibid., n.p. (13, my pagination).
61. PIJR, 'Quarterly Report July–September 1963', 4–5.
62. Rosenberg, *4-H Harvest*, 194–204.
63. Jones, 'Rural Youth Programs', 46.
64. Fundación Nacional 4-H de los Estados Unidos, 'Seminario Interamericano', n.p.
65. Ibid., n.p. (9, my pagination).
66. Henry Goethals, 'Agricultural Training to Be Probed', *Daily News-Post* (Monrovia), 25 August 1964, 2.
67. PIJR, 'Make the Best Better', 3, 5–7.
68. PIJR, 'Quarterly Report September 1967', 3.
69. PIJR, 'Quarterly Report October/December 1967', 1.
70. IICA, 'Report to the W.K. Kellogg Foundation', xx.
71. PIJR, 'Boletín Informativo Juventud Rural, no.1, 1972', 5.
72. Rosenberg, 'Programa Interamericano', 9.
73. MAG, 'Memoria 1976', 8–15; MAG, 'Memoria 1979', 46–49.
74. IICA, *Manual para la organización de jóvenes rurales*, 6.
75. Lopes et al., '4-S Positive Youth Development', 5–6.
76. Consejo Nacional de Clubes 4S, 'Informe Annual 2018', 16.

Bibliography

'4-H Clubs Speak Spanish'. *Extension Service Review* 12(3) (1941), 37.

Bevilaqua Marin, Joel O., and Fátima Andreu. 'Juventud Rural: Una Invención del Capitalismo Industrial'. *Estudios Sociológicos* 27(80) (2009), 619–53.

Boardman, Margaret C. 'The Man, the Girl and the Jeep AIA: Nelson Rockefeller's Precursor Non-Profit Model for Private U.S. Foreign Aid'. *Mexico and the World* 6(1) (2001). Retrieved 22 November 2020 from http://www.profmex.org/mexicoandtheworld/vo lume6/1winter01/01boardman1.html.

Cobbs Hoffman, Elizabeth. *The Rich Neighbor Policy: Rockefeller and Kaiser in Brazil*. New Haven: Yale University Press, 1992.

Consejo Nacional de Clubes 4S. 'Informe Annual 2018'. San José: 2019.

Coto Cedeño, Wainer Ignacio. 'Historia de un Alimento Bendito: Producción y Consumo de Papa en Costa Rica (1943–2015)'. *HALAC – Historia Ambiental, Latinoamericana y Caribeña* 7(2) (2017), 10–31.

Dalrymple, Martha. *The AIA Story: Two Decades of International Cooperation*. New York: American International Association for Economic and Social Development, 1968.

Ekbladh, David. *The Great American Mission: Modernization and the Construction of an American World Order*. Princeton: Princeton University Press, 2011.

Fischer-Tiné, Harald. 'The YMCA and Low-Modernist Rural Development in South Asia, c.1922–1957'. *Past & Present* 240(1) (2018), 193–234.

Fox, James W. *U.S. Aid to Costa Rica: An Overview*. Arlington: Agency for International Development, 1996.

———. 'Real Progress: Fifty Years of USAID in Costa Rica'. USAID Program and Operations Assessment Report, 23. Arlington: US Agency for International Development, 1998.

Fundación Nacional 4-H de los Estados Unidos. 'Informe del Seminario Interamericano de Lideres de Juventedes Rurales: Intercambio Internacional de Juventudes Agrícolas'. San José, Turrialba: IICA, 1961.

Harwood, Jonathan. 'Peasant Friendly Plant Breeding and the Early Years of the Green Revolution in Mexico'. *Agricultural History* 83(3) (2009), 384–410.

Immerwahr, Daniel. *Thinking Small: The United States and the Lure of Community Development*. Cambridge, MA: Harvard University Press, 2018.

Inter-American Institute of Agricultural Sciences. 'Technical Meeting on Agricultural Extension, Turrialba, Costa Rica, August 23rd to September 3rd, 1949'. Turrialba: 1949.

———. 'Annual Report of the Inter-American Institute of Agricultural Sciences for the Year 1950'. Turrialba: Organization of American States, 1950.

———. 'Report to the W.K. Kellogg Foundation on the First Year of Operation of the Grant to Demonstrate the Significant Contribution That Rural Young People Can Make to Rural Development in Latin America'. San José: 1972.

Inter-American Institute for Cooperation in Agriculture. 'IICA – Fifty Years of History'. San José: 1993.

———. *Manual para la Organización de Jóvenes Rurales*. San José: 1997.

Jones, Earl. 'A Study of a Costa Rican Rural Education Center', MA thesis. Turrialba: Inter-American Institute for Cooperation in Agriculture, 1959.

———. *Clubes 4-S y Liderazgo: Materia del Curso para Líderes Voluntarios Dictado en Puriscal, Costa Rica*. Turrialba: Inter-American Institute for Cooperation in Agriculture, 1961.

———. 'A Study of Rural Youth Programs in the Americas (Except United States and Canada)', Ph.D. dissertation. Bozeman: Montana State University, 1962.

———. _Summary of Study of Rural Youth Programs in the Americas (Except United States and Canada)_. San José: Inter-American Rural Youth Program, 1962.

Langrod, Witold L. 'Community Development in Mexico'. _Community Development Bulletin_ 15(4–5) (1964), 122–39.

Latham, Michael E. _The Right Kind of Revolution: Modernization, Development, and US Foreign Policy from the Cold War to the Present_. Ithaca: Cornell University Press, 2011.

Lopes, Sandro, G. John Geldhof, Edmond P. Bowers and Asia Thogmartin. '4-S Positive Youth Development in Latin America: Professional Schools in Costa Rica'. _Journal of Extension_ 56(1) (2018), 1–9.

Ministerio de Agricultura e Industrias. 'Memoria'. San José: 1947–59.

Ministerio de Agricultura y Ganadería. 'Memoria'. San José: 1960–80.

Olsson, Tore C. _Agrarian Crossings: Reformers and the Remaking of the US and Mexican Countryside_. America in the World. Princeton: Princeton University Press, 2017.

Pernet, Corinne A. 'Between Entanglements and Dependencies: Food, Nutrition, and National Development at the Central American Institute of Nutrition (INCAP)', in Marc Frey, Sönke Kunkel and Corinna R. Unger (eds), _International Organizations and Development, 1945–1990_ (Basingstoke: Palgrave Macmillan, 2014), 101–25.

Picado, Wilson. 'En Busca de la Genética Guerrera: Segunda Guerra Mundial, Cooperación Agrícola y Revolución Verde en la Agricultura de Costa Rica'. _Historia Agraria: Revista de Agricultura e Historia Rural_ 56 (2012), 107–34.

Programa Interamericano para la Juventud Rural. 'Quarterly Report' (1961–73).

———. 'Make the Best Better: Proceedings of the 1966 Inter-American Rural Youth Leaders' Conference'. San José: 1966.

———. 'Boletín Informativo Juventud Rural, no.1, 1972'.

Rivas, Darlene. _Missionary Capitalist: Nelson Rockefeller in Venezuela_. Chapel Hill: University of North Carolina Press, 2003.

Rosenberg, Gabriel N. 'The Programa Interamericano para la Juventud Rural (Inter-American Rural Youth Program) and Rural Modernization in Cold War Latin America'. Working Paper. Durham, NC: 2011. Retrieved 22 June 2017 from https://roc karch.issuelab.org/resource/the-programa-interamericano-para-la-juventud-rural-in ter-american-rural-youth-program-and-rural-modernization-in-cold-war-latin-ame rica.html.

———. _The 4-H Harvest: Sexuality and the State in Rural America_. Philadelphia: University of Pennsylvania Press, 2015.

Streeter, Stephen M. 'Nation-Building in the Land of Eternal Counter-Insurgency: Guatemala and the Contradictions of the Alliance for Progress'. _Third World Quarterly_ 27(1) (2006), 57–68.

Vessuri, Hebe M.C. 'Foreign Scientists, the Rockefeller Foundation and the Origins of Agricultural Science in Venezuela'. _Minerva_ 32(3) (1994), 267–96.

Warren, Gertrude L. '4-H Clubs in the Americas'. _Agriculture in the Americas_ 4(10) (1944), 190–91.

Wieters, Heike. _Showered with Kindness? The NGO CARE and Food Aid from America, 1945–1980_. Manchester: Manchester University Press, 2017.

 PART III

On the Ground
Translating Bodies of Knowledge in Rural Communities

 CHAPTER 9

The Politics of Rural Domesticity in Segregationist South Africa, 1902–48

Julia Tischler

In the first half of the twentieth century, many women in rural South Africa came into contact with new education programmes in domestic science. In the so-called African or native reserves in the eastern region of the Cape Province, middle-class black women organized classes in food preservation and home beautification, while state-employed male agricultural officers promoted vegetable gardening and nutritious recipes. Meanwhile, white women in the Orange Free State (OFS) province organized themselves into associations and called on the national government's home demonstration officers to show them how best to protect their families' health.[1] Domestic science education, often initiated by women's organizations and supported – albeit rather modestly – by the state, formed part of a larger rural education movement. However, most of the South African government's policies and measures in this regard revolved around agricultural production and exclusively targeted men.[2] The far fewer educational services that were available to black and white rural women followed supposed European norms, projecting complementary yet hierarchical gender roles: while the male farmer, as head of a monogamous household, was in charge of agricultural production, his wife's duties consisted of reproductive tasks in the home.

These ideals resonated with similar education movements across the world that were teaching women to conduct domestic chores according to 'scientific' principles. In different parts of the globe, domestic science was a patriarchal response to women's increasing urban migration and entry into wage labour, particularly after each of the two World Wars, with male experts and officials attempting to relegitimize the supposedly traditional role of women in unpaid, reproductive work. However, this chapter also emphasizes the ways in which rural women, both black and white, made use of domestic training to further their own ends or even wilfully transgressed the boundaries of domesticity.

Most of the existing literature has cast African encounters with domesticity as a clash between imposed 'European' gender norms and 'African' realities.[3]

However, this chapter argues that other cleavages, rooted in the economic patterns and labour processes of farming, played an even more important role in determining South African women's interactions with the domestic ideal. The chapter juxtaposes domestic education in the Transkei and Ciskei reserves in the eastern Cape Province – hence areas that were set aside for the settlement of black people – with similar initiatives for Afrikaans- and English-speaking women in the rural OFS, demonstrating significant overlaps in the parallel struggles of black and white women over domesticity. These findings echo recent explorations of rural domesticity elsewhere. Because their productive labour was crucial to the viability of farming, rural women in many parts of the world would not be reduced to reproductive work within the home.[4]

Gendering the 'Home' and the 'Farm' in the Transkei and the Ciskei

In the interwar period, problems of overcrowding, soil erosion and starvation in the South African reserves fed into widespread alarmist debates on the 'native problem'. Among other measures, white officials in charge of administering the Transkei and the Ciskei mused over the potential benefits of offering domestic science education as a means of 'rehabilitating' African rural communities. After about twenty years of experimenting with agricultural education directed exclusively at men, which had found some degree of acceptance but without improving agricultural conditions in the reserves to a significant degree,[5] several officials in the 1920s and 1930s identified women as key to rural improvement. Through homemakers' courses and other measures (see below), women were to be taught to 'take a greater pride in their homes', increase their wants and overcome 'idleness'. In so doing, they would become suitable marriage partners for educated African men as well as guardians of social cohesion who would dedicate their lives to the wellbeing of their communities.[6]

Such deliberations implied a – more or less conscious – reformulation of existing gendered divisions of labour. As in many other rural areas in colonial Africa, women in the eastern Cape Province were expected to cater to the needs of their children and husbands while also playing a crucial part in household production.[7] Among the largely Xhosa-speaking communities in the eastern Cape Province reserves, food production had traditionally been the domain of women, who cultivated the land and looked after poultry and small livestock, while men tended to larger animals. However, similar to what has been observed for different contexts in Africa, North America and Europe, governments and experts regarded modern commercial farming as a *male* domain. As such, commercialization went hand in hand with a 'marginalization of women's work'.[8] Across colonial Africa, increasing numbers of men became involved in so-called improved farming, which introduced the use of ploughs and other implements, from the late nineteenth century onwards.[9] Male officials actively supported men's increased participation in farming, which they regarded as a sign of progress. At the same time, they styled themselves as protectors of African women and vowed to ease their heavy workload, allowing them to concentrate on their domestic role.[10]

As in other parts of the world, the ideal of the rural housewife was also a response to the increasing migration of women to urban areas.[11] As Bradford and Bozzoli assert, the rise of male-dominated peasant farming and male labour migration was deeply interwoven with 'domestic struggles'.[12] Whereas an increasing number of African men were spending a good part of the year toiling in gold or diamond mines or on white-owned farms, women and girls were to be taught domestic skills so that they would 'remain at home and not follow the men to the towns'.[13] White employers had an interest in confining black women to the rural areas to ensure the reproduction of the migrant industrial labour force, and many African husbands and fathers shared this concern with restricting women's mobility.[14]

The notion of black rural domesticity echoed earlier Victorian norms that missionaries had set out to introduce in southern Africa and beyond in the nineteenth century.[15] Missionaries judged polygynous marriages and the labour burden of African women as immoral and exploitative.[16] Instead, they envisaged clearly distinct yet complementary roles for men, who would be engaged in productive work, and women, who would be responsible for reproductive, domestic tasks.[17] These older missionary discourses were revived in the interwar period, when US philanthropic organizations started to take an interest in rural development in South Africa. The New York-based Phelps-Stokes Fund, already a central player in African-American education policy, assumed a leading role in shaping colonial education policy in Africa (see Mark-Thiesen in this volume) by invoking racist analogies: Africans could supposedly learn a lot from 'their brethren' in the US South, who had progressed on the ladder of civilization through their exposure to white culture. The kind of education that US experts and philanthropists were promoting was practically oriented, serving the needs of a supposedly yet uncivilized race.[18]

A 1924 inquiry into 'native education' in Africa funded by the Phelps-Stokes Fund described women as the 'starting point of the social order' and cast their existing workload as a sign of 'primitivism'. Instead of running a separate household with her children, a wife and mother should be living together with her husband in a 'proper' home.[19] For this purpose, women had to be taught new tasks, including how to prepare nutritious meals, make elaborate clothes and decorate their homes. It was equally clear to the US commissioners that cash crops were the 'sphere of the men'.[20] The education programmes for which the commission appealed had little to do with education in an academic or professional sense. Instead, the commission report reproduced missionary ideas that women required less education and different forms of instruction in comparison to men, thereby disregarding women's hitherto central role in agricultural production.[21]

Women also became the focus of official attention in conjunction with new discourses on nutrition. Reflecting broader trends, nutrition became a prominent topic of debate among South African administrators in the 1930s amid the global Great Depression as well as local droughts and food shortages. Medical officers became preoccupied with malnutrition in rural areas, spurred by concerns over the productivity of migrant workers.[22] In this context, white Transkeian and Ciskeian officials shifted their emphasis in rural development away from earlier, more ambitious ideas of inculcating 'civilization' through improved farming to much narrower goals of food security, which allowed women to feature more prominently in local programmes.[23]

This new concern translated into a variety of educational measures, including vegetable gardening schemes, which a high-ranking official described as 'the only solution to the persistent cry for more land'.[24] Given South Africa's segregationist legislation, members of the African majority were permitted to farm independently on only 12 per cent of the country's territory. Rather than distributing land more proportionately, the government insisted that Africans be taught to make more of their current share.[25] Vegetable gardening, by providing the reserve populations with a mineral-, protein- and vitamin-rich diet, would enhance the migrant labour force's productivity. The acting principal of Fort Cox Agricultural School in the Ciskei made the state's interest in black manpower very clear: bodies were 'human machines', which 'must have fuel poured into them to make them do useful work'.[26] Similar to what has been observed for the settler-colonial context of Southern Rhodesia, domestic education constituted one of several efforts to make the principle of spatial segregation work in practice.[27]

Vegetable gardens were thus established both at schools and in private homes. By 1939, lecturers at Fort Cox had planned and laid out about one hundred such gardens.[28] A specially appointed officer helped women to set up and manage their own vegetable plots. This scheme was reportedly met with great 'enthusiasm and interest'; indeed, many more women than anticipated applied to participate. Agricultural officers also assisted women's organizations with running gardening competitions on a regular basis.[29] Other measures that sought to instruct women in nutritional issues included 'malnutrition and health meetings' as well as short courses at agricultural colleges on gardening, nutrition, cooking, poultry keeping and the slaughtering of pigs.[30] In October 1941, the first so-called Women's Day at Fort Cox attracted approximately two hundred female participants, many of whom were said to have exclaimed in 'delight' when they were shown the school's extensive gardens.[31]

Officials also devised more ambitious schemes to reach rural women. Although these never came to fruition, they nevertheless reveal administrative ideals of domesticity and the ways in which these ideals were (partially) renegotiated in light of ongoing shifts in gendered labour divisions. With the increased absence of men due to wage labour on the mines or in urban areas, women shouldered an even heavier labour burden in farming, but they also likely gained increased control over domestic resources.[32] More and more women managed fields and gardens independently from their husbands.[33] In this context, administrators struggled to define where the domestic sphere began and where it ended. One of the Transkeian administration's plans for an ambitious 'homemakers' course', for instance, included not only traditional subjects, such as cooking, sewing, laundry, hygiene, home improvement and childcare, but also an 'agricultural course' and instruction in petty crafts to enable women to earn a small amount of 'pin money'.[34]

As in other rural contexts, the bourgeois-industrial ideal of domesticity was thus renegotiated in light of the realities in the reserves. At times, there were even experts who challenged this ideal wholesale. The Phelps-Stokes commissioner Homer Shantz, contradicting some of the findings of the main report, warned against leading women away from the 'healthful and important work' of agriculture towards 'home duties'.[35] Similarly, a delegation from the International Labour Organization (ILO), which had been sent to South Africa to study Africans' working conditions, observed in passing that women, rather than men, should be trained in improved farming techniques.[36] Yet, officials could never bring themselves to pursue this path, even when the Second World War was exacerbating food shortages in the reserves and draining ever more men away from rural areas.[37]

Instead, South Africa's Native Affairs Department (NAD) started training home welfare demonstrators from the 1930s onwards. Following the model of the so-called Jeanes teachers, South African administrators and their US advisors adopted yet another educational model from the US South on the basis of supposed racial commonalities between black South Africans and African Americans. In 1907, the white Quaker Anna Jeanes had instituted a fund to enhance levels of basic education among African Americans by employing education supervisors to visit homes and schools in Southern communities.[38] To assist the South African authorities with implementing a similar programme, the Phelps-Stokes Fund paid several grants that allowed staff members of the All Saints mission school in the Transkei to study the Jeanes teachers at work in the United States and subsequently train local women. In the late 1930s, four African Jeanes teachers were thus sent to various locations to teach hygiene, 'mothercraft' and domestic science.[39]

Figure 9.1. Xhosa woman demonstrating how to bathe a baby, Transkei, South Africa. Photograph by Constance Stuart Larrabee, 1947, EEPA 1998-061334, Constance Stuart Larrabee Collection, Eliot Elisofon Photographic Archives, National Museum of African Art, Smithsonian Institution

After the Second World War, the newly opened Mears Training Institution for Home Welfare Officers trained sixteen women each year to become home welfare officers in the service of the Transkeian Territories General Council.[40] Their primary duties included providing instruction in health and hygiene, childcare and agricultural matters, especially vegetable and fruit cultivation, dairying and poultry keeping. Home welfare officers were told to demonstrate rather than 'preach', be sympathetic and have an intimate knowledge of the communities in which they were working.[41] For this purpose, they were usually stationed in their own homes, which they used to host demonstrations.[42]

Mears Institution was a manifestation of the growing dominance of discourses promoting educational segregation and African ruralness. A dense network of administrators and experts in the United States and South Africa, closely connected with the Phelps-Stokes Fund and Teachers College at Columbia University, had been debating the concept of 'educational adaptation', which favoured replacing earlier universalist notions with supposedly more modern concepts of a special education for black youth that would befit their predefined roles in society.[43] Proponents of a women's school emphasized 'simplicity'; home welfare officers should instil 'love of the simple life' rather than inspire ambition.[44] Domestic training, in fact, should not be 'too much related to the way Europeans lived'.[45] '[L]et us keep the standard of education down', the national Director of Native Agriculture demanded, lest African women became 'dissatisfied with their lot!'[46]

The home demonstrators, Jeanes teachers and home welfare officers received highly favourable comments in official reports for generating interest in domestic improvement and serving 'a definite need'.[47] In its first years, Mears Institution continuously attracted more suitable applicants than it could accommodate, reflecting women's interest in this new career field.[48] However, by the late 1940s, the fifty positions that had been reserved for home welfare officers in the Transkei were almost all filled, worsening future graduates' career prospects.[49] In addition, Mears Institution ran into financial difficulties and shifted from the authority of the Transkeian Council to the NAD and thus from local to central government control.[50] Under the new apartheid system from 1948, the NAD grew increasingly critical of the school, which it accused of only benefiting a small elite.[51] Echoing some of the central tenets of the apartheid Bantu education policy, officials declared the costs of the school unjustifiable and closed it at the end of 1955.[52]

Domestic Challenges in the Transkei and the Ciskei

Measures and programmes for black rural women appear to have been met with generally positive responses, convincing officials that women in the Transkei and Ciskei were 'intensely keen to learn'.[53] The available short courses continuously attracted a higher number of attendees than expected.[54] Women's associations and improvement societies (see below) were reported to be thriving.[55] Agricultural shows, in which farmers exhibited their livestock and produce, were particularly well attended by women, who were attracted by the special women's sections. *Umcebisi*, the Transkeian Council's agricultural journal, 'entered upon a new stage of influence' once it started to also address women.[56]

Many women thus seem to have been responsive to rural education, despite the fact that the framework of domesticity not only sat uneasily with their role in a reserve economy but also barred them from the more profitable branches of agriculture. Apparently, several measures did correspond to urgent local needs. Fort Cox's short courses for women, for instance, emphasized the growing and cooking of food at a time when high commodity prices made many everyday goods unaffordable.[57] Furthermore, women incorporated aspects of the state-led programmes into existing local movements. In the eastern Cape

Province in the 1920s and 1930s, several rural associations were established and led by mission-educated women. They focused on practical skills, including farming, cooking, sewing, hygiene, childcare and healthcare. Similar to the farmers' associations for African men, these organizations emphasized self-help and material uplift while shunning outright political activism.[58] 'Zenzele' – the Xhosa word for 'help yourself' – was the name of a leading organization that had been formed in the early 1920s and achieved a membership of approximately 600 women by the late 1930s.[59] Farming ranked high on Zenzele's agenda, which aimed to assist 'the African women of the Transkei in all matters concerning the development of agriculture and industry, particularly in the development of the homestead site'. Zenzele organized lectures, demonstrations and discussions that emphasized specific aspects of agriculture, including fruit and vegetable cultivation, poultry keeping and dairying[60] – activities that arguably went beyond the domestic. Several associations taught women how to raise poultry and pigs for sale, use cow manure to fertilize maize fields and grow vegetables. From the 1930s, women's organizations were present at agricultural shows, where they displayed vegetable and livestock exhibits.[61]

Women's associations drew on Christian notions of domesticity, condemning polygyny and *lobola* (bridewealth), yet at the same time emphasizing cultural autonomy.[62] Florence Jabavu, who was a leading figure in and the (likely) founder of the African Women's Self-Improvement Association, embodied this tension between assimilation and cultural distinctiveness.[63] Jabavu had been educated at the Lovedale missionary school, where part of her instruction involved being trained for domestic service in white homes, a field of work that she would nevertheless always avoid.[64] To make 'anti-Western' and anti-assimilationist statements, Higgs has argued, Jabavu would at times showcase 'traditional' elements in her work for the association – for instance, by wearing Xhosa dress on special occasions.[65]

Ostentatiously embracing both Western domesticity as well as African 'traditional' gender roles were strategies that were applied by women in various rural colonial contexts. As Epprecht has shown for colonial Lesotho, women's organizations were 'sometimes reactionary'[66] by not opposing women's subordinate status in society, but they did provide their members with a sense of direction and accomplishment.[67] Domestic education entrenched existing gender hierarchies, but it also offered new opportunities for women to organize, socialize, enhance their social status and gain an income.[68] In segregationist South Africa, rural domestic training represented a compromise that needs to be evaluated within the context of the limited choices available to African women. Rural development, however inadequate, still provided opportunities for them to organize, exchange knowledge and confront some of the hardships of life in the reserves. Given the socioeconomic context of the eastern

Cape Province in the 1920s and 1930s, where women ran family farms under conditions of severe environmental and economic stress but could not own land themselves, networks of solidarity were especially important.[69] Labour migration put a strain on marital relationships, as reflected in the rising rate of divorce. Furthermore, with fewer and fewer men being able to afford the cattle necessary to pay *lobola* in order to marry, many women entered into informal relationships that further undermined their social status and protection.[70]

Moreover, women's rural development activities were enmeshed in the politics of social distinction. Mears Institution only trained women with a high level of prior education, usually teachers or nurses whose husbands were often teachers or clerks, and who were active members of the Zenzele organization.[71] Leading organizers and many of the participants at agricultural shows, short courses and demonstrations were from Christian, formally educated and comparatively wealthy families.[72] Florence Jabavu, for instance, was not only the wife of the Ciskei's leading progressive farmer and first African professor, but she also originated from a prominent Christian African family and had trained as a teacher.[73] Jabavu's correspondence shows that she was in contact with other women from privileged backgrounds.[74] By contrast, many potential participants seem to have been excluded from the agricultural colleges' short courses for women for financial reasons, especially not being able to afford tuition fees and transport, board and lodging costs.[75]

Class deeply impacted the politics of rural women more broadly. Examining boycotts and strikes in the Herschel district in the Transkei in the 1920s and 1930s, Beinart has highlighted the ways in which African women protested against issues that had an immediate impact on their everyday lives, including high commodity prices during and after the First World War, while turning increasingly against the state and espousing notions of Africanism and black religious separatism. However, most of the self-consciously progressive and wealthier families continued to collaborate with white officials and missionaries, steering clear of populist politics.[76] Thus, similar to what Neth has observed for the US Midwest, rural domesticity was at least partly a middle-class, 'conservative' alternative to more radical women's movements.[77] While women improvers professed to reach out to the 'masses' and help their 'poor neighbours',[78] the domestic ideal was an expression of the social stratification within the eastern Cape Province reserves. Women's rural organizing was therefore a complex mix of social change goals and conservative strategies, 'traditional' culture and new practices of Western domesticity as well as social distinction and social inclusion.

Rural women's activities in the eastern Cape Province echoed similar programmes in the US South, which African women organizers adapted, and African-American missionary wives as well as white administrators helped to promote in South Africa. For instance, Susie Yergan arrived together with her

Baptist missionary husband in the eastern Cape Province in 1916 and founded several homemakers' clubs as well as the Bantu Women's Home Improvement Association.[79] Home economics had constituted an integral component of the segregated US extension service since 1913.[80] Female home demonstration agents, who usually teamed up with a male county agent, were responsible for teaching 'the latest scientific information' on topics such as vegetable gardening, fruit and vegetable canning, food preparation, healthcare and childcare.[81] In the early 1930s, home demonstration agents constituted about 40 per cent of all rural extension agents,[82] including 127 who served African American communities.[83] Black South African women organizers were inspired in particular by the Women's Club at the Tuskegee Institute in Alabama, a leading institution of higher education for African Americans in the Jim Crow South (see the Introduction and Mark-Thiesen in this volume). Margaret Murray Washington, wife of Tuskegee's principal, Booker Washington, organized regular 'mothers' meetings' and founded a Women's Industries Division at the institute, where she taught domestic subjects.[84]

While domestic science in the eastern Cape Province did not come close to matching the extent of institutionalization that it enjoyed in the United States, the gendered divisions of knowledge and labour that it promoted in a context of racial segregation were very similar.[85] Moreover, the politics of African-American women echoed the strategies of moderation and self-help of their South African counterparts. Murray Washington championed 'motherhood and wifehood', believing that stable, Christian households were nurturing places for racial improvement after slavery had deprived African-American women of such virtues. Murray Washington and other black middle-class reformers allied themselves with white Northern friends and did not attack segregation directly, but they still conceived of their work as a form of black empowerment and self-determination.[86] Similar to what has been observed for black home economics leaders in the eastern Cape Province, the US Jeanes teachers' schemes and home demonstration agents navigated a minefield between reform and conservatism. As research on the US South has shown, their education and activities 'marked them as potential agitators' and raised white landowners' suspicions.[87] At the same time, their willingness to accommodate white supremacy rather than challenge it directly has caused scholars to decry their work as 'nonconfrontational'.[88]

Educating Farmers' Wives and Mothers in the OFS

Domestic science also proliferated among the white minority in the early twentieth-century OFS, a time when rural Afrikaner families were particularly affected by the recent upsurge in female wage labour. Scores of Afrikaner women, particularly the young and unmarried, left for the cities with the aim of sending remittances home.[89] As in other parts of the globe, women's wage labour gave rise to a 'moral panic' among officials and urban intellectuals, with debates in the 1910s and 1920s revolving around prostitution, 'miscegenation' and the alleged promiscuity of urban women. Furthermore, hard industrial labour was said to weaken female physical and moral strength.[90] The ideal of the rural mother, catering to her husband and children in a healthy and safe environment, became a powerful counterimage.

South Africa's white domestic science movement was primarily driven by rural women's unions, with organizers following models from Canada, where the first 'women's institutes' had been formed in the late nineteenth century. These women's institutes set up committees and organized regular meetings with demonstrations on cooking, child welfare, horticulture and poultry keeping.[91] The South African state, for its part, looked to the US extension service and the important role played by its home agents.[92] Following the US example, but without ever reaching its level of sophistication, the South African Department of Agriculture appointed home demonstration agents, whose services were eagerly sought-after by the women's branches.[93] However, this home demonstration service was severely understaffed, and the five officers employed to cover the entire country could not keep up with the visits requested by women's branches as well as with correspondence, short courses, farmers' days, agricultural shows and other external requests.[94]

Home demonstration agents were unmarried and worked from one of South Africa's white agricultural colleges. They had undergone academic training, which at least in the early 1920s still usually implied a degree in the United States or Canada.[95] Their few surviving accounts provide scattered insights into their self-perceptions. Representing a higher socioeconomic standing than most of their rural clientele, the agents found rural women to be underprivileged compared to urban women. One officer, a Miss Daniotsz, reported on how she and her colleagues were promoting what they regarded as useful knowledge. She recounted that women's branches often asked her to instruct them in tasks that she considered to be beyond their members' standing, such as making fancy icing for cakes.[96] For Daniotsz, her work also had a disciplining component: new timesaving methods would help rural women to devote more time to 'cultural and social aspects of life', including needlework, art, interior decorating and dressmaking.[97] Home demonstration officers described themselves as civilizational pioneers, dedicated to raising the 'standard of the farm home' and lifting rural families out of their supposed state of destitution and isolation.[98]

In the interwar period, following intensive exchange between educators and administrators in South Africa and the United States, this rhetoric became suffused with eugenic theories concerning rural 'poor whites' – a politically explosive term to describe destitute Afrikaner families. As Heinemann has shown for the 1930s Great Depression in the United States, when many men lost their jobs and status as sole breadwinner, experts and officials reminded women of their traditional role to reproduce and raise 'fit' offspring for the nation.[99] The state's promotion of motherhood as a patriotic duty climaxed in New Deal programmes that intervened in the domestic sphere to restore traditional gender roles.[100] Similar tendencies could be witnessed in the depressed and drought-ridden rural areas of South Africa, where domestic education became part of policing women's contribution to the nation. As demonstrated by the 1929 Carnegie Commission of Investigation on the Poor White Question in South Africa, a commission of US and South African experts looking into poverty among whites, as well as debates on 'adapted education' (see below), eugenic thought reshaped older approaches to social reform and highlighted women's supposed duties of motherhood. Leading protagonists of the eugenic movement celebrated domesticity as a corrective to female wage work, which they believed was leading to a 'degeneration of the [white] race'.[101]

In this context, the South African government directed its attention more closely towards the education of white rural girls. Domestic science instruction was incorporated into the activities of children's clubs.[102] Vocational schools for domestic science (*huishoudskole*), educating future 'farmers' wives', were also seen as a way to combat the poor white problem.[103] The 660 girls enrolled in such schools by 1936 studied cooking, nutrition, needlework, clothes-making, hygiene and childcare alongside more academic subjects such as English and Afrikaans.[104]

According to numerous comments in the surviving records, many rural women seem to have welcomed domestic education. Home demonstration officers were fully booked months in advance and received far more requests for their services than they could accommodate.[105] Women's organizations in rural communities increased their membership rapidly, while officers judged the interest of women in home economics as 'phenomenal'.[106] Glen College of Agriculture near Bloemfontein offered short courses for women that aroused interest from across the province to such an extent that the college found itself obliged to construct new, well-equipped buildings to accommodate more students.[107] Principals from different schools reported that women were even 'more enthusiastic than the men' about education, constantly organizing events and requesting advice and support.[108]

Previous studies have pointed to examples of self-interest and transgression of domestic ideals that women brought to home economics programmes, for instance, by seeking career opportunities or developing a profound interest in the science.[109] Discussing the philanthropic work of Afrikaner women, du Toit has argued that notions of (rural) domesticity were conservative yet still actively shaped by the women themselves. For many white women, domesticity was a platform from which to influence social policy debates while gaining recognition as wives, mothers and social workers.[110] Furthermore, domesticity was not an apolitical void, interlaced as it was with Afrikaner nationalism. During the 1920s, women's philanthropic movements, such as the Afrikaans Christian Women's Organization (Afrikaanse Christelike Vroue Vereniging [ACVV]), used the 'domesticated space of home' as 'key to the construction of a racialized, Afrikaans cultural-political subjectivity'.[111]

The poor white issue of the late 1920s and early 1930s further linked rural motherhood and ethnic nationalism. The reproductive work of the so-called *volksmoeder* ('mother of the nation'), an ideal of motherhood projected in Afrikaner organizations, magazines and farm novels, not only determined the cultural level of a family but also the future of the whole Afrikaner *volk* ('nation' or 'people').[112] Domestic training for women thus fed into the context of a popular elaboration of white rural motherhood in which white male officials and middle-class female philanthropists but also many farmwomen were all participating. Devarenne has discussed the ways in which the *volksmoeder* ideal celebrated an 'unchanging' rural Afrikaner identity, with rural housewives portrayed as 'mothers of the nation', whose virtue, self-sacrifice, religiousness and self-reliance were saving the *volk* from degeneration.[113] Although the *volksmoeder* formed part of male, patriarchal discourse, it also represented an avenue for women to actively produce Afrikaner culture.[114]

M.E. Rothmann, the only female coauthor of the Carnegie Poor White study report, represented this cohort of nationalist women who took up positions in maternalist organizations.[115] As an Afrikaner nationalist who was at the same time an internationally renowned expert serving on a prominent US commission, Rothmann also reflected the ways in which national and transnational conversations on whiteness and domesticity coalesced. Rothmann was a feminist who promoted white female suffrage and became a highly influential social scientist and organizer.[116] Through her work for the Carnegie Commission, Rothmann simultaneously helped to promote patriarchal and classist notions of rural motherhood, a campaign that Willoughby-Herard has labelled as 'intraracial violence'.[117] Rothmann was particularly concerned with the racial status of poor white women. From the late 1920s, she and other middle-class maternalists advocated 'modernized maternity care' as a way to improve rural communities' social status and uphold socioeconomic boundaries between whites and blacks.[118]

In her function as a Carnegie commissioner, Rothmann visited numerous homes to observe and interview families. She also talked to church ministers, teachers, doctors, municipal officials and women organizers. Her widely read report *The Mother and Daughter of the Poor Family* tapped into a specific type of eugenic language that emphasized poor families' educability and the effects of environmental, rather than genetic, factors. Indigent women required 'simple instruction' on how to prepare food and grow vegetables on top of lessons on healthcare, nursing, childcare and housekeeping economics.[119] Their duty towards the nation was to raise children in such a way that the latter would become 'a benefit and not a burden to the state'.[120] Rothmann was strictly opposed to women working outside the home and deplored the fact that many mothers had to assist in farm work.[121] Her partly empathetic, partly aggressively voyeuristic report pleaded for greater state involvement in rural education, even if this meant overriding the opinions of families, who often regarded 'home-craft school[s]' with 'doubt and suspicion'.[122]

Not only was the notion of the domestic both political and public; the strict division that it projected between productive and reproductive work was porous in practice – analogous to what scholars have established for other rural contexts.[123] Numerous comments in official records describe the difficulties facing experts in defining what exactly fell into the realm of rural domesticity. Poultry keeping, vegetable gardening and elements of dairy farming, for instance, were commonly regarded as women's tasks, even though they did not take place inside the home.[124] Officers' comments reflect that, out of economic necessity alone, women's contributions often went beyond tasks relating to basic sustenance and reproduction. For instance, Glen College's 1931–32 annual report, written at the height of the Great Depression, mentions that women's work in the farmhouse was crucial in helping to 'augment the farm income'.[125] Home economists also emphasized 'home industries', such as the canning and preserving of food, 'so that these products could be marketed'.[126]

Women Farmers in the OFS?

OFS women not only negotiated the boundaries between the private and the public as well as between domestic labour and productive farm work, but they also challenged the idea of separate spheres altogether. In 1924, Esther Bell-Robinson, together with four hundred supporters, petitioned the national Department of Agriculture to admit women to the agricultural diploma course at Glen College. Bell-Robinson, a teacher from Ireland, had moved to the Orange River Colony after the Second South African War (1899–1902) as part of the British reconstruction administration's scheme to establish the English school system in the former Boer republics. She subsequently committed herself to 'uplifting' Afrikaner children and women – especially war widows – through agricultural development.[127] Bell-Robinson explained that many women inherited or shared farms; training them to use agricultural machinery would make these farms more productive. Obtaining an agricultural diploma also made sense for farmers' wives, as two trained experts – a husband together with his wife – were better than one.[128] Similarly, in 1921, the

National Council of Women, a white, middle-class organization that pushed for greater gender equality but professed to be apolitical,[129] officially requested the government to open up agricultural training.[130] 'Year by year, the number of women farmers is increasing', its members argued, '[and] women are anxious to take their part in the development of the resources of our country'.[131] The 1926 census indicated that 4,100 women were working as farmers, horticulturists or in managerial positions on farms.[132]

Officials, although not entirely dismissive, remained sceptical. Several argued that as long as there was a shortage of agricultural education for men, women could not be included.[133] The Secretary for Agriculture claimed that women with a degree in agriculture would marry and thus waste their training.[134] Finally, and most crucially, in contrast to many other countries, farming in South Africa implied 'deal[ing] with natives as workmen', which supposedly made it 'practically impossible' for a woman to manage a farm on her own.[135]

Women who wanted an agricultural diploma had the opportunity to obtain one at the privately run Boschetto Agricultural College near Harrismith in the OFS, at the time the only women's agricultural school in South Africa.[136] Boschetto was founded in the mid-1920s along the lines of Studley Agricultural College for Women in the English county of Warwickshire.[137] On Boschetto's 400 acres of land, female lecturers taught fifteen to twenty students in dairying, poultry keeping, horticulture and crop cultivation, preparing them for a one-year certificate or a two-year diploma.[138]

The staff included Boschetto's founder and owner, Norah Miller, who invested all of her capital in the college.[139] Her fellow lecturers were unmarried women from Europe, especially the United Kingdom.[140] During its thirty-four years of existence, Boschetto's body of students was similarly international, consisting of white women from the United Kingdom, Southern Rhodesia, South West Africa and other English-speaking territories.[141] The number of students from South Africa rose over time.[142] Students generally had better-off parents, mostly farmers. There were also students from prominent families, such as the daughters of the Southern Rhodesian Prime Minister Howard Moffat. Annual enrolment numbers ranged from fifteen to twenty-four; by 1959, about five hundred young women had trained at Boschetto.[143]

Initially, the college's main mission was to train women who wished to farm independently.[144] Several of Miller's students had come equipped with capital or the prospect of inheriting a farm and would subsequently become independent 'woman farmers'.[145] Other graduates secured professional employment, including leading management positions on commercial farms or in cheese factories or other agriculture-related businesses. The demand for trained graduates was high, according to Miller, who warned that 'we have not got sufficient girls trained to supply all the posts offered'.[146] Although her graduates typically received multiple offers of employment, salaries remained low.[147] In addition, a Boschetto diploma did not make graduates eligible for a post in the Department of Agriculture.[148]

Despite serving an obvious need, Boschetto was always on a tight budget and came to depend on the national Department of Agriculture's support, which in turn meant government inspections, control and criticism.[149] In particular, officials pressured the principal on the school's lack of white male staff. The 'girls' did much of the physical work themselves, which did not comply with white South African conventions;[150] even worse, 'white girls [were] working with natives'.[151] Miller, by contrast, criticized dominant South African gendered and racialized divisions of labour, insisting that women could do physical work themselves and were also capable of 'handling the native labour'.[152] Furthermore, she declared, white South African women 'had far too much unproductive leisure'.[153] However, forced to yield to the Department of Agriculture's pressure, Miller eventually hired a domestic science teacher who would add courses in cookery and house management to the curriculum.[154] She would nonetheless insist on continuing to offer a full agricultural course analogous to those at the state agricultural colleges for men.[155]

Over Boschetto's three-and-a-half decades in existence, the male agricultural bureaucracy constantly negotiated with Miller over the aims, methods and content of her course, contesting her principle that rural women should be able to acquire the same competences as their male counterparts.[156] While she seemed to have convinced at least some officials that women could perform productive agricultural work,[157] the government continued to be miserly in its support. On Miller's passing, Boschetto closed its doors in 1960, despite still receiving many enquiries and applications.[158] Meanwhile, the idea of a public women's school of agriculture, a recurring concern of the South African Women's Agricultural Union, chaffed against the Department of Agriculture's firm position that there was 'more urgent need for maximum facilities for men'.[159]

Conclusion

This chapter has examined rural domestic education for women – the counterpart to agricultural education for men – in order to trace the development of separate spheres and notions of domesticity as they evolved during South African agriculture's commercial take-off.[160] While Africanist scholarship has debated domesticity largely in terms of a clash of cultures between Western-imposed concepts and African realities, white communities in the OFS – and elsewhere in the world – experienced similar struggles and contestations as black communities in the eastern Cape Province reserves. Among rural Afrikaner families, divisions between productive and reproductive work corresponded at least partly to established household roles. Yet, although most Afrikaner women were traditionally not as centrally involved in productive agricultural work as black women were,[161] both groups experienced similar conflicts surrounding domestic training – as did rural communities elsewhere. As scholarship on Europe and North America has shown, the state-supported rise of scientific and commercial farming 'increasingly constructed the kitchen and the market as separate spheres', relegated women to roles that were 'not regarded as belonging to the economy' and devalued their work.[162] Hence, many observations made by Africanist scholars on 'new distinctions between home and work' in fact echo more universal experiences of agrarian transition.[163]

Rural women renegotiated the bourgeois domestic ideal in ways that were heavily dependent on their economic circumstances and class position. Many white and black women welcomed domestic education as a career path, an avenue to middle-class distinction and/or a platform for conservative social politics. Black women in the eastern Cape Province, similar to African American women in the Jim Crow South, instrumentalized rural domestic culture as a cautious political strategy with which to carve out a space for themselves in a segregationist context as well as a form of self-help and a path to respectability. In the case of Afrikaner communities in the OFS, national and transnational debates on whiteness coalesced, concentrating on the rural as a site of improvement and protection of racial purity under the guardianship of white maternalists. Economically strained women, both black and white, embraced aspects of domestic education that proved useful in their daily struggles to feed their families. Others aimed for qualifications beyond household science that would enable them to run their own farms or obtain skilled agricultural employment. In any case, the boundaries between the private and the public, the social and the political, as well as productive and reproductive work all remained porous.

Julia Tischler is Associate Professor of African history and co-director of the Centre for African Studies at the University of Basel, Switzerland. With a focus on the history of Southern Africa, she has published on questions of development, settler colonialism, environmental history, race and agriculture. Her first monograph dealt with the history of the Kariba Dam on the border between Zambia and Zimbabwe. She is currently working on a monograph on the history of agricultural progressivism in South Africa.

Notes

1. I use 'white' to refer to Afrikaans- or English-speaking persons who, in the period under investigation, would have regarded themselves as being of European descent.

I use 'black' or 'African' for persons who would have been recognized as being of African ancestry.

2. Women could not obtain a diploma at state agricultural colleges, nor could they work as agricultural extension agents.

3. See e.g. Hansen, *African Encounters*; Gaitskell, 'Housewives, Maids or Mothers'; Gaitskell, 'Devout Domesticity?'

4. On the United States, see Neth, *Preserving the Family Farm*; Grey Osterud, *Putting the Barn before the House*. On African-American communities, see Jones-Branch, 'African American Demonstration Agents'. On the idea of separate spheres in German rural contexts, see Grey, *Productive Men*. I thank Juri Auderset for helping me to develop my arguments in this regard.

5. Tischler, 'Education'.

6. Cullen Library, University of the Witwatersrand, Johannesburg (CUL), AD 1438, Box 2, Native Economic Commission, minutes of oral evidence, S.G. Butler, Umtata, 14 November 1930, 3315-8.

7. For similar gendered divisions of labour among the Yoruba people in colonial Nigeria, see Denzer, 'Domestic Science Training'.

8. Osterud, *Putting the Barn before the House*, 23. See also Neth, *Preserving the Family Farm*.

9. Bundy's classic *The Rise and Fall of the South African Peasantry* depicted black men's increased involvement in agricultural pursuits as a response to new economic opportunities, while Bradford has interpreted this trend as a sign of economic crisis (Bradford, 'Peasants, Historians, and Gender').

10. On German colonial discourse on the 'lazy' African husband, see e.g. Koponen, *Development for Exploitation*, 327–28.

11. According to Gaitskell, 'in late nineteenth-century rural society in South Africa, there was no such thing as a black housewife. Rural women had always been productive workers and continued to be involved in cultivation' (Gaitskell, 'Housewives, Maids or Mothers', 243).

12. Bozzoli, 'Marxism, Feminism and South African Studies', 135.

13. National Archives of South Africa, Kingwilliamstown repository, Qonce (KWT), N8/19/8, 145/9, vol. I, 'Mears Appeals to Bantu Women. Says They Must Lead the Men on the Land', newspaper clipping, newspaper not indicated [n.d., c. 1946].

14. Ibid.

15. By 1880, Christianity was 'relatively well established' in most densely populated areas of southern Africa (Gaitskell, 'Devout Domesticity?', 252).

16. Ibid., 254.

17. Comaroff and Comaroff, 'Home-Made Hegemony'.

18. Colonial authorities and experts increasingly advocated practical, rural education for Africans instead of academic instruction. This shift towards a racially differentiated education was informed by Social Darwinist ideas, school reforms in the United Kingdom and models from the US South. See e.g. Kallaway and Swartz, 'Introduction'. See also Domosh, 'Race, Biopolitics and Liberal Development'.

19. Jones, *Education in East Africa*, 339–40.

20. Ibid., 341.

21. Cock, 'Domestic Service and Education', 88.
22. Unger, 'Agrarwissenschaftliche Expertise und ländliche Modernisierungsstrategien', 562. On colonial constructions of the problem of 'malnutrition', see Hodge, *Triumph of the Expert*; Worboys, 'The Discovery of Colonial Malnutrition'.
23. Tischler, 'Education'. See also Staples, *The Birth of Development*.
24. National Archives of South Africa, Pretoria (SAB), NTS 7514, 662/327, P.[?] de Beyer, Acting Assistant Director of Native Agriculture, Kingwilliamstown, to Director of Native Agriculture, Pretoria, 7 November 1940.
25. On land reforms as catalysts for rural development and new education policies, see the Introduction to this volume.
26. SAB, NTS 7514, 662/327, A.G. Vanderplank, Principal, Fort Cox Agricultural School, Middledrift, to Director of Native Agriculture, Pretoria, Annex G, 8 November 1940.
27. Ranchod-Nilsson, 'Educating Eve', 201.
28. SAB, NTS 7514, 662/327, 'General Progress Report: Fort Cox', E. Wyatt Sampson, Principal, Fort Cox, 1 January 1938–31 October 1939.
29. SAB, NTS 7514, 662/327, P.[?] de Beyer, Acting Assistant Director of Native Agriculture, Kingwilliamstown, to Director of Native Agriculture, Pretoria, 7 November 1940.
30. National Archives of South Africa, Mthatha repository (MTHA), 'UTTGC Proceedings and Reports, 1941', 46; SAB, NTS 7514, 662/327, 'Review of the Services and Activities of the Fort Cox Agricultural School: Period October 1939 to October 1940', A.G. Vanderplank to Director of Native Agriculture.
31. SAB, NTS 7541, 759/327, 'Women's Day: Fort Cox', A.G. Vanderplank to Chief Native Commissioner, 1 November 1941.
32. Beinart, 'Women in Rural Politics', 347.
33. Ibid., 349.
34. UNISA. 'Written Evidence Presented to the Native Economic Commission', evidence by S.G. Butler (see note 6 above).
35. Shantz, 'Supplementary Chapter', 369–70.
36. Rhodes House Library, University of Oxford (RHL), MSS Brit Emp, S 22, G 597, 'Delegation to Union of South Africa, 1938-9', ILO Governing Body, confidential draft report, 10[?] May 1939. The delegation's aim was to 'inform themselves at first hand on Native labor conditions in South Africa' following 'discussions of the problems of contract labor' during an international labour conference (ibid.).
37. KWT, N8/19/2, Principal, Fort Cox, to Chief Native Commissioner, Kingwilliamstown, 23 August 1939.
38. Littlefield, 'Agency and Constructions of Political Identity', 23.
39. CUL, A920, 'A Preliminary Survey of the Agricultural and Nutritional Problems of the Ciskei and Transkeian Territories with Special Reference to Their Bearing on the Recruiting of Labourers for the Gold Mining Industry', by F. William Fox and Douglas Back, 1937.
40. SAB, NTS 2837, 300/302, Part I, Chief Native Commissioner, Kingwilliamstown, to Secretary for Native Affairs, 29 August 1944. The council system was a form of limited self-government through which African men were supposed to grow into administrative roles; see Evans, *Bureaucracy and Race*, 184–86.

41. SAB, NTS 2837, 300/302, Part I, UTTGC, 'Duties of Home Welfare Officers', forwarded by Chief Magistrate, Transkei, to W.G. Mears, Secretary for Native Affairs, 30 November 1945.

42. SAB, NTS 2837, 300/302, Part I, 'Mears School for the Training of Home Welfare Officers: Mbuto, Tsolo', [n.a.], 25 September 1946.

43. Kallaway and Swartz, 'Introduction'.

44. SAB, NTS 2837, 300/302, Part I, Wyatt Sampson, Principal, Fort Cox, to Chief Native Commissioner, 23 August 1939.

45. SAB, NTS 2837, 300/302, Part I, Ciskeian General Council debate, 20 September 1939.

46. SAB, NTS 2837, 300/302, Part I, Memorandum, by T.G.W. Reinecke, 14 October 1939.

47. SAB, NTS 2837, 300/302, Part II, 'Inspection Report Mears School', by W. du Rand, Chief Social Welfare Officer, Department of Social Welfare, 2 June 1948; SAB, NTS 2837, 300/302, Part I, 'Tour No. 36: Ciskei', Director of Native Agriculture, 9 May–24 September 1942.

48. SAB, NTS 2837, 300/302, Part I, V.M. de Villiers, Chief Magistrate, Transkei, to Chief Native Commissioner, Kingwilliamstown, 9 November 1944.

49. SAB, NTS 2837, 300/302, Part I, Chief Magistrate, Transkei, to Secretary for Native Affairs, 23 June 1947.

50. SAB, NTS 2837, 300/302, Part I, Principal Accountant to Secretary, Cape Town, 10 January 1948.

51. SAB, NTS 2820, 232/302, Part I, 'Toekoms van die Mearsskool', Memorandum, [n.a.], 23 April 1954.

52. SAB, NTS 2820, 232/302, Part I, 'Opsoming van Bespreking oor die Mearsskool', [n.a.], 4 May 1954.

53. KWT, N8/19/2, Principal, Fort Cox, to Chief Native Commissioner, Kingwilliamstown, 23 August 1939. See also National Archives of South Africa, Cape Town repository (KAB), AFC 6, N8/19/4/10, Vice Principal, Fort Cox, to Mrs F.T. Jabavu, 21 April 1936; KAB, 1/BIZ 6/128, N10/15/2, Extract from general report, R.A. Bennie, Agricultural Supervisor, 5 January 1938; SAB, NTS 2417, 73/287 – 25, 'Annual Report', J.R.A. Matheson, Principal, Teko School of Agriculture, 1946.

54. SAB, NTS 7539, 742/327, 'Acting Principal's Address, Women's Short Course, Fort Cox Agricultural School', 23–26 June 1942.

55. SAB, NTS 2417, 73/287, 'Future of Council Schools of Agriculture', United Transkeian Territories General Council, Annual Reports and Accounts for 1946, Estimates of Revenue and Expenditure, 1946.

56. MTHA, 'UTTGC Proceedings and Reports, 1941', 30.

57. SAB, NTS 7539, 742/327, Bunga session, [n.a.], [n.d., c. 1940].

58. Charman, 'Progressive Élites in Bunga Politics', 171; Higgs, 'Zenzele', 122.

59. Charman, 'Progressive Élites in Bunga Politics', 172.

60. SAB, NTS 2837, 300/302, Part II, 'Constitution of the Zenzele Women's Association of the Transkei', annexed to Secretary for Social Welfare to Secretary for Native Affairs, 27 July 1948.

61. Higgs, 'Zenzele', 128–29.

62. Ibid., 129.
63. See Higgs, *The Ghost of Equality*. The African Women's Self-Improvement Association was founded in Alice in 1927 (Higgs, 'Helping Ourselves', 62).
64. Higgs, 'Helping Ourselves', 122; see also Cock, 'Domestic Service and Education', 90.
65. Higgs, 'Zenzele', 124.
66. Epprecht, 'Domesticity and Piety', 223.
67. Ibid., 222–23.
68. For colonial Yorubaland, see Denzer, 'Domestic Science Training'; for colonial Uganda, see Musisi, 'Colonial and Missionary Education', 186. Gaitskell has advanced similar arguments on Christianity as a 'contradictory package' for African women ('Devout Domesticity?', 254). Jones-Branch described home demonstration activities and clubs in the US South as 'safe, women-centred spaces' ('African American Demonstration Agents', 162).
69. Higgs, 'Zenzele', 132.
70. Higgs, 'Helping Ourselves'.
71. Most trainees were married with children, whom they left in the care of relatives (SAB, NTS 2837, 300/302, Part II, 'Inspection Report Mears School', by Chief Social Welfare Officer, Department of Social Welfare, 2 June 1948).
72. Charman, 'Progressive Élites in Bunga Politics', 170–72. See also MTHA, 'UTTGC Proceedings and Reports, 1941', 46.
73. Higgs, 'Zenzele', 121.
74. See e.g. KAB, AFC 6, N8/19/4/10, Mrs Jabavu to Vice Principal, Fort Cox, 14 April 1936.
75. KAB, AFC 6, N8/19/4/10, Isaac Ngaki, Agricultural Demonstrator, to Principal, Fort Cox, 7 June 1932; KAB, AFC 6, N8/19/4/10, Principal, Teko, to Principal, Fort Cox, 9 March 1932.
76. Beinart, 'Women in Rural Politics', 328–30.
77. Neth, *Preserving the Family Farm*, 215.
78. Schomburg Library, New York (SCHOM), 42/9, D.D.T. Jabavu to Anson Phelps Stokes, 26 April 1932; KWT, N8/19/2, Principal, Fort Cox, to Chief Native Commissioner, Kingwilliamstown, 23 August 1939; Charman, 'Progressive Élites in Bunga Politics', 170.
79. Higgs, 'Zenzele', 61–62. Another promoter of Southern-style rural education for black women was the Natal-born organizer Sibusisiwe Makanya (Marks, *Not Either an Experimental Doll*, 32–34).
80. Hoffschwelle, *Rebuilding the Rural Southern Community*, 91.
81. Carnegie Corporation Archives, Butler Library, New York (CCNY), III.A, 158.4, 'Agricultural Extension Work and Vocational Education in Agriculture in White and Negro Schools in the Southern States of America', by R. Dudley Hampton, Carnegie Visitors' Grant Report 1932, 16–17.
82. In 1931, there were 128 female home agents and 171 male agricultural agents (SAB, NTS 10168, 57/419, 'Agricultural Economics among American Negroes. Report of a Visit to the United States of America under the Auspices of the Visitors' Grants Committee of the Carnegie Corporation of New York', by Bernard Huss, 1931).

83. Figures for 1932 (CCNY, III.A, 158.4, 'Agricultural Extension Work', by R. Dudley Hampton – see note 81 above).
84. Neumann, Caryn. 'Washington, Margaret Murray', *American National Biography Online*, April 2004. Retrieved 15 November 2022 from http://www.anb.org/view/10 .1093/anb/9780198606697.001.0001/anb-9780198606697-e-1501301.
85. Hoffschwelle, *Rebuilding the Rural Southern Community*, 91.
86. Rouse, 'Out of the Shadow of Tuskegee'.
87. Jones-Branch, 'African American Demonstration Agents', 157.
88. Littlefield, 'Agency and Constructions of Political Identity', 18–19, 22–23.
89. Keegan, *Rural Transformations*, 38. By 1935, women constituted 73 per cent of the industrial labour force in South Africa; Bonner, 'South African Society and Culture', 291.
90. Bonner, 'South African Society and Culture', 292.
91. SAB, LTD 240, R 2278/1, Home Economics Officer to Secretary for Agriculture, 27 February 1928. In 1897, women in Ontario had formed the first branch of a women's institute; Ambrose, 'Women's Institutes'.
92. SAB, LDB 3513, R 4165, vol. I, 'Part-Time Agricultural Education in the USA', Agricultural Attaché's Office, British Embassy, Washington DC, forwarded 18 February 1948.
93. Established in 1913, the home demonstration service was operating in almost every state by the early 1930s (CCNY, III.A, 158.4, 'Agricultural Extension Work', by R. Dudley Hampton – see note 81 above).
94. SAB, LTD 240, R 2278/1, Draft Notice, 'Home Economics Service', E.M. Ferguson, addressing Chief, Division of Agricultural Education and Extension, 11 February 1928. In the 1920s, there were about 100 women's institute branches (SAB, LTD 240, R 2278/1, [M.J. Daniotsz or Davidtsz] to Chief, Division of Extension and Agricultural Education, 9 September 1926).
95. Kok, 'The Home Economist'.
96. SAB, LTD 240, R 2278/1, [M.J. Daniotsz or Davidtsz], Lecturer and Demonstrator, Home Economics, to Public Service Inspector, 2 June 1927.
97. Kok, 'The Home Economist'.
98. SAB, LDB 1050, R 157.12, vol. I, Senior Extension Officer to Chief, Division of Agricultural Extension and Education, 28 April 1932.
99. Heinemann, *Wert der Familie*, 101.
100. Ibid., 105.
101. For the US context, see ibid., 105, 116–23.
102. SAB, LON 236, A 138/4, vol. II, 'Agricultural Club Work', Head of Education Department, January 1938.
103. SAB, LON 236, A 138/6, 'Experiment at Tweespruit', *The Friend*, 20 April 1944.
104. VAB, PAE 44, E2458/1 [2], Brochure 'Beroepsonderwys', Union Education Department, 1936.
105. SAB, LTD 240, R 2278/1, Chief, Division of Agricultural Education and Extension, to Secretary for Agriculture, 13 February 1928.
106. VAB SLT 1/19, A44/4, vol. I, 'Glen School of Agriculture, Annual Report, 1931–1932'.
107. Kok, 'The Home Economist'.

108. VAB, SLT 1/2 – A14 – vol. II, 'Minutes of Conference of Principals Held at Glen School of Agriculture', 14–15 August 1933.
109. Elias, *Stir It up*.
110. Du Toit, 'The Domesticity of Afrikaner Nationalism', 155–57.
111. Ibid., 156.
112. Devarenne, 'Nationalism and the Farm Novel'.
113. Ibid., 627–33. See also van Niekerk, 'Afrikaner Woman and Her "Prison"'.
114. Du Toit, 'The Domesticity of Afrikaner Nationalism', 175.
115. Ibid., 155. McClintock argues that the *volksmoeder* ideal highlighted 'the power of (white) motherhood', but at the same time reflected 'gender containment' (*Imperial Leather*, 378).
116. Davie, *Poverty*, 91; du Toit, 'The Domesticity of Afrikaner Nationalism', 159.
117. Willoughby-Herard, *Waste of a White Skin*, 146.
118. Du Toit, 'The Domesticity of Afrikaner Nationalism', 169–76.
119. Rothmann, *The Mother and Daughter in the Poor Family*, xv–xvi.
120. Ibid., 170–72.
121. Ibid., 173.
122. Ibid., 198.
123. See e.g. Neth, *Preserving the Family Farm*, 6–31; Osterud, *Putting the Barn before the House*, 14–23, 105–7.
124. See e.g. VAB, SLT 1/2 – A14 – vol. II, 'Minutes of Conference of Principals Held at Glen School of Agriculture', 14–15 August 1933; SAB, LDB 1050, R 157.12, vol. I, Senior Extension Officer to Chief, Division of Agricultural Extension and Education, 28 April 1932.
125. VAB SLT 1/19, A44/4, vol. I, 'Glen School of Agriculture, Annual Report, 1931–1932'.
126. Kok, 'The Home Economist'. Similarly, many rural women in the United States were frustrated by the fact that home agents instructed women only in domestic skills, whereas farm agents were providing information on crops and animals exclusively for men; Danbom, *Born in the Country*, 175.
127. Labuschagne, 'Esther Bell-Robinson', 41–45.
128. SAB, LON 10, A27/1, Esther Bell-Robinson to Colonel du Toit, 19 April 1924.
129. Walker, *Women and Resistance*, 54, 79.
130. SAB, CEN 735, EN 10/26, President, National Council of Women of South Africa, 20 September 1921.
131. Ibid.
132. SAB, LDB 1050, R 157.12, vol. I, Senior Extension Officer to Chief, Division of Agricultural Extension and Education, 28 April 1932. In 1935, women reportedly made up between 3 and 4 per cent of South Africa's independent farmers (SAB, LDB 2418, R3681, vol. I, Confidential Report by Principal, Glen College, to Chief, Division of Agricultural Education and Extension, annexed to letter, 18 March 1935).
133. SAB, CEN 735, EN 10/26, Minutes of Proceedings, Conference on Higher Agricultural Education, Union Buildings, Pretoria, 21 July 1921 (third day: first quotation; fifth day: second quotation).
134. COR, MS 17 753, Folder 5, Minutes of Proceedings, Conference on Higher Agricultural Education, 30 September 1921.

135. Ibid.
136. SAB, LON 207, A120, vol. 1, Mrs Herold to Principal, Cedara, 25 January 1945; SAB, LDB 2419, R3681, Part III, 'Boschetto College Prize-Giving', *The Friend*, 13 December 1947.
137. LSEWL, 1SOS/01/27, Extraordinary Meeting of the Africa Committee, 29 May 1935.
138. SAB, LDB 2418, R3681, vol. I, Boschetto Agricultural College, [n.a.], [n.d.].
139. SAB, LDB 2418, R3681, Part III, Principal, Boschetto, to Minister for Agriculture, 2 January 1948.
140. SAB, LDB 2418, R3681, vol. I, Confidential Report by Principal, Glen College, to Chief, Division of Agricultural Education and Extension, 18 March 1935; TAB, MGH 581/55, 17.
141. One-third of the student body came from the United Kingdom. Many of those who arrived in the period from 1929 to 1939 came under the auspices of the Society for the Oversea Settlement of British Women (SOSBW), a society that encouraged the emigration of 'superfluous' women after the First World War (see e.g. LSEWL, 1SOS/01/27, Africa Committee Meeting, 4 July 1933).
142. See e.g. ibid.
143. SAB, LDB 2418, R3681, vol. I, Prospectus 'Boschetto College of Agriculture', [n.a.], [n.d., c. 1930]; SAB, LDB 2418, R3681, vol. II, Report by A.J. du Plessis, Division of Economics, Department of Agriculture, [n.d., c. November 1943]. The fees ranged between £100 in the early 1930s and £200 in 1959 (SAB, LDB 2418, R3681, Part III, 'Boschetto Landboukollege vir Dames', Report, [n.a., Department of Agriculture?], 1959); LSEWL, 1SOS/01/27, Africa Committee Meeting, 4 July 1933.
144. Glen College's principal highlighted that Boschetto was training 'women farmers (vroue-boere)' rather than 'farmers' wives (boerevroue)' (VAB, SLT 1/2 – A14 – vol. III, 'Notule van Konferensie van Prinsipale van Landboukolleges', Pretoria, 20–22 February 1940).
145. LSEWL, 1SOS/02/04, 'The SOSBW, Annual Report 1928'.
146. SAB, LDB 2418, R3681, vol. II, Principal, Boschetto, to Secretary for Agriculture, 19 October 1943.
147. LSEWL, 1SOS/01/07, SOSBW Council Minute Book, 10 July 1935.
148. SAB, LDB 2418, R3681, vol. II, M.J. Joubert to Jean Robertson, Sea Point, Cape Town, 27 December 1940.
149. LSEWL, 1SOS/01/27, Extraordinary Meeting of the Africa Committee, 29 May 1935; SAB, LDB 2418, R3681, vol. I, Secretary for Agriculture to Secretary for Finance, 26 September 1934.
150. SAB, LDB 2418, R3681, vol. I, Confidential Report by Principal, Glen College, to Chief, Division of Agricultural Education and Extension, annexed to letter, 18 March 1935.
151. SAB, LDB 2418, R3681, vol. II, Director, Agricultural Research Institute, Pretoria, to Secretary for Agriculture and Forestry, 2 November 1943.
152. SAB, LDB 2418, R3681, vol. II, Principal, Boschetto, to Secretary for Agriculture, 19 October 1943.
153. SAB, LDB 2419, R3681, Part III, 'Boschetto College Prize-Giving', *The Friend*, 13 December 1947.

154. LSEWL, 1SOS/01/27, Extraordinary Meeting of the Africa Committee, 29 May 1935.
155. SAB, LDB 2418, R3681, vol. I, Principal, Glen College, to Principal, Boschetto, 20 April 1933; SAB, LDB 2418, R3681, vol. I, Principal, Boschetto, to Colonel Williams, 14 November 1929; SAB, LDB 2418, R3681, vol. I, Chief, Division of Agricultural Education and Extension, to Principal, Boschetto, 23 April 1931.
156. SAB, LDB 2419, R3681, Part III, Memorandum, 'Boschetto Agricultural College', Director of Agriculture, 15 April 1959.
157. SAB, LDB 2419, R3681, Part III, Notes for a Speech by the Minister for Agriculture at the Boschetto Agricultural College, 10 December 1947.
158. See correspondence, late 1950s, SAB, LDB 2419, R3681, Part III.
159. SAB, LDB 889, R595/5A, Secretary for Agriculture to M.J. Stofberg, SA Women's Agricultural Union, 18 June 1947; see also further correspondence in this file from the early 1950s; SAB, LDB 2419, R3681, Part III, Memorandum, 'Boschetto Agricultural College', Director of Agriculture, 15 April 1959 (quotation).
160. Jeeves and Crush, 'Introduction'.
161. Bozzoli, 'Marxism, Feminism and South African Studies', 130–34; Keegan, *Rural Transformations*, 38.
162. Grey, *Productive Men*, 275, 278. Grey locates the origins of this dichotomy already in the pre-industrial period (ibid., 9–10). See also, Neth, *Preserving the Family Farm*, 5.
163. Hansen, 'Introduction', 6. Moreover, Jones-Branch has argued that extension work in the US South reflected 'an idealized gender division of labor based on the assumption that farm women focused solely on home-based projects, although that was seldom the reality' ('African American Demonstration Agents', 159).

Bibliography

Ambrose, Linda. 'Women's Institutes in Canada and the United Kingdom: The Weighty Matters of Domestic Science, Home Economics, and Food Security', in Linda Ambrose and Joan Jensen (eds), *Women in Agriculture: Professionalizing Rural Life in North America and Europe 1880–1965* (Iowa City: University of Iowa Press, 2017), 120–35.

Beinart, William. 'Women in Rural Politics: Herschel District in the 1920s and 1930s', in Belinda Bozzoli (ed.), *Class, Community, and Conflict: South African Perspectives* (Johannesburg: Ravan Press, 1987), 324–58.

Bonner, Philip. 'South African Society and Culture, 1910–1948', in Robert Ross, Anne Mager and Bill Nasson (eds), *The Cambridge History of South Africa* (Cambridge: Cambridge University Press, 2011), 254–318.

Bozzoli, Belinda. 'Marxism, Feminism and South African Studies', in William Beinart and Saul Dubow (eds), *Segregation and Apartheid in Twentieth-Century South Africa* (New York: Routledge, 1995), 139–71.

Bradford, Helen. 'Peasants, Historians, and Gender: A South African Case Study Revisited, 1850–1886'. *History and Theory* 39(4) (2000), 86–110.

Bundy, Colin. *The Rise and Fall of the South African Peasantry*. 2nd edn. Cape Town: David Philip, 1988.

Charman, Andrew. 'Progressive Élites in Bunga Politics: African Farmers in the Transkeian Territories, 1904–1946', Ph.D. dissertation. Cambridge: University of Cambridge, 1998.

Cock, Jackely. 'Domestic Service and Education for Domesticity: The Incorporation of Xhosa Women into Colonial Society', in Cherryl Walker (ed.), *Women and Gender in Southern Africa to 1945* (Cape Town: David Philip, 1990), 76–96.

Comaroff, Jean, and John Comaroff. 'Home-Made Hegemony: Modernity, Domesticity, and Colonialism in South Africa', in Karen Tranberg Hansen (ed.), *African Encounters with Domesticity* (New Brunswick, NJ: Rutgers University Press, 1992), 37–74.

Danbom, David. *Born in the Country: A History of Rural America*. Baltimore: Johns Hopkins University Press, 2006.

Davie, Grace. *Poverty Knowledge in South Africa: A Social History of Human Science, 1855–2005*. New York: Cambridge University Press, 2015.

Denzer, LaRay. 'Domestic Science Training in Colonial Yorubaland, Nigeria', in Karen Tranberg Hansen (ed.), *African Encounters with Domesticity* (New Brunswick, NJ: Rutgers University Press, 1992), 116–39.

Devarenne, Nicole. 'Nationalism and the Farm Novel in South Africa, 1883–2004'. *Journal of Southern African Studies* 35(3) (2009), 627–42.

Domosh, Mona. 'Race, Biopolitics and Liberal Development from the Jim Crow South to Postwar Africa'. *Transactions of the Institute of British Geographers* 43(2) (2018), 312–24.

Du Toit, Marijke. 'The Domesticity of Afrikaner Nationalism: *Volksmoeders* and the ACVV, 1904–1929'. *Journal of Southern African Studies* 29(1) (2003), 155–76.

Elias, Megan. *Stir It up: Home Economics in American Culture*: Philadelphia: University of Pennsylvania Press, 2008.

Epprecht, Marc. 'Domesticity and Piety in Colonial Lesotho'. *Journal of Southern African Studies* 19(2) (1993), 202–24.

Evans, Ivan. *Bureaucracy and Race: Native Administration in South Africa*. Berkeley: University of California Press, 1997.

Gaitskell, Deborah. 'Housewives, Maids or Mothers: Some Contradictions of Domesticity for Christian Women in Johannesburg, 1903–39'. *Journal of African History* 24(2) (1983), 241–56.

———. 'Devout Domesticity? A Century of African Women's Christianity in South Africa', in Cherryl Walker (ed.), *Women and Gender in Southern Africa to 1945* (Cape Town: David Philip, 1990), 251–72.

Goldstein, Carolyn. *Creating Consumers: Home Economists in Twentieth-Century America*. Chapel Hill: University of North Carolina Press, 2012.

Grey, Marion. *Productive Men, Reproductive Women: The Agrarian Household and the Emergence of Separate Spheres during the German Enlightenment*. New York: Berghahn Books, 2000.

Grey Osterud, Nancy. *Putting the Barn before the House: Women and Family Farming in Early Twentieth-Century New York*. Ithaca: Cornell University Press, 2012.

Hansen, Karen Tranberg. 'Introduction: Domesticity in Africa', in Karen Tranberg Hansen (ed.), *African Encounters with Domesticity* (New Brunswick, NJ: Rutgers University Press, 1992), 1–36.

——— (ed.). *African Encounters with Domesticity*. New Brunswick, NJ: Rutgers University Press, 1992.

Heinemann, Isabel. *Wert der Familie: Ehescheidung, Frauenarbeit und Reproduktion in den USA des 20. Jahrhunderts*. Berlin: De Gruyter, 2018.

Higgs, Catherine. *The Ghost of Equality: The Public Lives of D.D.T. Jabavu of South Africa, 1885–1959*. Athens, OH: Ohio University Press, 1997.

———. 'Helping Ourselves: Black Women and Grassroots Activism in Segregated South Africa, 1922–1952', in Catherine Higgs, Barbara Moss and Earline Ferguson (eds), *Stepping Forward: Black Women in Africa and the Americas* (Athens, OH: Ohio University Press, 2002), 59–72.

———. 'Zenzele: African Women's Self-Help Organizations in South Africa, 1927–1998'. *African Studies Review* 47(3) (2004), 119–41.

Hodge, Joseph. *Triumph of the Expert: Agrarian Doctrines of Development and the Legacies of British Colonialism*. Athens, OH: Ohio University Press, 2007.

Hoffschwelle, Mary. *Rebuilding the Rural Southern Community: Reformers, Schools, and Homes in Tennessee, 1900–1930*. Knoxville: University of Tennessee Press, 1998.

Jeeves, Alan, and Jonathan Crush. 'Introduction', in Alan Jeeves and Jonathan Crush (eds), *White Farms, Black Labor: The State and Agrarian Change in Southern Africa, 1910–50* (Oxford: James Currey, 1997), 1–28.

Jones, Thomas Jesse. *Education in East Africa: A Study of East, Central and South Africa by the Second African Education Commission under the Auspices of the Phelps-Stokes Fund, in Cooperation with the International Education Board*. London: Edinburgh House Press, 1925.

Jones-Branch, Cherisse. 'African American Demonstration Agents in the Field and Rural Reform in Arkansas, 1914–1965', in Linda Ambrose and Joan Jensen (eds), *Women in Agriculture: Professionalizing Rural Life in North America and Europe 1880–1965* (Iowa City: University of Iowa Press, 2017), 156–73.

Kallaway, Peter, and Rebecca Swartz. 'Introduction', in Peter Kallaway and Rebecca Swartz (eds), *Empire and Education in Africa: The Shaping of a Comparative Perspective* (New York: Peter Lang, 2016), 1–29.

Keegan, Timothy. *Rural Transformations in Industrializing South Africa: The Southern Highveld to 1914*. Basingstoke: Macmillan, 1987.

Kok, A.E. 'The Home Economist in the O.F.S. Region'. *Farming in South Africa* 45(8) (Special Edition: 'Golden Jubilee Glen College of Agriculture') (1969), 71–75.

Koponen, Juhani. *Development for Exploitation: German Colonial Policies in Mainland Tanzania, 1884–1914*. Helsinki: Finnish Historical Society, 1994.

Labuschagne, Pieter. 'Esther Bell-Robinson, the Irish Rebel and the Hendrik van Loon Letters'. *South African Journal of Cultural History* 23(2) (2009), 38–57.

Littlefield, Valinda. 'Agency and Constructions of Political Identity', in Catherine Higgs, Barbara Moss and Earline Ferguson (eds), *Stepping Forward: Black Women in Africa and the Americas* (Athens, OH: Ohio University Press, 2002), 17–27.

Marks, Shula. *Not Either an Experimental Doll: The Separate Worlds of Three South African Women*. Bloomington: Indiana University Press, 1987.

McClintock, Anne. *Imperial Leather: Race, Gender, and Sexuality in the Colonial Contest*. New York: Routledge, 1995.

Musisi, Nakanyike. 'Colonial and Missionary Education: Women and Domesticity in Uganda, 1900–1945', in Karen Tranberg Hansen (ed.), *African Encounters with Domesticity* (New Brunswick, NJ: Rutgers University Press, 1992), 172–94.

Neth, Mary. *Preserving the Family Farm: Women, Community, and the Foundations of Agribusiness in the Midwest, 1900–1940*. Baltimore: Johns Hopkins University Press, 1995.

Ranchod-Nilsson, Sita. '"Educating Eve": The Women's Club Movement and Political Consciousness among Rural African Women in Southern Rhodesia, 1950–1980', in Karen Tranberg Hansen (ed.), *African Encounters with Domesticity* (New Brunswick, NJ: Rutgers University Press, 1992), 195–217.

Rothmann, Mary Elizabeth. *The Mother and Daughter in the Poor Family: Part B of the Sociological Report of the Carnegie Commission's Report on the Poor White Problem in South Africa*. Stellenbosch: Pro-Ecclesia-Drukkery, 1932.

Rouse, Jacqueline. 'Out of the Shadow of Tuskegee: Margaret Murray Washington, Social Activism, and Race Vindication'. *Journal of Negro History* 81 (1996), 33–38.

Shantz, Homer. 'Supplementary Chapter: Agriculture in East Africa', in Thomas Jesse Jones, *Education in East Africa. A Study of East, Central and South Africa by the Second African Education Commission under the Auspices of the Phelps-Stokes Fund, in Cooperation with the International Education Board* (London: Edinburgh House Press, 1925), 358–401.

Staples, Amy. *The Birth of Development: How the World Bank, Food and Agricultural Organization, and World Health Organization Changed the World, 1945–1965*. Kent, OH: Kent State University Press, 2006.

Tischler, Julia. 'Education and the Agrarian Question in South Africa, c. 1900–40'. *Journal of African History* 57(2) (2019), 251–70.

Unger, Corinna. 'Agrarwissenschaftliche Expertise und ländliche Modernisierungsstrategien in der internationalen Entwicklungspolitik, 1920er bis 1980er Jahre'. *Geschichte und Gesellschaft* 41(4) (2015), 552–79.

Van Niekerk, Marlene. 'Afrikaner Woman and Her "Prison": Afrikaner Nationalism and Literature', in Robert Kriger and Ethel Kriger (eds), *Afrikaans Literature* (Amsterdam: Rodopi, 1996), 141–54.

Walker, Cherryl. *Women and Resistance in South Africa*. Cape Town: David Philip, 1991.

Willoughby-Herard, Tiffany. *Waste of a White Skin: The Carnegie Corporation and the Racial Logic of White Vulnerability*. Oakland: University of California Press, 2015.

Worboys, Michael. 'The Discovery of Colonial Malnutrition between the Wars', in David Arnold (ed.), *Imperial Medicine and Indigenous Societies* (Manchester: Manchester University Press, 1988), 208–25.

 CHAPTER 10

Between War and Productivity

Facets of Agricultural Training and Land Restoration in the Villages of Northern Greek Macedonia from the Civil War to the AMAG Programmes, 1944–53

Kalliopi Geronymaki

By the spring of 1950, nine months had passed since the official end of the Greek Civil War (1946–49). In Northern Greece, the continuing conflict among rural dwellers over access to cultivable land echoed the enduring political polarization. A report by the Prefecture of Serres, which was sent to the General Directorate of Northern Greece in Thessaloniki, emphasized that the Greek state's new allowances for land acquisition by the residents around Lake Kerkini were irrevocable, citing the argument that these acted as a guarantee of political loyalty:

> It is not possible to cancel the administrative eviction of all those who culti-
> vated arbitrarily on the plot of land around Lake Kerkini, because the eviction
> of all those who cultivated has already been executed, thus making allowance
> for the inhabitants of the village of Anō Porroia to develop intensive agricul-
> ture. The claim by the inhabitants of Akritohōri that the eviction deprived
> them of their already sown plots is not true. The truth is that all those who
> sowed did so without permission and had occupied the land arbitrarily …
> It should be noted that the inhabitants of Anō Porroia are among the most
> heroic of our Commune, having fought for three years against the Slavic-led
> bandits without abandoning their village.[1]

'Arbitrary growers' and 'heroic inhabitants' framed the political divisions around which agricultural education evolved during the passage from a state of war to the economic recovery of the early Cold War era. Ministerial decrees from the governing authorities in Athens and Thessaloniki designed agricultural policies and the allocation of humanitarian aid around the targeting of Communists and leftist partisans, who were perceived as enemies of the state and land invaders.

War and agriculture went hand in hand in Northern Greece. The agriculturally rich provinces of Northern, Central and Western Greek Macedonia were the ultimate theatre of Greek political polarization during the Civil War and its aftermath.[2] The presence of agronomists in these territories reflected political tensions that arose as a result of the Greek authorities' attempts to thread an ambivalent passage between advancing anti-communist political priorities and adhering to international demands for food safety and market-oriented agricultural production. Set against this context, it is the aim of this chapter to explore the trajectory of agronomic development in Northern Greece. Furthermore, in their aforementioned report, the regional authorities also prioritized 'developing intensive agriculture' within a system of self-reliant village economies based on autoconsumption. As this chapter will argue, these parallel aims gave rise to social and economic controversies. Reflecting the first signs of Cold War polarization, the agricultural consequences of both the outbreak of the Greek Civil War and the modernizing plans proposed by the American Mission for Aid in Greece (AMAG) within the context of the United States' Marshall Plan (also known as the European Recovery Program [ERP]) found expression in Greek agronomic science.

The purpose of this chapter is to interpret the tasks and responsibilities that Greek agronomists assumed against the backdrop of a period of Civil War, political polarization and eventual economic restoration. It is structured into four sections. The first section searches for the interwar policies that reformed the agronomic profession in Greece. The second section briefly discusses the historical context of the Second World War and its aftermath, in particular the period from 1944 to 1946, as a basis for exploring how agronomic aid was reshaped as Greece dealt with the devastation left behind by the Axis occupation. The third section concerns the period during the Civil War from 1947 to 1949 when Greece's national and regional agronomic services distributed land and assistance more systematically in an effort to create maps of political loyalty in the war-torn areas of Northern Greece. The final section focuses on the international programmes launched first by the United Nations Relief and Rehabilitation Administration (UNRRA) and then by AMAG. Whereas UNRRA's main task was to distribute food aid and basic goods to the victims of the Civil War, the Marshall Plan authorities and AMAG planned new developmental agendas for long-term economic growth. In Greece, AMAG thus reflected the international turn towards market-oriented farming as well as the United States' support for the sector through its counterpart funds strategy.[3] This policy was consolidated through a series of directives in the period from 1948 to 1953, creating permanent new features of the agronomic profession in Greece.

Studying a span of eight years, the present analysis alternates between exploring instructive examples from the villages of five Northern provinces in Central and Western Greek Macedonia (Florina, Thessaloniki, Chalkidiki,

Kilkis and Serres) and analysis of Greek government and US agricultural development and agronomic planning.

Institutional Legacies of Agronomy in Greece: From Nationhood to Science

During the second half of the 1940s, the interwar divisions between intellectual agronomic elites and rural agronomists – or highly educated experts and local state officials – still determined the manner in which vocational training penetrated Greece's rural communities. An analysis of specific agronomic practices that were introduced during the interwar years provides an insight into the origins of postwar policies.

There was an immediate strong bond between agronomic science and the construction of national identity on land that the Greek state had annexed during the Balkan Wars (1912–13) and the First World War. From 1911 to 1920, the Greek government framed its proposals for land re-allocation by invoking the rhetoric of the peasant as patriot, defender of the soil and owner of the small family plot. This was reinforced by a 1911 law that introduced communal agronomists (*Nomogeōponoi*) as village instructors. These developments all had enduring political implications. From the interwar years, a young generation of Greek agronomists attached their professional profile to the politics of national identity. Moreover, in the Greek countryside, the doctrine of the diachronic 'autochthonous' origins of Greek farmers, who had been on their land since antiquity, placed pedagogical values at the centre of the agronomic profession.

The foundation of the Greek Ministry of Agriculture in 1917 made land re-allocation and access to loans the government's central strategy for the long-term development of the peasant economy. The main focus of land and credit reform now became the Northern departments of Greek Macedonia and Thrace. These territories, also known as the 'New Lands', had been annexed to Greece in the aftermath of the Balkan Wars, having previously been part of the Ottoman Empire. Agronomists were given the responsibility of introducing small landowners to new production methods as instructors in a nexus that also incorporated local village agricultural cooperatives and an expanding banking network.[4] Agronomic knowledge underpinned village economies in these territories. In this centralizing agenda, communal agronomists acquired a special role in implementing the modernizing agenda of the early governments of Prime Minister Eleutherios Venizelos.[5] In 1920, the new nucleus of their work became the recently established (primary-level) lower agricultural schools.[6] These institutions placed agronomists at the centre of village communities by offering gardening and cultivation classes to schoolchildren and by hosting short professional seminars for adult farmers. However, the 1920 foundation of Greece's first agronomic university, the Agricultural School of Athens, intensified a parallel circulation of more advanced agricultural knowledge among an educated stratum of young experts who were professionally alienated from the rural agronomists.[7]

In the early 1920s, driven by the rising contemporary discourse in many Eastern European countries on 'the peasantry' as an autonomous social stratum, the Greek government tasked agronomists with launching the 'reagrarianization of society', a trend that Spyridon Ploumidis has defined as 'peasantist nationalism'.[8]

During the Great Depression, the government introduced a pro-agrarian discourse to support the turn towards strong state interventionism in agriculture. It was at this juncture that Venizelos' final full-term government (1928–32) combined the pedagogical figure of 'the village agronomist' with a revised, modernizing agenda for agricultural vocational training. Law 4142/1929 offered a systematic attempt to improve farming methods through the foundation of vocational schools that were independent from the existing schooling system.[9] The legislation established a new Agricultural Directorate (Dieuthinsē Georgikōn Efarmogōn kai Propagandas) within the Ministry of Agriculture, which was to be dedicated to agricultural vocational training. However, the new legislation's most important legacy was the administrative division of Greece into twelve agricultural peripheries (districts), each with its own agricultural directorate. An agricultural inspector served as the head of each periphery and reported back to the Ministry of Agriculture in Athens. This new framework reinforced the previous centralized model for agricultural education by binding together the agricultural schools in different villages in the name of technological innovation. Following the end of the Second World War, these agronomic policies would bring village agronomy under centralized political control, thereby strengthening the centripetal administrative structure of the interwar period.

During the interwar years, the central government's political reform agenda had been manifest in the provinces of Northern Greece. In Central and Western Greek Macedonia, the official campaign of national irredentism attached agricultural state aid programmes to the Hellenization of Slavic-speaking populations.[10] The government launched a strategy of ethnic homogenization through a campaign of educational and ideological propaganda in cooperatives, schools and political associations. Administrative resources were also distributed on the basis of 'Greek' ethnicity. In the nationalistic atmosphere of mid-1920s 'agrarianism', cooperatives needed the approval of state agricultural inspectors to authorize their founding.[11]

In parallel to the national political agronomic project, a transnational exchange of expertise brought together agronomists from different countries in Northern Greece during the interwar period. For example, reclamation work on flooded land was an expert field that saw Greek agronomists working alongside foreign counterparts. Even before the passing of Law 4142, similar scientific exchanges had been encouraged in order to support the interwar development of public agricultural infrastructure. In Northern Greece, young agronomists very often found themselves working for foreign-owned private companies that had been contracted by the Greek state to undertake the realization of large-scale public works projects. The epicentre of this international cooperation became the marshy territories of the above-mentioned 'New Lands', which during the 1920s and 1930s were still seen as 'landscapes of disease', especially malaria.[12] The Greek authorities considered this vast area covered by lakes, swamps and rivers as being in urgent need of drainage, both for the benefit of public health and to allow for the future restitution of additional land for cultivation. In 1928, the government assigned a project to drain and irrigate the Strymon River as it passed through the Serres plain to the US companies John Monks & Sons and Henry Ulen,[13] with Greek engineers and agronomists also involved in the project. Drainage work was among the first fields in which Greek agronomists acquired the profile of 'experts', thereby combining their image of national pedagogical carrier with that of scientific expert in a field with irredentist implications.

Other agricultural activities, such as transhumance, were not considered in governmental planning. Local livestock breeders typically formed an economic landscape that during the 1920s and 1930s remained to a great extent isolated from the parallel professional universe of experts who were working on land reclamation. Nomadic or semi-nomadic herding in the Pindos mountains followed a seasonal itinerary from winter to summer pastures and supported a peasant economy based on subsistence farming. However, from 1920, some of these itineraries began to disappear due to the forced expropriation of peasant-used grazing lands that were to be incorporated into the land reform process in the 'New Lands'.[14] From 1923 onwards, this land was given to landless inhabitants and recent refugees from the population exchange with Turkey. As people settled on their new land, many herders began losing access to grazing locations due to the numerous new small, fenced-off properties that upended the erstwhile continuity of grazing land and marked a shift in government policy on the public sharing of environmental resources. As the following sections will analyse, the Greek government bolstered this policy direction in the early 1950s in order to reinforce new identity constructions in the aftermath of the Civil War.

Agronomy against a Backdrop of Institutional Emergencies, 1944–46

Military Emergencies

From 1944 to 1946, political tensions gradually shifted from the capital, Athens, to mountainous Northern Greece, turning land and natural resources into contested elements in the conflict between the Greek state and Communist rebels. Although 1944 had marked the end of the Second World War in Greece, it did not signify the end of war on Greek territory. On 3 December 1944, only two months after the Liberation celebrations, the Greek right-wing militant organization X/Chites, in coordination with the British and Greek armies, clashed violently with the regrouped Communist forces of the National Liberation Front (EAM) on the streets of Athens.[15] Upon EAM's subsequent withdrawal from this urban guerrilla warfare in January 1945, the Communist rebels transferred the bulk of their military actions into the countryside, with their focal point being the mountainous Northern provinces. However, on 12 February 1945, the EAM leadership signed the Treaty of Varkiza, consenting to discharge its military wing in exchange for the clearance of the corpses of Nazi collaborators and free elections. With the Greek Communist Party (KKE) having also entered into a period of overt political marginalization from official politics, many EAM members rejected this disbandment and preserved their military equipment.

Immediately after the Liberation, Greek territories that had been under Bulgarian occupation (1941–44) had briefly turned into epicentres of open conflict between the dispersed Communist forces and paramilitary groups made up of former Nazi collaborators. These hostilities resumed in March 1946 with the first open battle at Litochoro (Pieria, Western Greek Macedonia), a result of the rising incidents of 'white terror' in the countryside that would pave the way for the spread of the military conflict in the following months and years. 'White terror' refers to the violence and persecution to which civilians who showed solidarity with or were suspected of joining the Communist forces in the countryside were subjected by right-wing military or paramilitary groups with the support of the state's paramilitary security services. Especially in Western Greek Macedonia, this form of state-sponsored terrorism affected entire villages and their inhabitants.[16] The agronomic services and the agricultural cooperatives offered a wide range of services to 'trustworthy' citizens but discriminated against sympathizers of EAM and its military branch, the Greek People's Liberation Army (ELAS).

In 1945–46, the mounting political and military polarization dictated which villages received humanitarian aid or agronomic support from the Greek state and the representatives of the British authorities in Athens. Aid was only distributed to villages that offered refuge to 'bandit-stricken' populations, as they were characterized in the government's anti-communist rhetoric. Over the course of the following two years, political tensions in the five Northern provinces rose, paving the way for an open military conflict over who did and who did not have the right to dwell on and be fed by the land.

Administrative divisions influenced the manner in which agronomic aid was channelled. The highest regional institution in Greek Macedonia was the General Directorate of Northern Greece, which coordinated the activities of the decentralized agricultural directorates and oversaw the supervisory responsibilities of the agronomists. At a lower level, the provinces were divided into large municipal units (such as Thessaloniki, Kilkis, Pella, Florina and Chalkidiki), which in turn were made up of communes (*Nomoi*). Supplementary organs to the communes were the prefectures (*Nomarxies*), which functioned as intermediaries between the national government and the communes. Prefectures were responsible for disseminating circulars that arrived via the General Directorate from the Ministry of Agriculture in Athens. The community (*Koinotēta*), namely the village administrative unit, was placed at the centre of agricultural and agronomic policy on the lowest rung of the hierarchy after the prefectures and the communes. The presidents of the communities received and distributed circulars from their prefecture, the agricultural directorates and other supervisory bodies. Agronomists played the role of intermediaries in this structure, signing approvals for public works projects or for the distribution of seeds or hybrids but without enjoying the authority to act independently of government-approved schemes.

Under a framework of administrative centralization, control over the land and systems of land tenure was the top priority of the first postwar government in 1945. With Emergency Order 5156/1945, Prime Minister Petros Voulgaris' government made local agricultural security officers responsible for evicting any 'trespassers' from 'common lands' for unauthorized occupation. The government characterized as 'public' or 'common' all land that had been occupied by 'outlaw' cultivators during the Occupation.[17] Through this official condemnation of 'land trespassers', the Voulgaris government endorsed the paramilitary violence of the 'white terror', which saw senior military officers and gendarmes attack any civilian suspected of materially supporting EAM guerrilla fighters.[18]

Emergency Order 5156/1945 targeted the Northern provinces because of their mountainous terrain, which formed an ideal landscape in which to hide and from which to fight guerrilla war. However, from an agricultural perspective, George Margaritis has argued that the EAM/ELAS forces occupied the least productive and most isolated land, having been driven back from the plains and other highly fertile land by government forces.[19] Moreover, the territories that had been liberated by the Communists during the Second World War and which they continued to occupy remained cut off from UNRRA or

Greek Red Cross aid, thus forcing local inhabitants to pay the price for their solidarity with the EAM/ELAS fighters.

In a November 1945 letter, the Directorate of Agricultural Security warned its administrative officials and agronomists to ensure that state ownership rights over public land were protected.[20] The document's use of the term 'outlaw cultivators', despite its vagueness, shows that the government wanted to strip leftist partisans or their potential sympathizers of their land rights. This tactic also demonstrates that the authorities feared EAM's popularity in villages, including a scenario in which it would gain control over both the land and local cultivators. In response to this concern, the government began the four-year resettlement of almost 700,000 inhabitants from Northern Epirus and Greek Macedonia to the nearest urban centres or lowland villages.[21] From this point onwards, political loyalty (*ethnikofrosynē*) became a *sine qua non* in state land re-allocation programmes.

Economic Emergencies

During the four years of Axis occupation, half of Greece's agricultural infrastructure had been destroyed, while annual production levels for the period from 1941 to 1944 were about 40 per cent lower than those of 1939.[22] The December 1944 unrest generated further political destabilization and negatively impacted upon government policy-making in relation to economic recovery.[23] By the end of 1944, Greece was facing an inflation crisis, a lack of liquidity and continuous currency revaluations.[24] In 1945, the government was still funding more than 75 per cent of public spending with loans. Furthermore, domestic traders, with deep roots in black market activities, continued to undermine the restoration of agriculture and industry across Greece. The British delegation pushed hard for the implementation of moderate state intervention to ease the flow of goods within the Greek market, but this potential solution remained unrealized in 1946.

In the countryside, humanitarian aid was complemented by an embryonic government structural aid package for farmers, while UNRRA also offered capital to farmers with which to purchase agricultural equipment.[25] This type of aid implied long-term economic commitments on the part of the Greek authorities that revived the key prewar role of the Greek banking system in the country's agriculture – especially the Agricultural Bank of Greece (Agrotiki Trapeza tēs Ellados [ATE]), which provided loans to individual farmers for new farming equipment. Apart from food aid, ATE also signed contracts with the Greek state to distribute pesticides, seeds and phytosanitary equipment that had been provided by UNRRA. However, as Lykogiannis observes, UNRRA's intervention did not alter the trend of local agricultural production being channelled into the hands of fewer and fewer producers and merchants, mostly black market dealers. In terms of supplies of both food and equipment, UNRRA thus did not succeed in limiting the monopolies of the commercial networks that had been established during the Second World War.[26]

UNRRA's failures widened the gap between the producers who had monopolized the local market and local farmers whose operations had barely survived the war. Before the war, the agricultural producers of Northern Greek Macedonia were focused primarily on tobacco, raisins and cereal production.[27] Tobacco and local raisin varieties, in particular, had been staple products for the Greek export economy. After the war, the stocking of wheat became an urgent government priority.[28] In November 1945, the General Directorate of Central Greek Macedonia began working together with the Gendarmerie to requisition wheat from merchants or proprietors of threshing machines while also making machines available to poorer farmers or those whose farms had been damaged.[29]

But access to wheat, seeds or equipment went hand in hand with the infliction of 'white terror' as the police continued to impose intensified controls over local inhabitants. As of July 1946, the community of Sindos in Thessaloniki was warning its farmers not to pass through public works construction sites with their livestock or risk being apprehended by the police.[30] Using the protection of public infrastructure as a pretext, the police now possessed the right to inspect, arrest and interrogate any 'suspicious' civilian.

War and Agronomy in Northern Greece, 1947–49: Land, Cooperatives and the Supervision of 'Conscience'

New legislation in April 1947 gave shape to the transitional land regimes in Northern Greece. The central government attempted to establish control of the land reform process by issuing a new decree, according to which the ten-year lease of publicly owned land to landless farmers was to become mandatory for village and other local authorities and, under certain conditions, for monasteries.[31] In September 1947, the Ministry of Agriculture prolonged the period for the re-allocation of plots to landless inhabitants of Thessaloniki and requested all agronomists working at the level of the village authorities to work attentively on 'land security'. However, land re-allocation was not without preconditions. Membership of a local agricultural cooperative became compulsory for anyone seeking to acquire a plot in Northern Greek Macedonia. Whereas other cooperatives were 'productive', focusing on the collective selling of the local harvest, 'credit' and 'compulsory' cooperatives in Northern Greek Macedonia allocated land and loans exclusively to villagers who were cooperative members. 'Compulsory' village cooperatives elected a president and a council, but they remained strictly bound to official state policy and did not have the authority to modify the status of their members autonomously. It was the task of the agronomists to identify only these 'eligible' farmers as potential beneficiaries of the re-allocation of agricultural land:

> For the rapid adoption of our decision, each communal agronomist shall draw up a nominal table with all the beneficiaries of temporary land concessions. [For this task] they shall collaborate with the Mayor of the relevant commune or the Village President or – in their absence – with the chairman of the local credit cooperative and conduct hearings on the stakeholders' interests. He shall also consider the land concessions that have been released during the previous years, 1946–1947.[32]

State surveillance increased in 1948 following ELAS raids on villages in Western Greek Macedonia in search of food, clothing and young fighters.[33] The practice of transforming agronomists into social proctors went hand in hand with new emergency laws, which evaluated inhabitants' political profiles to ensure that they had denounced or were wholly alienated from communism.[34] Like other state employees, agronomists also had to offer proof of their distance from and condemnation of communism. In order to assess the political beliefs of farmers and villagers during the Civil War, the government created so-called Local Councils of Loyalty. These organs collaborated with their local police stations to examine the political profile of every inhabitant who applied for a plot of land. Rural policemen, village mayors and even the officers of the national Hellenic Army General Staff interrogated applicants by asking questions such as: 'Have you ever joined or morally supported the resistance groups?' or 'Where was your place of residence on 1 May 1941?' (implying an obligation to justify any subsequent relocations as unrelated to political activity).[35] Upon satisfactory answers to an interrogation, the government issued individual certificates of social beliefs that were essential for access to basic civil rights. Finally, the government required individuals who had joined or assisted left-wing groups or had been in any way associated with left-wing resistance during the Occupation to sign a declaration of penitence.

As the Civil War continued to escalate, the authorities reorganized the agricultural cooperatives into the primary organs for the propagation of new agricultural methods. Since the beginning of the twentieth century, these collective bodies had been principally responsible for offering credit services to farmers and implementing government decisions on village economic planning. During the Civil War, their traditional alignment with the state's policies took a new twist. The cooperatives' dissemination of agricultural knowledge was presented as a reward for villagers who were deemed to have been 'bandit-stricken' and were now being promised a new life upon 'repatriation' to their villages, from where they had been removed to prevent them from becoming supportive of the resistance forces.

Cooperative supervisors roamed the provinces overseeing the financial performance of the cooperatives as well as the profile of cooperative members. Pro-cooperative political propaganda reached its peak in March 1949, when the official cooperative press collectively celebrated 'Farmers' Day'. For example, the magazine *Voice of Cooperatives* addressed repatriated peasants in the 'bandit-stricken' villages with a special illustrated issue that relayed the following promise: 'Hold strong. No matter how much you are stricken, the Cooperative will assist you … It is not going to let you return to the village empty-handed.'[36]

Beyond this propagandistic façade, economic circumstances hampered the main function of agricultural cooperatives to distribute state loans and implement government policies. With private wholesalers controlling almost half of total purchasable agricultural production output, cooperatives conceded considerable ground to their commercial competitors. As such, cooperative members could seldom achieve a shared profit through their collective selling.[37]

The Ministry of Agriculture formally linked land ownership to cooperative membership with the proclamation of a new Rural Code in December 1949.[38] New recipients of land in Northern Greece were now obliged by law to register as members of their local cooperative, which had been especially established for this purpose. Farmers who refused membership would be expelled from their plots under a protocol of administrative eviction. In the same month, the Ministry of Agriculture issued a new circular ordering the resumption of the unfinished drainage work in Northern Greece.[39] However, by this time, land recovery and restoration had acquired new features that followed the US Marshall Plan's directives on increased productivity.

Agricultural Development after the Civil War, 1948–53: AMAG and Greek Government Expectations in Northern Greece

With the agricultural sector undergoing significant damage during the Civil War, the Greek government expected foreign aid to underpin the establishment of long-term recovery programmes. In 1947, one crucial development paved the path for the introduction of more permanent economic recovery policies. This was the British withdrawal from the Greek political and economic context, which was crucially followed by the arrival of the American Mission for Aid in Greece in July 1947.[40] AMAG and its leader, Dwight Griswold, planned a sector-by-sector approach to public policy-making, including in the agricultural and industrial sectors, in close coordination with the United States' economic oversight organ in Greece, the Monetary Committee (Nomismatikē Epitropē).[41]

In AMAG's agenda, the reconstruction of agricultural infrastructure (especially rural roads, irrigation systems and harvest storage facilities in villages) gradually displaced the UNRRA priority of mitigating the food security emergency in the Greek countryside. Consequently, UN humanitarian aid decreased as the focus shifted onto long-term economic recovery. This developmental agenda was particularly centred on the Civil War combat zones of Western Greek Macedonia, where the government saw the potential to establish political and economic control over displaced populations and to shape their beliefs.

From April 1948, AMAG raised the issue of the income security of agricultural populations in Northern Greece. In line with its planned shift from humanitarian aid to a long-term income agenda, all sectors of the national economy, especially agriculture and industry, would gradually come to depend less and less on public spending. Griswold explicitly encouraged businesses to rely less on state funding or Monetary Committee loans. During a speech at the Federation of Industries of Greece, Griswold discussed farmers and industrial workers as income groups whose output would have a decisive impact on the agreed-upon timetable for the reduction of public expenditure:

> Many Greek citizens in rural areas are already suffering from the loss of income, the loss of their homes and livelihoods, and even the loss of family members. Industrial workers would be able to achieve further [income] concessions only at the expense of those people whose situation is already much worse than their own [i.e. farmers]. The Government must make every possible effort to limit its expenses to the minimum necessary. Agriculture has already contributed its share through increased production and its relatively low prices. Commercial interests must provide their share.[42]

Griswold argued that farmers, despite being victims of both war and low market prices, had achieved a level of productivity that had allowed them to decrease their dependence on foreign aid and loans. Industry, he concluded, should follow this example, especially given the rising concerns about a potentially unsustainable dollar deficit across postwar Europe. Ensuring increased agricultural and industrial production in Greece would entail less dependence on foreign capital (as distributed by the Monetary Committee) and more purchasing capacity within domestic markets.

To further these goals in the agriculture sector, AMAG entered into an infrastructure aid agreement with the Ministry of Agriculture in March 1948. This foresaw the drainage of 100,000 acres of Greek farmland, the construction of irrigation projects, the expansion of fruit plantations, the installation of cooling systems and the restoration of agricultural machinery.[43] In November 1948, the central government communicated to the Prefecture of Thessaloniki that 'the state, with the support of the American Mission, has planned small jobs for the bandit-stricken populations gathered in the various centres, which will help them to become efficient and stop being a burden for the public care [humanitarian aid] budget'.[44] Access to employment on public works projects was expected to gradually relieve AMAG's budget of the costs of direct emergency humanitarian aid. However, in the same 1948 letter, the Ministry of Agriculture noted significant hindrances to the programme. One implicit obstacle was that local authorities' payment of salaries to farmers and labourers on public works projects was financed out of limited state loans. These loans were also insufficient for improving farmers' poor access to technical assistance and agricultural equipment. As such, the long-term sustainability of the programme – and, in turn, the continuing collaboration of the local population – appeared doubtful, a problem that becomes further evident in other sources discussed below.

Indeed, while the provision of agricultural loans was a milestone in Greece's modernizing process, their flow was strictly supervised. In its own evaluations, the Agricultural Bank of Greece emphasized that its recommendations on annual loan budgets had never been approved in their entirety by the Monetary Committee or its oversight partner, the Bank of Greece (Trapeza tēs Ellados). ATE commented that the resulting limited annual budget for loans had consequently impaired the 'productive efforts of our farmers during the years 1945–1950'.[45] A related problem was that capital for short-term loans far exceeded long-term credit for improving agricultural infrastructure (1,164 versus 359 million drachmas).[46] ATE argued that the comparatively high number of short-term loans was indirectly discouraging farmers from improving their agricultural methods and knowledge.

The passing of new legislation marked a turning point for Greece's agronomic services. Twin 1950 and 1951 laws shifted the agronomists' activity from providing basic village education to offering specialized vocational services specifically targeted at improving farming methods.[47] The Ministry of Agriculture revoked the interwar policies by which agronomists were recruited to teach at so-called practical agricultural schools (*syllogoi agrotopaidōn*) for children.[48] The new model for disseminating agricultural expertise followed the US emphasis on increasing agricultural productivity, thereby shifting priority from ideological indoctrination to the amelioration of material conditions.[49] Following the example set in the United States, Greek agronomic science was thus now conceived as a scientific advisory and supervisory service in which agronomists took on the role of agricultural experts rather than mere village educators.[50]

Following AMAG's directives, the 1950 and 1951 laws set five principal goals for agricultural vocational training. The first was centred on land reclamation work. Under the new framework, drainage projects remained an important instrument for fostering political loyalty by distributing land to participants and by creating an expectation for innovative and intensive farming methods. In the commune of Lagkadas in Thessaloniki, the local union of cooperatives called for a meeting with the village authorities to propose a project to drain 15,000 acres of 'most fertile land' around Lake Vrōmolimnes.[51] In its appeal, the union praised the return of residents to their villages, which they had previously abandoned due to the war, as well as their efforts to restore their economic means. It then made the following observation: 'We were closely watching your efforts ... and we realized that one of the most basic needs of your Region is the drainage of Vrōmolimnes.'[52] This project would aim for the eradication of malaria, which the document characterized as 'one of the main enemies of our People' before declaring that 'peace and calm are now consolidating in our country'.[53] Drainage projects had been common in Greek Macedonia during the interwar years; now they offered an opportunity to restore social consensus and orientate public opinion away from recent painful memories of war.

A second aim of the two new laws was the improvement of farming methods. However, in Northern Greece, this agenda was met with reluctance and a sluggish uptake among local communities. Nevertheless, alongside supporting the cultivation of traditional crops such as tobacco and raisins, ATE proceeded with the importation of seeds and tree nurseries in order to encourage intensive arboriculture. Starting in 1951, the bank launched experimental cultivation of grafted trees and tested their productive capacity in different soils. In relation to these plans, as well as the establishment of a grape juice agro-industry in Greek Macedonia, ATE experts commented positively and anticipated further progress by the early 1960s.[54]

Third, professionalizing the commercial practices of Northern Greek farmers also meant transforming social attitudes towards the agricultural profession itself. This is evident in ministerial records that proclaimed a new tree planting campaign in 1953 that was expected to last for the next four years.[55] The announcement of this campaign included a stated government aim to transform peasant superstition towards specific tree species into an enthusiasm for their cultivation and an appreciation of their potential as a source of income. By February 1953, agronomists had sent tree nurseries to various arboriculture stations, which in turn distributed new cultivable varieties to the communes. The planting campaign began with walnut, hazelnut and chestnut trees arriving at Chalkidiki and Rodopi.

By being designated with the responsibility for overseeing this transformation of the cultivated landscape, agronomists were tasked with not only improving farmers' economic means but also 'demystifying' modern plantations from common 'peasant' beliefs:

> The realization of this project will be entrusted to the agronomists of Agricultural Directorates, who, by means of available expedients (farming

clubs, agricultural organizations, lectures, etc.), are going to cultivate the appropriate psychological climate for the farmers and stimulate their interest in these fruit trees. The propagandistic campaign must aim for the end of the conflictual superstitions about planting walnut trees ... [Agronomists] must accentuate the economic importance of tree nut production as supplementary income for the producer.[56]

This call to agronomists associated modernization plans with the diffusion of a new commerce-centred mentality in the countryside. Meanwhile, its emphasis on income support reflected the attitudes that the AMAG experts and Dwight Griswold himself had sought to inculcate since 1948. However, in reality, the campaign was less ambitious, as the nurseries were not used to form large-scale commercial orchards. Instead, the young trees occupied small sections of farmers' plots or were planted alongside rural roads.

In the livestock economy, AMAG's plans for the professionalization of the sector attempted to develop supplementary sources of income. In the summer of 1951, AMAG recommended the division of land in Northern Greece into different categories in order to separate agricultural zones from barren or forested ones. However, formalized control over land – whether flat, mountainous or barren – was in direct conflict with the traditions of the pastoral economy in the villages of Northern Greece.[57] As discussed above, livestock breeders in the Pindos mountains had traditionally followed seasonal transhumant circuits.[58] This form of nomadic or semi-nomadic livestock husbandry was central to villagers' social organization and mobility. In AMAG's 1951 report, by contrast, the term 'controlled grazing' prevailed in the technical vocabulary of the US experts,[59] for the realization of which AMAG's Directorate of Food and Agriculture proposed three strategies. First, it opted to delimit pastoral zones and thus enforce alternate grazing methods. Second, the plan advised that sheep and goats would benefit from irrigated clover plantations, a nutritious plant that was ideal for foraging and would boost local meat production. Third, AMAG imagined that pastoral activity in mountainous areas would follow the example of the US Civilian Conservation Corps (CCC).[60] The CCC, which had formed part of President Franklin D. Roosevelt's New Deal policies in response to the Great Depression, aimed to bring unemployed young men into semi-permanent professional service working on the development of parks and forests and the construction of public infrastructure.[61] According to AMAG, such 'organizations were crowned with such success in the United States',[62] a clear hint at the policy path that Greece was advised to follow in order to create new employment opportunities for its rural youth.

Like youth involvement in pastoral activities, the fifth and final aim of the 1950 and 1951 laws was for villagers of all ages to contribute their labour towards the realization of Greece's forestry plans. Already in 1948, the state was financing vast reforestation projects as part of its expenditure on public infrastructure in the countryside. In the same year, in three communities in Thessaloniki (Peraia, Neoi Epivates and Agia Trias), the government spent a total of 20 million drachmas on forest tree nurseries and fencing. Local residents were expected to assist in long-term maintenance by digging holes for tree planting and irrigating the forests during the summer.[63] The same source suggests that they were offered no financial incentives for their labour and were reluctant to carry out this maintenance work. Two years later, the Ministry of Agriculture sent out a severe warning, castigating them for their reluctance to sustain the state project:

> Unfortunately, your contribution offered very little to the whole project, not to mention that some people displayed complete indifference. For the expansion of the already existing reforestation programme, a forester is going to work with you to devise a work schedule for the current year [1951]. We are also eager to support you if you wish to fully comprehend the importance of this project for your communities and likewise to support our efforts, because it is not possible for the state to afford the total expenses for projects of such [a vast] nature.[64]

If local residents remained indifferent, the authorities thus warned, the state would immediately cease reforestation work in the area.

With 1952 marking the end of both AMAG's activities and Greece's access to ERP funding, short-term aid to the country ceased. US experts turned their attention to the planning of long-term development programmes under the auspices of the North Atlantic Treaty Organization (NATO) and the Organisation for European Economic Co-operation (OEEC), which were coordinating economic support programmes in several Southern European countries (including Greece as well as Portugal, Spain, Turkey and Yugoslavia). Ultimately in Greece, besides a long-term OEEC economic development aid package,[65] other foreign and domestic aid programmes proceeded in the form of loans for the purchase of industrial agricultural equipment, such as cold storage equipment and machinery for the processing of raw materials. After the devaluation of the drachma on 4 April 1953, ATE commented positively that agricultural exports were increasing and more foreign capital was entering the country.

However, neither AMAG nor the Greek commercial banks ever questioned the quality of the loans that the producers were receiving. Long-term indebtedness and lack of income from small-scale farming forced many farmers out of the agricultural profession. A new wave of rural exodus from Greek Macedonia began in the early 1950s, following those that had already occurred during the almost constant armed conflict of the 1940s.[66] Moreover, this last wave did not stimulate the concentration of farming plots into larger, more profitable ones, as international productive standards were already recommending.[67] For their part, most agronomists continued to offer their services in the villages and did not make farms the epicentre of their activity, as US experts might have preferred.

Conclusion

In the years before and after the Second World War, the main fields of activity for Greek agronomists became land re-allocation and miscellaneous projects focusing on inculcating new farming methods and other forms of environmental development. The implementation of these plans encountered and then clashed with peasants' subsistence practices before ultimately resulting in peasant incorporation into an economically insecure environment through the provision of agricultural loans.

Back in the interwar period, agronomists who worked on annexed land in Northern Greece had been assigned pedagogical tasks in local villages. Some had also been seen as nascent specialists in the modernization projects that were launched by the Venizelist governments during the 1920s and 1930s. After the liberation of Greece in 1944, the state resumed the implementation of land reform and agricultural modernization policies in the period leading up to and during the Civil War. During this phase, agronomists were drawn into state control of political beliefs as both agents and objects of surveillance. In its recruitment of agronomists, the government applied the criteria of political loyalty to support its fight against Communist rebels, thus paving the way for a 'patriotic' project of land reform and economic restoration of 'bandit-stricken' villages. However, the introduction of the ERP and AMAG, which were implemented from 1948 to 1953, saw the advent of new regimes of productivity that were underpinned by the image of the peasantry as both the 'pillar' of the nation and a new professional class in Greek commercial agriculture. AMAG envisioned farmers as forming a labour force that could secure a steadily rising income through increased productivity in an otherwise chaotic era of inflation and monetary instability for the Greek economy. For their part, despite having featured as both village educators and up-and-coming experts, Greek agronomists were nevertheless limited to ambivalent, often invisible roles in archival sources from the interwar period. Although the Second World War had frozen this double-sided nature of the agronomic profession in place, its mutation towards a significantly more visible role during the immediate post-Civil War era provides a unique lens through which to historicize the intertwining of social and agrarian policy in Greece.

Kalliopi Geronymaki is a historian and associate researcher at the University of Florence. Her research focuses on the history of the European Common Agricultural Policy through the lens of comparative welfare and rural development in France, Italy and Greece. Her Ph.D. dissertation (European University Institute, 2021) is entitled 'Regional Paths to the Fruit and Vegetable Common Market Organization: Structural and Financial Impact of the European Common Agricultural Policy in Provence, the Delta of Po and Peloponnese (1957–1972)'. She is currently working on the European Research Council project 'HumanEuroMed – Humanitarianism and Mediterranean Europe: A Transnational and Comparative History (1945–1990)', in which she specializes in Greece and Cyprus as donor countries.

Notes

1. General State Archives/Historical Archives of Macedonia, General Directorate of Northern Greece (GSA/HAM, GDNG, http://arxeiomnimon.gak.gr), D25/6/232. Author's translation.
2. I use the term 'Greek Macedonia' to refer to the geographical region of Macedonia in Northern Greece. All Greek-language terms and titles are transcribed in Latin characters.
3. The counterpart funds programme was funding provided by the United States and converted into Greek currency (drachmas). This was intended to ensure monetary stability and a positive balance of payments in domestic agriculture. See Coutsoumaris and Westebbe, *Analysis and Assessment*, 43.
4. In the 'New Lands', village cooperatives (known as first-degree cooperatives) were gradually established from 1915 to assist in land re-allocation. Their tasks were primarily linked to the distribution of bank loans to cooperative members, namely local farmers.
5. With reference to their educational responsibilities, agronomists have also been viewed as 'organic intellectuals'. See Sotiropoulos and Panayotopoulos, 'Eidikoi Dianooumenoi', 121–50; Gilbert, *Planning Democracy*, esp. 256.
6. Law 2203 peri Katōterōn Geōrgikōn Sxolōn, FEK (Efimeris tēs Kyvernyseōs) 136/A (24 June 1920).
7. Panayotopoulos, 'Georgiki Ekpaideusi kai Anaptyksi', 84–97. Chrysos Evelpidis (1895–1971), an agronomist and professor at the Agricultural School of Athens, argued in 1923 that the network of rural agronomists in village schools needed to be further strengthened; Evelpidis, *Systēma Ellēnikēs Agrotikēs Politikēs*, 121.
8. Ploumidis, '"Peasantist Nationalism"', 111–29.
9. Tzardis, 'Georgikē Epaggelmatikē Ekpaideusē', 55.
10. Karakasidou, *Fields of Wheat, Hills of Blood*, 187–88; Kontogiori, *Population Exchange in Greek Macedonia*, 165 ff.
11. In 1928, the agricultural inspector in the province of Thrace, Constantinos Cholevas, provided an overview of this legal procedure without mentioning its underlying purpose of political indoctrination; Choleva, *Praktikos Odēgos*, 7–17.

12. Gardikas, *Landscapes of Disease*, 124–25.
13. Theodoridou-Sotiriou in Theodoridou-Sotiriou, *H Ektropē tou Strymona*, 63.
14. Psychogios and Papapetrou, 'Oi Metakinēseis tōn Nomadōn Ktinotrofōn', 11.
15. Charalambidis, *Dekembriana 1944*, 82–83.
16. Margaritis, *Hēstoria tou Ellēnikou Emphyliou Polemou 1946–1949*, 168.
17. This land is not to be confused with 'the commons', namely common pastures for grazing or other land for collective use within the transhumant economy.
18. Close, *Greece since 1945*, 28–29, 31.
19. Margaritis, *Hēstoria tou Ellēnikou Emphyliou Polemou 1946–1949*, 61–62.
20. GSA/HAM, GDNG, D25-1/25/26/27; GSA/HAM, GDNG, D-25-1-1/18, 20.
21. Laiou in Baerentzen et al., *Studies in the History of the Greek Civil War*, 74.
22. Besides damage to harvesting equipment and other machinery, many livestock had been killed and rotational planting and harvesting schedules disrupted. See Stathakis, *To Dogma Truman*, 100; Vlavianos, *Greece, 1941–1949*, 22.
23. Smith and Iatrides, *Studies in the History of the Greek Civil War*, 9–40.
24. Chadjiiosif in Kremmydas, *Eisagogē stē Neoellēnikē Oikonomikē Hēstoria*, 288–318.
25. Stathakis, *To Dogma Truman*, 52.
26. Lykogiannis, 'Why Did the "Varvaressos Experiment" Fail?', 134.
27. Petmezas, *Prolegomena gia tēn Ellēnikē Agrotikē Oikonomia sto Mesopolemo*.
28. According to John MacCallum, a 'staple product' requires sufficient external demand in order to sustain its continued production in its region of origin; MacCallum, *Unequal Beginnings*, 115.
29. GAK, GDNG, D25-1/32.
30. GAK, GDNG, D25-2/19.
31. Legislative Decree 327, peri Anagkastikēs Misthōseōs Gaiōn yper Aktimonōn Geōrgōn kai Ktēnotrofōn, FEK 84/A (19 April 1947).
32. GSA/HAM, GDNG, D25/3/35. Agricultural Directorate of Thessaloniki/Department of Settlement, 'Extremely Urgent Letter: Time Limits of Cultivation', 21 September 1947. The number of first-degree cooperatives continued increasing throughout the period under consideration in this chapter. In December 1950, the departments of Central and Western Macedonia registered a total of 1,142 active cooperatives, constituting approximately one-sixth of all 6,358 active cooperatives in Greece at the time. Klēmēs, *Oi Synetairismoi stēn Ellada, Vol. IV*, 65.
33. Gerasis, *Politikē, Koinōnia kai Politismos stē Florina*, 147.
34. Mandatory Law 516, peri Elenchou Nomimofrosynis ton Demosiōn klp. Ypallelōn kai Yperetōn, FEK 6/A (8 January 1948).
35. GSA/HAM, GDNG D25/8.2/7, 'Certificates of Social Beliefs/Directorate of Agriculture' (undated).
36. *The Voice of Cooperatives* [*Hē Fōnē tōn Synetairismōn*] 50 (March 1949).
37. Stathakis, *To Dogma Truman*, 254.
38. Agrotikos Kōdix, FEK – 342/A (Athens, 6 December 1949).
39. '[G]iven that the guerilla war has now been defeated and we dispose of sufficient loans for the Agricultural Directorates': GSA/HAM, GDNG, D25/6/49, 30 December 1949.
40. Voglis, 'O Paul Porter', 285–300; Zachariou, 'Implementing the Marshall Plan in Greece', 303–18.

41. Thomadakis, 'Truman Doctrine', 23–51.
42. Syndesmos Ellēnōn Viomichanōn, *H Ellēnikē Viomichania*, 10–11.
43. George Stathakis has commented that this programme offered only a very limited time horizon for the recovery of Greek agriculture; Stathakis, *To Dogma Truman*, 211–12. Indeed, the ambitious modernizing aims of the programme would have appeared unrealistic for the population of a region that was still suffering from the devastating after-effects of war. AMAG officials seldom discussed farmers' achievements with any appreciation for the structural challenges and technological deficiencies that they had needed to overcome, including a lack of basic agricultural equipment.
44. GAK, GDNG, D25-6/54.
45. ATE, 'To Ergo mias Dekaetias', 36.
46. Ibid.
47. Mandatory Law 1547, peri Systaseōs Dieuthinseōn Georgikōn Efarmogōn kai Ekpaideuseōs para to Ypourgeio Geōrgias, FEK 249/A (29 October 1950); Law 1643, peri kyroseos, tropopoieseos kai symploseros tou 1547/1950 Anagkastikou Nomou 'peri Systaseōs Dieuthinseōn Georgikōn Efarmogōn kai Ekpaideuseōs para to Ypourgeio Geōrgias', FEK 12/A (9 January 1951).
48. Mandatory Law 1547.
49. Danforth and van Boeschoten, *Children of the Greek Civil War*, 105.
50. ATE, 'To Ergo mias Dekaetias', 93. For its part, ATE started sending top executive officials – agronomists and forestry scientists – to receive specialized training in the United States, France, the Netherlands or the Scandinavian countries.
51. GSA/HAM, GDNG, D25/6/261, Enōsis Georgikōn Synetairismōn Lagkada, 'Egkyklios 15', 4 May 1950. One acre is equivalent to 10,000 hectares (ha).
52. Ibid.
53. Ibid.
54. ATE, 'To Ergo mias Dekaetias', 149–50.
55. GSA/HAM, GDNG, D28/2, 6 February 1953.
56. GSA/HAM, GDNG, D28/1, 6 February 1953.
57. Directorate of Food and Agriculture Mission of AMAG, 'To Programma gia tēn Axiopoiēsē', 29.
58. Psychogios and Papapetrou, 'Oi Metakinēseis tōn Nomadōn Ktinotrofōn', 3–23.
59. Directorate of Food and Agriculture Mission of AMAG, 'To Programma gia tēn Axiopoiēsē', 30.
60. Ibid.
61. For a general study of the CCC's activities, see Paige, *The Civilian Conservation Corps*.
62. AMAG, 'To Programma', 30.
63. GSA/HAM, GDNG, D28/4, Service of Reforestation and Torrents to the Communities of Peraias, Anō Epivatōn and Agias Triados, 18 December 1950.
64. Ibid.
65. Stathakis, *To Dogma Truman*, 418.
66. Greece's rural population dropped by 6 per cent in the period from 1940 to 1951 and by another 3.7 per cent by 1961. Antonopoulou, 'Ekviomēchanisē, Agrotikē Exodos', 165; Kotzamanēs, 'H Kinētikoteta tou Agrotikou Plēthysmou', 97–126.
67. Damianakos, 'The Ongoing Quest for a Model of Greek Agriculture', 203.

Bibliography

Agricultural Bank of Greece (ATE). 'To Ergo mias Dekaetias'. Athens: 1963.

Antonopoulou, Sofia. 'Ekviomēchanisē, Agrotikē Exodos kai to Zētēma tēs Stegēs stis Chōres tēs Perifereias kata tē Metapolemikē Periodo'. *Epitheōrēsē Koinōnikōn Ereunōn* 69 (1988), 156–76.

Baerentzen, Lars, et al. *Studies in the History of the Greek Civil War, 1945–1949*, 3rd edn. Athens: Olkos, 2002.

Chadjiiosif, Christos. *Hēstoria tēs Elladas tou Eikostou Aiōna 1940–1945, Vol. 3.2*. Athens: Bibliorama, 2007.

Charalambidis, Menelaos. *Dekembriana 1944: H Machē tōn Athēnon*. Athens: Alexandreia, 2014.

Choleva, Constantinou. *Praktikos Odēgos tōn Geōrgikōn Synetairismōn*. Athens: Dēmētrakos, 1928.

Close, David H. *Greece since 1945: Politics, Economy and Society*. Abingdon: Routledge, 2014.

Coutsoumaris, George, Richard M. Westebbe et al. *Analysis and Assessment of the Economic Effects of the U.S. PL 480 Program in Greece*. Athens: Center of Planning and Economic Research, 1965.

Damianakos, Stathēs. 'The Ongoing Quest for a Model of Greek Agriculture'. *Sociologia Ruralis* 37(2) (1997), 190–208.

Danforth, Loring M., and Riki van Boeschoten. *Children of the Greek Civil War: Refugees and the Politics of Memory*. Chicago: University of Chicago Press, 2012.

Directorate of the Food and Agriculture Mission of AMAG in Greece, 'To programma gia tēn axiopoiēsē tōn edafōn tēs Ellados'. Athens: 1951.

Evelpidis, Chrysos. *Systēma Ellēnikēs Agrotikēs Politikēs: Agrotiko Programma*, Athens: 1923.

Gardikas, Katerina. *Landscapes of Disease: Malaria in Modern Greece*. Budapest: CEU Press Studies, 2018.

Gerasis, Nikolaos. 'Politikē, Koinōnia kai Politismos stē Florina tou Emphyliou Polemou (Martios 1945 – Augoustos 1949) mesa apo tis Pēges tēs Topikēs Hēstorias', Master's thesis. Florina: University of Western Macedonia, 2019.

Gilbert, Jess. *Planning Democracy: Agrarian Intellectuals and the Intended New Deal*. New Haven: Yale University Press, 2015.

Karakasidou, Anastasia. *Fields of Wheat, Hills of Blood: Passages to Nationhood in Greek Macedonia (1870–1990)*. Chicago: University of Chicago Press, 1997.

Klēmēs, Aristeidis. *Oi Synetairismoi stēn Ellada, Vol. I*. Athens: I. Pitsilos, 1985.

———. *Oi Synetairismoi stēn Ellada, Vol. IV (1946–1960)*. Athens: SEKAP, 1996.

Kontogiori, Elisabeth. *Population Exchange in Greek Macedonia: The Rural Settlement of Refugees, 1922–1930*. Oxford: Oxford University Press, 2006.

Kotzamanēs, Byrōn. 'H Kinētikoteta tou Agrotikou Plēthysmou stēn Ellada tē Dekaetia 1940–1950-…'. *Epitheōrēsē Koinōnikōn Ereunōn* 77 (1990), 97–126.

Kremmydas, Vassilis. *Eisagōgē stē Neoellēnikē Oikonomikē Hēstoria (18os – 20os aiōnas)*. Athens: Typophyto, 2000.

Lykogiannis, Athanasios. 'Why Did the "Varvaressos Experiment" Fail?' *Journal of Modern Greek Studies* 19(1) (2001): 117–42.

MacCallum, John. *Unequal Beginnings: Agriculture and Economic Development in Quebec and Ontario until 1870.* Toronto: University of Toronto Press, 1980.

Margaritis, Giorgos. *Hēstoria tou Ellēnikou Emphyliou Polemou 1946–1949, Vol. I.* Athens: Bibliorama, 2001.

Paige, John C. *The Civilian Conservation Corps and the National Park Service (1933–1942): An Administrative History.* Washington DC: US Department of the Interior, 1985.

Panagiotopoulos, Vasilis (ed.). *Hēstoria tou Neou Ellenismou (1770–2000), 7: O Mesopolemos (1922–1940).* Athens: Ellēnika Grammata, 2004.

Panayotopoulos, Dimitris. 'Georgiki Ekpaideusi kai Anaptyksi: ē Symvolē tēs Anōtatēs Geoponikēs Sxolēs Athinōn', Ph.D. dissertation. Corfu: Ionio Panepistimio, 2003.

Petmezas, Socrates. *Prolegomena gia tēn Ellēnikē Agrotikē Oikonomia sto Mesopolemo.* Athens: Alexandreia, 2012.

Ploumidis, Spyridon. '"Peasantist Nationalism" in Interwar Greece (1927–41)', *Byzantine and Modern Greek Studies* 37(1) (2013), 111–29.

Psychogios, Dimitris, and Georgia Papapetrou. 'Oi Metakinēseis tōn Nomadōn Ktinotrofōn'. *Epitheōrēsē Koinōnikōn Ereunōn/Greek Review of Social Research* 53 (2016), 3–23.

Smith, Ole, and John Iatrides. *Studies in the History of the Greek Civil War (1945–1949).* Copenhagen: Museum Tusculanum Press, 1987.

Sotiropoulos, Dimitris, and Dimitris Panayotopoulos. 'Eidikoi Dianooumenoi kai Thylakes Xeirafetēsēs sto Mesopolemo: Metarythmistes Geoponoi kai Mēxanikoi stēn Ypaithro kai sto Asty'. *Mnēmōn* 29 (2008), 121–50.

Stathakis, George. *To Dogma Truman kai to Schedio Marshall.* Athens: Bibliorama, 2004.

Syndesmos, Ellēnōn Viomichanōn. *H Ellēnikē Viomichania kai to Programma Europaikēs Anorthōseōs: Anakoinōseis tou Archigou tēs AMAG D. Griswold/Apantēsis tou Syndesmou Ellēnōn Viomichanōn,* Athens: Syndesmos Ellēnōn Viomichanōn, 1948.

Theodoridou-Sotiriou, Lila (ed.). *H Ektropē tou Strymona: Ta Megala Exygiantika Erga tou Mesopolemou.* Serres: Library of Central Macedonia, 2017.

Thomadakis, Stavros. 'Truman Doctrine: Was There a Developmental Agenda?' *Journal of Modern Hellenism* 5 (1989), 23–51.

Tzardis, Myron. 'Georgikē Epaggelmatikē Ekpaideusē: Hē Periptōsi tou Praktikou Georgikou Sxoleiou Gortynas Messaras Krētēs', Master's thesis. Patras: Greek Open University, 2012.

Vlavianos, Haris. *Greece, 1941–1949: From Resistance to Civil War.* New York: Palgrave Macmillan, 1992.

Voglis, Polymeris. 'O Paul Porter kai ē Amerikanikē Oikonomikē Apostolē stēn Ellada (18 Ianouariou – 22 Martiou 1947)'. *Mnēmōn* 27 (2005), 285–300.

Zachariou, Stelios. 'Implementing the Marshall Plan in Greece: Balancing Reconstruction and Geopolitical Security'. *Journal of Modern Greek Studies* 27(2) (2009), 303–18.

 CHAPTER 11

The Sociability of Scientific Knowledge Exchange in British Farming, 1950–90

Sally Horrocks, John Martin and Paul Merchant

From the 1950s to the 1980s, the output and efficiency of British agriculture increased more dramatically than in earlier periods of 'revolutionary change', notably 1560–1670 and 1750–1880.[1] Yields of arable crops increased up to threefold, and there were significant increases in production in the livestock sector.[2] It is clear from existing research that these achievements depended on the application of scientific and technical knowledge.[3] What is less clear is *how* this knowledge was translated into practice on Britain's farms. We know little about how farmers were encouraged to plant certain crop varieties, to apply fertilizers and agrochemicals, to alter timings and methods of husbandry or to invest in a wide variety of machinery. This chapter uses oral history to explore one important means by which this encouragement occurred: personal interactions between scientists, farmers and agricultural advisers.

Studies of agricultural science in Britain in the period under investigation have tended to focus on the history of the science itself as it played out within key institutions, leaving any extension work or external communication to be assumed.[4] Meanwhile, agricultural historians have noted – but have not explored in any detail – the influence of agricultural advisers on British farms. For example, Holmes tells us that even before the Second World War, state and especially commercial advisers were significant sources of 'information'.[5] Howkins observes that there are many possible explanations for changes in farming practices after the war, but suggests that the National Agricultural Advisory Service (NAAS) 'played its part' in promoting applications of science.[6] Even an insider history of NAAS up to 1971 remains vague, suggesting on the basis of its size alone that NAAS must have had 'at least as much effect as any other single group'.[7] If advisers contributed to dramatic changes in the agricultural environment of Britain in the period under review, we lack accounts of how they did so.[8] For historians of science or agriculture, the problem is partly a matter of sources: much of agricultural advisory work was oral and cannot be reconstructed through archive work.[9] This chapter turns to oral history interviews with British farmers, agricultural advisers and scientists in order to explore details of their interactions in the period from 1950 to 1990: on farms, in field trials and at demonstrations, and at public meetings and talks.[10]

Research in the history and social studies of science emphasizes the work required to secure agreement about what counts as reliable knowledge and to enable that knowledge to move between specific local contexts.[11] A few contributions to this literature have considered this process in relation to British agricultural research and advice, but they have tended to concentrate on these relationships from only one or, at most, two perspectives.[12] Studies of agricultural extension and advice in other countries in the same period have explored the mismatch between science developed in state or colonial centres and the physical, social and economic settings in which its application was attempted – with strong echoes in parts of this chapter.[13] However, with some exceptions, these studies tend not to take us to the level of interaction between advisers and farmers.[14] This means that we overlook some important implications of Krige's observation that the movement of scientific knowledge is a 'social accomplishment'.[15] In this chapter, by remaining close to the details of advisory practice as experienced by scientists, advisers and farmers, we are able to show that the process of knowledge exchange was shaped by the personal and social relationships involved.

We first outline relevant details of British farming and agricultural advice in the period from 1950 to 1990, setting this briefly within a longer history of agricultural knowledge exchange. We then consider accounts in life story interviews of the three main modes of interaction between scientists, farmers and advisers: conversations and farm visits; trials and demonstrations; and talks to farmers' groups.

British Farming, 1950–90

In earlier periods, British farming had been influenced by what might be termed technical or expert agricultural knowledge. Local agricultural societies, concerned in part with improvements in practice, existed from the late seventeenth century, while the nineteenth century saw the formation of the Royal Agricultural Society and Britain's first experimental station for agriculture, Rothamsted, along with the first university departments of agriculture.[16] Such developments engaged only a minority of farmers directly. Agricultural education developed in local agricultural colleges and farm institutes from the 1890s and then from 1910 through a new state-funded network of agricultural research centres, a so-called Provincial Advisory Service and a separate County Advisory Service. The limited scale of these advisory systems, which together had fewer than 550 staff by the 1930s, meant that in Holmes' judgement, they provided less information to farmers than the large feed and fertilizer manufacturers.[17]

Britain was far more reliant on imported food than almost any other European country at the outbreak of the Second World War.[18] Wartime concerns for food security led to state direction of British farming through county War Agricultural Executive Committees (WAECs), which promoted the expansion of the arable area through ploughing of pasture and marginal land, mechanization and increased use of artificial fertilizer and lime.[19] Agricultural production remained a government priority after the war within a context of national and international food shortages and Britain's weak financial position. The Agriculture Act of 1947 established a system of price controls and direction of farmers by County Agricultural Executive Committees (CAECs).[20] The control of prices, Martin argues, provided an incentive for farmers to maximize food production by linking state support to farm output.[21] Martin and others also point to the moral pressure on farmers, first to increase production – in light of national and international food shortages that lasted until the mid-1950s – and then to improve efficiency, given continued state and later European Economic Community (EEC) spending on agricultural support.[22]

In 1946, alongside the introduction of price controls and the CAECs, the British government established NAAS as a new agricultural advisory service for England and Wales, combining and enlarging the County and Provincial systems.[23] NAAS operated independently of the CAECs, although there was some sharing of local intelligence and some farmers may have associated it with the CAECs and indeed the wartime WAECs.[24] By 1962, NAAS employed 500 District Officers and a further 850 staff, some of whom were scientific specialists at regional centres or scientific officers in a network of twelve Experimental Husbandry Farms (EHFs).[25] The key duties of NAAS District Officers were to advise farmers on technical questions and farm management, liaising as necessary with scientific specialists at regional headquarters; to conduct experimental work on commercial farms and EHFs; to assist farmers in taking advantage of grant schemes offered by the Ministry of Agriculture; and to deliver talks to farmers' groups. They also contributed to local newspapers as well as radio and television programmes.[26] In 1971, NAAS was amalgamated with three other bodies and renamed the Agricultural Development and Advisory Service (ADAS), which continued providing free advice to farmers until it was privatized in the 1990s.[27] Throughout the period under investigation, NAAS/ADAS District Officers operated in a reasonably crowded arena with many competing sources of information, including other farmers, the farming press, radio and television content, and representatives of companies selling inputs. The largest of the latter was Imperial Chemical Industries (ICI), which employed Development Officers across Britain to advise not just on fertilizers and pesticides but also on farm management.[28]

McCann's history of NAAS presents the advisory services of other countries as examples of parallel development rather than sources of inspiration or collaboration, but he does report that NAAS advisers had access to scientific specialists who kept up to date with research work at stations 'here and abroad' and that senior NAAS staff were sometimes seconded to governments in Africa or elsewhere in the Commonwealth. Some took courses at US universities or studied on fellowships that offered overseas work experience, which all helped to 'prevent the Service from becoming too introspective'.[29] Even if the majority of NAAS staff – including those whose interviews we consider in this chapter – were not directly involved with overseas postings or contacts, they were communicating scientific knowledge that was produced, in part, through international links. Cooke's history of the Agricultural Research Council includes many examples of international collaboration at agricultural research stations across Britain, especially in plant breeding, computing, grassland management and dairy farming.[30] Furthermore, the advisory services operated within a wider ecosystem of agricultural knowledge exchange that looked beyond Britain. As we see in this chapter, NAAS District Officers and ICI Development Officers were active in giving talks to local Young Farmers' Clubs, which had been established in the 1920s by individuals inspired by the work of the 4-H clubs in the United States and Canada.[31] Meanwhile, grassland scientists and farmers communicated through the British Grassland Society, which had been formed in 1945 and was actively involved in international congresses, exchange visits and European tours. [32]

Advisers encountered a very diverse farming community across Britain. Geographically, southern and eastern England tends to favour arable farming, while the north and west are more suited to pastoral farming. At the beginning of our period, there were about 300,000 agricultural holdings. The majority were under 100 acres and employed fewer than four workers.[33] Sixty per cent of farmers were tenants, and most had no formal agricultural training.[34] Writing in 1962, Self and Storing suggested that British farms fell between the small-scale peasant holdings in much of Europe and the large-scale mechanized holdings of North America or Australia. Many remained too small to fully realize the economies of scale that modern machinery could support.[35] From the 1960s to the 1980s, British farms tended to become larger, more specialized and more likely to be owned rather than tenanted.[36] By the late 1980s, holdings of below 50 acres had declined by 60 per cent, while those over 550 acres had increased by 30 per cent. Specialization took various forms, including a continuing trend towards specialized dairy farms, the development of large pig and poultry units, and a shift to arable-only farms.[37]

Conversations and Farm Visits

Advisers devoted the majority of their time to one-to-one conversations with farmers, some of which took place over the telephone. NAAS District Officer Jim Orson recalls that he spent 'an awful lot of time' telephoning farmers:

> You had to get to know when they're going to be in for breakfast, when they're going to be in for lunch, and sometimes when they get in, in the evening, and ring them then … to give them … a response to some advice or something.[38]

Other conversations between NAAS advisers and farmers were conducted at the local NAAS office. For NAAS District Officer Robert Hart, working in south Shropshire in the 1960s, market day was also 'surgery day' at his office in the town of Craven Arms: 'On market days there would be a queue sometimes, like a doctor's surgery, there would be a queue at the office … in the corridor.'[39] NAAS advisers and the advisory staff of agricultural supply companies also visited farms to speak to farmers. These on-farm conversations are remembered with reasonable consistency across interviews with NAAS District Officers, ICI Development Officers and farmers. Hart recalls that 'farmers liked having you there because you were part of the scene and it was something different for them and so they were never in a rush to get rid of you and if you weren't careful you could be there well into the evening on farms'.[40] David Morris, remembering his time as an ICI Development Officer in Cumberland and Westmorland in 1963 and 1964, echoes this: 'Many of them like a visitor anyhow; they've only seen the postman [laughs]. Very rarely were you told to go away … They got to know you … they were pleased to see you.'[41] Farmer Poul Christensen recalls that one memorable aspect of his father's work as a farm manager in Sussex in the 1950s was frequent visits from the 'NAAS Officer':

> Father developed a really close relationship with him. I suppose, in modern parlance, he [father] would be described as an early developer of this new technology … I mean John Dalton, he was the local guy, he used to come and sit in the kitchen.[42]

Another farmer, John Conant, paints a similar picture of valued friendship in his memories of his interactions with the local NAAS Officer:

> There was a chap called J.D. [David] Laurance, who became a great friend, and I went to him a lot for advice … David would come out to your farm and give you free advice. Wonderful really.[43]

These accounts point to the way in which encounters with advisers could provide farmers with distraction and social interaction that could be enjoyable without being frivolous; they were firmly part of farm *work*. They also suggest that advisers were well aware that success in communicating scientific and technical knowledge depended on their ability to establish themselves as a welcome presence in farmers' homes, in town on market day, and in the wider community.

There is evidence that NAAS, as an organization, understood the importance of interpersonal and social factors in its efforts to influence farmers. District Officers were recruited not just on the basis of their technical knowledge but also for their ability to 'impress and communicate with farmers'.[44] This ability was further developed by in-service training. Robert Hart recalls that he attended a three-week course at the University of Reading's Agricultural Extension Centre that was concerned with 'the whole psychology of interpersonal relationships and the principles behind education and teaching ... not so much a practical public speaking type thing but a lot more the theory background of how to influence people'.[45]

The interviews allow us to begin to appreciate the nature of conservations between advisers and farmers around kitchen tables or in fields. What seems to have been the aim of the advisers was to work together with farmers to reach agreement on key decisions based on shared expertise and common concerns. Jim Orson remembers potato crop walking with farmers in order to judge whether existing or new seed should be planted the following year:

> We'd take a mutual decision ... because, that's how it should be in many ways. And so he probably would do his assessment, and I would do my assessment, and then we'd have a chat about it at the end.[46]

This collaborative process is recalled from a farmer's point of view by Nicholas Watts:

> ADAS crop advisors ... used to come and look at things ... and between you, you could work out why the crop was failing, or whatever ... He will say one thing, and I'll say, 'Well it's not that because of this', and, you can quite quickly come to an answer.[47]

This does not seem simply to have been a strategy for involving farmers in decision-making or merely a display of respect for farmers' judgement. Instead, Jim Orson suggests that experience of local circumstances could substantially alter the advice given, even if this contradicted the position of scientists at NAAS county headquarters:

In Cambridge, we had a series of specialist disciplines ... agronomy, pathology, entomology, microbiology ... And sometimes you would say, you know, people in Cambridge say this, but, with experience I would say this, you know. So, but that came with experience, to sort of modify the, the central edicts for want of a better word, into a local bit of information.[48]

What emerges here is a complicated distribution of expertise. Advisers were not necessarily viewed by other actors, or by themselves, as 'experts' (in the sense in which Hodge, for example, uses this term).[49] Instead of *being* experts, advisers *had* access to expertise of different kinds, including the knowledge of head office specialists as well as the local knowledge of farmers.

While technical questions could be dealt with in relatively short interactions, advice on farm management involved extended conversations, often with accounts and data at hand. Where farm expansion was not possible, farmers were often advised to concentrate on a limited range of enterprises that were likely to be the most profitable. John Conant describes the experience of 'doing costings' with an ICI adviser:

He used to come about once a week and ... at the end of the year or whatever, they produced accounts which ... showed pretty well what paid and what didn't pay and then we set about acting accordingly.[50]

From the perspective of ICI Development Officer David Morris, this process is recalled as an intense focus on a small number of farms: 'I had to do five costed farms, which you visited every month and did detailed costings of their enterprise.'[51] NAAS District Officers also worked intensively with certain farmers on farm management: 'I used to ask farmers as many questions as they asked me I think: you know, 'why are you doing that ... is there a good reason for doing it like that or could it be done in some other way ... always anxious to change things for the better.'[52]

Because we are drawing on interviews with successful farmers and successful advisers, there is a significant danger that these memories present an overly harmonious picture of fruitful collaboration. It is therefore important to be alert to statements in the interviews that recall lack of success in communication, incomplete coverage and resistance to change. Advisers speak of being unsure whether their advice was followed: 'You go on a farm, comment on a situation, go away, and you wouldn't hear for a long time.'[53] Although advisers can point to examples of when advice was followed, they are aware that farmers were often not convinced of the need to make changes. Jim Orson remembers that when new fungicides for cereals became available in the mid-1970s, 'it was sometimes difficult to convince farmers they should spray', because the fungicides were relatively expensive and the farmers 'weren't familiar with the technology'.[54] Poul Christensen says of his experience of using ICI's Mascot computer program with farmers to calculate the most profitable use of their land that 'then they could sit down and decide what they wanted to do, which very often was nothing [laughs]'.[55] According to Hart, advisers transferred postings regularly to ensure that they did not 'get comfortable and sort of give up trying to change them [farmers] if you like – accept the fact that that's how they do it and they're always going to do it like that'.[56]

Finally, there is evidence to support Martin's view that advice was much more readily sought and followed by farmers with certain characteristics. Although our sample is small, some of the interview accounts do suggest that it was younger farmers and those who were in some respects unusual, or originally from outside the farming industry, who were especially keen to work with advisers.[57] John Conant refers indirectly to his age and his degree in agriculture from Cambridge when he talks of being much more interested in advice than other local farmers. He was also different in being the son of the owner of the estate of which his farm was a part:

> *Interviewer: When you started in 1949, were you aware that any … of the neighbouring farms were also working with … NAAS?*
>
> I think it's unlikely that they did because they were happy with their way of farming, they didn't want to change it … so I imagine they didn't, but I never asked David Laurance [the adviser]. I mean I must have been quite useful to him, because I was an avid searcher after advice, probably too – I don't know – perhaps too much. But I was very keen. I came from Cambridge for my farm and I was a very keen farmer, yes. Keen to, keen to make some money.[58]

By contrast, Conant's neighbours had 'been on their farms all their lives' and had direct experience of the less convivial approach to agricultural advice of the wartime WAECs, which had, he says, 'bullied farmers into doing things which they didn't like to grow more food'.[59]

Further support for the hypothesis that new or younger farmers might have been more amenable to advice comes from NAAS's Robert Hart. Asked to recall examples of successful work with farmers in the 1960s, he refers to a hill farmer who had started farming after a career in medicine and another whose father had died unexpectedly:

> He [the second of these] found himself running this sizeable farm … and he … had the feeling that it probably could be done better … and I got involved with him, we were more or less the same age … and I was able to have a big impact on him: a) in getting him to think about how farms should be managed and so on if you like almost if you like educating him, and b) then redesigning the farm.[60]

Advisers, though confident of the value of the scientific and technical advice to which they provided access, were conscious that the transfer of knowledge was a social accomplishment that was achieved more successfully in some cases than in others. Indeed, we cannot rule out the possibility that advisers were attracted to working with those farmers who were most receptive to advice, as Harwood suggests has been the case in other contexts.[61]

Trials and Demonstrations

In the period under investigation, a small cohort of British farmers engaged with scientists and advisers by allowing trials and experiments to take place on their fields. Some of these trials were led by scientists based at research stations who needed to conduct trials in areas with certain soils, weather conditions or disease prevalence. In these cases, it was farmers' local environments that seem to have been valued rather than their local knowledge. For example, while working on new potato varieties at the Scottish Plant Breeding Station in the 1970s, George Mackay sought sites on the west coast of Scotland where he could test blight resistance: 'if you didn't get blight there, you'd never get it anywhere'. Elsewhere, it was a farmer's relatively frost-free ground (suitable for early growing potato varieties) that made the required travel worthwhile:

> I need[ed] to get some trials of some of the advanced clones in a first early growing area … and, I had heard about this chap McCrone … So I went over to, to see him, and [he said] 'Oh yes, we'd love to work with you again'. So, we would go across there in spring and plant them … go and visit them during the growing season and see how they were growing, and harvest them and bring them back … We went over one time, and the plots were a bit bedraggled, and there was this seagull's wing sitting in the middle of a plot. And he said, 'I just wanted to mark that one: that's a winner, that's a good'un'. 'Yes', I said, 'thank you very much.' [It was] one of the controls [laughs].[62]

Although this farmer had significant experience of growing potatoes, including new varieties, the details of the randomized, multifactorial experiment were not known to him. As such, he was unable to interpret the results – as manifested overtly by his enthusiasm for one of the experimental controls (an existing variety rather than one of the new clones).[63] Similarly, potato farmers on the Breeding Station's advisory board or those who attended so-called Potato Days (open days organized by seed potato suppliers) were not necessarily regarded as producers of valuable knowledge:

> I remember one old Welsh boy came up to me and asked who I was, and I
> told him … 'Oh', he said, 'I've got a few potatoes of my own.' 'Oh yes?' And he
> pulls out this piece of paper, and he said, 'Look at this' … Some of the variet-
> ies were brand new! … It was their life, they loved it, you know, playing about
> with these old tatties [potatoes].[64]

The results of their 'playing about' with potatoes was perhaps not taken especially seriously, although Mackay accepts that commercial farming often
revealed problems with potatoes that were not recognized under scientific
testing regimes: '[S]omething happens in the agriculture scenario that we can't
sometimes recognise in trial … Once farmers get their hands on them and
start growing dozens of acres and lifting hundreds of tons, something you've
not picked up may suddenly appear.'[65]

The trials conducted by Mackay did not have an immediately educational
role; they were instead designed to produce data for scientists. By contrast,
NAAS District Officers – like the US Farm Advisers studied by Henke – were
involved in trials and experiments that tended to mix knowledge production
and persuasion, data collection and demonstration.[66] District Officers remember conducting fieldwork that produced new agricultural knowledge despite
NAAS representing itself officially as applying the 'results of research' rather
than doing research itself.[67] Robert Hart describes fieldwork on swedes (a root
vegetable) as 'almost the start of experimenting; I wasn't doing experiments as
such, but it was observing very closely what was happening, collecting some
data, and then interpreting that data and then seeing if we could change things
for the better.'[68] Jim Orson describes his own trials work as a District Officer in
Essex in the 1970s in a way that underlines more forcefully the extent to which
new knowledge was being produced:

> We were unusual in having such a high proportion of winter barley in the
> area. And because of that, there was no information … on how to use …
> fungicides … on winter barley. So I decided to do my own trials … Because
> nobody else was producing the data for them [farmers] at that time … I was
> recording huge responses … the proof was there in the data, of their value.[69]

Where scientific knowledge was already available, but not being used by farmers, NAAS District Officers conducted fieldwork that was intended to demonstrate that this knowledge was useful. Robert Hart was involved in what he
calls 'extensions' of research conducted at the nearby Terrington EHF.[70] He
describes one such project:

> Terrington did a whole series of experiments over a number of years where
> they established the optimum seed rates for each of the major varieties of

potatoes and it was clear to us in the field that that information was not actually being used by the farmers ... Somebody had said years back that a tonne to the acre was the optimum so that's what they did but it clearly wasn't and we had tonnes of information to show that it wasn't. So we each [District Officer in Lincolnshire] got a group of our own farmers ... and they bought their potato seed ... and then we got them to actually do what we said.[71]

Having demonstrated to these farmers that using the variable seed rates made a positive difference, he set about designing what might be regarded as a 'boundary object',[72] which would allow knowledge to move to many other farmers:

Then I designed a plastic wheel thing with windows in it ... so as a farmer you had this wheel – I bet there are still some around in Lincolnshire – and you could count how many seeds per hundredweights you'd got and you knew what the variety was and you dialled these things in and eventually in a little window down here it told you what the plant spacing was that you needed to do. The advisory aids people ... worked it up from my rough cardboard model into a posh plastic job and we made a few thousand of them and dished them out to potato growers.[73]

In this section, we have thus far been concerned with field trials and experiments in which scientists and advisers interacted with a single farmer or small groups of farmers. We now move on to 'demonstrations' and 'open days' – occasions when larger groups of farmers were invited to observe new technology, techniques and approaches developed at research stations or on experimental farms. David Morris says of the University of Newcastle's Cockle Park Experimental Farm, where he was Assistant Director from 1964 to 1968, that 'there were ... very big open days where things in progress were looked at – one of them was, when I was there, we had about 2,000 people in a day'.[74] The National Institute of Agricultural Engineering also hosted 'open days at regular intervals'.[75] At these events:

Almost everything was got out of the cupboard. You know, in addition to lively experiments and so on there would also have been a display of the experimentation we had, the computing power we had ... we would have shown the single wheel tester, we would have shown the rolling resistance rig, we'd have shown the tractor with the suspended cabin on it, we would have shown some wheels we'd developed.[76]

One interviewee, Nigel Young, remembers demonstrations at the Grassland Research Institute in Berkshire in the 1960s of what was called 'an intensive system of lamb production from temporary grassland'. This system, which he had helped to devise, involved laying out small 'paddocks' of sown, fertilized grass that were divided by moveable fences with gaps at the bottom that were sufficiently big to allow for 'forward creep' grazing by lambs. With the aim of feeding large numbers of sheep on grass alone, this approach was developed on the Institute's own land and then scaled up on a neighbouring farm to demonstrate that it worked at farm scale. Here, Young hosted visits from groups of farmers:

> And I always remember, we had French farmers over, because we were always showing different [people] … They didn't believe us … You know, 'Où est le troughs, monsieur?' No, no, no. They didn't believe that we could produce that number of lambs from that pasture.[77]

Even if these particular farmers 'didn't believe' the evidence in front of their eyes, a key purpose of the demonstration was to allow farmers to see for themselves that a system developed in a research institute could work in practice on a farm. Similarly, in his role as Director of Gleadthorpe EHF in the late 1970s and early 1980s, Robert Hart divided the site into an 'experimental farm', where trials took place, and 'a demonstration farm', where the results of these experiments were applied to generate field-scale results that were readily comprehensible to farmers:

> Farmers on the whole were not terribly interested in standing in front of a batch of experimental plots and listening to somebody tell them about this that and the other. Farmers are much more interested in looking at farms. And I remember one … evening standing on a trailer – load of farmers – and it had been a particularly difficult winter and spring. We went into the field … and it was winter barley and it looked absolutely fantastic … and I heard one farmer say to another one 'bloody hell … I never thought I'd see winter barley looking like that this year'. And I knew then that I'd got it right, because he was all ears wasn't he from now; he wanted to know how on Earth it got like that.[78]

Hart's observation that farmers found the farm more engaging than 'experimental plots' points to another purpose of demonstrations. There is strong evidence in the interviews that open days and demonstrations were a form of entertainment and social occasion for farmers. Speaking of his role in organizing summer meetings of the British Grassland Society, Nigel Young remembers:

> What they [farmers] loved to do was to go and see other grassland farmers who were doing it better than they were and learning from them. And this is

where the summer meetings were a huge success ... You all get together in a residential place, probably a college or something like that, about forty, fifty people ... and you'd go out on farm visits, probably three farms in a day.[79]

Describing the Grassland Research Institute's demonstrations of the intensive system of lamb production on temporary grassland, as observed by the visiting French farmers, Young recalls:

> There were a lot of farm discussion groups and they're always looking for places to go, you know, something a bit innovative, a bit different. So we'd have coach-loads ... or they'd come in several cars and we'd take them up there and my impression was that they loved it. Now, the interesting thing is though, did they do it back on their own farm? Unfortunately, no.
> *Interviewer: Why do you think that that was the case?*
> I think it was the case because they didn't see the value in putting up a system with all these separate, subdividing their fields. They had what was known as set stocking, or a more lax approach to rotational grazing.[80]

There are two points to emphasize here. First, Nigel Young states that a perfectly rational response for most farmers who saw this particular demonstration of intensive livestock farming was to do nothing. Just like those British farmers who continued to plant potentially suboptimal varieties of barley in the early 1960s or farmers across the world who were selective in their uptake of 'Green Revolution' offerings, Young's guests reached their own conclusions about the 'value' of the work involved in recreating this intensive grazing system on their own farms.[81] Second, it is clear that – for Young and the farmers who attended – the success of the demonstration was not measured in terms of uptake or impact on farming practice. A demonstration afforded farmers an enjoyable day out with work-related content – an end in itself.

Talks to Farmers' Groups

> The vast majority of my talks were evening meetings, with the overhead projector light looking into this black of a village hall filled with farmers.[82]

During the winter, scientists and advisers gave talks to farmers' discussion groups, including the Young Farmers' Clubs, that were often held in village halls. Robert Hart came to regard the training that he received during his postgraduate diploma in farm management as ideal coaching for the job of NAAS District Officer: '[O]nce a week we all trekked off to the education department and learnt about how people learn and how to lecture and how to teach and so on ... only one hour a week but incredibly valuable.'[83] Once in post, NAAS District Officers received training in public speaking: 'It was a core part of the grade 4 training for everybody. I remember going on a public speaking course at Newcastle ... which was ... very useful.'[84] Jim Orson recalls that: 'Everybody in ADAS went on a speaker's course, and we were told to keep, you know, slides simple, and, so many lines, you know, so many words in a phrase, and all that kind of thing.'[85] Orson's wife often helped by using her 'beautiful script writing' on acetate slides, and each district had a dedicated advisory aids service that provided visual aids.[86]

Trained and equipped, advisers drove out to village halls to communicate recent scientific findings. Robert Hart's approach was as follows:

> If someone asked me to give a talk at a farmers' discussion group ... I would simply go and get out results of experiments or a review from some EHF or other, find a couple of experiments that produced something that was interesting and relevant and simply talk about that. So as an intermediary between the research and the farming that was what we were about really so ... the results of experiments from EHFs was my basic raw material – that was what I was peddling – I was their salesman in many ways.[87]

Hart is unable to judge the likely impact on farmers of his talks. However, he does remember that any transfer of knowledge was lively and contested:

> In any audience there will always be the sceptic ... who just don't want to believe anything you say. One of the best stories – it wasn't me actually – this was a chap called John Warnock who was in Shropshire ... and the fashionable things he'd gone to talk about was quick haymaking and the virtues of dehorning cattle ... And apparently he thought it had all gone fairly well until one farmer in the audience stood up at the end and said, 'I reckon thou had best leave horns on those cattle', he said, 'to shake bloody mould out of the hay you've been making [laughs]'.[88]

Similarly, while Jim Orson says of his talks on the results of his own trials of fungicides for winter barley that 'farmers lapped it up really' and that this was in line with their general willingness to act on 'facts', he suggests that facts were not merely handed over as farmers nodded in silent appreciation. Instead, expert knowledge was interrogated through animated discussion:

> I always left plenty of time for questions ... and, farmers being farmers, they asked the questions. I mean they didn't, they didn't hold back quietly ... So I had some superb questions and some superb evenings.[89]

It was not enough for scientific findings simply to be displayed or shared. As with other modes of communication, successful talks to farmers' groups depended on effective social interaction. Perhaps this is why agricultural scientist John Matthews was disappointed with the apparent impact of one of his talks:

> The pamphlet I had put on every chair … had … eight or nine examples of where we were working or where we could have worked and the cost benefit of doing so. And that went down like a damp squib, and I'm not sure why. I didn't think it could possibly do other than have a considerable effect, that everybody had this to take home and they could see if they did something with the piggery they were going to save forty pounds a pig, or whatever. But it didn't work terribly well.[90]

Successful knowledge transfer seems to have been reliant on more than achieving clarity or providing useful information. When David Morris remarks that popular winter evening speakers at the NAAS headquarters in Wales were 'plain-speaking scientists who put it over very, very well', he emphasizes the quality of the performance rather than of the information itself.[91] There was much for the presenter to consider. As well as being able and willing to engage in lively discussion, it was important not to claim complete knowledge. In Jim Orson's view, 'if you don't know, you say you don't know, and, then, you get back to them. And they respect that … if you try and bluster your way through, you're dead.'[92] With such difficult performances required, perhaps it is no wonder that scientists at the Grassland Research Institute were, according to Nigel Young, often reluctant to give talks to farmers' groups: '[T]hey didn't particularly want to go and talk to farmers … they weren't competent in the company of farmers … in case they got caught out, [were] asked a question which they couldn't answer.'[93] However, Young felt able to strike the right note:

> When I was doing the sheep system, I think it wouldn't be too grandiose to say that I was probably one of the top sheep speakers in the country … I just love translating technical subjects, and some of the work which the scientists was doing were very technical stuff, I used to love translating it into farmers' language.[94]
>
> I once did a talk, 'Why is managing grass a pain in the arse?'[95]

As with the conversations, open days and demonstrations discussed above, what emerges from recollections of organized talks is the movement of scientific knowledge in the context of moments and events that had other functions. The winter talks were social occasions; as Robert Hart remarks, 'groups would ask you to come and talk about anything; they don't mind what you talk about they just want a night out'.[96] David Morris offers a description of the talks that took place at the NAAS headquarters in Wales:

> There'd be a hundred people there. And again, a social event, I suppose. But well worth it … They were extremely valuable … for learning, for farmers who were in the job. Many of them hadn't had any formal training whatsoever.
>
> *Interviewer: When you say it was a social occasion, what happened before and after the talk itself?*
>
> Not a lot … They came. Farmers have a lonely life, they like a night out, you know. And if it's good as well, it's all the better.[97]

And perhaps for most members of the Young Farmers' Clubs, talks given by NAAS staff, representatives of commercial companies or scientists were not the main motivation for membership.[98] Writing in the late 1950s, Bracey observed that the Young Farmers' Clubs had 'a threefold appeal – social, vocational and educational', with the first of these factors often the most important.[99] When Christensen remembers his enthusiasm for attending meetings of his local Club in the 1950s, it was not merely for the exposition of the latest in science-based agricultural improvement:

> You go and listen to a plant breeder and you suddenly realise that this wasn't just a bit of seed that you got from somewhere and planted it; it was a result of years and years of plant breeding, selection, cross-breeding and all that sort of thing … Artificial insemination was beginning to be used on farms, which gave you a real opportunity to … select the best genetics in not just the country, but in the world … and all this was developing, and a very exciting time and I couldn't wait to go to Young Farmers'. And of course then we had dances. And then you start seeing girls … so that became quite attractive as well.[100]

Talks to farmers' groups thus provided opportunities for enjoyment and even outright fun. Like conversations with advisers or days out on demonstration farms, these could nevertheless be regarded as being an extension of work and therefore a sensible use of time.

Conclusion

Long before the birth of the field of 'science communication', agricultural advisers seem to have been well aware of the importance of personal and social relationships to the application of scientific and technical knowledge in farming. They had degrees in agriculture, but were recruited as much for their ability to form effective relationships with farmers as for their agricultural knowledge. NAAS trained its District Officers in public speaking and communication skills, suggesting that it was well recognized by those in charge that moving knowledge between scientists, advisers and farmers was a social accomplishment. In matters such as the application of agrochemicals, potato planting seed rates or farm management, it was widely accepted that *who* said it and *how* were as important as *what* was said.

The existence of farmers' groups – including the Young Farmers' Clubs – whose members were interested in summer demonstrations and winter talks certainly helped advisers to reach more of their target audience. Their communication of scientific and technical knowledge on these occasions depended on awareness of the role that they had as opportunities for social contact between farmers. Furthermore, the material presented in this chapter strongly suggests that, for many farmers in attendance, talks and meetings represented an opportunity for social interaction as much as for engaging with the findings of various fields of agricultural science. We might even hypothesize that the demise of ADAS in the 1990s is one of the many factors that has contributed to challenges around mental wellbeing in the British farming community.

The communication of scientific and technical knowledge in British farming in the period under investigation depended on forms of interpersonal and group sociability. This does not mean that this process was necessarily benign, harmonious or – in Harwood's term – 'peasant friendly'.[101] We wish to avoid what Fitzgerald has described as a tendency to assume that in Western contexts, agricultural change is more consensual than in 'development' projects elsewhere.[102] A number of additional points should be made. First, the advisers working for NAAS or ICI were operating within a general paradigm in which increases in production afforded by scientific and technical inputs were assumed to be valuable, sensible and even necessary; the advisers shared a belief in what Fitzgerald calls 'the linkage between technology and the ideology of progress'.[103] Second, the material presented in this chapter suggests that, like the extension workers in different contexts in the period discussed by Harwood, advisers may have found it easier to work with farmers whose farms and personal circumstances predisposed them to be willing and enthusiastic to 'experiment'. One implication thereof may have been that the benefits of agricultural advice were not shared equally.[104] Third, although advisers were aware of the need to adjust scientific and technical knowledge to fit particular local environments and farms, they were usually concerned with knowledge that had been developed *somewhere else*: at a state research station or on an experimental farm, at a university department or in one of ICI's laboratories. Fourth, there is no evidence from any interview that what might be called 'local' knowledge – derived from or with the input of farmers – fed back into the work of agricultural scientists. Scientific and technical knowledge was adapted, refined and sometimes produced in interactions between advisers and farmers, but this knowledge seemingly stayed with these 'local' advisers and farmers without travelling back to centres of agricultural science. In Kloppenburg's words, it remained 'in the heads' of local actors, unable to inform or reform the work of agricultural scientists involved in '*formal* knowledge production for agriculture'.[105]

We stay with Kloppenburg in this final reflection. Although the work of agricultural advisers may have done little to break down the distinction between agricultural science, on the one hand, and farming practice, on the other, their work does perhaps offer one model for those interested in reducing this separation through 'dialogue':

> Farmers know something that agricultural scientists do not know and cannot completely know; and vice versa. Articulations between these different ways of knowing need to be established … to permit mutually beneficial dialogue. The problem is not one of choosing between scientific knowledge or local knowledge, but of creating conditions in which these separate realities can inform each other.[106]

Sally Horrocks is Associate Professor of Contemporary British History at the University of Leicester. Since 2011, she has been the senior academic adviser to National Life Stories at the British Library, a role in which she has worked on various history of science and technology projects, including 'An Oral History of Farming, Land Management and Conservation in Post-War Britain'. Her published work concentrates on the history of women in science and engineering, industrial research, and science and food manufacturing. From 2010 to 2012, she was President of the British Society for the History of Science.

John Martin is Visiting Professor of Agrarian History at the Museum of English Rural Life, University of Reading. His research focuses on agriculture, rural life and the transformation of the countryside in Britain. He is particularly interested in the issue of food security with reference to the impact and legacy of the state-sponsored agricultural revolution during and after the two World Wars and the effects of weather on food production. He has acted as an adviser and consultant for BBC and ITV television programmes and is a member of the Advisory Committee to 'An Oral History of Farming, Land Management and Conservation in Post-War Britain', a research project of the British Library's National Life Stories oral history fieldwork charity.

Paul Merchant holds the position of Oral Historian and Researcher within National Life Stories at the British Library. His published work is concerned with oral histories of the earth and environmental sciences, the relationship between science and religion, and the use of oral history in the historiography of science and technology.

Notes

1. Short et al., *Front Line*, 1–2; Holderness, *British Agriculture*, 92–120; Holderness, 'Third Agricultural Revolution', 68–69.
2. Martin, *Development of Modern British Agriculture*, 94–132; Short et al., *Front Line*, 9.
3. Brassley, 'Output and Technical Change'; Martin, *Development of Modern British Agriculture*; Howkins, *Death of Rural England*. This is not to say that scientific knowledge had not long been applied in British agriculture, but we do accept Holderness' argument that there was an unprecedented 'envelopment of agriculture with science and technology' from the 1950s onwards; Holderness, 'Third Agricultural Revolution', 70.
4. De Jager, 'Pure Science'; Thirtle et al., 'Organisation of Agricultural Research'; Palladino, 'Science, Technology, and the Economy'; Holmes, 'Crops in a Machine'; Garcia-Sancho, 'Animal Breeding'.
5. Holmes, 'Science and the Farmer', 83.
6. Howkins, *Death of Rural England*, 153.
7. McCann, *Story of the National Agricultural Advisory Service*, 72–73.
8. There are brief references to advisers in sociological studies of particular rural communities, such as Frankenberg, *Communities in Britain*, and in autobiographies of farmers, such as Ruck, *Place of Stones*.
9. Hoyle points to limitations in what survives of the NAAS/ADAS archives; Hoyle, *Farmer in England*, 38.
10. Interviews were recorded for 'An Oral History of Farming, Land Management and Conservation in Post-War Britain', a project undertaken by National Life Stories at the British Library and supported by the Arcadia Fund. For other uses of oral history in the history of agriculture and development, see e.g. Riley and Harvey, 'Oral Histories, Farm Practice'; Slim and Thompson, *Listening for a Change*; Jones and Osterud, 'Breaking New Ground'.
11. Latour, *Science in Action*; Latour, *Pandora's Hope*; Secord, 'Knowledge in Transit'; Krige, *How Knowledge Moves*.
12. Wynne, 'Misunderstood Misunderstanding'; Gieryn, *Cultural Boundaries*, 233–335; Parolini, 'Pursuit of a Science of Agriculture'.
13. Fitzgerald, 'Beyond Tractors'; Fitzgerald, *Every Farm a Factory*; Hodge, *Triumph of the Expert*; Harwood, *Europe's Green Revolution*.
14. Exceptions include Arce and Long, 'Bridging Two Worlds' and Henke, 'Making a Place for Science'.
15. Krige, *How Knowledge Moves*, 5.
16. Colyer, *Man's Proper Study*, 20–22. By the late 1950s, there were about five hundred graduates in agriculture each year, with about one hundred going on to become farmers or farmworkers; Bracey, *English Rural Life*, 221.
17. Holmes, 'Science and the Farmer', 77–83.
18. Short et al., *Front Line*, 1.

19. Ibid., 4–8.

20. Self and Storing, *State and the Farmer*, 111–16.

21. Martin, 'British Agriculture in Transition'.

22. Ibid.; Self and Storing, *State and the Farmer*, 121–35; Holderness, *British Agriculture*, 18.

23. Winnifrith, *Ministry of Agriculture*, 83–84.

24. Self and Storing, *State and the Farmer*, 152.

25. Winter, *Rural Politics*, 98; Winnifrith, *Ministry of Agriculture*, 84; McCann, *Story of the National Agricultural Advisory Service*, 19–20; Jones, 'Information and Advice', 64.

26. Winnifrith, *Ministry of Agriculture*, 85; McCann, *Story of the National Agricultural Advisory Service*, 23; Jones, 'Information and Advice', 54–56.

27. Blaxter and Robertson, *From Dearth to Plenty*, 261; Winter, *Rural Politics*, 110.

28. Jones, 'Information and Advice', 56–57. On the success of ICI's Agricultural Division in the 1970s, see Pettigrew, *Awakening Giant*.

29. McCann, *Story of the National Agricultural Advisory Service*, 70.

30. Cooke, *Agricultural Research*, 127–34.

31. Bracey, *English Rural Life*, 229.

32. Powell et al., 'History of the British Grassland Society', 6–23.

33. Martin, *Development of Modern British Agriculture*, 131; Self and Storing, *State and the Farmer*, 30–33.

34. Self and Storing, *State and the Farmer*, 33–34.

35. Ibid., 32.

36. McCann, *Story of the National Agricultural Advisory Service*, 20; Holmes, 'Science and the Farmer', 84; Holderness, 'Third Agricultural Revolution', 82; Martin, *Development of Modern British Agriculture*.

37. Howkins, *Death of Rural England*, 154–56.

38. Interview with Jim Orson, 2019, C1828/07, Track 5, British Library Sound Archive.

39. Interview with Robert Hart, 2019–2021, C1828/13, Track 5, British Library Sound Archive.

40. Ibid.

41. Interview with David Morris, 2019, C1828/11, Track 5, British Library Sound Archive.

42. Interview with Poul Christensen, 2019, C1828/08, Track 1, British Library Sound Archive.

43. Interview with John Conant, 2019, C1828/10, Track 1, British Library Sound Archive.

44. McCann, *Story of the National Agricultural Advisory Service*, 21.

45. C1828/13, Track 5.

46. C1828/07, Track 4.

47. Interview with Nicholas Watts, 2019, C1828/14, Track 3, British Library Sound Archive.

48. C1828/07, Track 6.

49. Hodge, *Triumph of the Expert*.

50. C1828/10, Track 2.

51. C1828/11, Track 5.

52. C1828/13, Track 4.

53. C1828/07, Track 13.
54. Ibid.
55. C1828/08, Track 2.
56. C1828/13, Track 6.
57. Martin, *Development of Modern British Agriculture*, 129.
58. C1828/10, Track 1.
59. Ibid.
60. C1828/13, Track 5.
61. Harwood, *Europe's Green Revolution*.
62. Interview with George Mackay, 2019, C1828/04, Track 7, British Library Sound Archive.
63. This was an example of the type of trial introduced to agricultural science from the 1920s that, because it required statistical analysis for a result, was unpopular with agricultural experts concerned with the 'demonstration' of effects to farmers; Parolini, 'Pursuit of a Science of Agriculture', 263.
64. C1828/04, Track 7.
65. Ibid.
66. Henke, 'Making a Place for Science'.
67. McCann, *Story of the National Agricultural Advisory Service*, 67.
68. C1828/13, Track 4.
69. C1828/07, Track 4.
70. C1828/13, Track 6.
71. Ibid.
72. Star and Griesemer, 'Institutional Ecology'.
73. C1828/13, Track 6.
74. C1828/11, Track 5.
75. Interview with John Matthews, 2019, C1828/02, Track 5, British Library Sound Archive.
76. C1828/02, Track 6.
77. Interview with Nigel Young, 2019–2020, C1828/12, Track 3, British Library Sound Archive.
78. C1828/13, Track 8.
79. C1828/12, Track 3.
80. Ibid.
81. Martin, *Development of Modern British Agriculture*, 99; Harwood, *Europe's Green Revolution*.
82. C1828/07, Track 8.
83. C1828/13, Track 3.
84. C1828/13, Track 5.
85. C1828/07, Track 8.
86. McCann, *Story of the National Agricultural Advisory Service*; C1828/13, Track 5.
87. C1828/13, Track 6.
88. C1828/13, Track 8.
89. C1828/07, Track 8.
90. C1828/02, Track 2.

91. C1828/11, Track 4.
92. C1828/07, Track 8.
93. C1828/12, Track 7.
94. Ibid.
95. C1828/12, Track 3.
96. C1828/13, Track 8.
97. C1828/11, Track 4.
98. David Morris suggests that speakers at his Young Farmers' Club in Wales included representatives of ICI, Fisons and Shell; see C1828/09, Track 1.
99. Bracey, *English Rural Life*, 229.
100. C1828/08, Track 1.
101. Harwood, *Europe's Green Revolution*.
102. Fitzgerald, 'Beyond Tractors', 125.
103. Ibid.
104. Harwood, *Europe's Green Revolution*.
105. Kloppenburg, 'Social Theory and the De/Reconstruction of Agricultural Science', 519 and 531, emphasis added.
106. Ibid., 540.

Bibliography

Arce, Alberto, and Norman Long. 'Bridging Two Worlds: An Ethnography of Bureaucrat-Peasant Relations in Western Mexico', in Mark Hobart (ed.), *An Anthropological Critique of Development: The Growth of Ignorance* (London: Routledge, 1993), 179–208.

Blaxter, Kenneth, and Noel Robertson. *From Dearth to Plenty: The Modern Revolution in Food Production*. Cambridge: Cambridge University Press, 1995.

Bracey, H.E. *English Rural Life: Village Activities, Organisations and Institutions*. London: Routledge, 1959.

Brassley, Paul. 'Output and Technical Change in Twentieth-Century British Agriculture'. *Agricultural History Review* 48(1) (2000), 60–84.

Colyer, Richard J. *Man's Proper Study: A History of Agricultural Education in Aberystwyth 1878–1978*. Llandysut: Gomer Press, 1982.

Cooke, George W. (ed.). *Agricultural Research 1931–1981*. London: Agricultural Research Council, 1981.

De Jager, Timothy. 'Pure Science and Practical Interests: The Origins of the Agricultural Research Council, 1930–1937'. *Minerva* 31(2) (1993), 129–50.

Fitzgerald, Deborah. 'Beyond Tractors: The History of Technology in American Agriculture'. *Technology and Culture* 32(1) (1991), 114–26.

———. *Every Farm a Factory: The Industrial Ideal in American Agriculture*. New Haven: Yale University Press, 2003.

Foreman, Susan. *Loaves and Fishes: An Illustrated History of the Ministry of Agriculture, Fisheries and Food 1889–1989*. London: HMSO, 1989.

Frankenberg, Ronald. *Communities in Britain: Social Life in Town and Country*. Harmondsworth: Penguin, 1970.

Garcia-Sancho, Miguel. 'Animal Breeding in the Age of Biotechnology: The Investigative

Pathway behind the Cloning of Dolly the Sheep'. *History and Philosophy of the Life Sciences* 37(3) (2015), 282–304.

Gieryn, Thomas F. *Cultural Boundaries of Science*. Chicago: University of Chicago Press, 1999.

Harwood, Jonathan. *Europe's Green Revolution and Its Successors: The Rise and Fall of Peasant-Friendly Plant Breeding*. Abingdon: Routledge, 2012.

Henke, Christopher R. 'Making a Place for Science: The Field Trial'. *Social Studies of Science* 30(4) (2000), 483–511.

Hodge, Joseph M. *Triumph of the Expert: Agrarian Doctrines of Development and the Legacies of British Colonialism*. Athens, OH: Ohio University Press, 2007.

Holderness, B.A. *British Agriculture since 1945*. Manchester: Manchester University Press, 1985.

———. 'Apropos the Third Agricultural Revolution: How Productive Was British Agriculture in the Long Boom, 1954–1973?', in P. Mathias and J.A. Davis (eds), *Agriculture and Industrialization: From the Eighteenth Century to the Present Day* (Oxford: Blackwell, 1996), 68–85.

Holmes, Colin J. 'Science and the Farmer: The Development of the Agricultural Advisory Service in England and Wales, 1900–1939'. *Agricultural History Review* 36(1) (1988), 77–86.

Holmes, Matthew. 'Crops in a Machine: Industrialising Barley Breeding in Twentieth-Century Britain', in Jon Agar and Jacob Ward (eds), *Histories of Technology, the Environment and Modern Britain* (London: UCL Press, 2018), 142–60.

Howkins, Alun. *The Death of Rural England: A Social History of the Countryside since 1900*. London: Routledge, 2003.

Hoyle, Richard W. (ed.). *The Farmer in England, 1650–1980*. Farnham: Ashgate, 2007.

Jones, Gwyn E. 'Sources of Information and Advice Available to United Kingdom Farmers: Description and Appraisal'. *Sociologia Ruralis* 3(1) (1963), 52–68.

Jones, Lu Ann, and Nancy Grey Osterud. 'Breaking New Ground: Oral History and Agricultural History'. *Journal of American History* 76(2) (1989), 551–64.

Kloppenburg Jr., Jack. 'Social Theory and the De/Reconstruction of Agricultural Science: Local Knowledge for an Alternative Agriculture'. *Rural Sociology* 56(4) (1991), 519–48.

Krige, John. (ed.). *How Knowledge Moves: Writing the Transnational History of Science and Technology*. Chicago: University of Chicago Press, 2019.

Latour, Bruno. *Science in Action: How to Follow Scientists and Engineers through Society*. Cambridge, MA: Harvard University Press, 1987.

———. *Pandora's Hope: Essays on the Reality of Science Studies*. Cambridge, MA: Harvard University Press, 1999.

Martin, John. *The Development of Modern British Agriculture: British Farming since 1931*. Basingstoke: Macmillan, 2000.

———. 'British Agriculture in Transition: Food Shortages to Food Surpluses, 1947–1957', in Carin Martiin, Juan Pan-Montojo and Paul Brassley (eds), *Agriculture in Capitalist Europe, 1945–1960: From Food Shortages to Food Surpluses* (Abingdon: Routledge, 2016), 107–24.

McCann, Neil Frank. *The Story of the National Agricultural Advisory Service: A Mainspring of Agricultural Revival, 1946–1971*. Ely: Providence Press, 1989.

Palladino, Paolo. 'Science, Technology, and the Economy: Plant Breeding in Great Britain, 1920–1970'. *The Economic History Review* 49(1) (1996), 116–36.

Parolini, Giuditta. 'In Pursuit of a Science of Agriculture: The Role of Statistics in Field Experiments'. *History and Philosophy of the Life Sciences* 37(3) (2015), 261–81.

Pettigrew, Andrew M. *The Awakening Giant: Continuity and Change in Imperial Chemical Industries*. Abingdon: Routledge, 1985.

Powell, R.A, A.J. Corrall and R.G. Corrall. 'A History of the British Grassland Society, 1945–1995', in G.E. Pollott (ed.), *Grassland into the 21st Century* (Dunston: British Grassland Society, 1995), 2–30.

Riley, Mark, and David Harvey. 'Oral Histories, Farm Practice and Uncovering Meaning in the Countryside'. *Social and Cultural Geography* 8(3) (2007), 391–415.

Ruck, Ruth J. *Place of Stones*. London: Faber & Faber, 1961.

Secord, James A. 'Knowledge in Transit'. *Isis* 95(4) (2004), 654–72.

Self, Peter, and Herbert J. Storing. *The State and the Farmer*. London: George Allen & Unwin, 1962.

Short, Brain, Charles Watkins and John Martin (eds). *The Front Line of Freedom: British Farming in the Second World War*. Exeter: British Agricultural History Society, 2006.

Slim, Hugo, and Paul Thompson. *Listening for a Change: Oral Testimony and Development*. London: Panos, 1993.

Star, Susan Leigh, and James R. Griesemer. 'Institutional Ecology, "Translations" and Boundary Objects: Amateurs and Professionals in Berkeley's Museum of Vertebrate Zoology, 1907–39'. *Social Studies of Science* 19(3) (1989), 387–420.

Thirtle, Colin, Paolo Palladino and Jenifer Piesse. 'On the Organisation of Agricultural Research in the United Kingdom, 1945–1994: A Quantitative Description and Appraisal of Recent Reforms'. *Research Policy* 26(4–5) (1994), 557–76.

Winnifrith, John. *The Ministry of Agriculture, Fisheries and Food*. London: George Allen & Unwin, 1962.

Winter, Michael. *Rural Politics: Politics for Agriculture, Forestry and the Environment*. London: Routledge, 1996.

Wynne, Brian. 'Misunderstood Misunderstanding: Social Identities and Public Uptake of Science'. *Public Understanding of Science* 1(3) (1992), 281–304.

 CHAPTER 12

Creating 'Bungereza' in Former 'Bukedi'

Landscape, Languages and Markets in Southeastern Uganda, 1870s–2000s

John Doyle-Raso

As farmers in the village of Doho in Bunyole County, southeastern Uganda, expanded rice cultivation during the 1980s, 'a slogan [emerged] calling the village "Bungereza" meaning England' because of the '[b]icycles, clothes and othe domestic utensiles [*sic*]' that its inhabitants were buying.[1] Farmers grew rice primarily to obtain cash – and because, unlike most crops, rice is cultivable in wetlands, which cover much of the region. Bungereza was the site of the Doho Rice Scheme (DRS), a demonstration farm that was a product of a 1965 agreement between the governments of Uganda and the People's Republic of China (PRC). Bungereza reflected Ugandan farmers' relationships with traders and officials as well as their experimentation with rice and wetlands. The village's nickname referenced Doho's colonial history, including rice projects that started in the 1910s; it did not denote the Chinese–Ugandan relationships associated with the postcolonial agreement or the precolonial introductions of rice in Uganda by Arab, Ganda, Indian and Swahili traders. Bungereza represented local interest in cash cropping and the colonial histories of certain imports. Yet, it also reflected tensions in farmers' experiences with traders and PRC officials, whose direct engagements contrasted with the indirect roles of British colonial officials.

Demonstration farms resulted from colonial and postcolonial government investment in rice cultivation as a means of limiting expenditure on one of Uganda's main imports; however, they also represented government officials' dependence on farmers to extend cultivation. Extending cultivation into wetland interiors required farmers to construct drainage and irrigation channels using manual labour, whereas government projects were mechanized. Establishing demonstration farms also depended on local farmers, who for decades had experimented with multiple rice varietals in environments ranging from hilltops to wetlands. Farmers were key informants when Chinese and Ugandan officials surveyed Uganda in search of a site for a first demonstration farm, and they petitioned officials to sponsor a second. Farmers modulated rice cultivation based on ecological and economic changes, with production peaking at approximately 1,300 tons in 1924, between 4,000 and 5,000 in 1943, and over 4,000 again by 1971 – followed by oscillations during violent instabilities in Uganda in the 1970s and 1980s.[2] This chapter connects changes in landscape, languages and markets to analyse exchanges of knowledge. It argues that farmers' experimentation was crucial to the creation of, and agricultural extension from, demonstration farms. Except for additional pressures during the Second World War and President Idi Amin's so-called Double Production campaign in the early 1970s, cultivation depended more on farmers' agricultural experimentation than on input by the central government.

Rather than framing demonstration farms as disseminators of knowledge, this chapter examines multidirectional exchanges. Scholarship about Chinese projects abroad analyses African and Chinese labour and political thinking, but it says little about farmers' environmental thinking.[3] Jennifer Bess reveals that demonstration farms in the United States depended on Indigenous farmers for 'knowledgeable and flexible labor' while subjecting them to exploitation and causing the loss of their other forms of agricultural knowledge.[4] This chapter builds on these findings by showing that officials depended on local farmers' knowledge to establish and operate demonstration farms, and that farmers in turn experimented with the techniques demonstrated there to cultivate wetlands.

Historicizing environmental knowledge builds on anthropological scholarship about gendered and socioeconomic tensions at DRS. Scholars find that rice farming became a point of conflict based on the following factors: food production (traditionally seen as women's work) overlapping with cash acquisition (traditionally seen as men's work); rice displacing other foods, although claims by local officials in nearby districts about rates of starvation being higher in Bunyole were unfounded; women acquiring land; and socioeconomic inequalities widening because of the costs of controlling labour and the water level in a rice plot.[5] However, this scholarship attributes intellectual advances to PRC officials. Whyte argues that in 1990 Bunyole farmers '[we]re not better … than they were fifteen or twenty years [earlier] – nor ha[d] they acquired more local knowledge'.[6] Yet, a longer perspective shows how farmers expanded cultivation: not by acquiring more local knowledge, but by using it to experiment with the cultivation of varietals in different environments and to develop drainage techniques. Advances in knowledge thus came at least as much from farmers as from officials.

Much scholarship about international exchanges of knowledge uses a binary framework that labels claims to 'locally valid' knowledge expressed in local languages as 'tradition' and claims to 'universally valid' knowledge

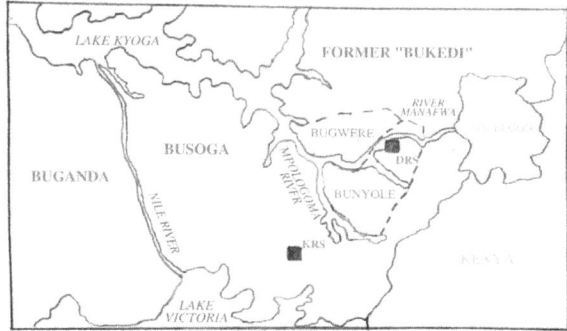

Figure 12.1. Map of southeastern Uganda © John Doyle-Raso

expressed in outside languages as 'science'. Critiques of this binary respond by identifying 'negotiated development', indigenous and 'vernacular' sciences, 'national sciences', as well as the role of intermediary individuals and countries.[7] Analysing demonstration farms in Uganda reveals that they depended on farmers' experimentation, the results of which officials incorporated into their own knowledge through iterative and inequitable exchanges. Farmers and officials conducted international exchanges involving forms of knowledge that were already in conversation, in which outsiders had incorporated farmers' knowledge into their own demonstrations.

In addition to experimentation, farmers learnt about rice cultivation through exchanges with waves of outsiders, including Arab, Ganda, Indian and Swahili traders and agricultural instructors, British and Ugandan agricultural officers, and Chinese technical officials. Their exchanges linked local and global changes by translating between numerous languages, including: Lunyole, spoken in Bunyole County; Lusoga, the language of Busoga; Luganda, the language of Ganda people and understood throughout Uganda; Kiswahili, the language of the Swahili people and a lingua franca in East Africa; and the globally influential Chinese and English languages (see Figure 12.1). Additionally, workers at the Kibimba Rice Scheme (KRS) – the first Ugandan-Chinese project – created 'Kibimba Language', combining elements from the above languages to speak with one another without interpreters. Historicizing place names, terminologies for rice and translations of key concepts relating to environmental change reveals the power dynamics that shaped and were shaped by exchanges of knowledge.

This chapter begins by analysing colonial cash cropping. It examines the derisive nature of the place name 'Bukedi', the introductions of rice, and farmers' experimentation with multiple varietals on hills and along wetland edges. The second and third sections of this chapter historicize KRS and DRS, the two Ugandan-Chinese demonstration farms. Unlike British officials in southeastern Uganda, PRC officials brought with them knowledge of 'swamp reclamation', i.e. the digging of channels at the low ends of wetlands to drain their interiors. In 1967, work began on the 728-hectare KRS based on Chinese and Ugandan officials' translations of local farmers' knowledge and usage of varietals that the farmers had developed themselves. In 1975, farmers and officials started construction on the 1,012-hectare DRS, leading to tensions over labour, land and other issues that manifested themselves at points of translation. By 2000, farmers had extended reclamation across almost 75 per cent of the wetland area in eastern Uganda.[8] After colonial officials and merchant settlers had institutionalized cash cropping in Bukedi District, local farmers ultimately succeeded in recasting the position of Doho in the global market through extensive experimentation and renamed it 'Bungereza'.

Cash Cropping and Colonialism, 1870s–1962

Rice farming for currency preceded colonialism in the region of present-day Uganda, but the British quickly came to depend on it. Colonialists promoted cash cropping based on farmers' experimentation with foreign upland varietals on hills and along wetland edges. Both rice farming and British influence expanded through the use of Kiswahili as a lingua franca – and even after Luganda became the language of 'subordinate administration' under colonialism, Kiswahili-loaned terminologies for rice endured in Ugandan languages. Cultivation boomed during the 1920s and the Second World War, even though by the late colonial era, officials were still learning basic knowledge about rice. At each stage, they depended on farmers experimenting in different environments using varietals such as Bungalla, Senna and Sindano.

'Bukedi' in the Colonial Hierarchy

Colonialism in southeastern Uganda started at the turn of the twentieth century under military administrators from the Kingdom of Buganda, which would become central Uganda after British annexation. Previously, through raiding and trade, Buganda had established its influence in the region that became southeastern Uganda. This area included Busoga – comprising small states populated mainly by Soga people speaking dialects of Lusoga (the Soga language) – and the ethnic borderlands further east of Busoga yet west of the Gisu-dominated Mount Elgon region. The borderlands incorporated small-scale communities and small states, including Bunyuli (known later as Bunyole). By the nineteenth century, Ganda people derisively called the borderlands 'Bukedi', meaning 'Place of Naked People'.[9] Under British rule through 'Ganda agents', these regions became Busoga District and Bukedi District, the latter of which included Bunyole County.[10]

In an effort to justify colonialism in Busoga, British officials stereotyped farmers' intelligence. During the famine in 1908 and 1909, possibly 'the worst ever experienced' there, one official claimed that Busoga had previously been 'the garden of the Protectorate, and the people were industrious, if stupid'.[11] He identified the cause of the famine not as changes under colonialism, but as farmers supposedly having become 'improvident', asserting that 'a Famine Tax should be imposed' to reimburse the colonial government for the costs of famine relief.[12] In the late colonial era, officials who failed to meet economic targets reproduced this stereotyping.[13] One agricultural official referred to Soga farmers as 'slow[er] than many agriculturalists', blaming them for allegedly rendering farm planning a 'dead duck' there.[14] Another official called them 'a lazy lot'; yet, the same official had recently recorded them extending rice cultivation by thousands of hectares within a single year.[15] As officials tried to justify the limitations of colonial interventions, they were slower to read the landscape than farmers were to experiment with new crops.

Further east, precolonial stereotyping manifested itself in the demonyms 'Mukedi' and 'Bakedi' and the toponym 'Bukedi'. The British reproduced these categories despite residents of the borderlands 'not lik[ing] to be called Bakedi … the people in Bunyuli County call themselves *Banyuli*', today spelt Bunyole and Banyole respectively. Because of their opposition, '[t]he name Mukedi [wa]s dying out in the Eastern Province' by 1955.[16] Nonetheless, colonial and postcolonial officials administered Bukedi District as an official jurisdiction until 1991, when it was decentralized into multiple districts. A colonial tax official explained the employ of Ganda proxies as 'the best means we can at present adopt to excite among Bakedi chiefs … co-operation with the Government'.[17] Colonialism therefore expanded east from Busoga through the power of Buganda and the reproduction of precolonial stereotyping.

However, Bunyole farmers critiqued the wealth that chiefs obtained through their roles facilitating colonial exploitation. In 1960, decades after the British began appointing Nyole chiefs and two years before Ugandan independence, farmers across Bunyole protested against taxation. Farmers damaged 15 local government headquarters and 1,121 homesteads, the majority of which belonged to chiefs, as well as two cars owned by chiefs (at least one had a Mercedes-Benz in 1964); the British responded by suspending taxation in Bunyole.[18] Car ownership generated anger in a region where, for many residents, even bicycle ownership remained aspirational.[19] While farmers to the east of Busoga opposed stereotyping by outsiders as well as the wealth that chiefs obtained by overseeing agricultural production, they pursued cash cropping as a means of accessing the global markets that traders and officials embodied.

Introducing Rice

Rice farming in the region of present-day Uganda began with, and facilitated, the nineteenth-century expansion of large-scale trade between the East African coast and the interior. According to the historian Erik Gilbert, rice farming in the interior was limited to estates owned by coastal traders, who discussed it in Kiswahili.[20] In Buganda, British explorers reported that Arab traders had introduced rice following their arrival in around 1844. By 1875, rice cultivation 'was still in the hands of the traders and the Ganda remained untutored [therein]'.[21] For coastal traders in the interior, 'rice, like Islam ... evoked worldliness'.[22] However, British observers in Uganda sometimes failed to distinguish between Arab, Indian and Swahili people.[23] Furthermore, distinctions between Arab, Indian and Swahili people were often 'fuzzy' in this context, as some individual traders represented mixed heritages and/or loose cultural distinctions.[24] Regardless of their identities, communications with outsiders in 1870s Buganda occurred in Kiswahili and occasionally Arabic.[25] As traders moved inland, they used their knowledge of farming and Kiswahili to meet their own demands for rice.

Kiswahili was instrumental in the introductions of rice and colonialism. Kiswahili terminology for rice at successive stages of its production (*mpunga*, then *mchele*, then *wali*) became loan words in the terminologies of languages across East and Southern Africa, including Luganda, Lunyole and Lusoga, which use *omupunga*, then *omucele*, *omutyere* and *omutyele* respectively.[26] Lunyole also uses *obwali*. The terms *omupunga*, *omucele/omutyere/omutyele* and *obwali* correspond to what English-language sources call unprocessed rice, dried rice and rice respectively (although in Kiswahili, *wali* means rice cooked with coconut milk).

Terminologies for rice reflect local differences in the histories of its introductions and/or consumption. Lusoga loaned rice terminology from Luganda. Coastal traders entered Buganda from the south, bypassing Busoga, where they employed Ganda proxies until the 1880s.[27] Furthermore, during the 1880s and 1890s, many Ganda Muslims moved east following their defeat in the religious wars in Buganda during the British annexation. Some became interpreters for the colonial government, as most British officials knew only English and Kiswahili.[28] Ganda agents also 'populariz[ed] Swahili foods'.[29] In Busoga, interpreters and traders thus used Kiswahili and rice to assert their statuses under colonialism.

Different terminologies reflect local histories. In Bunyole, as the anthropologist David Kyaddondo noted, '[f]armers in Doho recall that rice was introduced to the area by the Indians'.[30] Yet, Lunyole uses the Kiswahili-loaned roots *-punga/-tyere/-wali*, which indicates that either Indian traders hired Swahili workers to teach farmers rice cultivation, Indians taught farmers in Kiswahili, or Ganda agents introduced rice and farmers later attributed this to the traders who purchased it. In each scenario, as in Buganda and Busoga, farmers loaned terminology to describe rice at successive stages of production. However, they also created the word *obwali*, indicating the influence of Swahili cuisine and/ or traders on trends in consumption. Bunyole farmers grew and ate more rice than their counterparts in Busoga, who may have been less interested in rice after its use as famine relief during the traumas of 1908–9.[31] To the east of Busoga, by contrast, farmers had cultivated rice before its use as famine relief.[32] Although this was primarily to sell, they did increase their own rice consumption when prices were low.[33] Despite local differences, farmers across southeastern Uganda grew large amounts of rice primarily for sale, eating different amounts based on culinary preferences and market conditions.

Hills and Wetlands in the Imperial Cash Economy

Increasing rice sales reflected farmers' interest in exchanging currency with traders. Farmers started growing rice to sell to traders in the late nineteenth century, experimenting with Bungalla, Sindano and other varietals on hills and along wetland edges. By 1899, rice cultivation had expanded to the point that officials counted it among the 'Indian rations [that] can be supplied locally'.[34] Colonial officials purchased rice using successive currencies (varying by time period), another recent introduction.[35] Although coastal traders had introduced cowrie shells as a method of payment to the east of Buganda in the nineteenth century, the historian Frederick Batala-Nayenga 'doubt[s] whether they really were in wide-spread use … even during the latter half of the nineteenth century [because] trade by barter was carried on alongside trade by cowrie'.[36]

Officials used commercial exchanges between farmers and traders to establish control of the local economy through monetization and, from 1901, taxation. The British disliked cowries: one official "'wish[ed] to burn them'". Officials insisted that farmers sell cowries to traders in exchange for Indian rupees, which they in turn would use to pay taxes.[37] Therefore, in addition to meeting officials' interest in securing a reliable supply of rations, purchasing rice facilitated taxation by circulating cash.

Demand for rice increased following a drought and imperial economic expansion. In 1899, because of drought, British officials 'suddenly f[ou] nd [them]selves out of [rice]'. In 1900, they initiated a standing order from India, to which they soon added imports from Britain, the Congo Free State and German East Africa.[38] Southeastern Uganda imported tons of rice each month, as the number of traders continued growing with the construction of the Uganda Railway during the 1890s and 1900s.[39] After 1904, with the completion of its initial stage, which ended in western Kenya, thousands of labourers from British India arrived in southeastern Uganda. Many traders expanded existing trading centres in Busoga, increasing demand "'for clothing other than bark-cloth'".[40] This period also saw the first recorded bicycle ride in Uganda, by a missionary in 1897.[41] Although an official wrote in 1902 that residents of a major Busoga town had never seen a bicycle, by 1912 a market had emerged in Bukedi District for a class of bicycles that traders sold but did not ride themselves.[42] Farmers were thus capitalizing on the growing demand for rice to buy imports, including bicycles.

As demand increased following the completion of the railway, officials sponsored rice instructors and farmers continued expanding cultivation. Touring Busoga in 1906, a regional subcommissioner identified traders as sources of knowledge for African farmers who were seeking to grow rice.[43] In '[a]bout 1909 the Government employed Swahili and Indian staff to teach' rice cultivation.[44] By 1910, farmers across Busoga were growing rice.[45] In 1917, an agricultural officer found rice 'cultivated in fresh parts almost every time he [went] on tour'.[46] That year, officials in Bunyole observed '[a] considerable quantity … being grown [and] find[ing] a ready sale among the Indian community'.[47] The government then concentrated '[t]he rice instructor's time' on Bunyole County and its northern neighbour, Bugwere County.[48] In 1918, there were roughly 4,000 plots in Bunyole, the largest cluster of which was 900 in Mazimasa Subcounty (including Doho); Bukedi District had the most plots of any district in Uganda.[49] By 1922, Bunyole County was Uganda's main rice-producing area.[50] Cultivation there was mainly along wetland edges using the Bungalla and Sindano varietals, which East African farmers had developed.[51] Bunyole farmers, who were at the core of this expansion, focused on varietals that performed best in wetlands.

Small-scale farmers were crucial for rice cultivation because traders prioritized coffee, cotton and tea cultivation on their estates, which they acquired on hilltops. Traders profited more by exporting these crops than by facilitating import substitution for rice.[52] Reports from the 1920s noted rice being grown almost exclusively on African-held lands.[53] Traders' export crops grew well on hills, which like the wetlands in the valleys between them are numerous in Busoga; Bunyole is less hilly. The physical and social foundations of Soga society are *mitalla*, namely '[r]ise[s] of land between swamps' or simply 'villages'.[54] The anthropologist Lloyd Fallers observed that 'one lives "on" (*ku*) a *mutalla*, not "in" (*mu*) it'. Soga farmers saw hilltops as their prime land, but also cultivated wetlands, esteeming '[a] holding running down from the high part of the village land, combining areas of all these types of soil' as 'ideal'.[55] As traders acquired hilltop land, wetlands became increasingly important for farmers. Nonetheless, even years later, Busoga officials still observed rice being cultivated primarily on hills rather than along wetland edges. The most prominent upland varietal was Buyu.[56] Throughout the colonial era (except during the Second World War production drive from 1942 to 1943; see 'Booms and

Busts' below), unlike farmers in Bunyole, Busoga farmers reserved wetland edges for other crops.

Booms and Busts

After the emergence of wetland edges in Bunyole as the core of colonial Uganda's rice industry, farmers modulated cultivation in relation to ecological and economic conditions. In the 1910s and 1920s, the extension of the railway to Uganda increased the number of traders and connections to Indian Ocean trade.[57] By 1919, markets in southeastern Uganda had several varietals with different geographic origins and prices. In Busoga, Asian varietals were the most expensive.[58] In Bunyole, a varietal with a Bantu name – Bungalla – that officials classified as 'local' was the priciest.[59] While traders and their families remained the primary consumers of rice, farmers were eating increasing amounts. In 1925, officials observed rice 'rapidly taking its place as one of the staple foods' in southeastern Uganda.[60] They estimated that farmers were eating one-third to half of their rice harvests.[61] Bunyole had over 15,000 of Uganda's 16,000 hectares of rice cultivation.[62] Officials reported production across Bunyole totalling 900–1,300 tons per season, although '[i]t [wa]s practically impossible to give anything like an accurate estimate'.[63]

After the expansion of rice cultivation throughout the 1920s, ecological and economic disasters prompted farmers to shift their labour to focus on other crops. In 1929, with the start of the Great Depression, commodity prices plummeted globally. Farmers became less able to compete with rice imports, which officials were now also less compelled to substitute. Moreover, throughout the 1930s, locusts resurged regionally for the first time since 1920, devouring rice and other grains.[64]

Yet, in 1942, rice prices increased following Japan's entry into the Second World War, which disrupted Asian trade. Famine in Bengal in the same year further limited supplies.[65] To compensate, officials across the British Empire promoted wetland rice cultivation.[66] Officials in Uganda visited Kenya to learn about wetland varietals, where they discovered that Kenyan farmers prioritized varietals that Ugandan farmers were already growing, particularly Bungalla, Sindano and Buyu. The visiting officials declared 'Faya' and Senna to be the 'most satisfactory' varietals.[67] Officials in Uganda then began to promote Afaa (to which 'Faya' possibly referred), Bungalla and Senna, particularly by offering higher prices for the latter two,[68] and encouraged farmers to cultivate wetlands rather than hills.[69] Officials also sold seeds, but many farmers 'object[ed] to having their names written down' as part of the wartime system for tracking cultivation.[70] Despite the minimal role of the government in circulating seeds, Busoga farmers expanded production from approximately 700 tons in 1942 to 4,000–5,000 tons in 1943.[71] Most of this planting – including the wetland-friendly varietal Senna – was on hills, although farmers also grew substantial quantities along wetland edges.[72] Bungalla and especially Senna were the most popular varietals.[73] Responding to the wartime price increase, farmers expanded cultivation through experimentation with varietals, including along wetland edges.

Officials also sought to extend cultivation through demonstration and experimental farms. They established the Nakamimi Rice Scheme in Bugiri County (the future jurisdiction of KRS) as well as a farm at Doho.[74] Officials obtained ideas for experiments by reading publications from across the British Empire.[75] The simplicity of the experiments inspired by their reading of these texts – such as soaking seeds before planting – suggests that British officials still had much to learn about rice.[76] Nonetheless, farmers increased production severalfold by using their knowledge of their local environment to experiment with the basic techniques that officials were demonstrating. After the Second World War, Asian exporters regained their leading positions in the global market, in response to which Ugandan farmers shifted their labour to other crops. In the 1950s, British officials began planning to drain wetland interiors across Uganda.[77] However, in 1962, Uganda attained independence before the British could promote this plan.

Interpreters and Seeds, 1965 to the 1980s

During the establishment of KRS, the first major rice scheme in postcolonial Uganda, officials faced new language barriers in comparison to their colonial predecessors. After its completion, farmers experimented with a new technique: drainage, also known as reclamation. When Uganda gained its independence, it had roughly 2,000 hectares under rice cultivation.[78] In 1965, the government signed an agreement with the PRC to popularize rice farming. When PRC officials surveyed Kibimba wetland, farmers contributed local environmental knowledge via an interpreter. However, KRS workers and officials soon spoke across language barriers and without the aid of interpreters by creating what they called Kibimba Language. This finding adds to Jamie Monson's observation that Chinese and Tanzanian workers combined sign language, Chinese and Kiswahili to speak with one another during railway construction work.[79] Kibimba Language was vital in overcoming the challenge of having only one interpreter at a time on a 728-hectare Ugandan-Chinese project. Beyond language, seeds of wetland varietals – particularly Sindano – evidenced officials' dependence on farmers' knowledge for the establishment and operation of KRS. In turn, after the opening of this mechanized scheme, nearby farmers experimented with the knowledge demonstrated there to drain wetlands manually.

Figure 12.2. Chinese and Ugandan officials exchanging documents in front of a portrait of President Obote. Uganda Broadcasting Corporation Film Negative Archive (UBCFNA), File 2802, Image 003

Under its agreement with the PRC, the Ugandan government exported 'agricultural and other primary products' to the PRC in exchange for agricultural machinery and technical expertise.[80] The archival record does not specify which country initiated the agreement. However, viewing this agreement in light of the Republic of China (ROC) having offered an alternative partner in wetland rice farming – as it vied with the PRC for global influence – indicates the potential of the Ugandan government to have selected a different partner. President Milton Obote's politics aligned more with the anti-imperialism and communism advocated by the PRC than with the ROC's projects, which involved connections to the US government.[81] The PRC had developed its approach to reclamation based on demonstrations by officials from the Soviet Union before sending its own technicians abroad; rather than having wholly invented their approach, PRC officials had developed it through iterative exchanges of knowledge.[82] The Ugandan government used KRS to pursue exchanges of knowledge about rice through anti-imperialist and communist networking. The state newspaper claimed that 'the colonialists [had] barred the development of paddy fields there'.[83] It lauded Prince Sihanouk of Cambodia for visiting KRS and thanking

Uganda for its support against US aggression.[84] Uganda also negotiated with North Korea to construct additional rice schemes.[85]

After signing the Uganda–PRC agreement, the decision on where to site the farm depended on local-level exchanges. Chinese technicians visited several swamps and proposed Kibimba, where they started work on KRS in 1967. Before the creation of the scheme, the local environmental conditions were 'virtually unknown' to the state; a 1964 report had noted a near-total lack of data on the area.[86] KRS officials thus depended on local farmers for knowledge about the environment. Because Chinese and Ugandan officials would have to interview Soga farmers for the environmental survey, the Commissioner for Agriculture instructed the Regional Agricultural Officer to send a Soga official ('a Musoga') to interpret between Lusoga and English.[87] As a result, farmers could use Lusoga to share with Chinese and Ugandan officials their knowledge about 'rainfall intensity and duration and temperature variations'.[88]

Language barriers influenced the construction of KRS. As Douglas Ngobi, an agricultural science student who interviewed workers there, described:

> [T]he Chinese Experts did not know English. The Ugandan officials … did not know Chinese or [Lusoga]. The local people knew neither Chinese nor English and few of them knew any Kiswahili. However, there was one Chinese interpreter who knew English. This one man had to co-ordinate all the Chinese personnel and the Ugandan officials. In turn, Ugandan officials acted as middlemen between Chinese and Soga people.[89]

Beyond Chinese and Ugandan officials' need for translations of farmers' knowledge, language barriers were therefore also prevalent between officials.

In response, KRS workers created Kibimba Language. Despite leaving no archival record beyond the General Manager's farewell address to PRC officials, it enabled them to rework the landscape by exchanging knowledge across language barriers:

> [T]he society here managed to narrow down the communication barrier by develping [*sic*] a new language called 'Kibimba Language'. This is a language hypridized [*sic*] with the Chinese, Englishe [*sic*], Swahili, Luganda and other local languages. For a number of years now, staff, workers and the experts have been communicating easily and comfortably without having to strain the only one interpreter we had. It is true that we may have had disagreements here and there. to [*sic*] this, we sincerely apologise to the experts – there was no ill-intention meant.[90]

Ugandan officials framed Kibimba Language as an opportunity for cooperation amid tensions with Chinese officials. Despite the dearth of records detailing Chinese–Ugandan relations at KRS, the archives of the Doho Irrigation Farmers Cooperative Society Limited (DIFACOS) describe similar tensions at DRS (see 'Bungereza and "Hi China", 1972 to the 2000s' below).

Farmers' experimentation with varietals along wetland edges became crucial to postcolonial officials' experimentation with reclamation in wetland interiors. In the late 1960s, rice cultivation at KRS began after the government had obtained seeds of wetland varietals from western Kenya.[91] In 1967 and 1968, PRC officials tested five varietals.[92] These tests indicated that Bungalla and Sindano – the main varietals grown by Bunyole farmers along wetland edges – were the best options.[93]

Officials also noted increasing production along wetland edges outside KRS.[94] The main varietals that farmers cultivated were Bungalla and especially Sindano, which by 1969 was receiving the highest price.[95] Farmers, particularly to the east of Busoga, obtained Sindano seeds from Kenya via Indian traders.[96] Following Amin's 1972 expulsion of Ugandan Indians, officials required farmers with Sindano seeds to supply not just other farmers who had none, but also KRS officials as they lacked a supply, despite it being their recommended varietal.[97] Officials thus relied on farmers identifying, obtaining, developing and distributing seeds.

In 1977, KRS officially opened as a farm for demonstrating irrigation techniques and producing rice under a PRC-controlled parastatal. At the inaugural ceremony, representatives toured the site behind Amin (see Figure 12.3). It is unclear if the Chinese interpreter could speak Kiswahili, Amin's preferred language for government affairs, or whether he, like the interpreter present during the construction of KRS, spoke English. By 1984, records evidence a Chinese interpreter at DRS named 'Huang' or 'Wang' who spoke Kiswahili; if the 'Wang' referenced as an interpreter in a 1977 letter to DRS management was the same person, he was in Uganda when KRS opened.[98] Regardless, most farmers spoke neither English nor Kiswahili.[99] Whereas Amin and other officials learnt about KRS as an international parastatal corporation in English and/or Kiswahili, farmers learnt about rice in Lusoga and Luganda. Among the 'outgrowers' – nearby independent rice farmers – Lusoga would have been particularly prevalent.

Labour methods differed more than language when comparing the farmers at KRS with those in nearby wetlands. Whereas KRS was mechanized, outgrowers reclaimed wetland interiors using manual labour.[100] In 1988, the geographer Victoria Mwaka explained that although cotton had been the main local cash crop, it had collapsed 'due to low prices'. Mwaka observed outgrowers using trial and error to experiment with rice cultivation methods based on their local environments and the technologies that they could access, with '[d]rainage of swamps and flooding of gardens [becoming] widely practiced by small-scale farmers'. Mwaka estimated that by 1980, there were over

Figure 12.3. Ugandan and PRC representatives watch on as President Amin and an interpreter discuss a model of KRS. UBCFNA, File 5598, Image 036

100 such farmers and in 1988 approximately 350. Furthermore, she found that outgrowers sometimes rejected KRS officials' recommendations. For example, those with larger plots broadcast seeds rather than transplanting seedlings from nurseries.[101] Outgrowers were thus successful in using manual labour and knowledge of their local environments to experiment with techniques that had been demonstrated at KRS, eventually using them to reclaim most of the wetland area in Busoga.

Reclamation changed the ecological and economic significances of wetland interiors in Busoga. Whereas during the colonial period rice cultivation was limited to wetland edges, in the postcolonial era farmers developed techniques for manually draining wetland interiors.[102] The drainage of land on which to cultivate cash crops conflicted with other uses of wetland interiors, particularly the gathering of grasses under communal access rights for the construction of buildings and the manufacturing of household items. The clearing of wetland grasses meant that farmers would have to import materials for these tasks instead of being able to use freely gathered materials. However, for rice farmers, rather than the need to buy imports being an unfortunate byproduct of their work, the ability to buy imported goods was a crucial part of the appeal.

Bungereza and 'Hi China', 1972 to the 2000s

The name 'Bungereza' (meaning England) indicated the colonial rather than postcolonial history of the area, but Kyaddondo heard farmers calling DRS's offices 'hi China'.[103] DRS began partly as a response by farmers to government pressure to expand land under cultivation. The extension of rice production beyond DRS has depended on farmers experimenting with wetland cultivation in the surrounding areas, thereby trying to reproduce the high incomes earned at Doho. There were conflicts between PRC and Ugandan officials, as well as between PRC officials and farmers, over labour and land. These manifested themselves in instances of translation at the DRS buildings. PRC officials de-emphasized the economic and social tensions underpinning these tensions by arguing that they were caused by translation errors. However, archival records regarding relationships between farmers and PRC officials attest almost solely to conflict, with no indication of direct cooperation beyond the state newspaper's claim that farmers initially tried to learn Chinese and PRC officials' claim that farmers begrudgingly accepted certain Chinese farming techniques.[104] In this context, it is hard to interpret the name 'hi China' as anything but an expression of frustrations. The place names 'Bungereza' and 'hi China' reflected aspirations that Bunyole farmers have had since the early colonial era for economic advancement through rice cultivation – as well as the tensions with PRC officials that farmers experienced while pursuing these aspirations. Regardless, farmers continued rice cultivation at DRS, which they called a '"factory"'.[105] Furthermore, conflicts emerged over land and water as farmers near DRS extended the area of reclaimed wetland.

In early postcolonial Bunyole, farmers recalled with frustration the connection between bicycles, cash cropping and colonialism. In 1970, Whyte recorded a story about a Nyole man who returned from Kampala with a bicycle:

> A local tinker (*omubuti*) looked carefully … and decided to make one for himself … using metal and wood and banana fibers … to sell to Nyole … But then one day the D.C. (District Commissioner) … took the tinker off to jail [and] told the people that, should they want bicycles, they must cultivate cotton and earn money and buy the bicycles from [Indian] Asian traders.

As Whyte observes: 'Before the imposition of the D.C.'s contract, it is not clear which is center and which is periphery. Relationships are apparently symmetrical; both can build bicycles. After the imposition of the contract, asymmetry is established.'[106]

To assert their positions within the globalized markets of bicycles and rice, Bunyole farmers used their knowledge of their local environments to experiment with cultivation methods. This assertion gained a new form – rice cultivation in wetland interiors – soon after the first high-profile interactions in postcolonial Bunyole between farmers and government officials. In 1972, officials toured the region, promoting Amin's so-called Double Production campaign. Amin targeted export crops to boost foreign exchange earnings as well as wheat and rice 'to make Uganda self-sufficient' in these foods.[107] Officials advocated both 'extensive and intensive agriculture', the latter incorporating the use of fertilizers, pesticides and other inputs.[108] However, Amin's government offered farmers few resources. In practice, the campaign depended on farmers using their own initiative and resources to extend agriculture into forests and wetlands. Officials promoted extension based on the finite extent of these areas, warning that '[a]nyone who did not fully utilize their land would lose the surplus to an active neighbor'.[109] Prior to reclamation, access to wetlands had been communal (or reserved for government foresters). Yet, as increasing numbers of farmers reclaimed sections of wetlands, other farmers came under rising pressure to reclaim sections for themselves.

In 1974, responding to the push to extend cultivation, farmers petitioned the government to sponsor a rice scheme. They lodged this petition through Bunyole County Chief Azaliya Wanjala.[110] The only archival source detailing Wanjala's request is an application for a DRS plot that a farmer submitted approximately seventeen years later. The applicant, W.K. Birehire, wrote that he had 'convince[d]' Wanjala to pursue the idea after Birehire had visited KRS and an irrigation scheme in western Uganda. 'At the beginning many people abused Mr. Wanjala and he gave up. But [Birehire] encouraged [Wanjala]' based on Birehire's experiences touring irrigation schemes – and a memory from the colonial era:

> [I]t was in 1944, when the District Commissioner Bukedi asked Bunyole county council to allow the Government [to] plant Trees in Namunasa Swamp [to drain it for silviculture]. Luckily, I was present, though very young. … The father of UNUSU MIYA (Haji) … told the D.C. that we shall not agree. Bunyole is a small county, therefore Namunasa has to be Reserved for our children and Grandchildren. After having Enough Education, they will be able to use the swamp. The Request was rejected. Sir, with those words ringing in my head, I determined to inform Wanjala to implement the idea, and here we are.[111]

According to Birehire, Bunyole farmers solicited the establishment of DRS as a result of intergenerational planning for educational and environmental changes. It began with their rejection of a colonial government proposal for a silviculture scheme and a promise to preserve the wetland until the 'children and Grandchildren' of the area had more education; it culminated with their appeal to the government to sponsor a cash-cropping project. In response to this solicitation, Ugandan and PRC officials agreed to build a second rice scheme, which was ultimately to be run by the farmers rather than as a parastatal. Surveying and the construction of channels began in 1975.[112] Despite the Forestry Department's objection, which claimed that the land formed part of a forest reserve, construction continued.[113] Farmers had thus successfully asserted their collective power by both rejecting colonial officials' silviculture proposal as well as opposing the Forestry Department's appeal that the area should be maintained as a Protected Area.

Constructing DRS reproduced issues that had featured during the establishment of KRS. Initially, officials knew little about the local environment, having first recorded the temperature there in 1970.[114] Furthermore, 'communication [wa]s a problem as there [we]re no telephones in the area'.[115] The presence of only one interpreter on site at a time, interpreting Lunyole into English or Kiswahili, further limited communication.[116] Considering that only a decade earlier even many schoolteachers in Bukedi District did not know English, there were few opportunities to exchange knowledge in foreign languages.[117] However, there is no evidence of a 'Doho Language'.

Instead, to prove that farmers were cooperating with PRC officials, the state newspaper lauded farmers for 'try[ing] to learn the language of the Experts'.[118] Furthermore, within months farmers had dug enough channels to irrigate about 120 hectares.[119] Additionally, '[t]he construction of the sluice gate and ... bridge needed 21 tons of sand, which the farmers collected from the river nearby without [government] spending a single cent'.[120] However, farmers' contributions of unpaid labour and natural resources were likely responses to the pressures they faced under Amin's production campaign, and their need for cash, rather than their own push for intercultural cooperation.

Tensions over labour, land and other issues developed, particularly at points of translation and intercultural communication. For instance, farmers opposed the use of Chinese weighing scales because of 'a belief that they were being cheated'.[121] A PRC report describes further early tensions, acknowledging that '[a]t the beginning ... there were some unavoidable misgivings' regarding unpaid labour. PRC officials claimed that 'Bunyole farmers never had the experience of doing such a thing in such a manner' and therefore worried about 'the benefit going to the government [or] farmers from other places'. PRC officials also noted that farmers circulated claims 'that the government had allocated money to pay the farmers for their day-to-day labour ... but the money was rumoured to have gone to the pocket of chieves [*sic*] or local officials'.[122] As farmers questioned inequities, PRC officials thus began explaining away socioeconomic conflicts as mere misunderstandings in intercultural interpretation.

DRS expanded quickly despite these tensions. Moreover, nearby farmers began growing rice. However, reclaiming or renting a wetland plot required considerable labour and/or money. By 1983, Ugandan officials were boasting that '[t]he rice farmers in Doho are regarded by their non-rice growing friends as rich people', thereby ignoring the barriers to rice cultivation.[123] In 1985, the Bunyole chief exhorted farmers 'to aid in the final development of the place such that it will eventually look like the "Real Bungereza"'.[124] In around 1987, Whyte and Whyte heard residents around Doho 'referr[ing] to [DRS] as "little Europe" because of its money'.[125] Even before DRS was complete, farmers at two nearby wetlands petitioned for similar schemes.[126] By 1986, 'most of the swamps in [Bunyole and Bugwere] ha[d] been opened up for rice growing'.[127] As such, an increasing number of farmers with relatively high levels of access to labour and money were pursuing rice cultivation based on the DRS model.

Tensions over inequities and issues of interpretation also emerged between PRC and Ugandan officials. In 1987, the year after DRS opened, Ugandan officials lost their offices, which PRC officials dismantled. These offices were in a separate building from those of the PRC officials, who blamed errors in interpretation for the dismantling. The DRS manager 'inquired from the Chinese as to why the uniport he had erected for use by African staff, had been dismantled. It was discovered that it was due to error [*sic*] in interpretation. The Chinese said that due to money problems and the need to complete the project by the end of the year, it [wa]s not possible' to re-erect the uniport.[128] Even central administrative tasks did not necessarily receive close translative attention at 'hi China', and PRC officials were unwilling to spend the money required to rectify the issue.

Ugandan workers expressed their displeasure when they unsuccessfully requested interpretations. They went on strike within a year of DRS opening. Healthcare was a key issue, with workers noting that: '[W]hen the Interpreter is not present [during medical examinations], the doctor doesn't understand. Also when the workers are given a note from the site the doctor miss-handles [*sic*] them in fear of contracting a disease'.[129] In response, PRC officials 'advised [the Ugandans to] get a Ugandan medical staff [member] to assist the Chinese Doctor', insisting that Chinese interpreters would not provide translations for Ugandan workers during their medical examinations. [130] As regards labour and land, economic and social inequities at DRS manifested themselves in officials' selectivity about which medical knowledge they translated.

Two years after the opening of DRS, Ugandan officials rented out more plots. To ease any 'misgivings' farmers had, officials promised that land 'would be distributed according to the principle of greater efforts, more land and bigger contribution, earlier distribution' – meaning that the more land a farmer helped to drain, the earlier he or she would receive a plot and the larger it would be.[131] Nevertheless, officials' distribution of the new plots was not necessarily proportional to the amount of labour that farmers contributed. Additional requirements included being aged 20–45 and having 'some formal Education for easy extension communication'. Yet, the possibility of enforcing the latter was limited, as officials later complained of '[l]ow levels of literacy among majority farmers [*sic*]'.[132] Plot applications required sending a letter, although sometimes farmers asked other people to write these for them; letters often arrived in sets written on the same date, in the same village, by the same hand and with the same phrasing.[133] Farmers obtained English versions of their applications for land to circumvent officials' attempts to maintain hierarchies of education and language.

Meanwhile, conflicts arose between DRS and outgrowers, which resulted in the invention of a new Lunyole term: *ohuligulula amaaji*, meaning to 'maliciously divert water; open a water channel to prevent water from flowing into neighbours' rice fields'.[134] Into the 1970s, farmers in Bukedi District had grown upland varietals along wetland edges.[135] After the creation of DRS, they began cultivating wetlands using drainage and irrigation channels based on river flows. In 1993, a farmer hired KRS engineers to design a project called Lwoba Irrigation Farm. He requested permission from DRS to access water downstream along the River Manafwa, but built irrigation channels upstream instead. In response, unknown farmers sabotaged Lwoba infrastructure at night-time.[136] This DRS-Lwoba conflict exemplified the new term *ohuligulula amaaji*, which farmers invented to reflect their knowledge about creating irrigation infrastructure and the social tensions associated with this practice.

Conflicts between different groups of farmers became entrenched because rice was a crucial source of cash. Many farmers near DRS turned to rice after losing their cattle – which they needed for ploughing cotton fields, long the main cash crop in Bunyole – during the 1970s and 1980s under Amin's presidency (1971–79) and the Ugandan Civil War (1980–86).[137] By 1983, DRS farmers had found a market in 'individual businessmen some of whom come from Kampala'.[138] The researcher Gariyo Zie interviewed DRS farmers in 1990, finding that 'some of them remarked "the swamp has become our factory" in view of the "waves" of people from the more than 20 surrounding villages, some as far as 12 miles and beyond, descending on it every morning and leaving it every afternoon'.[139] In 1988, as Mwaka observed, Busoga farmers rented plots 'as far away as 5 to 10 km from their homes', commuting by bicycle.[140] This state of affairs differed markedly from the assertion of a colonial official in 1940 that rice was 'not a popular crop [because] it cannot be grown near [farmers'] houses'.[141] By the late twentieth century, farmers were willing to travel by bicycle to rented plots, using a part of the proceeds from these plots to ensure continued cash cropping.

In the late 1980s, Ugandan officials took over DRS from their PRC counterparts, who began leaving. The Ugandan government paid the airfares of the departing PRC officials, negatively impacting the country's foreign exchange reserves.[142] The year 1989 saw the 'informal handover' of DRS, coinciding with a broader shift in PRC approaches to international development, in which Chinese officials withdrew from maintaining large overseas presences.[143] Their departure from DRS gave rise to tensions over accounting records.[144] Initially, the Chinese interpreter claimed that 'he had no time to translate them'. He relented after Ugandan officials emphasized 'the difficulties of checking accounting books written in Chinese' and the challenges of '[t]he Chinese Accountant ha[ving] his own system for of [*sic*] keeping books which is difficult for us to understand'.[145] The act of translation thus remained conten-tious at 'hi China' until the end.

In the early twenty-first century, Ugandan officials began applying addi-tional knowledge about rice farming. By this point, DRS had hosted consul-tants and delegations from Egypt, South Korea, various European countries and elsewhere.[146] In 2002, facing the recurring problem of farmers not clear-ing channels, the Irrigation Officer endorsed a proposal by a Japanese con-sultant 'to cut off even the little water so that farmers miss a season if they don't [clear channels]'.[147] DRS officials' control of the infrastructure enabled them to exchange knowledge with infrastructure managers from around the world regarding how to control farmers' labour. Meanwhile, farmers outside DRS continued extending rice cultivation across southeastern Uganda using a range of varietals in wetlands. This extension has continued in the twenty-first century. However, based on government interest in wetland conservation as a response to the ecological impacts of widespread drainage, farmers have also grown increasing amounts of rice on hilltops since the 1990s.[148]

Conclusion: Exchanging Knowledge

The extension of rice cultivation into wetlands across southeastern Uganda was a manifestation of farmers' needs for cash, traders' demand for rice, and colonial and postcolonial officials' interest in import substitution. Farmers expanded cultivation based on local demand in a globalized market, mitigated the challenges of economic and ecological changes, experimented with vari-etals in different environments and developed reclamation techniques. Their work often aligned with government fiscal planning; traders provided a link between farmers' experimentation and officials' planning. Farmers in postco-lonial Bunyole saw traders' control of the circulation of bicycles as vital in the institutionalization of cash cropping. Furthermore, Bunyole farmers identified traders as exploitative of their efforts to improve their positions in globalized markets: '"[w]e're working for the traders", said one man' to the anthropolo-gists Whyte and Whyte.[149] Nonetheless, rice farming continued to be one of the most common means of purchasing the bicycles, clothes and other imports that marked 'Bungereza'. Farmers also renamed the DRS buildings 'hi China'. These place names reflected the significance of colonialism in institutionaliz-ing rice cash cropping and the postcolonial tensions that emerged during the construction and operation of DRS, respectively.

Farmers' knowledge made them subject to exploitation by traders with access to global markets and by officials planning to change the position of Uganda in those markets. Interpreters and other intermediaries performed fraught work that facilitated these inequitable exchanges. British officials had preferred Ganda,

Indian and Swahili proxies to take on these roles, not only out of a desire to avoid interpersonal conflicts but also due to their limited knowledge about rice and of local languages. In the postcolonial era, PRC officials explained the conflicts that arose during the construction of DRS as being the results of translation misunderstandings rather than imbalances of power in exchanges of knowledge, rice and money. Nonetheless, farmers continued to participate in these exchanges because they enabled the creation of 'Bungereza' in former Bukedi, reasserting a symmetry that the 'D.C.'s contract' – under which farmers could only access bicycles and other goods by growing cash crops – had undermined.

Changes in the landscape of southeastern Uganda, the languages used there and the market availability of different rice varietals arose out of exchanges between farmers, officials and traders. During the creation and operation of demonstration farms, officials depended on farmers' knowledge. Furthermore, the extension of rice cultivation beyond demonstration farms required farmers to experiment with varietals on hills and in wetlands, including the eventual development of techniques to drain wetland interiors manually. Bringing this history into conversation with scholarship on exchanges of knowledge makes it possible to analyse the environmental significance of demonstration farms as well as emphasize the importance of farmers in originating and experimenting with the environmental thinking demonstrated there.

John Doyle-Raso is an assistant professor (fixed-term) at Michigan State University (MSU), where he obtained a Ph.D. in history. He received MSU's Gill-Chin Lim Award for Outstanding Doctoral Dissertation in Global Studies by analysing changes in knowledge about wetlands in Uganda, focusing on connections between community-based projects and scientific networks in relation to the country's world-leading national policy for wetland conservation. His additional research projects historicize the international governance of the Nile as well as the engagements of ecologists, fishers and craftspeople with invasive species in Lake Victoria.

Notes

I am grateful for the insights from many graduate students and faculty at Michigan State University, particularly my doctoral supervisor Laura Fair. I thank the African Studies Center, College of Social Science and Department of History at MSU for funding, the Uganda National Council for Science and Technology for research clearance (#SS4339), Wilberforce Segula for granting access to the records of the Doho Irrigation Farmers Cooperative Society Limited, and the Uganda Broadcasting Corporation for giving reproduction rights for the photographs.

1. 'Annual Meeting Held between Chinese Experts and Established Staff of Doho Rice Scheme on 22nd Dec. 1983', Doho Irrigation Farmers Cooperative Society Limited Archive (DIFACOS), DRS/9/42: 4.

2. These instabilities included the Ugandan Civil War and violence under Idi Amin's presidency.
3. Brautigam, *Chinese Aid and African Development*; Hsiao-pong, 'Planting Rice', 381–400; Lin, 'Martyrs of Development', 61–66.
4. Bess, 'The New Egypt', 498–500, 509; Bess, 'The Price of Pima Cotton', 171–89.
5. Whyte, 'The Process of Survival in South-Eastern Uganda', 121–45; Whyte, '"We Have No Cash Crops Any More"', 307–322; Whyte and Whyte, 'The Values of Development', 227–44; Kyaddondo, '"Rice Is a Jealous Crop"'.
6. Whyte, 'The Process of Survival in South-Eastern Uganda', 122, 125, 139–40.
7. Van Beusekom, *Negotiating Development*; Tilley, 'Global Histories', 110–19; Osseo-Asare, *Bitter Roots*; De la Cadena, *Earth Beings*; Tsing, *The Mushroom at the End of the World*, 218; Jacobs, *Birders of Africa*; Mavhunga, *What Do Science, Technology, and Innovation Mean from Africa?*; Frumer, 'Translating Words, Building Worlds', 326–32.
8. Arinaitwe, Pomeroy and Tushabe, *The State of Uganda's Biodiversity 2000*, 20–21, 42.
9. Reid, *Political Power in Pre-colonial Buganda*, 194.
10. Twaddle, *Kakungulu and the Creation of Uganda*. This form of government resembled that analysed by Moses Ochonu in *Colonialism by Proxy*.
11. T. Grant to Deputy Commissioner of Uganda, 12 May 1908, UNA-SMP, A44/214/1.
12. G. Wilson to H.H. Bell, 16 September 1908, UNA, President's Office – Confidential Collection, 41/003/7/enclosure 1: 11.
13. South Busoga District Officer-in-Charge of Resettlement, 'A Summary of Development to Date', August 1958, UNA, Jinja District Archives (JDA), Agriculture 59/1/11/enclosure: 7.
14. Agricultural Officer to Senior Agronomist of Kawanda Research Station, 9 January 1958, UNA-JDA, Agriculture 28/9/141.
15. T.R. Hayes to Bukedi, Busoga and Teso District Agricultural Officers, 4 March 1946, UNA-JDA, Agriculture 27/22/160A; Hayes to all Busoga County Chiefs, 22 October 1943, UNA-JDA, Agriculture 20/16/59.
16. Kagolo, 'Tribal Names and Customs in Teso District', 41.
17. A.H. Watson to Central Province Acting Subcollector, 14 November 1904, UNA, Secretariat Minute Papers, A10/4/34: 4.
18. Government Printer, 'Report of Commission of Inquiry into Disturbances in the Eastern Province', 4, 20, 72–73, Appendix 2:2; Twaddle, 'Politics in Bukedi', 276.
19. In 1970, anthropologists counted 0.6 bicycles per homestead (Whyte and Whyte, 'The Values of Development', 236).
20. Gilbert, 'Rice, Civilisation and the Swahili Towns', 180–83.
21. Reid, *Political Power in Pre-colonial Buganda*, 28.
22. Gilbert, 'Rice, Civilisation and the Swahili Towns', 180.
23. Twaddle, 'East African Asians through a Hundred Years', 153.
24. Gilbert, 'Rice, Civilisation and the Swahili Towns', 180.
25. Twaddle, 'Some Implications of Literacy in Uganda', 229.
26. Andras Rajki, 'Swahili Dictionary (with Etymologies)' (2005), 20, 22, 39. Retrieved 11 November 2022 from https://www.academia.edu/12788108/Swahili_Etymological_Dictionary; Musimami and Diprose, *Ehyagi hy'ebibono by'Olunyole Lunyole*

Dictionary, 144, 246, 372; Gonza, *Lusoga-English and English-Lusoga Dictionary*, 404; Awde, *Swahili-English English-Swahili Dictionary*, 265.

27. Lubogo, *A History of Busoga*, 61.
28. Pawliková-Vilhanová, 'White Fathers, Islam and Kiswahili', 211; Twaddle, *Kakungulu and the Creation of Uganda*, 107; Twaddle, 'Politics in Bukedi', 35–36.
29. Twaddle, *Kakungulu and the Creation of Uganda*, 222.
30. Kyaddondo, '"Rice Is a Jealous Crop"', 26.
31. Grant to Deputy Commissioner, 12 May 1908, UNA-SMP, A44/214/1.
32. H.M. Tarrant to H.H. Johnston, 13 November 1900, UNA-SMP A10/1/87; Bukedi District Acting Commissioner to Famine Relief Committee Chairman, 13 October 1919, UNA, Provincial Papers – Eastern Province 12/Z. 0419/unnumbered.
33. Department of Agriculture, Uganda Protectorate, 'Annual Report of the Department of Agriculture for the Year Ended 31st December, 1926', 10.
34. George Wilson, 'Memorandum to H.M Acting Commissioner', 17 June 1899, UNA-SMP, A5/9/113.
35. In 1906, the British made the rupee the official currency in Uganda before switching to the shilling in 1920 (Batala-Nayenga, 'An Economic History of the Lacustrine States', 238).
36. Ibid., 126–27.
37. Twaddle, *Kakungulu and the Creation of Uganda*, 167.
38. Johnston to D.J. Wilson, 15 February 1900, UNA-SMP, A5/9/88; Johnston to Wilson, 26 February 1900, UNA-SMP, A5/9/108; 'Toro District', n.d., UNA-SMP, A6/18/31/ enclosure: 3; D.L. Baines, 'Statement of Imports for the Month of December 1904', UNA-SMP, A10/4/11/enclosure.
39. 'Statement of Imports for the Month of October 1904', UNA-SMP, A10/4/179/enclosure; S. Hornsby, 'Imports for Bukedi District for January 1906', UNA-SMP, A10/5/27/ enclosure.
40. Twaddle, *Kakungulu and the Creation of Uganda*, 223.
41. Whyte, 'The Process of Survival in South-Eastern Uganda', 130.
42. Fraser, 'Cycle Trip in Usoga and Kavirondo', 73; Twaddle, 'East African Asians through a Hundred Years', 151.
43. Central Province Subcommissioner to Acting Commissioner of Uganda, 3 March 1906, UNA-SMP, A10/5/30: 3.
44. Biggs, 'Rice', 158.
45. G.M.I., 7 May 1910, UNA, Provincial Papers – Eastern Province, 20/Z. 1189/ minute 9.
46. Untitled, 16 August 1917, UNA-SMP, A46/689/18: 2.
47. Lynell Bruce, 24 October 1914, UNA-SMP, A46 Ref. 453, 26: 2; Untitled, 15 November 1917, UNA-SMP, A46/689/25: 2.
48. L. Hewett, 17 July 1917, UNA-SMP, A4/689/15: 2.
49. Untitled, 23 February 1918, UNA-SMP, A46/690/1: 2.
50. Department of Agriculture, Uganda Protectorate, 'Annual Report of the Department of Agriculture, Uganda Protectorate, for the Year Ended 31st December, 1922', 7.
51. Ibid., 7, 20–21; Department of Agriculture, Uganda Protectorate, 'Annual Report of the Department of Agriculture, Uganda Protectorate, for the Year Ended 31st December, 1924', 8.

52. A leading trader, Allidina Visram, bought 'large quantities' of rice from German East Africa, but he grew none himself despite 'having plenty of land to do so upon' (G. Wilson to E. Brown, 30 November 1907, UNA-SMP, A43/88/minute 10).

53. The highest annual total land under rice cultivation recorded on the farms of European and Indian landowners was 22 hectares, compared with 354 hectares under 'Native Agriculture' (R.G. Harper, 'Annual Report on the Government Seed Farms in Teso District for the Year Ended 31st December, 1920', UNA-SMP, A46/721X/9/enclosure: 52–55).

54. Batala-Nayenga, 'An Economic History of the Lacustrine States', xiii; Fallers, 'The Politics of Landholding in Busoga', 262.

55. Fallers, *Law without Precedent*, 206.

56. Hayes to Bukedi, Busoga and Teso District Agricultural Officers, 10 August 1944, UNA-JDA, Agriculture 27/22/45: 1.

57. Hill, *Permanent Way*, 443–75.

58. Eastern Province Acting Commissioner to Chief Secretary, 11 October 1919, UNA, Provincial Papers – Eastern Province, 16/N.0076/unnumbered.

59. Department of Agriculture, Uganda Protectorate, 'Annual Report of the Provincial Commissioner on the Eastern Province for the Year Ended 31st December 1923', UNA-SMP, A46/263/1/enclosure: 15; Department of Agriculture, Uganda Protectorate, 'Annual Report of the Department of Agriculture 1922', 20–21.

60. Department of Agriculture, Uganda Protectorate, 'Annual Report of the Department of Agriculture for the Year Ended 31st December 1925', 7.

61. W.B.S. Estcourt to Eastern Province Commissioner, 21 May 1924, UNA-SMP, A46/2679/125; A.R. Morgan to Director of Agriculture, 11 October 1924, UNA-SMP, A46/2679/128/enclosure.

62. Department of Agriculture, Uganda Protectorate, 'Annual Report of the Department of Agriculture 1925', 36.

63. Morgan to Director of Agriculture, 11 October 1924, UNA-SMP, A46/2679/128/enclosure; Department of Agriculture, Uganda Protectorate, 'Annual Report of the Department of Agriculture 1924', 8.

64. Hopkins, 'Locusts', 518; District Commissioner, Busoga, 'Native Agriculture for the Year Ended 31st December, 1931', UNA-JDA, Agriculture 36/24/136: 2.

65. Collingham, *The Taste of War*, 146–54.

66. Millington, 'Environmental Degradation, Soil Conservation and Agricultural Policies', 239; O'Gorman, *Wetlands in a Dry Land*, 113.

67. 'Notes on a Visit to Kisumu Rice Areas', n.d., UNA-JDA, Agriculture 34/4/195A.

68. Hayes to Bukedi, Busoga and Teso District Agricultural Officers, 22 December 1945, UNA-JDA, Agriculture 27/22/155.

69. Busoga District Agricultural Officer to all Busoga County Chiefs, 14 August 1944, UNA-JDA, Agriculture 20/16/102; Iganga County Assistant Agricultural Officer to Busoga District Agricultural Officer, 7 November 1944, UNA-JDA, Agriculture 27/22/105; G. Williams to E.D. Biruma, Y.K. Musitwa, Y.B. Walukamba and J.N. Sekimpi, 22 September 1943, UNA-JDA, Agriculture 34/4/129; Williams to Walukamba, 1 May 1945, UNA-JDA, Agriculture 35/6/66: 7.

70. Williams to all County Chiefs, 7 March 1945, UNA-JDA, Agriculture 20/16/124.

71. Acting Director of Agriculture, 'Note on the Present Position Regarding the

Production and Marketing of Various Crops August, 1942', UNA, Secretariat Topical – Agriculture, Forestry, Game and Veterinary 4/H. 336/35; Busoga District Commissioner to the Kyabazinga, 23 July 1943, UNA-JDA, Agriculture 20/16/15.

72. Hayes to Bukedi, Busoga and Teso District Agricultural Officers, 10 August 1944, UNA-JDA, Agriculture 27/22/45; Busoga District Agricultural Officer to County Chiefs, Butembe-Bunya and Luuka, 9 November 1945, UNA-JDA, Agriculture 20/16/137.

73. Williams to Biruma et al., 22 September 1943, UNA-JDA, Agriculture 34/4/129; Iganga County Assistant Agricultural Officer to Busoga District Agricultural Officer, 7 November 1944, UNA-JDA, Agriculture 27/22/105.

74. Hayes to Y.B. Walukamba and Y.K. Musitwa, 14 December 1943, UNA-JDA, Agriculture 20/16/69. Williams to Soroti Assistant Agricultural Officer, 28 November 1944, UNA-JDA, Agriculture 27/22/123; Zie, *Appropriate Technology, Productivity, and Employment*, 5.

75. Busoga District Agricultural Officer to Eastern Province Agricultural Officer, 24 November 1944, UNA-JDA, Agriculture 27/22/113.

76. Agricultural Officer to African Assistant Agricultural Officers, 27 November 1944, UNA-JDA, Agriculture 27/22/121.

77. Grehan, 'Annual Report of the Water Development Department for the Year Ended 31st December, 1959', 4.

78. Kirya to all County and Subcounty Chiefs, 17 August 1966, UNA-JDA, Agriculture 33/16/42: 2.

79. Monson, *Africa's Freedom Railway*, 61.

80. Mukasa, 'An Attempt at Swamp Reclamation', 4.

81. 'Ambassadors of the Farm', *Taiwan Today*, 1 November 1961. Retrieved 11 November 2022 from https://taiwantoday.tw/news.php?unit=8,8,29,32,32,45&post=14035.

82. Brautigam, *Will Africa Feed China?*, 40–41.

83. 'Rice Scheme Prospers', *Voice of Uganda*, 6 January 1977, 3.

84. 'Kibimba Scheme: A Pride', *Voice of Uganda*, 8 December 1975, 1, 3.

85. Eva Lubwama and Perez Owori, 'Envoy Hands over Rice Scheme', *Uganda Times*, 23 January 1982, 8.

86. Ngobi, 'A Study of the Kibimba Rice Scheme', 22; Sir William Halcrow and Partners, 'Report on the Feasibility of Irrigation in Uganda', 112.

87. F.X. Lubega to Regional Agricultural Officer, 16 January 1968, UNA-JDA, Agriculture 47/5/20.

88. Buyondo, 'An Evaluation of Kibimba Surface Irrigated Rice Scheme', 11.

89. Ngobi, 'A Study of the Kibimba Rice Scheme', 22–23.

90. 'Welcome Speech by the General Manager on the Occasion of Bidding Farewell to the Chinese Technical Team at Kibimba Rice Company Ltd on 20th March 1990', DIFACOS, DRS/2/85.

91. J.P. Oyende to Eastern Region Marketing Officer, 14 May 1965, UNA-JDA, Agriculture 33/16/36/enclosure; A.M. Kirya to Nyanza Province Marketing Board Senior Marketing Officer, 20 October 1966, UNA-JDA, Agriculture 33/16/50; Kirya to all County Agricultural Assistant Officers, 20 October 1966, UNA-JDA, Agriculture 33/16/51.

92. Maidment to Bukedi, Busoga and Teso District Agricultural Officers and Agricultural

Officer-in-Charge of Serere Research Station, 25 March 1947, UNA-JDA, Agriculture 27/22/154.

93. Kirya to all County and Subcounty Chiefs, 17 August 1966, UNA-JDA, Agriculture 33/16/42: 2.

94. Ibid., 1–2. G.L.M. Kagezi to Eastern Regional Agricultural Officer, 11 June 1969, UNA-JDA, Agriculture 23/19/10: 1–2; Kagezi to Eastern Regional Agricultural Officer, 15 August 1969, UNA-JDA, Agriculture 23/19/11.

95. P.S. Gubi to Busoga District Agricultural Officer, September 1969, UNA-JDA, Agriculture 33/16/119: 2; M.N. Ndugwa to Commissioner for Agriculture, 'Rice Report for July 1972 Eastern Region', UNA-JDA, Agriculture 33/16/unnumbered.

96. Kagezi to Eastern Regional Agricultural Officer, 11 June 1969, UNA-JDA, Agriculture 23/19/10: 2.

97. W.M. Okoche to Eastern Regional Agricultural Officer, 6 October 1971, UNA-JDA, Agriculture 33/16/154; Ndugwa to Eastern Regional Assistant Agricultural Officer-in-Charge of Rice, 28 August 1972, UNA-JDA, Agriculture 33/16/159; Ndugwa to Eastern Regional Agricultural Officer, 24 January 1973, UNA-JDA, Agriculture 33/16/unnumbered.

98. Wang to Rusoke, 12 September 1977, DIFACOS, DRS/7/9.

99. Ngobi, 'A Study of the Kibimba Rice Scheme', 22–23.

100. Ibid., iii.

101. Mwaka, 'The Diffusion of Irrigation Farming', 267, 272, 275, 285.

102. G.L.M. Kagezi to Commissioner for Agriculture, 25 January 1970, UNA-JDA, Agriculture 23/19/12: 2.

103. Kyaddondo, '"Rice Is a Jealous Crop"', 19.

104. Chinese Technical Team to the Ministry of Agriculture and Forestry, 4 February 1988, DIFACOS, DRS/2, attachment to folio 26: 5–6.

105. Zie, *Appropriate Technology, Productivity, and Employment*, 64.

106. Whyte, '"We Have No Cash Crops Any More"', 312–13.

107. Rice consumption totalled 10,000 tons annually, well above rice production, which averaged 4,000 tons (Government of the Republic of Uganda, 'Achievements of the Government of Uganda during the First Year of the Second Republic', 17; Ndugwa, 'Progamme of Work for the Rice Development Scheme in the Eastern Region, 1971', UNA-JDA, Agriculture 33/16/unnumbered).

108. Ndugwa to Commissioner for Agriculture, 29 February 1972, UNA-JDA, Agriculture 33/16/154/enclosure.

109. Kashambuzi, 'Once There Were Trees', 149.

110. Rusoke to District Team/Planning Committee, 2 April 1976, DIFACOS, DRS/2/6.

111. Capitalizations in original. W.K. Birehire to Officer-in-Charge, 17 March 1991, DIFACOS, DRS/PT-4-10/180: 1–2.

112. Rusoke, 'Notes about DRS Presented to the Officials from the E.E.C.', 24 August 1979, DIFACOS, DRS/conf-2/34: 2.

113. Forest Ranger to Assistant Agricultural Officer, 18 March 1976, DIFACOS, DRS/7/1.

114. George Omwatum to Commissioner for Agriculture, 9 January 1971, UNA-JDA, Agriculture 23/19/unnumbered.

115. Wegoye, 'Land Reclamation for Rice Production'.

116. 'Minutes of Meeting Held in the O/C's Office', n.d., DIFACOS, DRS/9/3. 'Meeting

between African Staff and Chinese Construction Preparatory Group Held on 14th May, 1985', DIFACOS, DRS/9/68.

117. 'Bukedi District Half Yearly Report January to June 1968', Makerere University Library Africana Collection, G EAU/BUK E3 (05) 1: 5.

118. 'Brief to Pressmen from *Voice of Uganda*', 16 September 1977, DIFACOS, DRS/2/27: 2.

119. C.A. Amone to DTFC Members, 24 March 1976, DIFACOS, File DRS/7/9.

120. Chinese Technical Team to Ministry of Agriculture and Forestry, 4 February 1988, DIFACOS, in DRS/2/26/enclosure: 2.

121. Rusoke to General Manager, Kibimba Rice Company, 25 June 1984, DIFACOS, unlabelled file, folio 123.

122. Chinese Technical Team to Ministry of Agriculture and Forestry, 4 February 1988, DIFACOS, DRS/2/26/enclosure: 2.

123. Rusoke to Zonal Agricultural Officer, Jinja/Tororo, 13 April 1983, UNA-JDA, Agriculture 2/8/59.

124. 'General Meeting between Farmers, County Chief, Agricultural Staff of DRS and Chinese Construction Prep. Team', 26 June 1985, DIFACOS, DRS/9/75: 4.

125. Whyte and Whyte, 'The Values of Development', 228.

126. 'Annual Meeting Held between Chinese Experts and Established Staff of Doho Rice Scheme on 22nd Dec. 1983', DIFACOS, DRS/9/42: 6, 7.

127. Rusoke to Minister of Agriculture and Forestry, 24 March 1986, DIFACOS, DRS/2/60.

128. 'Meeting with Chinese Experts and African Staff of Doho Rice Scheme to Resolve Workers Grievances', 11 August 1987, DIFACOS, DRS/9/92A: 4.

129. 'Minutes of Meeting Held between African Staff and Construction Team of Chinese, Held on 18th July', DIFACOS, DRS/9/88: 2.

130. Rusoke to Commissioner for Agriculture, 7 September 1987, DIFACOS, DRS/conf/2/72: 2.

131. Chinese Technical Team to Ministry of Agriculture and Forestry, 4 February 1988, DIFACOS, DRS/2/26/enclosure: 2.

132. J. Omudu to Commissioner for Land Resources and Development, 15 April 1996, DIFACOS, TRO/LCV/59/unnumbered: 3.

133. DIFACOS, DRS/10.

134. Musimami and Diprose, *Ehyagi hy'ebibono by'Olunyole Lunyole Dictionary*, 175.

135. Ndugwa, 'Progamme of Work for the Rice Development Scheme in the Eastern Region, 1971', UNA-JDA, Agriculture 33/16/unnumbered.

136. Rusoke to Managing Director, 30 July 1993, DIFACOS, DRS/36/50. Rusoke to A.N. Naleba, 31 August 1993, DIFACOS, DRS/36/53. Naleba to Director of Water Development, 1 September 1993, DIFACOS, DRS/36/56. Similar acts of sabotage resurged in the 2000s (Naleba to Kachonga Police Post, 7 January 2009, DIFACOS, DRS/36/unnumbered).

137. National Wetlands Programme, 'Wetland Status Report for Pallisa District', 12.

138. Rusoke to Zonal Agricultural Officer, Jinja/Tororo, 13 April 1983, UNA-JDA, Agriculture 2/8/59.

139. Zie, *Appropriate Technology, Productivity, and Employment*, 64.

140. Mwaka, 'The Diffusion of Irrigation Farming', 283.

141. Biggs, 'Rice', 159–60.

142. In 1988, tickets for just nineteen of the approximately one hundred PRC officials at DRS cost US$22,246 (Yang Xian-Da to Permanent Secretary, Ministry of Agriculture, 5 August 1988, DIFACOS, DRS/33/unnumbered; V. Sekitoleko to G. Kiyonga, 23 September 1988, DIFACOS, DRS/33/unnumbered).
143. Brautigam, *Will Africa Feed China?*, 38–39.
144. Rusoke to Commissioner for Agriculture, 28 November 1989, DIFACOS, DRS/2/83.
145. Rusoke to Permanent Secretary, Ministry of Agriculture, 4 July 1988, DIFACOS, DRS/33/unnumbered; Wang Jun-Gan to Rusoke, 8 August 1988, DIFACOS, File DRS/33/unnumbered.
146. 'Proposed Program of the Tour of the Team of Egyptian Agricultural Experts at DRS on 8th July 1987', 8 July 1987, DIFACOS, DRS/7/75; 'Minutes of Meeting between Chinese Construction Preparatory Group and African Staff', 28 May 1985, DIFACOS, DRS/9/69: 2; 'Notes about DRS Presented to the Officials from the E.E.C', 24 August 1979, DIFACOS, DRS/2/34.
147. Richard Mukandya to Officer-in-Charge, 15 February 2002, DIFACOS, DRS/36/unnumbered.
148. National Wetlands Programme, 'Wetland Status Report for Pallisa District', 11–14; Joshua Kato, 'Upland Rice Farmers' Prize', *New Vision*, 10 November 2004, 28.
149. Whyte and Whyte, 'The Values of Development', 229.

Bibliography

Arinaitwe, Harriet, Derek Pomeroy and Herbert Tushabe (eds). *The State of Uganda's Biodiversity 2000*. Kampala: National Biodiversity Data Bank, 2000.

Awde, Nicholas. *Swahili-English English-Swahili Dictionary*. New York: Hippocrene Books, 2010.

Batala-Nayenga, Frederick. 'An Economic History of the Lacustrine States of Busoga, Uganda', Ph.D. dissertation. Ann Arbor: University of Michigan, 1976.

Bess, Jennifer. 'The New Egypt, Pima Cotton, and the Role of Native Wage Labour on the Cooperative Testing and Demonstration Farm, Sacaton, Arizona, 1907–1917'. *Agricultural History* 88(4) (2014): 491–516.

———. 'The Price of Pima Cotton: The Cooperative Testing and Demonstration Farm at Sacaton, Arizona, and the Decline of the Pima Agricultural Economy, 1907–1920'. *Western Historical Quarterly* 46(2) (2015): 171–89.

Biggs, C.E.J. 'Rice', in J.D. Tothill (ed.), *Agriculture in Uganda* (London: Oxford University Press, 1940), 158–61.

Brautigam, Deborah. *Chinese Aid and African Development: Exporting Green Revolution*. New York: St Martin's Press, 1998.

———. *Will Africa Feed China?* Oxford: Oxford University Press, 2015.

Buyondo, F.J. 'An Evaluation of Kibimba Surface Irrigated Rice Scheme', Bachelor's thesis. Kampala: Makerere University, 1977.

Collingham, Lizzie. *The Taste of War: World War Two and the Battle for Food*. London: Penguin, 2011.

De la Cadena, Marisol. *Earth Beings: Ecologies of Practice across Andean Worlds*. Durham, NC: Duke University Press, 2015.

Department of Agriculture, Uganda Protectorate. 'Annual Report of the Department of Agriculture, Uganda Protectorate, for the Year Ended 31st December, 1922'. Entebbe: His Majesty's Stationery Office, 1924.

——. 'Annual Report of the Department of Agriculture, Uganda Protectorate, for the Year Ended 31st December, 1924'. Entebbe: His Majesty's Stationery Office, 1924.

——. 'Annual Report of the Department of Agriculture for the Year Ended 31st December, 1925'. Entebbe: His Majesty's Stationery Office, 1926.

——. 'Annual Report of the Department of Agriculture for the Year Ended 31st December, 1926'. Entebbe: His Majesty's Stationery Office, 1926.

Fallers, Lloyd A. 'The Politics of Landholding in Busoga'. *Economic Development and Cultural Change* 3(3) (1955), 260–70.

——. *Law without Precedent: Legal Ideas in Action in the Courts of Colonial Busoga.* Chicago: University of Chicago Press, 1963.

Fraser, A.G. 'Cycle Trip in Usoga and Kavirondo'. *Uganda Notes* 3(11) (1902), 72–75.

Frumer, Yulia. 'Translating Words, Building Worlds: Meteorology in Japanese, Dutch, and Chinese'. *Isis* 109(2) (2018): 326–32.

Gilbert, Erik. 'Rice, Civilisation and the Swahili Towns: Anti-commodity and Anti-state?', in Sandip Hazareesingh and Harro Maat (eds), *Local Subversions of Colonial Cultures: Commodities and Anti-commodities in Global History* (New York: Palgrave Macmillan, 2016), 170–86.

Gonza, Richard Kayaga. *Lusoga-English and English-Lusoga Dictionary.* Kampala: MK Publishers, 2007.

Government of the Republic of Uganda. 'Achievements of the Government of Uganda during the First Year of the Second Republic'. Entebbe: Government Printer, 1972.

Government Printer. 'Report of Commission of Inquiry into Disturbances in the Eastern Province'. Entebbe: Government Printer, 1960.

Grehan, M. 'Annual Report of the Water Development Department for the Year ended 31st December, 1959'. Entebbe: Government Printer, n.d.

Hill, Mervyn F. *Permanent Way: The Story of the Kenya and Uganda Railway.* Nairobi: East African Literature Bureau, 1961.

Hopkins, G.H.E. 'Locusts', in J.D. Tothill (ed.), *Agriculture in Uganda* (London: Oxford University Press, 1940), 518–21.

Hsiao-pong, Philip. 'Planting Rice on the Roof of the UN Building: Analysing Taiwan's "Chinese" Techniques in Africa, 1961–Present'. *China Quarterly* 198 (2009), 381–400.

Jacobs, Nancy. *Birders of Africa: History of a Network.* New Haven: Yale University Press, 2016.

Kagolo, B.M. 'Tribal Names and Customs in Teso District'. *Uganda Journal* 19(1) (1955), 41–48.

Kashambuzi, Eric. 'Once There Were Trees: Impacts of Agricultural Policy on Climate Change in Uganda'. *Whitehead Journal of Diplomacy and International Relations* 16(1) (2014), 147–54.

Kyaddondo, David. '"Rice Is a Jealous Crop": Subsistence, Markets and Morality in a Changing Economy in Eastern Uganda', Ph.D. dissertation. Copenhagen: University of Copenhagen, 2004.

Lin, James. 'Martyrs of Development: Taiwanese Agrarian Development and the Republic of Vietnam, 1959–1975'. *Cross-Currents: East Asian History and Culture Review* 33(1) (2019), 67–106.

Lubogo, Y.K. *A History of Busoga*. Kampala: East African Literature Bureau, 1960.

Mavhunga, Clapperton Chakanetsa (ed.). *What Do Science, Technology, and Innovation Mean from Africa?* Cambridge, MA: MIT Press, 2017.

Millington, Andrew. 'Environmental Degradation, Soil Conservation and Agricultural Policies', in David Anderson and Richard H. Grove (eds), *Conservation in Africa: Peoples, Policies and Practice* (Cambridge: Cambridge University Press, 1987), 229–48.

Monson, Jamie. *Africa's Freedom Railway: How a Chinese Development Project Changed Lives and Livelihoods in Tanzania*. Bloomington: Indiana University Press, 2009.

Mukasa, J.B. 'An Attempt at Swamp Reclamation in an Area: Kibimba Rice Scheme', Bachelor's thesis. Kampala: Makerere University, 1976.

Musimami, Sylvester N.M., and Martin Diprose. *Ehyagi hy'ebibono by'Olunyole Lunyole Dictionary: Lunyole-English with English Index*. Entebbe: Lunyole Language Association and SIL International, 2012.

Mwaka, Victoria Miriam. 'The Diffusion of Irrigation Farming in Iganga and Kamuli Districts', in Emmanuel G. Nabuguzi (ed.), *The Agrarian Question and Technological Change in Uganda* (Kampala: Makerere Institute of Social Research, 1990), 259–301.

National Wetlands Programme. 'Wetland Status Report for Pallisa District'. Kampala: National Wetlands Programme, 1996.

Ngobi, Douglas. 'A Study of the Kibimba Rice Scheme in General', Bachelor's thesis. Kampala: Makerere University, 1978.

O'Gorman, Emily. *Wetlands in a Dry Land: More-Than-Human Histories of Australia's Murray-Darling Basin*. Seattle: University of Washington Press, 2021.

Ochonu, Moses. *Colonialism by Proxy: Hausa Imperial Agents and Middle Belt Consciousness in Nigeria*. Bloomington: Indiana University Press, 2014.

Osseo-Asare, Abena Dove. *Bitter Roots: The Search for Healing Plants in Africa*. Chicago: University of Chicago Press, 2014.

Pawliková-Vilhanová, Viera. 'White Fathers, Islam and Kiswahili in Nineteenth-Century Uganda'. *Asian and African Studies* 13(2) (2004), 198–213.

Rajki, Andra. 'Swahili Dictionary (with Etymologies)'. 2005. Retrieved 11 November 2022 from https://www.academia.edu/12788108/Swahili_Etymological_Dictionary.

Reid, Richard. *Political Power in Pre-colonial Buganda: Economy, Society and Warfare in the Nineteenth Century*. Oxford: James Currey, 2002.

Sir William Halcrow and Partners. 'Report on the Feasibility of Irrigation in Uganda'. Entebbe: Ministry of Agriculture, 1964.

Tilley, Helen. 'Global Histories, Vernacular Science, and African Genealogies: Or, Is the History of Science Ready for the World?'. *Isis* 101(1) (2010): 110–19.

Tsing, Anna. *The Mushroom at the End of the World: On the Possibility of Life in Capitalist Ruins*. Princeton: Princeton University Press, 2015.

Twaddle, Michael. 'Politics in Bukedi, 1900–1939: An Historical Study of Administrative Change among the Segmentary Peoples of Eastern Uganda under the Impact of British Colonial Rule', Ph.D. dissertation. London: University of London, 1967.

———. 'East African Asians through a Hundred Years', in Colin Clarke, Ceri Peach and Steven Vertovec (eds), *South Asians Overseas: Migration and Ethnicity* (Cambridge: Cambridge University Press, 1990), 149–63.

————. *Kakungulu and the Creation of Uganda, 1868–1928.* London: James Currey, 1993.

————. 'Some Implications of Literacy in Uganda'. *History in Africa* 38 (2011), 227–55.

Van Beusekom, Monica M. *Negotiating Development: African Farmers and Colonial Experts at the Office du Niger, 1920–1960.* Portsmouth: Heinemann, 2002.

Wegoye, A.C. 'Land Reclamation for Rice Production: A Case Study of Do Ho Rice Scheme in Bukedi District', Bachelor's thesis. Kampala: Makerere University, 1978.

Whyte, Michael. 'The Process of Survival in South-Eastern Uganda', in M. Bovin and L. Manger (eds), *Adaptive Strategies in African Arid Lands* (Uppsala: Scandinavian Institute of African Studies, 1990), 121–45.

————. '"We Have No Cash Crops Any More": Agriculture as a Cultural System, 1969–1987', in Anita Jacobson-Widding and Walter van Beek (eds), *The Creative Communion: African Folk Models of Fertility and Regeneration of Life* (Uppsala: Uppsala Studies in Critical Anthropology, 1990), 307–22.

Whyte, Susan Reynolds, and Michael A. Whyte. 'The Values of Development: Conceiving Growth and Progress in Bunyole', in Hölger Bernt Hansen and Michael Twaddle (eds), *Developing Uganda* (Oxford: James Currey, 1998), 227–44.

Zie, Gariyo. *Appropriate Technology, Productivity, and Employment in Agriculture in Uganda: The Case Study of the Kibimba and Doho Rice Schemes.* Kampala: Centre for Basic Research, 1991.

 CHAPTER 13

Agrarian Colonization and Indigenous 'Integration'

The Cotoca Project in Eastern Bolivia, 1955–62

Georg Fischer

In 1955, three years into the Bolivian Revolution, a new rural development project in the municipality of Cotoca in eastern Bolivia attracted international attention. At the time, Bolivians and international observers often referred to Cotoca as a 'United Nations colony', as it was part of the Andean Indian Programme (AIP), in which several UN organizations were collaborating in an attempt to engender the economic 'integration' of indigenous peoples into their respective national societies. The Cotoca colony was the only AIP sub-project that involved the resettlement of Indigenous highland inhabitants in the tropical lowlands. Whereas historians have discussed Cotoca as a minor feature in the history of the AIP,[1] an example of frustrated expectations within the broader history of Bolivian frontier settlement[2] or a historical case study of social intervention in the age of development,[3] I focus specifically in this chapter on the transmission and application of agricultural knowledge and its entanglements with the shifting paradigms of indigenism. As some of the main actors in the project themselves declared, Cotoca was the result of a peculiar confluence of development discourses: on the one hand, it was intended to 'modernize' the habits of indigenous peoples in order to facilitate their physical adaptation to a new environment and their 'integration' into the Bolivian nation by means of socioeconomic uplift; on the other hand, it propagated particular organizational forms, namely the agrarian coopera-tive and the agrarian village, as the most promising means of achieving such change. This chapter looks into the practices of rural development and the visions of rurality and indigeneity that emerged at precisely this intersection. Agricultural knowledge, which stood at the centre of each of these visions and practices, was embedded within broader conceptualizations of modern rural life and hygiene as well as gender, race and class.

The chapter contributes to the growing historiography of twentieth-century rural development by approaching these themes mostly from the perspective of international development workers who wrote regular reports to their respective UN organizations in Rome, Geneva or Paris.[4] In recent years, historians have underscored the complexity and diversity of practices and discourses of rural development in the postwar era. Their histories cannot be reduced to simple formulas or master narratives such as the global Cold War, neocolonialism or the rise of the 'American Empire'. As a consequence, the richness of the recent historiography lies in how it showcases this complexity by focusing on local case studies, individual biographies or specific organizations and on the movement of actors, concepts and practices between different contexts. Such histories reveal the multiple origins and trajectories of rural development expertise.[5]

Indeed, transnational experts with diverse specializations and vantage points contributed to the creation of the Cotoca model village and the transfers of agricultural knowledge that I discuss in this chapter. For instance, Olen E. Leonard, Cotoca's director during a critical phase in its early development, began his career in the United States in the late 1930s as a researcher in a larger project on 'rural life studies'. He conducted fieldwork among Spanish-speaking communities in New Mexico, which prepared him for a research position in the Division of Extension and Training in the US Department of Agriculture's Office of Foreign Agricultural Relations. In this role, he conducted several studies on rural areas in Latin America and became the director of a cooperative agricultural station in Bolivia.[6] When he joined the AIP, Leonard had already published an impressive oeuvre covering rural transformation and village structures in Bolivia and other Latin American countries, and over time he became an authority on Latin American rural sociology, agricultural extension and community development.[7]

Another central figure was Jeanne Sylvain, a Haitian anthropologist, social worker and women's rights advocate who initially directed the social work programme in Cotoca and later became the AIP's head coordinator for social services. Sylvain had studied in the United States in 1942–43 on fellowships from the US Department of Labor's Children's Bureau and the University of Chicago's School of Social Service Administration before working as a researcher in a UNESCO rural development project in Haiti's Marbial valley that was headed by the renowned Swiss anthropologist Alfred Métraux. In this role, she studied cultural understandings of childhood diseases in her home country.[8] Other influential actors included Jef Rens, a Belgian trade union representative who in his role as the Deputy Director General of the International Labour Organization (ILO) followed the work of the AIP closely and gave it advice on practical matters of implementation, and Alejandro Quesada, an agronomist from Costa Rica who served as Cotoca's chief agricultural expert after being appointed by the Food and Agriculture Organization of the United Nations (FAO).[9] The diverse backgrounds of the project's main protagonists are illustrative of the wide range of professional experience that informed international rural modernization schemes such as the AIP.

I first contextualize the Cotoca project within the history of the state-led expansion of the agricultural frontier in eastern Bolivia in the 1950s. Second, I discuss how the project reflected and interacted with shifting notions of indigeneity and indigenous integration in Bolivian politics and within international organizations. Third, I examine Cotoca as both a model village intended to showcase a rural development vision as well as a concrete site where experts and colonists negotiated the implementation of a rural development intervention. Fourth, I discuss the significance of agricultural training and the transfer of organizational knowledge, namely in the form of the principles of cooperativism, as key ingredients of the envisioned modern Indigenous farming community that was to develop at Cotoca. As is common in histories of development interventions, the story of the Cotoca colony is rife with the unintended consequences of multidirectional knowledge transfers and social engineering, such as unforeseen transformations in gendered labour relations.

Colonizing the Oriente

The agrarian colonization of its eastern lowlands was a crucial element in Bolivia's mid-twentieth-century state-building projects and was, as such, embedded within broader social and political transformations.[10] The bloody Chaco War (1932–35), in which Bolivia lost most of its share of the Chaco Boreal region to Paraguay, was a catalytic event for fostering a political environment in which vigorous critiques of oligarchic rule and quasifeudal social structures grew louder. Successive Bolivian governments reacted to popular demands by applying a mix of strategies, including greater state control of extractive industries and the reform of labour relations, especially in rural areas dominated by large haciendas that relied on the labour of dependent Indigenous peasants. The government of President Germán Busch (1936–39) nationalized the oil industry and adopted measures to retain mining revenues in the country, while the Gualberto Villarroel (1943–46) government passed a decree to end forced servitude in the countryside.[11] However, Bolivian politics remained highly volatile, and the military frequently intervened in democratic processes with the support of influential economic interest groups, such as the three dominant tin mining companies.

The 1950s saw decisive shifts in Bolivian politics. After a long and steady ascent, the Movimiento Nacional Revolucionario (MNR, National Revolutionary Movement), supported by both left-wing and right-wing nationalist intellectuals and by large sections of the working class, including peasants and miners, came to power in 1952 with the promise to crush deeply rooted structures of inequality. Besides the nationalization of the tin mining industry, at the centre of its agenda was a land reform process that would become one of the most ambitious of its kind in Latin American history as well as the extension of voting rights to women and the illiterate, who comprised a large proportion of the rural Indigenous population. Under pressure from peasants and miners alike, MNR politicians considered access to land, healthcare services and citizenship rights for rural and Indigenous populations a key strategy for strengthening the movement's rural support base.[12]

At the same time, Bolivia's Revolution did not lead to a breakdown in the country's international relations. President Victor Paz Estenssoro adopted a moderate form of progressive-nationalist state capitalism in order to avoid provoking severe US antagonism.[13] As a consequence, the United States remained a major buyer of Bolivian tin and became a leading source of development funding and expertise that was also intended to soften the MNR's political agenda. For instance, a strategic highway between Cochabamba and Santa Cruz de la Sierra, the capital of the department of Santa Cruz, was paved using US money and machinery. From the early 1950s, international organizations such as the FAO, the ILO and UNESCO also implemented development projects in Bolivia, which was commonly seen as the poorhouse of Latin America.

The tropical lowlands of eastern Bolivia, often simply called the Oriente, acquired a special significance during the country's period of economic transformation and political upheaval from the 1930s to the 1950s. Alongside Bolivia's other two principal geographical zones – the Altiplano highlands and the central Andean mountains and valleys – the Oriente was of only marginal demographic and economic importance. An ecologically mixed region containing patches of savanna and the Bolivian section of the Amazon rainforest, the Oriente is largely characterized by dry forest or vegetation that typically marks the transition between the dry Chaco region and the tropical rainforest. Although the region had not been forgotten in previous decades – in the early twentieth century, rubber extraction in the departments of Beni and Santa Cruz had been a major contributor to the Bolivian economy, as was the emerging oil industry south of Santa Cruz – the Oriente remained 'underused', as government officials and international observers constantly pointed out in the early 1950s. In the eyes of many observers, its small population did not correspond to its vast land area, and its production was falling short of its economic potential – especially in the agricultural sector.

The agrarian colonization of the Bolivian Oriente had become a political priority around 1950 amid a context of rising political tension and rural unrest. The Bolivian government's dominant colonization strategy was based on attracting immigrants. With the help of the UN Relief and Rehabilitation Administration and the International Refugee Organization, several European states had set up targeted emigration schemes for their own rural inhabitants to resettle in Latin America.[14] A 1950 UN special mission headed by the Director General of the UN Technical Assistance Administration, Hugh L. Keenleyside, concluded that Bolivia did not quite meet the prerequisites for large-scale immigration projects because it needed 'to import skill (insofar as it can use it) rather than mass manpower'. However, the mission's report argued that circumstances in the Oriente were different, and '[i]f large-scale development works are undertaken in the plains, the introduction of fairly considerable numbers of foreign workers to carry out such projects may be found desirable'.[15] A list of 'colonizable zones' compiled by the Ministry of Government, Justice and Immigration divided Bolivia's territory up according to climate and topography, detailing which European nationalities would be best suited to settling in each region.[16] However, the Bolivian government ultimately proved financially incapable of supporting the establishment of immigrant colonies.[17]

Bolivia was a member of the Intergovernmental Committee on European Migration in its early years, and international organizations on the ground tried to channel and assist with migrant flows. In January 1951, the Bolivian government signed an agreement with the ILO that stipulated the drafting of a comprehensive immigration and colonization plan under the auspices of an ILO technical mission.[18] Yet, it was more common for the Bolivian state to respond to private initiatives that applied for land and funds. However, these private colonization schemes often disillusioned government officials, who complained that European immigrants generally came with 'speculative' intentions and lacked the necessary means and motivation to effectively 'colonize' the land that they acquired.[19]

Nevertheless, when the MNR government started implementing its new policies regarding land tenure and frontier expansion, important shifts were already underway in the Oriente. In 1953, the construction of a railway from the Brazilian border to Santa Cruz, a joint project by the two countries that was initiated in 1938, was nearing its completion. Although mainly envisioned as a route to transport oil from the Yacuiba oilfields in the Chaco, thereby connecting the Bolivian economy with the Atlantic via Puerto Quijarro on the Paraguay River, the railway also raised expectations that migrants would flock to the east of the country to undertake the agrarian colonization of that region. In May 1953, the newspaper *El Diario* reported that 'all these extensive and fertile lands, which until today have remained uncultivated, are now being populated, and along the railroad many rural villages have emerged, which … means progress and improvement'.[20] Indeed, private individuals, colonization companies, state agencies and the military all proposed colonies along the future transport corridor, often specifically designed for prospective settlers from particular countries.[21]

In 1954, the Paz Estenssoro government succeeded in attracting Mennonite settlers from Paraguay, who had gained a reputation as highly skilled farmers in environments similar to that of Santa Cruz, by granting them land and privileges such as the right to operate their own schools and to remain exempt from military service. Meanwhile, immigrants from Okinawa settled to the north of Santa Cruz de la Sierra, a programme supported by the US Civil Administration of the Ryūkyū Islands, the Japanese government and the Okinawan diaspora in Bolivia in response to the economic crisis on the islands in the aftermath of the Second World War, their limited arable land and a corresponding fear that communist ideas would spread under such conditions.[22]

Highland miners and peasants also subscribed to the idea of the Oriente as a land of promise. The Bolivian government received petitions from mining or rural labour unions for land concessions in Santa Cruz. One example is a colonization plan proposed by *campesinos* (peasants) from Oruro in the central Altiplano, who made an explicitly nationalistic case for migrating to the lowlands. In their proposal, domestic colonization of the Oriente was presented as an 'obligation as good Bolivians' to bring 'another degree of culture to the most hidden places of our homeland' and one way of overcoming a 'feeling of inferiority in all aspects in relation to strangers of our patria'.[23]

Whereas in the highlands land reform led to substantial redistribution of formerly idle hacienda land and the expansion of – often ill-equipped and underfunded – smallholder farming, in the lowlands large-scale agrarian enterprises whose land was deemed 'productive' were allowed to thrive.[24] As such, the priority in the Oriente was not land redistribution, but colonization. In a region that was seen as offering vast swathes of unoccupied, fertile land, such perceptions of the Oriente's geography and resource endowment intermingled with what can be interpreted as a genuine frontier discourse: the Oriente as a region that could ignite socioeconomic transformation, an area of settlement for migrants of diverse origins whose agrarian activities could feed the nation.

Indigenous Colonization

In 1952–53, there was a crucial convergence in the agendas of the Bolivian government and international organizations, which manifested itself in the creation of the AIP. The national government's interest in rural development stemmed from the need to appease Indigenous communities and rural unions and keep them within the MNR support base. It was also in line with the MNR's project of forging a 'modern' Indigenous peasantry – an idea rooted in the perception that Bolivian society was marked by a deep abyss between a dynamic, productive urban population and a static, unproductive rural/Indigenous population.

After the Second World War, the treatment of indigenous populations received increasing international attention, especially in relation to Latin America. In 1949, the UN General Assembly declared that 'there exists on the American continent a large aboriginal population and other under-developed social groups which face peculiar social problems'.[25] Guided by this declaration, a 1952 mission involving several UN organizations, which was headed by the New Zealand psychologist and ethnologist Ernest Beaglehole, visited the Andean region and proposed a series of recommendations for an ambitious technical assistance programme aimed at the social and economic 'integration' of the Indigenous populations of Bolivia, Peru and Ecuador.[26] Especially within the ILO, 'integration' evolved into the main paradigm guiding policies relating to indigenous peoples. After a 1953 report had denounced 'the persistence of certain semi-feudal practices in land tenure and, in many cases, social discrimination based on the assumption that aborigines are biologically incapable of attaining the degree of evolution necessary for integration into the national economic and labour system',[27] the concept of 'integration' was finally enshrined in the ILO Convention 107 of 1957.[28] This was in line with the broader paradigm that inspired the ILO's development assistance agenda under its then Director General, David Morse, and Assistant Director General, Jef Rens, who were both close followers of the implementation of the AIP: a version of modernization theory, under the guise of 'industrialism', that was intended to facilitate the adaptation of individuals and population groups to the conditions of life and work in industrial societies and that recognized the necessity of offering a democratic, market-oriented response to the state-centred Soviet development model.[29]

In Bolivia, this consensus resulted in an experiment in rural development that was seen as the testing ground for broader transformative policies: the resettlement of highland Indigenous people to the lowlands for the purpose of establishing an agrarian colony. At the time, the Bolivian army and various private initiatives had already initiated several of their own colonies of highland *campesinos* and miners on the plains of Santa Cruz. The Cotoca colony received special attention from the Bolivian government – which was represented by the state-controlled Corporación Boliviana de Fomento (CBF, Bolivian Development Corporation) – as well as the FAO, the ILO, the World Health Organization (WHO) and UNESCO, all of which were responsible for different aspects of the project. These agencies saw Cotoca as a crucial test of whether the adaptation of Altiplano Indigenous people to living and working conditions in the lowlands – with its different climate, soils and diet – was possible. The project planners all agreed that resettling Altiplano dwellers would improve their welfare, health and education levels in light of the highlands' limited economic opportunities due to overpopulation and shortage of fertile land. A successful pilot project in Indigenous resettlement would

Figure 13.1. Map of AIP projects in Bolivia that slightly misrepresents the geographical location of Cotoca, which in fact lies east of Santa Cruz de la Sierra. Courtesy of the ILO Historical Archives

foreshadow a solution to what observers perceived as the major impediments to Bolivia's national development: the uneven distribution of its population and the hitherto incomplete social and economic 'integration' of the country's Indigenous majority. With a demographic shift towards the lowlands, the agencies hoped that Bolivia would be able to produce sufficient food and raw materials domestically to feed its urban population and supply its industries.[30]

Initially, the AIP contemplated selecting both underemployed miners and seasonal agricultural workers for its tropical colony. Entrusted with the selection of colonists in the highlands and the establishment of services to facilitate and oversee their adaptation in Cotoca, Jeanne Sylvain and her assistants toured the mining districts of Oruro and Potosí, negotiated with state-owned mining companies and unions, and conversed with local physicians. Sylvain concluded that the AIP could not expect many colonists from the ranks of the miners, arguing that the sector's excess labour force comprised mainly sick and elderly workers who were unfit for the challenge. Difficulties in reaching agreements with the highly combative mining unions further contributed to the decision to focus instead on agricultural communities,[31] a group that promised better results. In July 1955, Sylvain and her team of bilingual or trilingual social workers visited Calcha, a predominantly Quechua-speaking *cantón* in the province of Nor Chichas, Potosí Department, where they sought contact with families whose male members frequently travelled to the Andean valleys or northern Argentina to work as seasonal agricultural labourers. The delegation gained access to the local population, the *calcheños*, with the help of the Franciscan missionary Gabriel Landini, who directed several schools in the region. From Sylvain's perspective, seasonal agricultural labourers and their families were interesting for three main reasons: they were already accustomed to a warm and humid climate; they had experience in tropical agriculture; and the women were more likely to be economically active due to the men's long periods of absence.[32]

Just like other parts of rural Bolivia, Calcha was experiencing a profound transformation in local power relations. The MNR government promoted the establishment of rural *sindicatos* (unions), and Indigenous organizational forms like the *ayllu* (a complex term denoting a place-based community) as well as traditional authorities now coexisted with *juntas rurales*, local committees responsible for carrying out land reform at the municipal level.[33] The relationship between these actors and institutions varied between different localities. Even if redistribution of land to former dependent hacienda workers (*colonos*) and restitution of dispossessed land to Indigenous communities (*ex-comunidades*) represented conflicting goals, both groups were united against the *hacendados* (hacienda owners) in their demands.[34] The mere fact that the MNR government opened legal channels for Indigenous communities to file land restitution claims went against its own assimilation policies and strengthened Indigenous identities.[35]

As happened elsewhere in Bolivia, the agrarian reform in Calcha tended to benefit the former *colonos* of the surrounding haciendas while failing to consolidate the land rights of Indigenous communities, let alone restitute the land that they had lost to the haciendas over the centuries.[36] Still, the rural unions supported the *ayllu*'s quest to diminish the power of the *vecinos*, mestizo landowners living in the villages, who had supported the erosion of the authority of *ayllu* leaders.[37] Some of these rural power struggles surface in Sylvain's reports. For instance, after a first group of colonists had settled in Cotoca, she described how members of Calcha's local elite and *junta rural* had actively worked against the AIP's second recruitment campaign:

[I]n two localities, we found upon arriving that all the candidates had changed their mind. It seems that vecinos from the pueblo of Calcha have been announcing that our colonists have died eaten by snakes and mosquitoes. We were informed that Sr. Iporre, Presidente de la Junta Rural of the Province of Vitichi had made a few bad hints which influenced defavourably the indian peasants whose confidence is so easily shaken.[38]

Although we lack details of their precise nature, such disagreements attest to the fact that international development experts did not enjoy easy access to local communities and had to negotiate with an array of stakeholders who were attempting to exert some level of control over Indigenous peasants.

In order to more effectively assist in the *calcheños'* resettlement, members of Sylvain's team stayed in Calcha to learn more about the social life and agricultural practices of the region's population. *Calcheños* typically planted corn and harvested pears or other fruit on small, family-owned private plots (*chacras*), which were up to 1 ha in size and were situated in a village (*ayllu menor* or *rancho*).[39] Traditional farming techniques included fallowing (*barbecho*), growing a combination of different crops (such as corn and cucurbits) and applying a mix of animal manure and humus.[40] On the collectively owned land surrounding the *chacras* but within the boundaries of the *ayllu menor*, villagers could collect firewood and pasakana cacti and let their animals graze.[41] At the time of the corn harvest, *chacra* owners invited neighbours and their families to take part in the *minka*, a festive, ritualized work party that followed certain rules of hospitality and reciprocity.[42] *Minkas* were convoked for sowing, manuring and harvesting as well as for building or repairing houses.[43] Because production cycles and community life were closely tied in with fiestas and Catholic holidays, the AIP recruitment team paid special attention to the significance of Calcha's calendar of festivities.[44]

From the outset, the Bolivian and international experts regarded the selection of colonists as a crucial decision that would have a decisive impact on the prospects of the colony. Accordingly, the participating parties invested significant amounts of time and money in the process. After comprehensive medical and psychological examinations of the selected candidates and their families, the men were instructed to travel to Cotoca, where each man would construct a house and prepare a farming lot in order to at least partially guarantee his family's subsistence by the time of his wife and children's arrival. Over the following months, the colonists were supposed to repay the debt that they had incurred in this process, which typically amounted to 15,000 bolivianos for transport and the construction of their houses. In addition, the CBF was entitled to keep 30 per cent of the first year's harvest to cover food provisions, seeds for the following year, and logistics and infrastructure expenses.[45]

Building a Tropical Model Colony

The Cotoca colony actually consisted of two settlements, El Campanero and La Enconada. Construction started in El Campanero, where the school buildings, the carpentry and mechanical workshops, a marketing cooperative, administrative offices, a depot and the medical centre formed the hub of the settlement. This centralized layout promised an active community life and better social integration than a scattered settlement with houses built on isolated plots, while also offering services to the wider population of the region. Alejandro Quesada highlighted the use of locally available materials such as adobe as well as the incorporation of Altiplano design elements. For instance, the patio, traditionally the centre of family life in the Andes, would, in Quesada's words, 'make the change less abrupt'.[46] To improve air circulation inside the houses, the Swiss architect Henri Fornallaz travelled to French and British colonies in West Africa to identify appropriate ventilation systems.[47] Proponents of a more scattered settlement pattern argued that if the colonists lived next to their fields, they would spend more time working on them. This approach inspired the construction of La Enconada, about 2 kilometres to the east of El Campanero, as an additional settlement in 1956 under the directorship of J.M. Texier. Quesada considered these initiatives a threat to the colonists' social integration, because long walking distances would prevent them from making effective use of the communal spaces and workshops. In addition, he judged as unsuitable the location of the La Enconada settlement, which was built on a large patch of sandy soil without access to water. In his opinion, these adverse ecological factors would complicate efforts to grow vegetables and raise livestock while impeding the production and construction of adobe bricks and walls respectively.[48]

Social assistance was a key feature of the project. A team of social workers was responsible for organizing activities and interventions that were aimed at equipping the colonists for life in the lowlands. These included household inspections and lessons to alter the colonists' personal and household hygiene habits, educational activities (especially for women, such as cooking and sewing courses) as well as community building and entertainment events such as storytelling or film evenings or holiday festivities at the colony's social club. In sum, the social workers' main task was to ensure that there was a low dropout rate from the colony, whose survival was constantly threatened by the colonists' inclination to return to their places of origin.

The endeavour to transform Indigenous habits in order to facilitate the colonists' adaptation to their new environment led to a degree of estrangement between the international experts and the colonists. These tensions are indicative of the various ways in which ideas and theories of modernization inspired development experts. For some observers, Cotoca was simply a place

The Cotoca Region

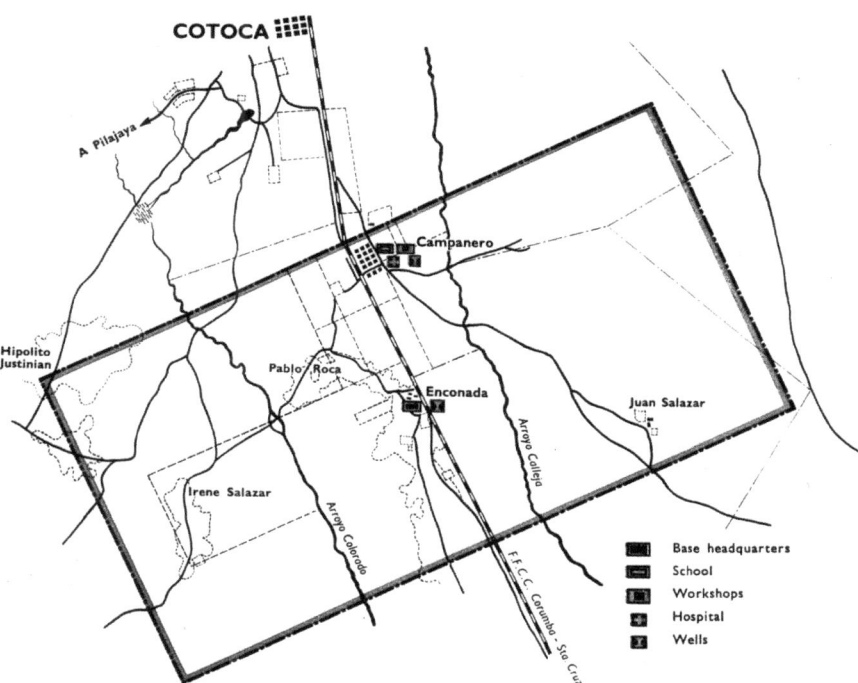

Figure 13.2. Map of the Cotoca colony. Courtesy of the ILO Historical Archives

where 'backward' highland 'Indians' were being transformed into 'modern' workers. These experts experienced gratification when colonists abstained from chewing coca leaves, a habit that in the eyes of Western observers was associated with hunger, poverty and outdated traditions. Integrating the colonists into the populations of surrounding villages was another declared goal, and Victor Bruce, the head of the FAO mission to Bolivia, reported that local volunteers were showing the colonists how to dress, cook and live 'a way of life adapted to the semi-tropical climate'. Nevertheless, Bruce still went on to remark how: 'One cannot help but smile at seeing the Altiplano Indians in the heat of Santa Cruz still wearing their heavy voluminous clothing which is so essential on the bitterly cold highlands. With these people, old habits die hard.'[49]

However, the colonists did not passively accept such derogatory paternalism. An article entitled 'It Is Much Better Here – Success of a Human Transplant', which was published in February 1957 in the international Spanish-language weekly *Visión* and included statements by Rubén González, the colony's doctor, painted an unflattering image of the colonists' mores and habits shortly after their arrival from Calcha. In particular, González boasted about the success of his interventions to improve the *calcheños'* personal hygiene, albeit not before ridiculing their initial reactions: 'Some of them believed that the bar of soap was of sugar, because it had the same color as the *chancaca* (a kind of turrón). One of them scratched it with his fingernails to taste it.'[50] The article portrayed the miraculous transformation of a population who had shortly before lived in abject poverty and uncleanliness without shoes, latrines or bathtubs into healthy and robust settlers. The education adviser Nieto informed UNESCO headquarters that the colonists, whom he described as 'simple, humble, but civilized', were deeply upset about the article.[51]

Other experts displayed a more nuanced understanding of the difficulties of modernization-inspired 'integration'. For Sylvain, the modernizers' challenge consisted in promoting forms of social organization that built upon or reinforced Altiplano *campesino* institutions and traditions. In addition to her AIP responsibilities, the young anthropologist taught seminars on Quechua and Aymara peasants as well as on pathways to social transformation at the Ministry of Education and Fine Arts' Department of Archaeology, Ethnography and Folklore in La Paz. One of these lectures shows the complexity with which Sylvain reflected on cultural patterns and social structures as they entered into a fragile tension with modernization processes just as the customary lifeworlds of peasants were disintegrating. Comparing Haitian and Aymara/Quechua peasants, Sylvain identified similarities:

> [Both groups] preserve primitive techniques to pluck the products of the soil, both depend on the force of the familial group as labour power, both groups – besides growing crops for their subsistence – assign some produce to be sold on the market, they believe in the efficacy of offerings to supernatural entities to protect their harvests, they prepare meals and pour beverages as a sacrifice before the first sowing, they must complement their marginal economy by means of trade and other resources, they have a latent admiration for everything mechanical and dream of a Singer machine and bicycles.[52]

Through the work of figures such as Sylvain or Olen Leonard, Cotoca's acting director in 1957 who was an active participant in international discussions on rural development intervention methods, the practices tested in and experiences derived from the colony informed the ways in which international experts thought about rural development globally.[53]

Even though the Cotoca project bore paternalistic traits and some of its experts held quite essentialist views of the Indigenous colonists and their farming skills, the implementation of its agricultural programme was a relatively open-ended process. The experts reacted to unforeseen challenges with a degree of flexibility, adapted some of their preconceived ideas to local realities and adjusted their plans to what they considered the limitations or preferences of the colonists. For instance, after some experimentation and many mechanical failures, Quesada came to the conclusion that the use of tractors was unviable in Cotoca. Instead, he ordered the purchase of mules and horses, arguing that the colonists were used to working with draught animals, not agricultural machinery. Furthermore, he reported, the animals would find an abundance of natural pasture in the surroundings and produce valuable manure that could be used to improve the sterile patches of sandy soil, the so-called *pampas blancas*, that were common in the area.[54]

These adjustments were an expression of an overall change of course that took place in 1956–57, when some of the shortcomings of the project had become apparent. Increasing production had become prioritized over what the Mexican UNESCO expert Angel Nieto Ramírez, who was responsible for Cotoca's rural education programme, called 'self-development'. In his March 1957 report, he criticized previous Cotoca administrators for adopting an excessive focus on productivity and for neglecting basic education and the transfer of practical skills. Moreover, the colonists were not yet living in their own homes, and the system of work rotation made it impossible for them to specialize in construction work or farming techniques. Nieto Ramírez regretted how the colonists referred to Cotoca not as a 'project', but as a 'company', a habit in which he identified a sign of missing community spirit and lack of identification with the project. According to him, Cotoca's underlying goal was about 'educating, not domesticating them'.[55] This shift in focus was also a response to the colonists' own initiatives to self-organize and exert greater influence on the management of the colony.[56]

'Integration' through Farming

The transfer of farming knowledge was at the heart of the different projects implemented under the framework of the AIP. Whereas the AIP centres in the Altiplano in Pillapi, Playa Verde and Otavi were aimed at reforming agricultural practices and increasing literacy rates among highland dwellers as well as offering them training in nontraditional crafts in their home environment, the Cotoca project was a pilot project in transregional migration and environmental adaptation through farming. The training of the colonists in farming techniques to boost agricultural productivity was intended to complement the redistribution of land and guarantee the enduring socioeconomic uplift of the beneficiaries.[57] Each aspect of the project was in one way or another related to the question of how to instil efficient and appropriate farming techniques among a group of settlers who arrived with little to no experience of tropical farming, who often had to learn Spanish and who constantly threatened to defect from the colony.

The process of integration through farming started with the choice of the crops that the colonists would plant in Cotoca. This selection reflected the project's four subgoals. First, cassava and corn harvests were seen as vital to reduce the colonists' reliance on food provisions from the CBF. Second, as key ingredients of basic lowland diets, cassava and plantains symbolized the envisioned adaptation process that the colonists would undergo. Third, worried that the colonists would develop the mentality of passive aid receivers, Quesada also considered it vital to increase the colony's sugar cane production, arguing that the colonists would otherwise grow accustomed to free sugar. Fourth, experimental plots would also be planted with cotton and tobacco, with a view to identifying viable cash crops.[58]

Agricultural production and the transfer of farming skills took place on plots assigned to individual families as well as on cooperative land that the colonists worked collectively. Cooperative principles played an important role within the AIP, representing a middle ground between collectivist ideals and approaches favouring private ownership. Disagreements over the best ownership model surfaced not only between the Bolivian government and Western donor countries but also among international experts. Quesada was convinced that family-owned farms 'would [even] in the best of cases increase the number of wretched peasants in the region'.[59] However, in the opinion of a dismayed Victor Bruce, Quesada was organizing a 'collective farm'. Suspicious of Quesada's political leanings, and despite not being formally involved in the Cotoca project, Bruce reminded his colleague of 'the unsatisfactory results that had been encountered elsewhere in the world from this type of operation'. The two FAO experts ultimately reached a compromise that stipulated a gradual shift from a collective model to cooperative or private farming, with the colonists being granted the right to decide on their own future after a period of 'continuous oversight and control' of approximately five years.[60]

If Cold War ideological cleavages affected the ways in which experts negotiated different proposals for the colony's future, another common argument was that the cooperative model was compatible with highland land-use practices and social institutions and would thus facilitate the *calcheños'* adaptation to lowland farming. Sylvain contended that Andean Indigenous communities represented 'structured' societies with strong communal organization that could be transformed through 'addition', rather than suppression, of organizational elements. Cooperatives could be one such additional element, although Sylvain lamented that in practice they had 'lent themselves to mystical propaganda without adapting to local necessities'.[61] As the ILO's Deputy Director, Abbas Ammar, emphasized, Cotoca was intended as a training ground for leaders of Indigenous agrarian cooperatives. In a condescending tone, he stated that 'our methods to develop these cooperatives among the Indians must be extremely modest, and [they] should not follow the forms traditionally applied in more developed countries'.[62]

Cooperative land in Cotoca was used for commercial agriculture, but also for the production of basic foodstuffs such as cassava and maize for the colony's subsistence. Work on cooperative land started with soil studies and soil preparation, and continued with ploughing, initially using tractors but later also with draught animals. The colonists received theoretical training in the form of evening talks that covered themes such as soil preparation or apiculture.[63] The experts also organized regular educational film screenings on agricultural topics at the colony's social centre using video material that had been provided by the US Information Agency.[64] However, they constantly complained about their lack of opportunities to provide systematic practical instruction. To remedy this shortcoming, they selected individual colonists – 'characterized by their interest' – with whom they would work together on planning the daily work schedule and evaluating the labour performance of the other colonists.[65] Some colonists also received instruction in specific tasks, such as collecting and interpreting evaporation data.[66] According to Nieto Ramírez, this incorporation of select colonists into planning roles was an early step in the gradual

Figure 13.3. Farming cooperative land. Courtesy of the ILO Historical Archives

transfer of responsibility to the colonists, thereby preparing the colony for its ultimate 'self-development' and 'self-determination'.[67]

In addition to working on cooperative land, each family of colonists was to receive their own plot of 10 hectares on which to grow crops for their subsistence and eventually for sale. While the cooperative land and the individual plots were located away from the village centre, the colonists could grow vegetables and spices, including lettuces, tomatoes, onions, carrots and cayenne pepper, in small lots that were directly attached to their houses.[68] The agricultural advisers and social workers regarded these private gardens as eminently important. They would secure the colonists a fresh supply of healthy food, help them to adapt to the regional diet, teach the children about agriculture and eventually genenerate some surplus produce that could be sold at local markets.[69] The gardens were regarded as being attached to the household realm and were thus associated with other domestic interventions, such as instruction in cooking techniques and family hygiene.[70] As a consequence, different forms of farming knowledge acquired markedly gendered connotations. Cooperative farming was a male domain, with only male colonists receiving training in the use of agricultural machinery. The private gardens became the domain of the nuclear family, but especially that of the women and girls. As Nieto Ramírez reported: 'This activity has aroused interest primarily among the ladies, the colonists' wives. Every [time] the *señoritas*, the teachers of the basic education service, meet with the housewives, they give special attention to these tasks. In this way, we will be able to improve the diet.'[71] While the men were assigned time in their labour schedules to work on their private plots, the gardens – as well as a collectively maintained pigsty and henhouse – were the main features of the agrarian education and daily lives of the women and children in the colony.[72] Although UNESCO funded literacy training and 'castellanization' courses, most women did not speak Spanish and were thus excluded from many other educational activities.[73]

As a consequence, Sylvain and María Luísa Covarrubias, the only Quechua-speaking social worker, cautioned against the 'demoralization' of the women in the colony.[74] Whereas the men's long absence during the Argentinian sugar planting season and the women's economic autonomy had been among the main reasons for recruiting families from Calcha, now the women saw their economic roles and social agency greatly diminished due to the gendered division of agricultural occupations in the colony. The social workers noticed that the shift to the cooperative farming model in conjunction with interventions aimed at reducing alcohol consumption negatively affected the social position of women, who were traditionally in charge of producing the *chicha* (a fermented beverage often made with corn) for the *minka*. The hotter climate also meant that their ability to make warm clothes became redundant. But it was particularly their exclusion from field labour on cooperative land as well as from decision-making within the cooperative that relegated them to the role of passive housewives:

Figure 13.4. The school garden. Courtesy of the ILO Historical Archives

With … the husband at home, the administration of the Center and the 'directiva' of the cooperative to carry on the main economic responsibilities, the women are left with little to do. Washing the children and the few clothes, cleaning one or two rooms, buying the food and cooking became suddenly their restricted universe. Some started a minuscule trade selling bananas, matches, kerosene, etc. Many took advantage of any truck going to the village to make a ride under any futile pretext. Two or three resorted to drinking.[75]

With the instruction of the next generation seen as a more promising path towards sustained agricultural change than the training of adults, agricultural knowledge played a central role in basic educational activities. As a result, the colony's agricultural and educational units started working together, for instance on the construction of a school garden and the hosting of workshops in apiculture at the primary school.[76] Schoolteachers organized activities in accordance with cooperative principles in order to provide the children with an understanding of the organizational aspects of cooperative farming.[77]

Conclusion

In order to fully understand the ideas and practices of rural modernization in Latin America in their international context, we need to be attentive to the ways in which the transfer of agricultural knowledge intersected with other state-building projects. In the case of revolutionary Bolivia, the international development community encountered a political context in which social and ethnic categories were undergoing decisive renegotiation. The strengthening of class-based group identities and concepts at the expense of ethnicity-based institutions was in line with the philosophy of indigenous 'integration' promoted by international development agencies. The goal of the Cotoca project was to contribute to the formation of a class of lowland farmers who would be organized into market-oriented cooperatives and versed in the use of modern machinery, thereby helping to feed the nation and – in time – the world. Yet, many instances in the history of the colony reveal that the agents who were to initiate the required transfer of knowledge, namely the international experts, were conscious of how the figure of the *campesino* at the heart of the AIP's vision was an abstraction. As a consequence, they often acted in the manner of those whom Jess Gilbert has termed 'low modernists' by paying attention to, rather than merely ignoring, local knowledge and traditions.[78] Indeed, what characterized the agricultural knowledge transfer in Cotoca was the experts' constant attempts to reconcile the high modernist ambition of a scalable experiment in agrarian colonization and spatio-demographic restructuring with the experiences and expectations of the communities that were supposed to become the bearers of a self-sustaining development process.

The legacy of the Cotoca colony is difficult to evaluate. Almost all posterior assessments emphasize the high desertion rates that impeded the development of stable community life. A study from 1973 stated that, of the 320 families who had settled in Cotoca, only eighty remained.[79] Observers like the German geographer Felix Monheim, who visited the region in 1962, argued that the Cotoca experience had in principle proven the adaptability of the highlanders. In his view, many of Cotoca's problems did not stem from a lack of skill or receptivity on the part of the colonists, but rather from the programme's overly generous investment in housing and land clearing as well as its general 'spoon-feeding' of the settlers.[80] Consequently, Monheim argued, the costs of desertion were low, and the colonists did not develop sufficient attachment to the land.

While Cotoca did not turn into the dynamic hub for further colonization that had been envisioned, Indigenous resettlement to the lowlands became an ever more important component of state-directed colonization in the 1960s. In particular, the regions to the north and northwest of Santa Cruz did in fact become, in the words of Ben Nobbs-Thiessen, a 'landscape of migration', attracting growing numbers of highlanders and foreigners alike. Indigenous resettlement remained a central element of international aid agreements, which had become increasingly funded by the Inter-American Development Bank, and Bolivian national development programmes under the auspices of the CBF. Looking back in 1964, Jef Rens attributed the strengthening of the integration paradigm within national development policies across the Andean region to the experiences gleaned in the context of the AIP. In his view, 'more than an effort to free these societies from the restraining vestiges of the past', the AIP represented a decisive step towards a fusion of policies aimed at indigenous integration and rural development.[81] Yet, understanding precisely how subsequent rural development practices drew inspiration from the Cotoca colony and similar development interventions is beyond the scope of this chapter and requires further research.

Georg Fischer has a Ph.D. in history from Freie Universität Berlin, where he also worked as a research assistant and lecturer at the Institute for Latin American Studies. Since 2014, he has been working at Aarhus University, Denmark, where he is Associate Professor for Brazilian Studies. Among his publications are a monograph and several articles on geological knowledge production and iron ore in nineteenth- and early twentieth-century Brazil along with several contributions on Latin America's place in current global history debates. His ongoing research deals with agricultural colonization in several South American countries from the 1950s to the 1980s.

Notes

1. Maurel, 'Le programme indien-andin'.
2. Nobbs-Thiessen, *Landscape of Migration*, 120–27; Fifer, 'The Search'.
3. Guthrie, 'The ILO'.

4. Complementary to the perspectives discussed here, Nobbs-Thiessen (*Landscape of Migration*, 120–27) presents an impressive array of sources produced by Indigenous project participants, mostly in the form of petitions and complaints to Bolivian state agencies.

5. Examples of this historiographical trend include Sackley, 'Village Models'; Pribilsky, 'Development and the "Indian Problem"'; Siegel, 'The Kibbutz and the Ashram'.

6. Leonard and Loomis, *Culture of a Contemporary Rural Community*; Loomis, 'Rural Sociologists'.

7. See e.g. Leonard, *Santa Cruz*; Leonard, *Canton Chullpas*; Leonard and Loomis, *Readings in Latin American Social Organization*; Leonard and Clifford, *La sociología rural*.

8. Sylvain, 'L'enfance paysanne'; Verna, *Haiti and the Uses of America*, 113–14; Bourguignon, 'Haiti and the Art', 183; Lenroot, 'The Training of Child Welfare Specialists'.

9. Other technical experts appointed by the ILO, the FAO, WHO and UNESCO came from France, the United Kingdom, the United States, Colombia and Switzerland; see Victor Bruce to Friedrich T. Wahlen, La Paz, 23 November 1955, FAO Archives (FAOA), Rome, RG 71.39, Series A1 – Missions to Bolivia, Outgoing Letters to FAO Staff 1951–1959.

10. The most comprehensive study of the 'march to the East' is Nobbs-Thiessen, *Landscape of Migration*.

11. Young, *Blood of the Earth*, 23–33.

12. Pacino, 'Bringing the Revolution to the Countryside'; Gotkowitz, *A Revolution for Our Rights*; Heath, Buechler and Erasmus, *Land Reform*; Soliz, *Fields of Revolution*; Alexander, *The Bolivian National Revolution*.

13. Zunes, 'The United States and Bolivia'; Siekmeier, *Aid, Nationalism and Inter-American Relations*.

14. Papadopoulos and Parsanoglou, 'European Land Settlement'.

15. Hugh L. Keenleyside, 'Report of the United Nations Mission of Technical Assistance to Bolivia', Lake Success, October 1950, FAOA, RG 71.39, Series 03 – Missions to Bolivia, Report of the UN Mission of T.A. to Bolivia 1950, p. 356.

16. 'Zonas colonizables e inmigrantes que conviene colocar allí', c. 1951, Archivo y Biblioteca Nacionales de Bolivia (ABNB), Sucre, IC 660.

17. United States Department of Commerce, *Economic Review of Bolivia*, 4; Bolivian Ministry of Agriculture, *Zonas colonizables*.

18. Ministerio de Agricultura, Ganadería y Colonización, 'Acuerdo entre la Oficina Internacional del Trabajo y el Gobierno de Bolivia para la elaboración de un plan específico de migraciones y colonizaciones', 17 January 1951, ABNB, IC 736.

19. Bolivian Ministry of Agriculture, *Zonas colonizables*, 28–29.

20. 'En agosto se entregará oficialmente el FF.CC. de Corumbá a Santa Cruz', *El Diario*, 10 May 1953, my translation.

21. Rojas Vásquez, *Región y poder dentral*, 246–50.

22. Iacobelli, *Postwar Emigration to South America*; Nobbs-Thiessen, *Landscape of Migration*, 65–101.

23. 'Plan presentado por los señores colonizadores del Depto. de Oruro', 8 December 1955, ABNB, IC 592.

24. Gotkowitz, *A Revolution for Our Rights*, 279.
25. Ibid., 361.
26. Beaglehole, 'A Technical Assistance Mission'.
27. International Labour Organization, 'Indigenous Peoples'.
28. International Labour Organization, 'Indigenous and Tribal Populations Convention'.
29. Maul, '"Help Them Move the ILO Way"', 393–95; Guthrie, 'The ILO and the International Technocratic Class', 115.
30. See e.g. Olen E. Leonard, 'Andean Indian Programme: Report Prepared by Mr. Olen E. Leonard on the Termination of His Mission as Chief of the Cotoca Project', 18 October 1957, UNESCO Digital Library, AIP/COTOCA/R.1, p. 3. Retrieved 15 November 2022 from https://unesdoc.unesco.org/ark:/48223/pf0000156345.
31. Jeanne Sylvain to Jean Richardot, 15 April 1955, p. 2, ILO Historical Archives (ILOA), Geneva, TAP-A, 15-13-1; Sylvain to Richardot, 26 May 1955, pp. 3–4, ILOA, TAP-A, 15-13-1; Sylvain to Richardot, 20 September 1955, ILOA, TAP-A, 15-13-1, pp. 4–5.
32. Sylvain to Richardot, 15 April 1955, p. 1; Sylvain to Richardot, 12 July 1955, ILOA, TAP-A, 15-13-1, p. 3.
33. Albó et al., *Para comprender las culturas rurales*, 51–52.
34. Soliz, *Fields of Revolution*, 120–40.
35. Ibid., 139.
36. The best study of socioeconomic conditions in Calcha is Frías Mendoza, *Mistis y mokochinches*.
37. Ibid., 32–36.
38. Sylvain to Richardot, 4 November 1955, ILOA, TAP-A, 15-13-1, pp. 3–4. On *vecino* resistance, see also Sylvain to Benjamin Hopenbayn, 12 July 1955, ILOA, TAP-A, 15-13-1, p. 2.
39. Frías Mendoza, *Mistis y mokochinches*, 58–59.
40. Ibid., 64–65.
41. Ibid., 87–92.
42. On *minka* and other forms of nonmonetary reciprocity in the Andes, see Albó et al., *Para comprender las culturas rurales*, 55–57.
43. Frías Mendoza, *Mistis y mokochinches*, 64–65.
44. Jeanne Sylvain to Jean Richardot, 20 September 1955, p. 6.
45. Lockwood, 'Indians of the Andes', 387–88.
46. Alejandro Quesada, 'Field Report No. 17', July–August 1956, ILOA, TAP-A, 15-6-1, p. 8.
47. Henri Fornallaz, 'Rapport trimestriel no. 1', 31 July 1956, ILOA, TAP-A, 15-44-1.
48. Quesada, 'Field Report No. 17', July–August 1956, p. 8.
49. Bruce to Wahlen, 23 November 1955.
50. 'Aquí es mucho mejor: Éxito de un transplante humano', *Visión*, 15 February 1957, 52.
51. Angel Nieto Ramírez, 'Informe trimestral enero–marzo, de las actividades desarrolladas como Jefe de la Sección de Educación Funtamental del Proyecto', Cotoca, 29 March 1957, UNESCO Digital Library, AIP/COTOCA/PR.3, p. 2, my translation. Retrieved 15 November 2022 from https://unesdoc.unesco.org/ark:/48223/pf0000159005.
52. Jeanne Sylvain, 'El campesino Aymara-Quechua', c. 1957, ILOA, TAP-A, 15-13, p. 1, my translation.
53. Jeanne Sylvain, 'Problems Arising in the Teaching of Cultural Anthropology to Social

Workers'. Paper presented at the UN/UNESCO Meeting of Experts on the Contribution of Social Science to Training in Social Work, Paris, 1960. UNESCO Digital Repository, UN/SS/Teach.Soc.Work/4, WS/0560.76. Retrieved 15 November 2022 from https:// unesdoc.unesco.org/ark:/48223/pf0000178073; Leonard and Clifford, *La sociología rural*.

54. Alejandro Quesada, 'Field Report No. 17', July–August 1956, ILOA, TAP-A, 15-6-1, p. 6.
55. Angel Nieto Ramírez, 'Informe trimestral enero–marzo', 29 March 1957.
56. Guthrie, 'The ILO and the International Technocratic Class', 125.
57. Rens, 'The Development of the Andean Indian Programme', 31.
58. Quesada, 'Field Report No. 17', p. 4.
59. Alejandro Quesada, 'Field Report No. 3', February 1955, ILOA, TAP-A, 15-6-1, p. 4.
60. Bruce to Wahlen, p. 3.
61. Jeanne Sylvain, 'El campesino Aymara-Quechua', p. 6, my translation.
62. Abbas Ammar to Jean Ambrosini, 21 February 1958, ILOA, TAP-A, 15–58.
63. Report by the agricultural adviser Mario Durán, in Angel Nieto Ramírez, 'Informe trimestral octubre–diciembre', Cotoca, 31 December 1957, UNESCO Digital Library, AIP/COTOCA/PR.3, p. 5.
64. Angel Nieto Ramírez, 'Proyecto Cotoca: Informe trimestral julio–septiembre 1957', Cotoca, 30 September 1957, UNESCO Digital Library, AIP/COTOCA/PR.3, p. 6.
65. Ibid., p. 6.
66. Ibid., p. 7.
67. Ibid., p. 2.
68. Report by the basic education adviser Victoria de Durán, in Nieto Ramírez, 'Informe trimestral octubre–diciembre', 31 December 1957; Olen E. Leonard, 'Cotoca Center – Inducement to Colonization of the Eastern Lowlands of Bolivia', September 1957, ILOA, TAP-A, 15-47-1, p. 3.
69. Report by the agricultural adviser Mario Durán, in Nieto Ramírez, 'Informe trimestral octubre–diciembre', 31 December 1957, p. 5.
70. Report by Victoria de Durán, in ibid., p. 6.
71. Angel Nieto Ramírez, 'Informe trimestral abril–junio, de las actividades desrrolladas como Jefe de la Sección de Educación Funtamental del Proyecto', Cotoca, 30 June 1957, UNESCO Digital Library, AIP/COTOCA/PR.3, p. 1.
72. On the gendered dimensions of rural development interventions, see Julia Tischler's chapter in this volume.
73. On Spanish-language and literacy courses, see Angel Nieto Ramírez, 'Resumen del informe anual (1958)', n.d., UNESCO Digital Library, AIP/COTOCA/PR.3, p. 2.
74. Sylvain to Bruno Leuschner, 2 July 1958, ILOA, TAP-A, 15-13-1, p. 6.
75. Ibid., p. 7. This assessment of the socioeconomic roles of female colonists from the highlands is in line with later findings from other eastern Bolivian colonies; see Kaltmeier, *Im Widerstreit der Ordnungen*, 152–53.
76. Report by Mario Durán, in Nieto Ramírez, 'Informe trimestral octubre–diciembre', 31 December 1957.
77. Nieto Ramírez, 'Resúmen del informe anual (1958)'.
78. Gilbert, 'Low Modernism', 131.

79. Stearman, 'Colonization in Eastern Bolivia', 286.
80. Monheim, 'Forschungsbericht', 334. A more detailed analysis of Cotoca is included in Monheim, *Junge Indianerkolonisation*, 51–64.
81. Rens, 'The Development of the Andean Indian Programme', 32.

Bibliography

Albó, Xavier, Kitula Libermann, Armando Godínez and Francisco Pifarré. *Para comprender las culturas rurales en Bolivia*. La Paz: MEC/CIPCA/UNICEF, 1989.

Alexander, Robert J. *The Bolivian National Revolution*. New Brunswick, NJ: Rutgers University Press, 1958.

Beaglehole, Ernest. 'A Technical Assistance Mission in the Andes'. *International Labour Review* 67(6) (1953), 520–34.

Bolivian Ministry of Agriculture. *Zonas colonizables: Bolivia*. La Paz: Ed. Kollasuyo, 1950.

Bourguignon, Erika. 'Haiti and the Art of Paul-Henri Bourguignon'. *Research in African Literatures* 35(2) (2004), 173–88.

Fifer, J. Valerie. 'The Search for a Series of Small Successes: Frontiers of Settlement in Eastern Bolivia'. *Journal of Latin American Studies* 14(2) (1982), 407–32.

Frías Mendoza, Víctor Hugo. *Mistis y mokochinches: Mercado, evangélicos y política local en Calcha*. La Paz: Ed. Mama Huaco, 2002.

Gilbert, Jess. 'Low Modernism and the Agrarian New Deal', in Jane Adams (ed.), *Fighting for the Farm: Rural America Transformed* (Philadelphia: University of Pennsylvania Press, 2002), 129–46.

Gotkowitz, Laura. *A Revolution for Our Rights: Indigenous Struggles for Land and Justice in Bolivia, 1880–1952*. Durham, NC: Duke University Press, 2007.

Guthrie, Jason. 'The ILO and the International Technocratic Class, 1944–1966', in Sandrine Kott and Joëlle Droux (eds), *Globalizing Social Rights: The International Labour Organization and Beyond* (Basingstoke: Palgrave Macmillan, 2013), 115–34.

———. 'The International Labor Organization and the Social Politics of Development, 1938–1969'. Ph.D. dissertation. College Park: University of Maryland, 2015.

Heath, Dwight B., Hans C. Buechler and Charles J. Erasmus. *Land Reform and Social Revolution in Bolivia*. New York: Praeger, 1969.

Iacobelli, Pedro. *Postwar Emigration to South America from Japan and the Ryukyu Islands*. London: Bloomsbury, 2017.

International Labour Organization. 'Indigenous Peoples: Living and Working Conditions of Aboriginal Populations in Independent Countries'. Geneva: 1953.

———. 'Indigenous and Tribal Populations Convention (No. 107)'. Geneva: 1957. Retrieved 1 April 2022 from https://www.ilo.org/dyn/normlex/en/f?p=NORMLEXPUB:12100:0::NO::P12100_ILO_CODE:C107.

Kaltmeier, Olaf. *Im Widerstreit der Ordnungen: Kulturelle Identität, Subsistenz und Ökologie in Bolivien*. Wiesbaden: Deutscher Universitäts-Verlag, 1999.

Lenroot, Katherine F. 'The Training of Child Welfare Specialists from the Other American Republics'. *Bulletin of the Pan American Union* 79(9) (1945), 499–504.

Leonard, Olen E. *Canton Chullpas: A Socioeconomic Study in the Cochabamba Valley of Bolivia*. Washington DC: United States Department of Agriculture, 1948.

——. *Santa Cruz: A Socioeconomic Study of an Area in Bolivia*. Washington DC: United States Department of Agriculture, 1948.

Leonard, Olen E., and Charles P. Loomis. *Culture of a Contemporary Rural Community: El Cerrito, New Mexico*. Washington DC: United States Department of Agriculture, 1941.

——. (eds). *Readings in Latin American Social Organization and Institutions*. East Lansing: Michigan State College Press, 1953.

Leonard, Olen E., and Roy A. Clifford. *La sociología rural para los programas de acción*. Havana: IICA, 1960.

Lockwood, Agnese N. 'Indians of the Andes: Technical Assistance on the Altiplano'. *International Conciliation* 31(508) (1956), 355–431.

Loomis, Charles P. 'Rural Sociologists in Latin America'. *Applied Anthropology* 4(4) (1945), 50–52.

Maul, Daniel. '"Help Them Move the ILO Way": The International Labor Organization and the Modernization Discourse in the Era of Decolonization and the Cold War'. *Diplomatic History* 33(3) (2009), 387–404.

Maurel, Chloé. 'Le programme indien-andin des Nations Unies (années 1950–1960)'. *Cahiers des Amériques Latines* 67 (2011): 137–61.

Monheim, Felix. 'Forschungsbericht über eine Reise nach Südperu und Bolivien'. *Geographische Zeitschrift* 51(4) (1963), 323–35.

——. *Junge Indianerkolonisation in den Tiefländern Ostboliviens*. Braunschweig: Westermann, 1965.

Nobbs-Thiessen, Ben. *Landscape of Migration: Mobility and Environmental Change on Bolivia's Tropical Frontier, 1952 to the Present*. Chapel Hill: University of North Carolina Press, 2020.

Pacino, Nicole. 'Bringing the Revolution to the Countryside: Rural Health Programmes as State-Building in Post-1952 Bolivia'. *Bulletin of Latin American Research* 38(1) (2017), 1–16.

Papadopoulos, Yannis G.S., and Dimitris Parsanoglou. 'European Land Settlement and Development in Latin America: The Evolution of an Idea from Interwar to the Early Post-WWII Years'. *Diálogos Latinoamericanos* 30 (2021), 1–15.

Pribilsky, Jason. 'Development and the "Indian Problem" in the Cold War Andes: "Indigenismo", Science, and Modernization in the Making of the Cornell-Peru Project at Vicos'. *Diplomatic History* 33(3) (2009), 405–26.

Rens, Jef. 'The Development of the Andean Indian Programme and Its Future'. *Ekistics* 18(104) (1964), 29–32.

Rojas Vásquez, Víctor Hernán. *Región y poder central en Bolivia: Santa Cruz de la Sierra 1938–1971*. Santa Cruz de la Sierra: Biblioteca del Museo de Historia, 2015.

Sackley, Nicole. 'Village Models: Etawah, India, and the Making and Remaking of Development in the Early Cold War'. *Diplomatic History* 37(4) (2013), 749–78.

Siegel, Benjamin. 'The Kibbutz and the Ashram: Sarvodaya Agriculture, Israeli Aid, and the Global Imaginaries of Indian Development'. *American Historical Review* 125(4) (2020), 1175–204.

Siekmeier, James F. *Aid, Nationalism and Inter-American Relations: Guatemala, Bolivia, and the United States 1945–1961*. Lampeter: Edwin Mellen Press, 1999.

Soliz, Carmen. *Fields of Revolution: Agrarian Reform and Rural State Formation in Bolivia, 1935–1964.* Pittsburgh: University of Pittsburgh Press, 2021.

Stearman, Allyn MacLean. 'Colonization in Eastern Bolivia: Problems and Prospects'. *Human Organization* 32(3) (1973), 285–293.

Sylvain, Jeanne. 'L'enfance paysanne en Haiti'. *Présence Africaine* 3(12) (1951), 88–111.

United States Department of Commerce. *Economic Review of Bolivia, 1949.* Washington, DC: US Government Printing Office, 1950 (International Reference Service 7, 57).

Verna, Chantalle F. *Haiti and the Uses of America: Post-U.S. Occupation Promises.* New Brunswick, NJ: Rutgers University Press, 2017.

Young, Kevin A. *Blood of the Earth: Resource Nationalism, Revolution, and Empire in Bolivia.* Austin: University of Texas Press, 2017.

Zunes, Stephen. 'The United States and Bolivia: The Taming of a Revolution, 1952–1957'. *Latin American Perspectives* 28(5) (2001), 33–49.

Index

Milton Keynes UK
Ingram Content Group UK Ltd.
UKHW021847300723
426044UK00004B/75